DATE DUE

COMMERCIAL SHIPPING HANDBOOK
SECOND EDITION

RELATED TITLES

Other titles in this series are:

Dictionary of Shipping Terms
4th edition
by Peter Brodie

COMMERCIAL SHIPPING HANDBOOK

SECOND EDITION

BY

PETER BRODIE
F.I.C.S., F.I.C.D.D.S.

informa

LONDON
2006

Informa Law
Mortimer House
37–41 Mortimer Street
London W1T 3JH
law.enquiries@informa.com

An Informa business

First edition 1999
Second edition 2006
© Peter Brodie 2006

British Library Cataloguing in Publication Data
A catalogue record for this book is available from the British Library.

ISBN 1-84311-531-X

Text set in 10/12 Postscript Plantin by
Tony Lansbury, Tonbridge, Kent
Printed in Great Britain by
MPG Books, Bodmin, Cornwall

To IB and SJB

Preface to the second edition

Since writing the first edition of this book, major changes have occurred to the industry, in particular in relation to security and the structure of the liner industry.

Security measures have been introduced gradually since the terrorist attacks on New York in September 2001; these measures were introduced firstly in the USA itself and then elsewhere around the world. This edition includes details of the International Code for the Security of Ships and Port Facilities, aimed at ships and shipping companies, port authorities and port facilities, and the role of governments. New requirements for cargoes, introduced in the USA, are also explained.

The liner industry has undergone structural changes, with more and more groupings of companies. There have also been changes to the way it is regulated in Europe; at the time of writing, the European Commission is in the throes of removing the block exemption from competition rules hitherto afforded to liner conferences. The different groupings, and the types of trade in which they are engaged, are explained.

The work of the many industry organisations evolves, and changes have been reflected in new sections for a number of these.

A number of new abbreviations and acronyms have sprung up reflecting these changes, and these have been incorporated.

Peter Brodie
February 2006

Preface to the second edition

Preface to the first edition

This book fills a need for a handbook which gives concise explanations of the many activities which comprise shipping. It is essentially a guide for the practitioner and student of both liner and tramp shipping. It explains the terms and how they inter-relate. The many areas covered include:

—documents used in international transport, for example the bill oflading and the charter-party – what they contain, the different types and examples of each;
generic types of ships, cargoes, containers and ports;
—the many organisations whose members contribute to international transport and the aims and objectives of those organisations;
—the many surcharges found especially in liner shipping;
—chartering terms, an explanation of each and their context;
—clauses appearing in bills of lading, in voyage and time charters;
—technical elements of shipping as they relate to the commercial operation of ships, for example tides and draughts;
—examples of principal documents.

The book is divided into concise entries, each one dealing with an individual topic, for which there is an alphabetical Table of Contents. In addition, there is an alphabetical index of over 1,250 terms, showing the entries in which they can be found, and list of over 200 abbreviations, showing the term in full and the entry or entries in which the abbreviation is explained.

Peter Brodie

Acknowledgements

I wish to acknowledge the contributions made by the following organisations and their agreement to reproduce documents:

Association of Ship Brokers and Agents (USA) Inc.
Baltic Exchange
Baltic and International Maritime Council
British International Freight Association*
British Shippers' Council
Bureau Veritas
Chamber of Shipping
CLECAT
European Sea Ports Organisation (ESPO)
European Shippers' Council
Federation of European Maritime Associations of Surveyors and Consultants
Federal Maritime Commission
Hydrographic Office
Institute of Chartered Shipbrokers
International Association of Classification Societies
International Association of Independent Tanker Owners (INTERTANKO)
International Association of Ports and Harbors (IAPH)
International Bunker Industry Association
International Cargo Handling Co-ordination Association (ICHCA)
International Federation of Freight Forwarders' Associations (FIATA)
International Harbour Masters' Association
International Maritime Organization
Institute of Marine Engineers
INTERCARGO
INTERTANKO
International Ship Managers' Association (ISMA)
International Ship Suppliers Association
International Transport Workers' Federation
Lloyd's of London
Lloyd's Register of Shipping
London Shipping Law Centre
London Tanker Brokers' Panel

* Redfern House, Browells Lane, Feltham, Middlesex TW13 7EP. Use of BIFA documents is restricted to BIFA members.

Acknowledgements

Maritime and Coastguard Agency
Nautical Institute
Organisation for Economic Co-operation and Development
Royal Institute of Naval Architects
Society of International Gas Tanker & Terminal Operators
Simpler Trade Procedures Board
United Nations Conference on Trade and Development
Weather Routing Inc.
WNI Oceanroutes
Worldscale Association (London) Limited

Facilitation forms on pp. 120–125 are reproduced by kind permission of the International Maritime Organization, London.

Material under the heading "Tides" (pp. 300–301) is reproduced from Admiralty Tide Tables (1999) by permission of Her Majesty's Stationery Office and the UK and the Hydrographic Office.

About the Author

Peter Brodie has been a Chartered Ship broker since 1979 and winner of the Baltic Exchange prize in the Fellowship examinations of the Institute of Chartered Shipbrokers. He has spent 30 years in shipping, as a shipper, ship operator, business analyst for a software company specialising in shipping applications, and, more recently, for an intermodal railway company.

Peter Brodie has been writing textbooks for over 25 years and is the author of four other books on shipping, including the *Dictionary of Shipping Terms*, a standard textbook published by Informa and now in its fourth edition.

Table of Contents

Table of Contents

Table of Contents

List of Illustrations

List of Abbreviations

Abbreviation	Meaning	See under
1sb	one safe berth	Berth
abt	about	Chartering—offer and counter-offer
a/c	account	Chartering—offer and counter-offer
ad	area differential	Liner surcharges
addcomm	address commission	Sundry charter-party clauses (found in both voyage and time charters)
ADP	Automatic Data Processing	Convention on Facilitation of International Maritime Traffic
AFRA	Average Freight Rate Assessment	London Tanker Brokers' Panel
aps	arrival pilot station	Delivery and re-delivery (time charter)
atdn	any time day or night	Delivery and re-delivery (time charter)
baf	bunker surcharge	Bunker surcharge, Bunkers
b/b	breakbulk	Cargo types
BCI	Baltic Capesize Index	Baltic Exchange indices
BCTI	Baltic Exchange Clean Tanker Index	Baltic Exchange indices
BDI	Baltic Dry Index	Baltic Exchange indices
BDTI	Baltic Exchange Dirty Tanker Index	Baltic Exchange indices
BHI	Baltic Handy Index	Baltic Exchange indices
BHMI	Baltic Exchange Handymax Index	Baltic Exchange indices
BIFA	British International Freight Association	British International Freight Association (BIMCO)
BIMCO	Baltic and International Maritime Council	BIMCO (Baltic and International Maritime Council), Dangerous goods, Ice clause
b/l	bill of lading	Bill of lading, Bill of lading as document of title, Bill of lading as evidence of contract of carriage, Bill of lading as receipt, Bill of lading—common clauses, Bookings, Charter-party, Forwarder's Certificate of Transport (FIATA FCT), Shipping documents
BLPG	Baltic Exchange LPG (index)	Baltic Exchange indices
b/n	booking note	Bookings
bol	bill of lading	Bill of lading as document of title
BPI	Baltic Exchange Panama Index	Baltic Exchange indices
b/s	bunker surcharge	Bunker surcharge, Bunkers, Liner surcharges
BSC	British Shippers' Council	British Shippers' Council (BSC)
BSI	Baltic Exchange Supramax Index	Baltic Exchange indices
BSPA	Baltic Exchange Sale and Purchase Association	Baltic Exchange indices
bw	brackish water	Draught
cabaf	currency and bunker adjustment factor	Bunker surcharge, Currency adjustment factor, Liner surcharges
cac	currency adjustment charge	Currency adjustment factor
caf	currency adjustment factor	Currency adjustment factor, Liner surcharges

List of Abbreviations

Abbreviation	Meaning	See under
cbl	combined bill of lading	Bill of lading
cbm	cubic metre	Weights and measures
CENSA	Council of European and Japanese National Shipowners' Associations	European Shippers' Council
c&f	cost and freight	Conventional freight and the export contract
CFR	cost and freight	Incoterms
cfs	container freight station	Cargo handling charges, Containers and associated ancillary charges
charts	charterers	Chartering—offer and counter-offer
cif	cost, insurance and freight	Conventional freight and the export contract, Incoterms
ciffo	cost, insurance and freight free out	Conventional freight and the export contract
CIP	carriage and insurance paid to	Incoterms
cl.	clause	Sundry voyage charter-party clauses
coa	contract of affreightment	Contract of affreightment
c/p	charter-party	Charter-party, Charter-party
cpp	clean petroleum products	Cargo types
CPT	carriage paid to	Incoterms
cs	congestion surcharge	Congestion
cso	company security officer	Security
cst	Centistokes	Worldscale
C-TPAT	Customs-Trade Partnership Against Terrorism	Security
DAF	delivered at frontier	Incoterms
DDU	delivered duty unpaid	Incoterms
DEQ	delivered ex quay	Incoterms
DES	delivered ex ship	Incoterms
DG	Dangerous Goods	Dangerous goods
DGN	Dangerous Goods Note	Dangerous goods, Shipping documents, Standard Shipping Note (SSN)
dic	delivered in charge	Cargo handling charges
d 1/2 d	despatch half demurrage	Penalties
dly	delivery	Charter documentation, Delivery and re-delivery (time charter), Time charter
doc	document of compliance	International Safety Management (ISM) Code, Ship's documents
dop	dropping outward pilot	Delivery and re-delivery (time charter)
dpp	dirty petroleum products	Cargo types
DSHA	Dangerous Substance in Harbour Area (Regulations)	Dangerous goods
dwat	deadweight all told	Ship's dimensions and capacities
dwcc	deadweight cargo capacity or deadweight carrying capacity	Ship's dimensions and capacities
dwt	deadweight	Ship's dimensions and capacities, Worldscale
ECSA	European Community Shipowners' Associations	European Shippers' Council
ECSI	Export Cargo Shipping Instructions	Shipping documents, Shipping instructions
ECU	European Currency Unit	Liner and conference tariffs
EDI	Electronic Data Interchange	Convention on Facilitation of International Maritime Traffic
ESC	European Shippers' Council	European Shippers' Council

Abbreviation	Meaning	See under
ESPO	European Sea Ports Organisation	European Sea Ports Organisation (ESPO), European Shippers' Council
eta	estimated time of arrival	Voyage charter—ship's position
etc	estimated time of completion	Voyage charter—ship's position
etd	estimated time of departure	Voyage charter—ship's position
etr	estimated time of readiness	Voyage charter—ship's position
ets	estimated time of sailing	Voyage charter—ship's position
EXW	ex works	Incoterms
fac	fast as can	Conventional freight and the export contract
fac	forwarding agent's commission	Forwarding agent
faccop	fast as can custom of the port	Conventional freight and the export contract
faf	fuel adjustment factor	Bunker surcharge, Bunkers
fak	freight all kinds	Container freight, Liner and conference tariffs
FAS	free alongside	Incoterms, Liner contracts
FCA	free carrier	Incoterms
f&cc	full and complete cargo	Charter freight terms, Ship's dimensions and capacities
fcl	full container load	British International Freight Association (BIFA), Change of destination, Container freight, Containers and associated ancillary charges, Dangerous goods, Liner and conference tariffs
FCR	Forwarder's Certificate of Receipt	Forwarder's Certificate of Receipt (FIATA FCR)
FCT	Forwarder's Certificate of Transport	Forwarder's Certificate of Transport (FIATA FCT)
fd&d	freight, demurrage and defence	Protection and Indemnity Club (P&I Club)
FEMAS	Federation of European Maritime Associations of Surveyors and Consultants	Federation of European Maritime Associations of Surveyors and Consultants (FEMAS)
FEPORT	Federation of European Port Operators	European Shippers' Council
feu	forty-foot equivalent unit	Containers and associated ancillary charges, Weights and measures
fwa	fresh water allowance	Freeboards and load lines
FFI	FIATA Forwarding Instructions	Forwarding Instructions (FIATA FFI)
fhex	Fridays and holidays excepted (or excluded)	Laytime—calculation
FIATA	International Federation of Freight Forwarders Associations	Dangerous goods, European Shippers' Council, Multimodal transport bill of lading, Shipping documents
FICS	Fellow of the Institute of Chartered Shipbrokers	Institute of Chartered Shipbrokers (ICS)
filo	free in liner out	Conventional freight and the export contract
filtd	free in liner terms discharge	Conventional freight and the export contract
fio	free in and out	Charter freight terms, Chartering – offer and counter-offer, Conventional freight and the export contract
fios	free in and out and stowed	Charter freight terms
fiot	free in and out and trimmed	Charter freight terms

List of Abbreviations

Abbreviation	Meaning	See under
flt	full liner terms	Conventional freight and the export contract
FMC	Federal Maritime Commission	Federal Maritime Commission (FMC)
fo	free out	Conventional freight and the export contract
fob	free on board	Containers and associated ancillary charges, Conventional freight and the export contract, Incoterms, Liner contracts
fob's	free on board charges	Breakbulk liner ancillary charges, Cargo handling charges
foc	flag of convenience	Flag, International Transport Workers' Federation (ITF)
FONASBA	Federation of National Associations of Shipbrokers and Agents	Institute of Chartered Shipbrokers (ICS)
fos	fuel oil surcharge	Bunker surcharge, Bunkers
frob	freight remaining on board	Security
frt	freight	Freight
fw	fresh water	Draught
fwa	fresh water allowance	Draught
FWR	FIATA Warehouse Receipt	FIATA Warehouse Receipt (FIATA FWR)
ga	general average	Bill of lading—common clauses
GISIS	IMO's Global Integrated Shipping Information System	Security
gp (container) or gp (box)	general purpose (container)	Containers and associated ancillary charges
gri	general rate increase	Liner and conference tariffs
grt	gross register tonnage or gross registered tonnage	Ship's dimensions and capacities
gt	gross tonnage	Ship's dimensions and capacities
gt	gross terms	Charter freight terms
HAT	highest astronomical tide	Tides
hla	heavy lift additional	Breakbulk liner ancillary charges
IACS	International Association of Classification Societies	Classification societies, International Association of Classification Societies (IACS), International Association of Dry Cargo Shipowners (Intercargo), International Association of Ports and Harbors (IAPH)
iaf	inflation adjustment factor	Liner surcharges
IBIA	International Bunker Industry Association Ltd	International Bunker Industry Association Ltd (IBIA)
ICC	International Chamber of Commerce	Forwarder's Certificate of Transport (FIATA FCT), ICC International Maritime Bureau (IMB), International Chamber of Commerce (ICC)
icd	inland container depot	Container freight
ICS	Institute of Chartered Shipbrokers	Institute of Chartered Shipbrokers (ICS)
ICS	International Chamber of Shipping	European Shippers' Council
IFF	Institute of Freight Forwarders	British International Freight Association (BIFA)
IFP	Institute of Freight Professionals	British International Freight Association (BIFA)
ifp	interim fuel participation	Bunker surcharge, Bunkers

Abbreviation	Meaning	See under
IHMA	International Harbour Masters Association	International Harbour Masters Association (IHMA)
IIL	ICHCA International Limited	ICHCA International Limited (IIL)
i/m	intermodal	Combined transport
IMB	International Maritime Bureau	ICC International Maritime Bureau (IMB), International Chamber of Commerce (ICC)
IMCO	Inter-Governmental Maritime Consultative Organization	International Maritime Organization (IMO)
IMDG Code	International Maritime Dangerous Goods Code	Dangerous goods
IMO	International Maritime Organization	Convention on Facilitation of International Maritime Traffic, International Maritime Organization (IMO), International Transport Workers' Federation (ITF), Security
ISM Code	International Safety Management Code	Ship's documents
ISMA	International Ship Managers' Association	InterManager—International Ship Managers' Association (ISMA), ISMA Code
ISPS	International Ship and Port Facility Security Code	International Association of Dry Cargo Shipowners (Intercargo), Security
ISSA	International Ship Suppliers Association	International Ship Suppliers Association (ISSA)
ISSC	International Ship Security Certificate	Security
ITF	International Transport Workers' Federation	International Transport Workers' Federation (ITF)
JBP	Joint Bulker Project	International Association of Dry Cargo Shipowners (Intercargo)
LASH	lighter aboard ship	Dry cargo ships
LAT	lowest astronomical tide	Tides
laycan	laydays cancelling	Chartering—offer and counter-offer
lbp	length between perpendiculars	Ship's dimensions and capacities
l/c	laycan	Cancellation of a charter, Chartering—offer and counter-offer, Laytime—commencement
lcl	less than container load	British International Freight Association (BIFA), Change of destination, Container freight, Containers and associated ancillary charges, Dangerous goods, Liner and conference tariffs
lifo	liner in free out	Conventional freight and the export contract
lla	long length additional	Breakbulk liner ancillary charges, Cargo handling charges
lm	lane metres	Ship's dimensions and capacities, Weights and measures
lng	liquid natural gas or liquefied natural gas	Tankers
loa	length overall	Ship's dimensions and capacities
loi	letter of indemnity	Bill of lading as document of title
lpg	liquid petroleum gas or liquefied petroleum gas	Tankers
ls	lump sum	Charter freight terms, Weights and measures

List of Abbreviations

Abbreviation	Meaning	See under
ls&d	landing, storage and delivery charges	Breakbulk liner ancillary charges, Cargo handling charges
lt	liner terms	Conventional freight and the export contract
lt	long ton	Weights and measures
MCA	Maritime and Coastguard Agency	Maritime engineering
MHWN	mean high water neaps	Tides
MHWS	mean high water springs	Tides
MICS	Member of the Institute of Chartered Shipbrokers	Institute of Chartered Shipbrokers (ICS)
min/max	minimum/maximum	Charter freight terms
MLWN	mean low water neaps	Tides
MLWS	mean low water springs	Tides
molchop	more or less in charterer's option	Charter freight terms, Chartering—offer and counter-offer
moloo	more or less in owner's option	Charter freight terms, Chartering—offer and counter-offer
MOU	Memorandum of Understanding	International Association of Dry Cargo Shipowners (Intercargo)
m/r	mate's receipt	Bill of lading as receipt
MSA	Marine Safety Agency	Maritime engineering
MSL	mean sea level	Tides
mt	metric ton	Weights and measures
MTL	mean tide level	Tides
MTO	multimodal transport operator	Combined transport, International Association of Dry Cargo Shipowners (Intercargo), Multimodal transport bill of lading, Shipping
nii	non intrusive inspection	Security
noe	not otherwise enumerated	Liner and conference tariffs
nos	Not Otherwise Specified	Dangerous goods, Liner and conference tariffs
nrt	net register tonnage or net registered tonnage	Ship's dimensions and capacities
nt	net ton or nett ton	Weights and measures
nt	net tonnage	Ship's dimensions and capacities
nvo, nvoc, nvocc	Non vessel owning common carrier, non vessel operating carrier, non vessel owning carrier	Carrier, Security, Shipping
obo	ore/bulk/oil carrier	Multipurpose ships
OECD	Organisation for Economic Co-operation and Development	European Shippers' Council, Liner shipping—how it is regulated, Organisation for Economic Co-operation and Development (OECD)
ohbc	open hatch bulk carrier	Bulk carriers
o/o	ore/oil carrier	Multipurpose ships
osb	one safe berth	Berth
osd	open shelter decker	Ship types
os&d (report)	over, short and damage report	Tally (to)
OSRA	Ocean Shipping Reform Act	Liner shipping—how it is regulated
o/t	overtime	Sundry voyage charter-party clauses
pandi	Protection and Indemnity	Protection and Indemnity Club (P&I Club)
pcc	pure car carrier	Vehicle carriers
pctc	pure car and truck carriers	Vehicle carriers

Abbreviation	Meaning	See under
pd	per day	Containers and associated ancillary charges
pfsa	port facility security assessment	Security
pfso	port facility security officer	Security
pfsp	port facility security plan	Security
pft	per freight ton	Conventional freight and the export contract
P&I	protection and indemnity	Protection and Indemnity Club (P&I Club), Sundry voyage charter-party clauses
pltc's	port liner term charges	Breakbulk liner ancillary charges
pp	posted price	Bunker surcharge
PSC	Port State Control	International Association of Dry Cargo Shipowners (Intercargo)
redly	redelivery	Charter documentation, Delivery and re-delivery (time charter)
redly cert	redelivery certificate	Delivery and re-delivery (time charter), Time charter
RINA	Royal Institution of Naval Architects	Royal Institution of Naval Architects (RINA)
rob	remaining on board	Bunkers, Sundry time charter-party clauses
ro-ro	roll-on/roll-off	Cargo types, Dry cargo ships, Multi-purpose ships, Vehicle carriers
rso	recognised security organisations	Security
RSS	Register of Shipping and Seamen	Maritime engineering
rtw	round the world	Liner shipping—trades
sb	safe berth	Berth
SCEA	Shipping Conferences Exemption Act	Liner shipping—how it is regulated
sd	single decker	Ship types
SDR	Special Drawing Rights	Multimodal transport bill of lading
shex	Sundays and holidays excepted	Chartering—offer and counter-offer, Laytime—calculation
shinc	Sundays and holidays included	Chartering—offer and counter-offer, Delivery and re-delivery (time charter), Laytime—calculation
sim. sub.	similar substitute	Chartering—offer and counter-offer, Voyage charter—ship's position
SITPRO	Simpler Trades Procedures Board	Dangerous goods, Shipping documents, SITPRO
SMS	safety management system	International Safety Management (ISM) Code
SOLAS	Safety of Life at Sea Convention	Security
s&p	sale and purchase	Sale & purchase (s&p)
ssa	ship security assessment	Security
sshex	Saturdays, Sundays and holidays excepted	Chartering—offer and counter-offer, Laytime—calculation
sshinc	Saturdays, Sundays and holidays included	Chartering—offer and counter-offer
sso	ship security officer	Security
ssp	ship security plan	Security
stc	said to contain	Bill of lading as receipt, Security
sub.	subject or substitute	Chartering - offer and counter-offer, Voyage charter—ship's position
sub. dets.	subject details	Chartering—offer and counter-offer
sw	salt water	Draught
tba	to be advised	Chartering—offer and counter-offer, Voyage charter—ship's position

List of Abbreviations

Abbreviation	Meaning	See under
tbn	to be nominated	Chartering—offer and counter-offer, Voyage charter—ship's position
t/c	time charter	Chartering, Charter-party, Time charter
tdw	tonnes deadweight	Ship's dimensions and capacities
teu	twenty-foot equivalent unit	Congestion, Containers and associated ancillary charges, Ship's dimensions and capacities, Weights and measures
thc	terminal handling charges	Cargo handling charges, Container freight
tpc	tonnes per centimetre	Ship's dimensions and capacities
tpi	tons per inch	Ship's dimensions and capacities
ubc	universal bulk carrier	Bulk carriers
uncon	uncontainerable, uncontainerisable	Cargo types
UNCTAD	United Nations Conference on Trade and Development	Liner shipping—how it is regulated, Multimodal transport bill of lading, United Nations Conference on Trade and Development (UNCTAD)
UIRR	International Union of combined Road-Rail transport companies	European Shippers' Council
ulcc	ultra large crude carrier	Tankers
v	voyage	Liner ship positions
v/c	voyage charter	Chartering, Charter-party, Voyage charter
vlcc	very large crude carrier	Tankers
voy	voyage	Liner ship positions
w/b	waybill	Charter-party, Shipping documents
WCO	World Customs Organisation	Security
wibon	whether in berth or not	Berth, Laytime—commencement
wifpon	whether in free pratique or not	Laytime—commencement
wipon	whether in port or not	Laytime—commencement
w/m	weight or measure(ment)	Conventional freight and the export contract, Weights and measures
wog	without guarantee	Chartering—offer and counter-offer
wp	weather permitting	Laytime—calculation
WTO	World Trade Organization	European Shippers' Council
wwd	weather working day	Laytime—calculation
wwr	when where ready	Delivery and re-delivery (time charter)
wwrcd	when where ready on completion of discharge	Delivery and re-delivery (time charter)

Arrived Ship

Requirement of all voyage charters that the ship must have arrived before laytime can commence. Where a berth or dock has been nominated by the charterer, the ship must have arrived at that berth or dock. When a port is nominated, the ship must have arrived at the port, although various legal decisions have defined a port differently in this context in cases where there is no berth available and the ship is obliged to wait.

When a ship arrives at a port from a foreign country, the authorities need to satisfy themselves as to the state of health of those on board and will then grant **pratique** or **free pratique**, that is, official permission for them to make physical contact with the shore. A ship which is the subject of such a permission is said to be **in free pratique**. Some charter-parties stipulate that lay time will start to count **whether (the ship is) in free pratique or not**.

The place to which the ship must have arrived is open to negotiation. The expression **whether in berth or not** signifies that laytime will start to count when the ship has arrived at the port whether she has reached the berth or not. The charter-party may even stipulate that lay time will start to count **whether in port or not**. In this case, the ship need only arrive at the anchorage, if outside the port, and tender notice of readiness.

Charter-parties normally require the shipowner, or master on his behalf, to issue a **notice of readiness** to the charterer. This states that the ship has arrived and is ready to load or discharge and for laytime to start to count. The clause containing this provision often stipulates the particular hours and days when this notice may be tendered and how soon afterwards lay time commences.

Gencon, BIMCO's general purpose voyage charter-party, treats the commencement of laytime as follows:

"Laytime for loading and discharging shall commence at 1 p.m. if notice of readiness is given before noon, and at 6 a.m. next working day if notice given during office hours after noon. Notice at loading port to be given to the Shippers named in Box 17.

Time actually used before commencement of lay time shall count.

Time lost in waiting for berth to count as loading or discharging time, as the case may be."

Arrived ship

Associated abbreviations:
nor notice of readiness
wibon whether in berth or not
wifpon whether in free pratique or not
wipon whether in port or not

Associated term:
to tender notice of readiness

Ballast

Heavy weight, often sea water, which gives a ship stability and improves handling when she is at sea and not carrying cargo. Such a ship is said to be steaming **in ballast** or **ballasting**.

Reasons for a ship having to steam in ballast include:

(a) no further cargo being available at the port where the ship discharged her previous cargo. Typically this happens in the case of tramp ships which are not on fixed schedules and are looking for further employment;

(b) in some trades, a ship may perform a series of voyages between two ports, very often on time charter or contract of affreightment, with a (suitable) cargo available in one direction only. This situation applies particularly in certain bulk trades where the ships are specialised and only suited to one type of cargo;

(c) in other instances, it may be more economical, after discharging a cargo, to steam empty to another port to pick up the next cargo than to take cargo which pays a low freight to that port.

That part of a ship's voyage during which she is not carrying a cargo is known as a **ballast leg**. It is useful for a shipowner or ship operator, when doing a voyage estimate, to separate ballast legs from parts of the voyage when the ship is carrying a cargo, known as **loaded legs**, in order to evaluate the profitability of the voyage and to assess requirements for bunkers, since a ship may consume less when in ballast.

A **ballast bonus** is a sum of money paid by a time charterer to a shipowner in recognition of the fact that the shipowner is unlikely to find a cargo near to the place of redelivery of the ship at the end of the period of the charter and is therefore obliged to ballast his ship elsewhere.

Ballast is also useful when it is important to keep the freeboard, that is, the distance from the waterline to the deck line of the ship, at a fixed level when loading. It is possible to achieve this by discharging ballast, or **deballasting**, simultaneously with loading. This operation may be crucial, for example, in the case of large bulk carriers which might be obliged to stop loading should deballasting not keep up with the rate of loading of the cargo. Similarly, deballasting can help keep the ramp of a roll-on roll-off ship at a fixed angle with the shore.

See also:
Contract of affreightment
Voyage estimate

Baltic Exchange

Shipping market, located in London, England, known widely as the Baltic, whose main function is to provide facilities for the chartering of ships by its members.

Founded some 250 years ago, the Baltic's original purpose remains to facilitate the business of international bulk shipping. In the early 1700s tallow shipped from the Baltic States was the major trade. Accordingly, in 1744, the London coffee house favoured by commodity dealers negotiating carriage with shipowners was renamed the "Virginia and Baltick". To combat wild gambling within the market and to ward off unscrupulous dealers, a number of senior coffee house regulars formed a committee to devise rules for the admission of members. After the committee had met on 1 May 1823, a private room with controlled entry was established. This tight, closed market became the framework for the modern-day Baltic Exchange.

The traders soon outgrew the coffee house and in 1857 they formed a limited company and moved into South Sea House—a larger building in Threadneedle Street. It was here, following a dispute over linseed oil, that a fundamental requirement of Baltic trading was established—that "a broker's word should be considered binding and trustworthy". The famous Baltic motto—"Our Word Our Bond"—reflects this principle and is still key today.

Membership continued to grow and in 1900 the Baltic merged with the London Shipping Exchange to form the Baltic & Mercantile Shipping Exchange Ltd. By 1903 a new Exchange had been built in St Mary Axe which remained home to the Baltic for almost 90 years. Many related organisations were founded here including the Institute of Chartered Shipbrokers, the London Corn Traders Association and the Baltic Air Charter Association.

The Baltic continued to thrive and by 1920 its members represented virtually all shipowners and cargo interests worldwide. The 1930s saw a rapid decline in world trade and, with the outbreak of the Second World War, government requisition policy reduced the Exchange to a ghost of its former self. After the War, the Baltic quickly regained its position at the heart of international bulk shipping—a position it retains to this day.

The Exchange is made up of members from over 40 nationalities, both corporate and individual, representing shipowners, brokers, agents, managers and operators, insurance brokers, protection and indemnity clubs, surveyors, lawyers and arbitrators, banks and finance houses, classification societies, commodity and futures traders, freight forwarders, port agents, air brokers and consultants and information providers.

Over 4.5 billion tonnes, or 98 per cent of world trade, is carried by sea. Coal, iron ore and crude oil predominate along with grain, sugar, rice, steel, timber, bauxite, phosphates and refined products of oil. These form the raw materials for the world's economy: fuels for industry and food for people. Baltic Exchange members arrange their transportation from the producing countries to their destination. It is the matching of ships and bulk cargoes that forms the cornerstone of the Baltic market today.

Under an exclusive contract for services with the UK Ministry of Defence, the Exchange employs a broker—the Government Freight Market Representative (GFMR)—to act for government departments and agencies in chartering vessels for dry cargo defence movements and specialist vessels, including for example salvage operations. The GFMR is charged with securing the best value for money for the UK taxpayer and usually there are no restrictions on the nationality or flag of vessels chartered.

The Baltic is the only international, self-regulated shipbroking market in the world. Brokers undertake to abide by a code of business conduct based on the motto "Our Word Our Bond" and those who breach the code are disciplined or expelled.

Baltic members continually trade information, either face to face on the Trading Floor or around the world by telephone, telex, fax or e-mail. On Monday lunchtime around 400 members gather on the Exchange Floor to exchange information. The Exchange also gathers, collates and distributes information to members unable to attend these sessions. Two freight indexes and the list of known dry bulk cargo fixtures are published daily.

The Baltic also acts as the world's foremost sale and purchase market. Over half the world's new and second-hand tonnage is bought and sold by Baltic members.

Air brokers are also represented. The Baltic Air Charter Association was formed at the Baltic in 1949, when the Exchange became the first air broking market. These niche brokers handle specialist air freight.

The Baltic acts as an intermediary in some types of commercial dispute involving a member, both disagreements between a member and a non-member and disagreements between two members. Such disputes are not those which would go to arbitration.

The Exchange has strong working relations with many other international shipping organisations. The Institute of Chartered Ship brokers was founded at the Exchange and, like Intercargo, is just a short walk away. Intertanko have a full time representative at the Exchange and BIMCO hold most of their London meetings there.

See also:
Baltic Exchange Indices
Shipbroker

Baltic Exchange indices

The Baltic Exchange collates and produces valuable market information. In particular, it publishes freight indices based on a variety of ship types and routes:

The **Baltic Dry Index** (BDI) is a daily index made up of 24 dry routes. The **Baltic Exchange Capesize Index** (BCI) is made up of 11 daily Capesize vessel assessments including voyage and time charter rates. The **Baltic Exchange Panama Index** (BPI) is made up of 7 daily Panamax vessels including voyage and time charter rates. The **Baltic Exchange Handymax Index** (BHMI) consists of 6 daily timecharter rates. The **Baltic Exchange Supramax Index** (BSI) consists of 7 daily time charter rates, and is intended to replace the Baltic Handymax Index. The **Baltic Handy Index** (BHI) covers handy-sized bulk carriers. The **Baltic Exchange Dirty Tanker Index** (BDTI) consists of daily Worldscale assessments of international dirty tankers. The **Baltic Exchange Clean Tanker Index** (BCTI) is made up of daily Worldscale assessments international clean tankers. The **Baltic Exchange LPG** (BLPG) index represents a single daily assessment. **Baltic Exchange Sale and Purchase Assessments** (BSPA) are two-weekly assessments of second ship values—Aframax, VLCCs, Capesize and Panamax.

Associated abbreviations:
BCI Baltic Capesize Index
BCTI Baltic Exchange Clean Tanker Index
BDI Baltic Dry Index
BDTI Baltic Exchange Dirty Tanker Index
BHI Baltic Handy Index
BHMI Baltic Exchange Handymax Index
BLPG Baltic Exchange LPG (index)
BPI Baltic Exchange Panama Index
BSI Baltic Exchange Supramax Index
BSPA Baltic Exchange Sale and Purchase Assessments

See also:
Baltic Exchange
Bulk carriers
Worldscale

Bareboat Charter

The hiring or leasing of a ship for a period of time during which the shipowner provides only the ship while the charterer provides the crew together with all stores and bunkers and pays all operating costs.

This type of charter is favoured by persons or companies who wish to own a ship for investment purposes but who do not have the desire or expertise to

Bareboat Charter

1. Shipbroker	**BIMCO STANDARD BAREBOAT CHARTER** **CODE NAME: "BARECON 2001"** PART I
	2. Place and date
3. Owners/Place of business (Cl. 1)	4. Bareboat Charterers/Place of business (Cl. 1)
5. Vessel's name, call sign and flag (Cl. 1 and 3)	
6. Type of Vessel	7. GT/NT
8. When/Where built	9. Total DWT (abt.) in metric tons on summer freeboard
10. Classification Society (Cl. 3)	11. Date of last special survey by the Vessel's classification society
12. Further particulars of Vessel (also indicate minimum number of months' validity of class certificates agreed acc. to Cl. 3)	

13. Port or Place of delivery (Cl. 3)	14. Time for delivery (Cl. 4)	15. Cancelling date (Cl. 5)
16. Port or Place of redelivery (Cl. 15)	17. No. of months' validity of trading and class certificates upon redelivery (Cl. 15)	
18. Running days' notice if other than stated in Cl. 4	19. Frequency of dry-docking (Cl. 10(g))	
20. Trading limits (Cl. 6)		
21. Charter period (Cl. 2)	22. Charter hire (Cl. 11)	
23. New class and other safety requirements (state percentage of Vessel's insurance value acc. to Box 29)(Cl. 10(a)(ii))		
24. Rate of interest payable acc. to Cl. 11(f) and, if applicable, acc. to PART IV	25. Currency and method of payment (Cl. 11)	

Printed and sold by Fr. G. Knudtzons Bogtrykkeri A/S,
Vallensbaekvej 61, DK-2625 Vallensbaek, Fax: +45 4366 0701

continued

Left margin: First issued by The Baltic and International Maritime Council (BIMCO), Copenhagen, in 1974 as "Barecon A" and "Barecon B". Revised and amalgamated 1989. Revised 2001

Left margin: Copyright, published by The Baltic and International Maritime Council (BIMCO), Copenhagen. Issued November 2001

Bareboat charter-party (Barecon 2001)

6

26. Place of payment; also state beneficiary and bank account (Cl. 11)	27. Bank guarantee/bond (sum and place)(Cl. 24)(optional)
28. Mortgage(s), if any (state whether 12(a) or (b) applies; if 12(b) applies state date of Financial Instrument and name of Mortgagee(s)/Place of business)(Cl. 12)	29. Insurance (hull and machinery and war risks)(state value acc. to Cl. 13(f) or, if applicable, acc. to Cl. 14(k))(also state if Cl. 14 applies)
30. Additional insurance cover, if any, for Owners' account limited to (Cl. 13(b) or, if applicable, Cl. 14(g))	31. Additional insurance cover, if any, for Charterers' account limited to (Cl. 13(b) or, if applicable, Cl. 14(g))
32. Latent defects (only to be filled in if period other than stated in Cl. 3)	33. Brokerage commission and to whom payable (Cl. 27)
34. Grace period (state number of clear banking days)(Cl. 28)	35. Dispute Resolution (state 30(a), 30(b) or 30(c); if 30(c) agreed Place of Arbitration <u>must</u> be stated (Cl. 30)
36. War cancellation (indicate countries agreed)(Cl. 26(f))	
37. Newbuilding Vessel (indicate with "yes" or "no" whether PART III applies)(optional)	38. Name and place of Builders (only to be filled in if PART III applies)
39. Vessel's Yard Building No. (only to be filled in if PART III applies)	40. Date of Building Contract (only to be filled in if PART III applies)
41. Liquidated damages and costs shall accrue to (state party acc. to Cl. 1) a) b) c)	
42. Hire/Purchase agreement (indicate with "yes" or "no" whether PART IV applies)(optional)	43. Bareboat Charter Registry (indicate "yes" or "no" whether PART V applies)(optional)
44. Flag and Country of the Bareboat Charter Registry (only to be filled in if PART V applies)	45. Country of the Underlying Registry (only to be filled in if PART V applies)
46. Number of additional clauses covering special provisions, if agreed	

PREAMBLE - It is mutually agreed that this Contract shall be performed subject to the conditions contained in this Charter which shall include PART I and PART II. In the event of a conflict of conditions, the provisions of PART I shall prevail over those of PART II to the extent of such conflict but no further. It is further mutually agreed that PART III and/or PART IV and/or PART V shall only apply and only form part of this Charter if expressly agreed and stated in the Boxes 37, 42 and 43. If PART III and/or PART IV and/or PART V apply, it is further agreed that in the event of a conflict of conditions, the provisions of PART I and PART II shall prevail over those of PART III and/or PART IV and/or PART V to the extent of such conflict but no further.

Signature (Owners)	Signature (Charterers)

Bareboat charter-party (Barecon 2001)

Bareboat Charter

1. **Definitions** 1
In this Charter, the following terms shall have the 2
meanings hereby assigned to them: 3
"*The Owners*" shall mean the party identified in Box 3; 4
"*The Charterers*" shall mean the party identified in Box 4; 5
"*The Vessel*" shall mean the vessel named in Box 5 and 6
with particulars as stated in Boxes 6 to 12. 7
"*Financial Instrument*" means the mortgage, deed of 8
covenant or other such financial security instrument as 9
annexed to this Charter and stated in Box 28. 10

2. **Charter Period** 11
In consideration of the hire detailed in Box 22, the 12
Owners have agreed to let and the Charterers have 13
agreed to hire the Vessel for the period stated in Box 21 14
("The Charter Period"). 15

3. **Delivery** 16
(not applicable when Part III applies, as indicated in Box 37) 17
(a) The Owners shall before and at the time of delivery 18
exercise due diligence to make the Vessel seaworthy 19
and in every respect ready in hull, machinery and 20
equipment for service under this Charter. 21
The Vessel shall be delivered by the Owners and taken 22
over by the Charterers at the port or place indicated in 23
Box 13 in such ready safe berth as the Charterers may 24
direct. 25
(b) The Vessel shall be properly documented on 26
delivery in accordance with the laws of the flag State 27
indicated in Box 5 and the requirements of the 28
classification society stated in Box 10. The Vessel upon 29
delivery shall have her survey cycles up to date and 30
trading and class certificates valid for at least the number 31
of months agreed in Box 12. 32
(c) The delivery of the Vessel by the Owners and the 33
taking over of the Vessel by the Charterers shall 34
constitute a full performance by the Owners of all the 35
Owners' obligations under this Clause 3, and thereafter 36
the Charterers shall not be entitled to make or assert 37
any claim against the Owners on account of any 38
conditions, representations or warranties expressed or 39
implied with respect to the Vessel but the Owners shall 40
be liable for the cost of but not the time for repairs or 41
renewals occasioned by latent defects in the Vessel, 42
her machinery or appurtenances, existing at the time of 43
delivery under this Charter, provided such defects have 44
manifested themselves within twelve (12) months after 45
delivery unless otherwise provided in Box 32. 46

4. **Time for Delivery** 47
(not applicable when Part III applies, as indicated in Box 37) 48
The Vessel shall not be delivered before the date 49
indicated in Box 14 without the Charterers' consent and 50
the Owners shall exercise due diligence to deliver the 51
Vessel not later than the date indicated in Box 15. 52
Unless otherwise agreed in Box 18, the Owners shall 53
give the Charterers not less than thirty (30) running days' 54
preliminary and not less than fourteen (14) running days' 55
definite notice of the date on which the Vessel is 56
expected to be ready for delivery. 57
The Owners shall keep the Charterers closely advised 58
of possible changes in the Vessel's position. 59

5. **Cancelling** 60
(not applicable when Part III applies, as indicated in Box 37) 61
(a) Should the Vessel not be delivered latest by the 62
cancelling date indicated in Box 15, the Charterers shall 63
have the option of cancelling this Charter by giving the 64
Owners notice of cancellation within thirty-six (36) 65
running hours after the cancelling date stated in Box 66
15, failing which this Charter shall remain in full force 67
and effect. 68
(b) If it appears that the Vessel will be delayed beyond 69
the cancelling date, the Owners may, as soon as they 70

are in a position to state with reasonable certainty the 71
day on which the Vessel should be ready, give notice 72
thereof to the Charterers asking whether they will 73
exercise their option of cancelling, and the option must 74
then be declared within one hundred and sixty-eight 75
(168) running hours of the receipt by the Charterers of 76
such notice or within thirty-six (36) running hours after 77
the cancelling date, whichever is the earlier. If the 78
Charterers do not then exercise their option of cancelling, 79
the seventh day after the readiness date stated in the 80
Owners' notice shall be substituted for the cancelling 81
date indicated in Box 15 for the purpose of this Clause 5. 82
(c) Cancellation under this Clause 5 shall be without 83
prejudice to any claim the Charterers may otherwise 84
have on the Owners under this Charter. 85

6. **Trading Restrictions** 86
The Vessel shall be employed in lawful trades for the 87
carriage of suitable lawful merchandise within the trading 88
limits indicated in Box 20. 89
The Charterers undertake not to employ the Vessel or 90
suffer the Vessel to be employed otherwise than in 91
conformity with the terms of the contracts of insurance 92
(including any warranties expressed or implied therein) 93
without first obtaining the consent of the insurers to such 94
employment and complying with such requirements as 95
to extra premium or otherwise as the insurers may 96
prescribe. 97
The Charterers also undertake not to employ the Vessel 98
or suffer her employment in any trade or business which 99
is forbidden by the law of any country to which the Vessel 100
may sail or is otherwise illicit or in carrying illicit or 101
prohibited goods or in any manner whatsoever which 102
may render her liable to condemnation, destruction, 103
seizure or confiscation. 104
Notwithstanding any other provisions contained in this 105
Charter it is agreed that nuclear fuels or radioactive 106
products or waste are specifically excluded from the 107
cargo permitted to be loaded or carried under this 108
Charter. This exclusion does not apply to radio-isotopes 109
used or intended to be used for any industrial, 110
commercial, agricultural, medical or scientific purposes 111
provided the Owners' prior approval has been obtained 112
to loading thereof. 113

7. **Surveys on Delivery and Redelivery** 114
(not applicable when Part III applies, as indicated in Box 37) 115
The Owners and Charterers shall each appoint 116
surveyors for the purpose of determining and agreeing 117
in writing the condition of the Vessel at the time of 118
delivery and redelivery hereunder. The Owners shall 119
bear all expenses of the On-hire Survey including loss 120
of time, if any, and the Charterers shall bear all expenses 121
of the Off-hire Survey including loss of time, if any, at 122
the daily equivalent to the rate of hire or pro rata thereof. 123

8. **Inspection** 124
The Owners shall have the right at any time after giving 125
reasonable notice to the Charterers to inspect or survey 126
the Vessel or instruct a duly authorised surveyor to carry 127
out such survey on their behalf:- 128
(a) to ascertain the condition of the Vessel and satisfy 129
themselves that the Vessel is being properly repaired 130
and maintained. The costs and fees for such inspection 131
or survey shall be paid by the Owners unless the Vessel 132
is found to require repairs or maintenance in order to 133
achieve the condition so provided; 134
(b) in dry-dock if the Charterers have not dry-docked 135
her in accordance with Clause 10(g). The costs and fees 136
for such inspection or survey shall be paid by the 137
Charterers; and 138
(c) for any other commercial reason they consider 139
necessary (provided it does not unduly interfere with 140

Bareboat charter-party (Barecon 2001)

Bareboat Charter

the commercial operation of the Vessel). The costs and 141
fees for such inspection and survey shall be paid by the 142
Owners. 143
All time used in respect of inspection, survey or repairs 144
shall be for the Charterers' account and form part of the 145
Charter Period. 146
The Charterers shall also permit the Owners to inspect 147
the Vessel's log books whenever requested and shall 148
whenever required by the Owners furnish them with full 149
information regarding any casualties or other accidents 150
or damage to the Vessel. 151

9. Inventories, Oil and Stores 152
A complete inventory of the Vessel's entire equipment, 153
outfit including spare parts, appliances and of all 154
consumable stores on board the Vessel shall be made 155
by the Charterers in conjunction with the Owners on 156
delivery and again on redelivery of the Vessel. The 157
Charterers and the Owners, respectively, shall at the 158
time of delivery and redelivery take over and pay for all 159
bunkers, lubricating oil, unbroached provisions, paints, 160
ropes and other consumable stores (excluding spare 161
parts) in the said Vessel at the then current market prices 162
at the ports of delivery and redelivery, respectively. The 163
Charterers shall ensure that all spare parts listed in the 164
inventory and used during the Charter Period are 165
replaced at their expense prior to redelivery of the 166
Vessel. 167

10. Maintenance and Operation 168
(a)(i)Maintenance and Repairs - During the Charter 169
Period the Vessel shall be in the full possession 170
and at the absolute disposal for all purposes of the 171
Charterers and under their complete control in 172
every respect. The Charterers shall maintain the 173
Vessel, her machinery, boilers, appurtenances and 174
spare parts in a good state of repair, in efficient 175
operating condition and in accordance with good 176
commercial maintenance practice and, except as 177
provided for in Clause 14(l), if applicable, at their 178
own expense they shall at all times keep the 179
Vessel's Class fully up to date with the Classification 180
Society indicated in Box 10 and maintain all other 181
necessary certificates in force at all times. 182
(ii) New Class and Other Safety Requirements - In the 183
event of any improvement, structural changes or 184
new equipment becoming necessary for the 185
continued operation of the Vessel by reason of new 186
class requirements or by compulsory legislation 187
costing (excluding the Charterers' loss of time) 188
more than the percentage stated in Box 23, or if 189
Box 23 is left blank, 5 per cent. of the Vessel's 190
insurance value as stated in Box 29, then the 191
extent, if any, to which the rate of hire shall be varied 192
and the ratio in which the cost of compliance shall 193
be shared between the parties concerned in order 194
to achieve a reasonable distribution thereof as 195
between the Owners and the Charterers having 196
regard, inter alia, to the length of the period 197
remaining under this Charter shall, in the absence 198
of agreement, be referred to the dispute resolution 199
method agreed in Clause 30. 200
(iii) Financial Security - The Charterers shall maintain 201
financial security or responsibility in respect of third 202
party liabilities as required by any government, 203
including federal, state or municipal or other division 204
or authority thereof, to enable the Vessel, without 205
penalty or charge, lawfully to enter, remain at, or 206
leave any port, place, territorial or contiguous 207
waters of any country, state or municipality in 208
performance of this Charter without any delay. This 209
obligation shall apply whether or not such 210

obligation shall apply whether or not such 210
requirements have been lawfully imposed by such 211
government or division or authority thereof. 212
The Charterers shall make and maintain all arrange- 213
ments by bond or otherwise as may be necessary to 214
satisfy such requirements at the Charterers' sole 215
expense and the Charterers shall indemnify the Owners 216
against all consequences whatsoever (including loss of 217
time) for any failure or inability to do so. 218
(b) Operation of the Vessel - The Charterers shall at 219
their own expense and by their own procurement man, 220
victual, navigate, operate, supply, fuel and, whenever 221
required, repair the Vessel during the Charter Period 222
and they shall pay all charges and expenses of every 223
kind and nature whatsoever incidental to their use and 224
operation of the Vessel under this Charter, including 225
annual flag State fees and any foreign general 226
municipality and/or state taxes. The Master, officers and 227
crew of the Vessel shall be the servants of the Charterers 228
for all purposes whatsoever, even if for any reason 229
appointed by the Owners. 230
Charterers shall comply with the regulations regarding 231
officers and crew in force in the country of the Vessel's 232
flag or any other applicable law. 233
(c) The Charterers shall keep the Owners and the 234
mortgagee(s) advised of the intended employment, 235
planned dry-docking and major repairs of the Vessel, 236
as reasonably required. 237
(d) Flag and Name of Vessel - During the Charter 238
Period, the Charterers shall have the liberty to paint the 239
Vessel in their own colours, install and display their 240
funnel insignia and fly their own house flag. The 241
Charterers shall also have the liberty, with the Owners' 242
consent, which shall not be unreasonably withheld, to 243
change the flag and/or the name of the Vessel during 244
the Charter Period. Painting and re-painting, instalment 245
and re-instalment, registration and re-registration, if 246
required by the Owners, shall be at the Charterers' 247
expense and time. 248
(e) Changes to the Vessel - Subject to Clause 10(a)(ii), 249
the Charterers shall make no structural changes in the 250
Vessel or changes in the machinery, boilers, appurten- 251
ances or spare parts thereof without in each instance 252
first securing the Owners' approval thereof. If the Owners 253
so agree, the Charterers shall, if the Owners so require, 254
restore the Vessel to its former condition before the 255
termination of this Charter. 256
(f) Use of the Vessel's Outfit, Equipment and 257
Appliances - The Charterers shall have the use of all 258
outfit, equipment, and appliances on board the Vessel 259
at the time of delivery, provided the same or their 260
substantial equivalent shall be returned to the Owners 261
on redelivery in the same good order and condition as 262
when received, ordinary wear and tear excepted. The 263
Charterers shall from time to time during the Charter 264
Period replace such items of equipment as shall be so 265
damaged or worn as to be unfit for use. The Charterers 266
are to procure that all repairs to or replacement of any 267
damaged, worn or lost parts or equipment be effected 268
in such manner (both as regards workmanship and 269
quality of materials) as not to diminish the value of the 270
Vessel. The Charterers have the right to fit additional 271
equipment at their expense and risk but the Charterers 272
shall remove such equipment at the end of the period if 273
requested by the Owners. Any equipment including radio 274
equipment on hire on the Vessel at time of delivery shall 275
be kept and maintained by the Charterers and the 276
Charterers shall assume the obligations and liabilities 277
of the Owners under any lease contracts in connection 278
therewith and shall reimburse the Owners for all 279
expenses incurred in connection therewith, also for any 280
new equipment required in order to comply with radio 281
regulations. 282

Bareboat charter-party (Barecon 2001)

Bareboat Charter

(g) Periodical Dry-Docking - The Charterers shall dry- 283
dock the Vessel and clean and paint her underwater 284
parts whenever the same may be necessary, but not 285
less than once during the period stated in Box 19 or, if 286
Box 19 has been left blank, every sixty (60) calendar 287
months after delivery or such other period as may be 288
required by the Classification Society or flag State. 289

11. **Hire** 290
(a) The Charterers shall pay hire due to the Owners 291
punctually in accordance with the terms of this Charter 292
in respect of which time shall be of the essence. 293
(b) The Charterers shall pay to the Owners for the hire 294
of the Vessel a lump sum in the amount indicated in 295
Box 22 which shall be payable not later than every thirty 296
(30) running days in advance, the first lump sum being 297
payable on the date and hour of the Vessel's delivery to 298
the Charterers. Hire shall be paid continuously 299
throughout the Charter Period. 300
(c) Payment of hire shall be made in cash without 301
discount in the currency and in the manner indicated in 302
Box 25 and at the place mentioned in Box 26. 303
(d) Final payment of hire, if for a period of less than 304
thirty (30) running days, shall be calculated proportionally 305
according to the number of days and hours remaining 306
before redelivery and advance payment to be effected 307
accordingly. 308
(e) Should the Vessel be lost or missing, hire shall 309
cease from the date and time when she was lost or last 310
heard of. The date upon which the Vessel is to be treated 311
as lost or missing shall be ten (10) days after the Vessel 312
was last reported or when the Vessel is posted as 313
missing by Lloyd's, whichever occurs first. Any hire paid 314
in advance to be adjusted accordingly. 315
(f) Any delay in payment of hire shall entitle the 316
Owners to interest at the rate per annum as agreed in 317
Box 24. If Box 24 has not been filled in, the three months 318
interbank offered rate in London (LIBOR or its successor) 319
for the currency stated in Box 25, as quoted by the British 320
Bankers' Association (BBA) on the date when the hire 321
fell due, increased by 2 per cent., shall apply. 322
(g) Payment of interest due under sub-clause 11(f) 323
shall be made within seven (7) running days of the date 324
of the Owners' invoice specifying the amount payable 325
or, in the absence of an invoice, at the time of the next 326
hire payment date. 327

12. **Mortgage** 328
(only to apply if Box 28 has been appropriately filled in) 329
*) (a) The Owners warrant that they have not effected 330
any mortgage(s) of the Vessel and that they shall not 331
effect any mortgage(s) without the prior consent of the 332
Charterers, which shall not be unreasonably withheld. 333
*) (b) The Vessel chartered under this Charter is financed 334
by a mortgage according to the Financial Instrument. 335
The Charterers undertake to comply, and provide such 336
information and documents to enable the Owners to 337
comply, with all such instructions or directions in regard 338
to the employment, insurances, operation, repairs and 339
maintenance of the Vessel as laid down in the Financial 340
Instrument or as may be directed from time to time during 341
the currency of the Charter by the mortgagee(s) in 342
conformity with the Financial Instrument. The Charterers 343
confirm that, for this purpose, they have acquainted 344
themselves with all relevant terms, conditions and 345
provisions of the Financial Instrument and agree to 346
acknowledge this in writing in any form that may be 347
required by the mortgagee(s). The Owners warrant that 348
they have not effected any mortgage(s) other than stated 349
in Box 28 and that they shall not agree to any 350
amendment of the mortgage(s) referred to in Box 28 or 351
effect any other mortgage(s) without the prior consent 352
of the Charterers, which shall not be unreasonably 353
withheld. 354

*) (Optional, Clauses 12(a) and 12(b) are alternatives; 355
indicate alternative agreed in Box 28). 356

13. **Insurance and Repairs** 357
(a) During the Charter Period the Vessel shall be kept 358
insured by the Charterers at their expense against hull 359
and machinery, war and Protection and Indemnity risks 360
(and any risks against which it is compulsory to insure 361
for the operation of the Vessel, including maintaining 362
financial security in accordance with sub-clause 363
10(a)(iii)) in such form as the Owners shall in writing 364
approve, which approval shall not be un-reasonably 365
withheld. Such insurances shall be arranged by the 366
Charterers to protect the interests of both the Owners 367
and the Charterers and the mortgagee(s) (if any), and 368
the Charterers shall be at liberty to protect under such 369
insurances the interests of any managers they may 370
appoint. Insurance policies shall cover the Owners and 371
the Charterers according to their respective interests. 372
Subject to the provisions of the Financial Instrument, if 373
any, and the approval of the Owners and the insurers, 374
the Charterers shall effect all insured repairs and shall 375
undertake settlement and reimbursement from the 376
insurers of all costs in connection with such repairs as 377
well as insured charges, expenses and liabilities to the 378
extent of coverage under the insurances herein provided 379
for. 380
The Charterers also to remain responsible for and to 381
effect repairs and settlement of costs and expenses 382
incurred thereby in respect of all other repairs not 383
covered by the insurances and/or not exceeding any 384
possible franchise(s) or deductibles provided for in the 385
insurances. 386
All time used for repairs under the provisions of sub- 387
clause 13(a) and for repairs of latent defects according 388
to Clause 3(c) above, including any deviation, shall be 389
for the Charterers' account. 390
(b) If the conditions of the above insurances permit 391
additional insurance to be placed by the parties, such 392
cover shall be limited to the amount for each party set 393
out in Box 30 and Box 31, respectively. The Owners or 394
the Charterers as the case may be shall immediately 395
furnish the other party with particulars of any additional 396
insurance effected, including copies of any cover notes 397
or policies and the written consent of the insurers of 398
any such required insurance in any case where the 399
consent of such insurers is necessary. 400
(c) The Charterers shall upon the request of the 401
Owners, provide information and promptly execute such 402
documents as may be required to enable the Owners to 403
comply with the insurance provisions of the Financial 404
Instrument. 405
(d) Subject to the provisions of the Financial Instru- 406
ment, if any, should the Vessel become an actual, 407
constructive, compromised or agreed total loss under 408
the insurances required under sub-clause 13(a), all 409
insurance payments for such loss shall be paid to the 410
Owners who shall distribute the moneys between the 411
Owners and the Charterers according to their respective 412
interests. The Charterers undertake to notify the Owners 413
and the mortgagee(s), if any, of any occurrences in 414
consequence of which the Vessel is likely to become a 415
total loss as defined in this Clause. 416
(e) The Owners shall upon the request of the 417
Charterers, promptly execute such documents as may 418
be required to enable the Charterers to abandon the 419
Vessel to insurers and claim a constructive total loss. 420
(f) For the purpose of insurance coverage against hull 421
and machinery and war risks under the provisions of 422
sub-clause 13(a), the value of the Vessel is the sum 423
indicated in Box 29. 424

Bareboat charter-party (Barecon 2001)

Bareboat Charter

14. Insurance, Repairs and Classification 425

(Optional, only to apply if expressly agreed and stated 426 *in Box 29, in which event Clause 13 shall be considered* 427 *deleted).* 428

(a) During the Charter Period the Vessel shall be kept 429 insured by the Owners at their expense against hull and 430 machinery and war risks under the form of policy or 431 policies attached hereto. The Owners and/or insurers 432 shall not have any right of recovery or subrogation 433 against the Charterers on account of loss of or any 434 damage to the Vessel or her machinery or appurt- 435 enances covered by such insurance, or on account of 436 payments made to discharge claims against or liabilities 437 of the Vessel or the Owners covered by such insurance. 438 Insurance policies shall cover the Owners and the 439 Charterers according to their respective interests. 440

(b) During the Charter Period the Vessel shall be kept 441 insured by the Charterers at their expense against 442 Protection and Indemnity risks (and any risks against 443 which it is compulsory to insure for the operation of the 444 Vessel, including maintaining financial security in 445 accordance with sub-clause 10(a)(iii)) in such form as 446 the Owners shall in writing approve which approval shall 447 not be unreasonably withheld. 448

(c) In the event that any act or negligence of the 449 Charterers shall vitiate any of the insurance herein 450 provided, the Charterers shall pay to the Owners all 451 losses and indemnify the Owners against all claims and 452 demands which would otherwise have been covered by 453 such insurance. 454

(d) The Charterers shall, subject to the approval of the 455 Owners or Owners' Underwriters, effect all insured 456 repairs, and the Charterers shall undertake settlement 457 of all miscellaneous expenses in connection with such 458 repairs as well as all insured charges, expenses and 459 liabilities, to the extent of coverage under the insurances 460 provided for under the provisions of sub-clause 14(a). 461 The Charterers to be secured reimbursement through 462 the Owners' Underwriters for such expenditures upon 463 presentation of accounts. 464

(e) The Charterers to remain responsible for and to 465 effect repairs and settlement of costs and expenses 466 incurred thereby in respect of all other repairs not 467 covered by the insurances and/or not exceeding any 468 possible franchise(s) or deductibles provided for in the 469 insurances. 470

(f) All time used for repairs under the provisions of 471 sub-clauses 14(d) and 14(e) and for repairs of latent 472 defects according to Clause 3 above, including any 473 deviation, shall be for the Charterers' account and shall 474 form part of the Charter Period. 475

The Owners shall not be responsible for any expenses 476 as are incident to the use and operation of the Vessel 477 for such time as may be required to make such repairs. 478

(g) If the conditions of the above insurances permit 479 additional insurance to be placed by the parties such 480 cover shall be limited to the amount for each party set 481 out in Box 30 and Box 31, respectively. The Owners or 482 the Charterers as the case may be shall immediately 483 furnish the other party with particulars of any additional 484 insurance effected, including copies of any cover notes 485 or policies and the written consent of the insurers of 486 any such required insurance in any case where the 487 consent of such insurers is necessary. 488

(h) Should the Vessel become an actual, constructive, 489 compromised or agreed total loss under the insurances 490 required under sub-clause 14(a), all insurance payments 491 for such loss shall be paid to the Owners, who shall 492 distribute the moneys between themselves and the 493 Charterers according to their respective interests. 494

(i) If the Vessel becomes an actual, constructive, 495 compromised or agreed total loss under the insurances 496 arranged by the Owners in accordance with sub-clause 497

14(a), this Charter shall terminate as of the date of such 498 loss. 499

(j) The Charterers shall upon the request of the 500 Owners, promptly execute such documents as may be 501 required to enable the Owners to abandon the Vessel 502 to the insurers and claim a constructive total loss. 503

(k) For the purpose of insurance coverage against hull 504 and machinery and war risks under the provisions of 505 sub-clause 14(a), the value of the Vessel is the sum 506 indicated in Box 29. 507

(l) Notwithstanding anything contained in sub-clause 508 10(a), it is agreed that under the provisions of Clause 509 14, if applicable, the Owners shall keep the Vessel's 510 Class fully up to date with the Classification Society 511 indicated in Box 10 and maintain all other necessary 512 certificates in force at all times. 513

15. Redelivery 514

At the expiration of the Charter Period the Vessel shall 515 be redelivered by the Charterers to the Owners at a 516 safe and ice-free port or place as indicated in Box 16, in 517 such ready safe berth as the Owners may direct. The 518 Charterers shall give the Owners not less than thirty 519 (30) running days' preliminary notice of expected date, 520 range of ports of redelivery or port or place of redelivery 521 and not less than fourteen (14) running days' definite 522 notice of expected date and port or place of redelivery. 523 Any changes thereafter in the Vessel's position shall be 524 notified immediately to the Owners. 525

The Charterers warrant that they will not permit the 526 Vessel to commence a voyage (including any preceding 527 ballast voyage) which cannot reasonably be expected 528 to be completed in time to allow redelivery of the Vessel 529 within the Charter Period. Notwithstanding the above, 530 should the Charterers fail to redeliver the Vessel within 531 the Charter Period, the Charterers shall pay the daily 532 equivalent to the rate of hire stated in Box 22 plus 10 533 per cent. or to the market rate, whichever is the higher, 534 for the number of days by which the Charter Period is 535 exceeded. All other terms, conditions and provisions of 536 this Charter shall continue to apply. 537

Subject to the provisions of Clause 10, the Vessel shall 538 be redelivered to the Owners in the same or as good 539 structure, state, condition and class as that in which she 540 was delivered, fair wear and tear not affecting class 541 excepted. 542

The Vessel upon redelivery shall have her survey cycles 543 up to date and trading and class certificates valid for at 544 least the number of months agreed in Box 17. 545

16. Non-Lien 546

The Charterers will not suffer, nor permit to be continued, 547 any lien or encumbrance incurred by them or their 548 agents, which might have priority over the title and 549 interest of the Owners in the Vessel. The Charterers 550 further agree to fasten to the Vessel in a conspicuous 551 place and to keep so fastened during the Charter Period 552 a notice reading as follows: 553

"This Vessel is the property of (name of Owners). It is 554 under charter to (name of Charterers) and by the terms 555 of the Charter Party neither the Charterers nor the 556 Master have any right, power or authority to create, incur 557 or permit to be imposed on the Vessel any lien 558 whatsoever." 559

17. Indemnity 560

(a) The Charterers shall indemnify the Owners against 561 any loss, damage or expense incurred by the Owners 562 arising out of or in relation to the operation of the Vessel 563 by the Charterers, and against any lien of whatsoever 564 nature arising out of an event occurring during the 565 Charter Period. If the Vessel be arrested or otherwise 566 detained by reason of claims or liens arising out of her 567

Bareboat charter-party (Barecon 2001)

Bareboat Charter

operation hereunder by the Charterers, the Charterers shall at their own expense take all reasonable steps to secure that within a reasonable time the Vessel is released, including the provision of bail. 568 569 570 571

Without prejudice to the generality of the foregoing, the Charterers agree to indemnify the Owners against all consequences or liabilities arising from the Master, officers or agents signing Bills of Lading or other documents. 572 573 574 575 576

(b) If the Vessel be arrested or otherwise detained by reason of a claim or claims against the Owners, the Owners shall at their own expense take all reasonable steps to secure that within a reasonable time the Vessel is released, including the provision of bail. 577 578 579 580 581

In such circumstances the Owners shall indemnify the Charterers against any loss, damage or expense incurred by the Charterers (including hire paid under this Charter) as a direct consequence of such arrest or detention. 582 583 584 585 586

18. Lien
The Owners to have a lien upon all cargoes, sub-hires and sub-freights belonging or due to the Charterers or any sub-charterers and any Bill of Lading freight for all claims under this Charter, and the Charterers to have a lien on the Vessel for all moneys paid in advance and not earned. 587 588 589 590 591 592 593

19. Salvage
All salvage and towage performed by the Vessel shall be for the Charterers' benefit and the cost of repairing damage occasioned thereby shall be borne by the Charterers. 594 595 596 597 598

20. Wreck Removal
In the event of the Vessel becoming a wreck or obstruction to navigation the Charterers shall indemnify the Owners against any sums whatsoever which the Owners shall become liable to pay and shall pay in consequence of the Vessel becoming a wreck or obstruction to navigation. 599 600 601 602 603 604 605

21. General Average
The Owners shall not contribute to General Average. 606 607

22. Assignment, Sub-Charter and Sale
(a) The Charterers shall not assign this Charter nor sub-charter the Vessel on a bareboat basis except with the prior consent in writing of the Owners, which shall not be unreasonably withheld, and subject to such terms and conditions as the Owners shall approve. 608 609 610 611 612 613

(b) The Owners shall not sell the Vessel during the currency of this Charter except with the prior written consent of the Charterers, which shall not be unreasonably withheld, and subject to the buyer accepting an assignment of this Charter. 614 615 616 617 618

23. Contracts of Carriage
*) **(a)** The Charterers are to procure that all documents issued during the Charter Period evidencing the terms and conditions agreed in respect of carriage of goods shall contain a paramount clause incorporating any legislation relating to carrier's liability for cargo compulsorily applicable in the trade; if no such legislation exists, the documents shall incorporate the Hague-Visby Rules. The documents shall also contain the New Jason Clause and the Both-to-Blame Collision Clause. 619 620 621 622 623 624 625 626 627 628

*) **(b)** The Charterers are to procure that all passenger tickets issued during the Charter Period for the carriage of passengers and their luggage under this Charter shall contain a paramount clause incorporating any legislation relating to carrier's liability for passengers and their luggage compulsorily applicable in the trade; if no such 629 630 631 632 633 634

legislation exists, the passenger tickets shall incorporate the Athens Convention Relating to the Carriage of Passengers and their Luggage by Sea, 1974, and any protocol thereto. 635 636 637 638

*) *Delete as applicable.* 639

24. Bank Guarantee
(Optional, only to apply if Box 27 filled in)
The Charterers undertake to furnish, before delivery of the Vessel, a first class bank guarantee or bond in the sum and at the place as indicated in Box 27 as guarantee for full performance of their obligations under this Charter. 640 641 642 643 644 645 646

25. Requisition/Acquisition
(a) In the event of the Requisition for Hire of the Vessel by any governmental or other competent authority (hereinafter referred to as "Requisition for Hire") irrespective of the date during the Charter Period when "Requisition for Hire" may occur and irrespective of the length thereof and whether or not it be for an indefinite or a limited period of time, and irrespective of whether it may or will remain in force for the remainder of the Charter Period, this Charter shall not be deemed thereby or thereupon to be frustrated or otherwise terminated and the Charterers shall continue to pay the stipulated hire in the manner provided by this Charter until the time when the Charter would have terminated pursuant to any of the provisions hereof always provided however that in the event of "Requisition for Hire" any Requisition Hire or compensation received or receivable by the Owners shall be payable to the Charterers during the remainder of the Charter Period or the period of the "Requisition for Hire" whichever be the shorter. 647 648 649 650 651 652 653 654 655 656 657 658 659 660 661 662 663 664 665 666

(b) In the event of the Owners being deprived of their ownership in the Vessel by any Compulsory Acquisition of the Vessel or requisition for title by any governmental or other competent authority (hereinafter referred to as "Compulsory Acquisition"), then, irrespective of the date during the Charter Period when "Compulsory Acquisition" may occur, this Charter shall be deemed terminated as of the date of such "Compulsory Acquisition". In such event Charter Hire to be considered as earned and to be paid up to the date and time of such "Compulsory Acquisition". 667 668 669 670 671 672 673 674 675 676 677

26. War
(a) For the purpose of this Clause, the words "War Risks" shall include any war (whether actual or threatened), act of war, civil war, hostilities, revolution, rebellion, civil commotion, warlike operations, the laying of mines (whether actual or reported), acts of piracy, acts of terrorists, acts of hostility or malicious damage, blockades (whether imposed against all vessels or imposed selectively against vessels of certain flags or ownership, or against certain cargoes or crews or otherwise howsoever), by any person, body, terrorist or political group, or the Government of any state whatsoever, which may be dangerous or are likely to be or to become dangerous to the Vessel, her cargo, crew or other persons on board the Vessel. 678 679 680 681 682 683 684 685 686 687 688 689 690 691 692

(b) The Vessel, unless the written consent of the Owners be first obtained, shall not continue to or go through any port, place, area or zone (whether of land or sea), or any waterway or canal, where it reasonably appears that the Vessel, her cargo, crew or other persons on board the Vessel, in the reasonable judgement of the Owners, may be, or are likely to be, exposed to War Risks. Should the Vessel be within any such place as aforesaid, which only becomes dangerous, or is likely to be or to become dangerous, after her entry into it, the Owners shall have the right to require the Vessel to leave such area. 693 694 695 696 697 698 699 700 701 702 703 704

Bareboat charter-party (Barecon 2001)

(c) The Vessel shall not load contraband cargo, or to 705
pass through any blockade, whether such blockade be 706
imposed on all vessels, or is imposed selectively in any 707
way whatsoever against vessels of certain flags or 708
ownership, or against certain cargoes or crews or 709
otherwise howsoever, or to proceed to an area where 710
she shall be subject, or is likely to be subject to a 711
belligerent's right of search and/or confiscation. 712
(d) If the insurers of the war risks insurance, when 713
Clause 14 is applicable, should require payment of 714
premiums and/or calls because, pursuant to the 715
Charterers' orders, the Vessel is within, or is due to enter 716
and remain within, any area or areas which are specified 717
by such insurers as being subject to additional premiums 718
because of War Risks, then such premiums and/or calls 719
shall be reimbursed by the Charterers to the Owners at 720
the same time as the next payment of hire is due. 721
(e) The Charterers shall have the liberty: 722
(i) to comply with all orders, directions, recommend- 723
ations or advice as to departure, arrival, routes, 724
sailing in convoy, ports of call, stoppages, 725
destinations, discharge of cargo, delivery, or in any 726
other way whatsoever, which are given by the 727
Government of the Nation under whose flag the 728
Vessel sails, or any other Government, body or 729
group whatsoever acting with the power to compel 730
compliance with their orders or directions; 731
(ii) to comply with the orders, directions or recom- 732
mendations of any war risks underwriters who have 733
the authority to give the same under the terms of 734
the war risks insurance; 735
(iii) to comply with the terms of any resolution of the 736
Security Council of the United Nations, any 737
directives of the European Community, the effective 738
orders of any other Supranational body which has 739
the right to issue and give the same, and with 740
national laws aimed at enforcing the same to which 741
the Owners are subject, and to obey the orders 742
and directions of those who are charged with their 743
enforcement. 744
(f) In the event of outbreak of war (whether there be a 745
declaration of war or not) (i) between any two or more 746
of the following countries: the United States of America; 747
Russia; the United Kingdom; France; and the People's 748
Republic of China, (ii) between any two or more of the 749
countries stated in Box 36, both the Owners and the 750
Charterers shall have the right to cancel this Charter, 751
whereupon the Charterers shall redeliver the Vessel to 752
the Owners in accordance with Clause 15, if the Vessel 753
has cargo on board after discharge thereof at 754
destination, or if debarred under this Clause from 755
reaching or entering it at a near, open and safe port as 756
directed by the Owners, or if the Vessel has no cargo 757
on board, at the port at which the Vessel then is or if at 758
sea at a near, open and safe port as directed by the 759
Owners. In all cases hire shall continue to be paid in 760
accordance with Clause 11 and except as aforesaid all 761
other provisions of this Charter shall apply until 762
redelivery. 763

27. **Commission** 764
The Owners to pay a commission at the rate indicated 765
in Box 33 to the Brokers named in Box 33 on any hire 766
paid under the Charter. If no rate is indicated in Box 33, 767
the commission to be paid by the Owners shall cover 768
the actual expenses of the Brokers and a reasonable 769
fee for their work. 770
If the full hire is not paid owing to breach of the Charter 771
by either of the parties the party liable therefor shall 772
indemnify the Brokers against their loss of commission. 773
Should the parties agree to cancel the Charter, the 774
Owners shall indemnify the Brokers against any loss of 775

commission but in such case the commission shall not 776
exceed the brokerage on one year's hire. 777

28. **Termination** 778
(a) Charterers' Default 779
The Owners shall be entitled to withdraw the Vessel from 780
the service of the Charterers and terminate the Charter 781
with immediate effect by written notice to the Charterers if: 782
(i) the Charterers fail to pay hire in accordance with 783
Clause 11. However, where there is a failure to 784
make punctual payment of hire due to oversight, 785
negligence, errors or omissions on the part of the 786
Charterers or their bankers, the Owners shall give 787
the Charterers written notice of the number of clear 788
banking days stated in Box 34 (as recognised at 789
the agreed place of payment) in which to rectify 790
the failure, and when so rectified within such 791
number of days following the Owners' notice, the 792
payment shall stand as regular and punctual. 793
Failure by the Charterers to pay hire within the 794
number of days stated in Box 34 of their receiving 795
the Owners' notice as provided herein, shall entitle 796
the Owners to withdraw the Vessel from the service 797
of the Charterers and terminate the Charter without 798
further notice; 799
(ii) the Charterers fail to comply with the requirements of: 800
(1) Clause 6 (Trading Restrictions) 801
(2) Clause 13(a) (Insurance and Repairs) 802
provided that the Owners shall have the option, by 803
written notice to the Charterers, to give the 804
Charterers a specified number of days grace within 805
which to rectify the failure without prejudice to the 806
Owners' right to withdraw and terminate under this 807
Clause if the Charterers fail to comply with such 808
notice; 809
(iii) the Charterers fail to rectify any failure to comply 810
with the requirements of sub-clause 10(a)(i) 811
(Maintenance and Repairs) as soon as practically 812
possible after the Owners have requested them in 813
writing so to do and in any event so that the Vessel's 814
insurance cover is not prejudiced. 815
(b) Owners' Default 816
If the Owners shall by any act or omission be in breach 817
of their obligations under this Charter to the extent that 818
the Charterers are deprived of the use of the Vessel 819
and such breach continues for a period of fourteen (14) 820
running days after written notice thereof has been given 821
by the Charterers to the Owners, the Charterers shall 822
be entitled to terminate this Charter with immediate effect 823
by written notice to the Owners. 824
(c) Loss of Vessel 825
This Charter shall be deemed to be terminated if the 826
Vessel becomes a total loss or is declared as a 827
constructive or compromised or arranged total loss. For 828
the purpose of this sub-clause, the Vessel shall not be 829
deemed to be lost unless she has either become an 830
actual total loss or agreement has been reached with 831
her underwriters in respect of her constructive, 832
compromised or arranged total loss or if such agreement 833
with her underwriters is not reached it is adjudged by a 834
competent tribunal that a constructive loss of the Vessel 835
has occurred. 836
(d) Either party shall be entitled to terminate this 837
Charter with immediate effect by written notice to the 838
other party in the event of an order being made or 839
resolution passed for the winding up, dissolution, 840
liquidation or bankruptcy of the other party (otherwise 841
than for the purpose of reconstruction or amalgamation) 842
or if a receiver is appointed, or if it suspends payment, 843
ceases to carry on business or makes any special 844
arrangement or composition with its creditors. 845
(e) The termination of this Charter shall be without 846
prejudice to all rights accrued due between the parties 847

Bareboat Charter

prior to the date of termination and to any claim that 848
either party might have. 849

29. Repossession 850

In the event of the termination of this Charter in 851
accordance with the applicable provisions of Clause 28, 852
the Owners shall have the right to repossess the Vessel 853
from the Charterers at her current or next port of call, or 854
at a port or place convenient to them without hindrance 855
or interference by the Charterers, courts or local 856
authorities. Pending physical repossession of the Vessel 857
in accordance with this Clause 29, the Charterers shall 858
hold the Vessel as gratuitous bailee only to the Owners. 859
The Owners shall arrange for an authorised represent- 860
ative to board the Vessel as soon as reasonably 861
practicable following the termination of the Charter. The 862
Vessel shall be deemed to be repossessed by the 863
Owners from the Charterers upon the boarding of the 864
Vessel by the Owners' representative. All arrangements 865
and expenses relating to the settling of wages, 866
disembarkation and repatriation of the Charterers' 867
Master, officers and crew shall be the sole responsibility 868
of the Charterers. 869

30. Dispute Resolution 870

*) (a) This Contract shall be governed by and construed 871
in accordance with English law and any dispute arising 872
out of or in connection with this Contract shall be referred 873
to arbitration in London in accordance with the Arbitration 874
Act 1996 or any statutory modification or re-enactment 875
thereof save to the extent necessary to give effect to 876
the provisions of this Clause. 877
The arbitration shall be conducted in accordance with 878
the London Maritime Arbitrators Association (LMAA) 879
Terms current at the time when the arbitration proceed- 880
ings are commenced. 881
The reference shall be to three arbitrators. A party 882
wishing to refer a dispute to arbitration shall appoint its 883
arbitrator and send notice of such appointment in writing 884
to the other party requiring the other party to appoint its 885
own arbitrator within 14 calendar days of that notice and 886
stating that it will appoint its arbitrator as sole arbitrator 887
unless the other party appoints its own arbitrator and 888
gives notice that it has done so within the 14 days 889
specified. If the other party does not appoint its own 890
arbitrator and give notice that it has done so within the 891
14 days specified, the party referring a dispute to 892
arbitration may, without the requirement of any further 893
prior notice to the other party, appoint its arbitrator as 894
sole arbitrator and shall advise the other party 895
accordingly. The award of a sole arbitrator shall be 896
binding on both parties as if he had been appointed by 897
agreement. 898
Nothing herein shall prevent the parties agreeing in 899
writing to vary these provisions to provide for the 900
appointment of a sole arbitrator. 901
In cases where neither the claim nor any counterclaim 902
exceeds the sum of US$50,000 (or such other sum as 903
the parties may agree) the arbitration shall be conducted 904
in accordance with the LMAA Small Claims Procedure 905
current at the time when the arbitration proceedings are 906
commenced. 907

*) (b) This Contract shall be governed by and construed 908
in accordance with Title 9 of the United States Code 909
and the Maritime Law of the United States and any 910
dispute arising out of or in connection with this Contract 911
shall be referred to three persons at New York, one to 912
be appointed by each of the parties hereto, and the third 913
by the two so chosen; their decision or that of any two 914
of them shall be final, and for the purposes of enforcing 915
any award, judgement may be entered on an award by 916
any court of competent jurisdiction. The proceedings 917
shall be conducted in accordance with the rules of the 918
Society of Maritime Arbitrators, Inc. 919

In cases where neither the claim nor any counterclaim 920
exceeds the sum of US$50,000 (or such other sum as 921
the parties may agree) the arbitration shall be conducted 922
in accordance with the Shortened Arbitration Procedure 923
of the Society of Maritime Arbitrators, Inc. current at 924
the time when the arbitration proceedings are commenced. 925
*) (c) This Contract shall be governed by and construed 926
in accordance with the laws of the place mutually agreed 927
by the parties and any dispute arising out of or in 928
connection with this Contract shall be referred to 929
arbitration at a mutually agreed place, subject to the 930
procedures applicable there. 931
(d) Notwithstanding (a), (b) or (c) above, the parties 932
may agree at any time to refer to mediation any 933
difference and/or dispute arising out of or in connection 934
with this Contract. 935
In the case of a dispute in respect of which arbitration 936
has been commenced under (a), (b) or (c) above, the 937
following shall apply:- 938
(i) Either party may at any time and from time to time 939
elect to refer the dispute or part of the dispute to 940
mediation by service on the other party of a written 941
notice (the "Mediation Notice") calling on the other 942
party to agree to mediation. 943
(ii) The other party shall thereupon within 14 calendar 944
days of receipt of the Mediation Notice confirm that 945
they agree to mediation, in which case the parties 946
shall thereafter agree a mediator within a further 947
14 calendar days, failing which on the application 948
of either party a mediator will be appointed promptly 949
by the Arbitration Tribunal ("the Tribunal") or such 950
person as the Tribunal may designate for that 951
purpose. The mediation shall be conducted in such 952
place and in accordance with such procedure and 953
on such terms as the parties may agree or, in the 954
event of disagreement, as may be set by the 955
mediator. 956
(iii) If the other party does not agree to mediate, that 957
fact may be brought to the attention of the Tribunal 958
and may be taken into account by the Tribunal when 959
allocating the costs of the arbitration as between 960
the parties. 961
(iv) The mediation shall not affect the right of either 962
party to seek such relief or take such steps as it 963
considers necessary to protect its interest. 964
(v) Either party may advise the Tribunal that they have 965
agreed to mediation. The arbitration procedure shall 966
continue during the conduct of the mediation but 967
the Tribunal may take the mediation timetable into 968
account when setting the timetable for steps in the 969
arbitration. 970
(vi) Unless otherwise agreed or specified in the 971
mediation terms, each party shall bear its own costs 972
incurred in the mediation and the parties shall share 973
equally the mediator's costs and expenses. 974
(vii) The mediation process shall be without prejudice 975
and confidential and no information or documents 976
disclosed during it shall be revealed to the Tribunal 977
except to the extent that they are disclosable under 978
the law and procedure governing the arbitration. 979
(Note: The parties should be aware that the mediation 980
process may not necessarily interrupt time limits.) 981
(e) If Box 35 in Part I is not appropriately filled in, sub-clause 982
30(a) of this Clause shall apply. Sub-clause 30(d) shall 983
apply in all cases. 984
*) *Sub-clauses 30(a), 30(b) and 30(c) are alternatives;* 985
indicate alternative agreed in Box 35. 986

31. Notices 987

(a) Any notice to be given by either party to the other 988
party shall be in writing and may be sent by fax, telex, 989
registered or recorded mail or by personal service. 990
(b) The address of the Parties for service of such 991
communication shall be as stated in Boxes 3 and 4 992
respectively. 993

Bareboat charter-party (Barecon 2001)

14

"BARECON 2001" Standard Bareboat Charter

PART III
PROVISIONS TO APPLY FOR NEWBUILDING VESSELS ONLY
(Optional, only to apply if expressly agreed and stated in Box 37)

1. Specifications and Building Contract

(a) The Vessel shall be constructed in accordance with the Building Contract (hereafter called "the Building Contract") as annexed to this Charter, made between the Builders and the Owners and in accordance with the specifications and plans annexed thereto, such Building Contract, specifications and plans having been countersigned as approved by the Charterers.

(b) No change shall be made in the Building Contract or in the specifications or plans of the Vessel as approved by the Charterers as aforesaid, without the Charterers' consent.

(c) The Charterers shall have the right to send their representative to the Builders' Yard to inspect the Vessel during the course of her construction to satisfy themselves that construction is in accordance with such approved specifications and plans as referred to under sub-clause (a) of this Clause.

(d) The Vessel shall be built in accordance with the Building Contract and shall be of the description set out therein. Subject to the provisions of sub-clause 2(c)(ii) hereunder, the Charterers shall be bound to accept the Vessel from the Owners, completed and constructed in accordance with the Building Contract, on the date of delivery by the Builders. The Charterers undertake that having accepted the Vessel they will not thereafter raise any claims against the Owners in respect of the Vessel's performance or specification or defects, if any. Nevertheless, in respect of any repairs, replacements or defects which appear within the first 12 months from delivery by the Builders, the Owners shall endeavour to compel the Builders to repair, replace or remedy any defects or to recover from the Builders any expenditure incurred in carrying out such repairs, replacements or remedies. However, the Owners' liability to the Charterers shall be limited to the extent the Owners have a valid claim against the Builders under the guarantee clause of the Building Contract (a copy whereof has been supplied to the Charterers). The Charterers shall be bound to accept such sums as the Owners are reasonably able to recover under this Clause and shall make no further claim on the Owners for the difference between the amount(s) so recovered and the actual expenditure on repairs, replacement or remedying defects or for any loss of time incurred.

Any liquidated damages for physical defects or deficiencies shall accrue to the account of the party stated in Box 41(a) or if not filled in shall be shared equally between the parties. The costs of pursuing a claim or claims against the Builders under this Clause (including any liability to the Builders) shall be borne by the party stated in Box 41(b) or if not filled in shall be shared equally between the parties.

2. Time and Place of Delivery

(a) Subject to the Vessel having completed her acceptance trials including trials of cargo equipment in accordance with the Building Contract and specifications to the satisfaction of the Charterers, the Owners shall give and the Charterers shall take delivery of the Vessel afloat when ready for delivery and properly documented at the Builders' Yard or some other safe and readily accessible dock, wharf or place as may be agreed between the parties hereto and the Builders. Under the Building Contract the Builders have estimated that the Vessel will be ready for delivery to the Owners as therein provided but the delivery date for the purpose of this Charter shall be the date when the Vessel is in fact ready for delivery by the Builders after completion of trials whether that be before or after as indicated in the Building Contract. The Charterers shall not be entitled to refuse acceptance of delivery of the Vessel and upon and after such acceptance, subject to Clause 1(d), the Charterers shall not be entitled to make any claim against the Owners in respect of any conditions, representations or warranties, whether express or implied, as to the seaworthiness of the Vessel or in respect of delay in delivery.

(b) If for any reason other than a default by the Owners under the Building Contract, the Builders become entitled under that Contract not to deliver the Vessel to the Owners, the Owners shall upon giving to the Charterers written notice of Builders becoming so entitled, be excused from giving delivery of the Vessel to the Charterers and upon receipt of such notice by the Charterers this Charter shall cease to have effect.

(c) If for any reason the Owners become entitled under the Building Contract to reject the Vessel the Owners shall, before exercising such right of rejection, consult the Charterers and thereupon

(i) if the Charterers do not wish to take delivery of the Vessel they shall inform the Owners within seven (7) running days by notice in writing and upon receipt by the Owners of such notice this Charter shall cease to have effect; or

(ii) if the Charterers wish to take delivery of the Vessel they may by notice in writing within seven (7) running days require the Owners to negotiate with the Builders as to the terms on which delivery should be taken and/or refrain from exercising their right to rejection and upon receipt of such notice the Owners shall commence such negotiations and/or take delivery of the Vessel from the Builders and deliver her to the Charterers;

(iii) in no circumstances shall the Charterers be entitled to reject the Vessel unless the Owners are able to reject the Vessel from the Builders;

(iv) if this Charter terminates under sub-clause (b) or (c) of this Clause, the Owners shall thereafter not be liable to the Charterers for any claim under or arising out of this Charter or its termination.

(d) Any liquidated damages for delay in delivery under the Building Contract and any costs incurred in pursuing a claim therefor shall accrue to the account of the party stated in Box 41(c) or if not filled in shall be shared equally between the parties.

3. Guarantee Works

If not otherwise agreed, the Owners authorise the Charterers to arrange for the guarantee works to be performed in accordance with the building contract terms, and hire to continue during the period of guarantee works. The Charterers have to advise the Owners about the performance to the extent the Owners may request.

4. Name of Vessel

The name of the Vessel shall be mutually agreed between the Owners and the Charterers and the Vessel shall be painted in the colours, display the funnel insignia and fly the house flag as required by the Charterers.

5. Survey on Redelivery

The Owners and the Charterers shall appoint surveyors for the purpose of determining and agreeing in writing the condition of the Vessel at the time of re-delivery. Without prejudice to Clause 15 (Part II), the Charterers shall bear all survey expenses and all other costs, if any, including the cost of docking and undocking, if required, as well as all repair costs incurred. The Charterers shall also bear all loss of time spent in connection with any docking and undocking as well as repairs, which shall be paid at the rate of hire per day or pro rata.

Bareboat Charter

PART IV
HIRE/PURCHASE AGREEMENT
(Optional, only to apply if expressly agreed and stated in Box 42)

On expiration of this Charter and provided the Charterers 1
have fulfilled their obligations according to Part I and II 2
as well as Part III, if applicable, it is agreed, that on 3
payment of the final payment of hire as per Clause 11 4
the Charterers have purchased the Vessel with 5
everything belonging to her and the Vessel is fully paid 6
for. 7

In the following paragraphs the Owners are referred to 8
as the Sellers and the Charterers as the Buyers. 9

The Vessel shall be delivered by the Sellers and taken 10
over by the Buyers on expiration of the Charter. 11

The Sellers guarantee that the Vessel, at the time of 12
delivery, is free from all encumbrances and maritime 13
liens or any debts whatsoever other than those arising 14
from anything done or not done by the Buyers or any 15
existing mortgage agreed not to be paid off by the time 16
of delivery. Should any claims, which have been incurred 17
prior to the time of delivery be made against the Vessel, 18
the Sellers hereby undertake to indemnify the Buyers 19
against all consequences of such claims to the extent it 20
can be proved that the Sellers are responsible for such 21
claims. Any taxes, notarial, consular and other charges 22
and expenses connected with the purchase and 23
registration under Buyers' flag, shall be for Buyers' 24
account. Any taxes, consular and other charges and 25
expenses connected with closing of the Sellers' register, 26
shall be for Sellers' account. 27

In exchange for payment of the last month's hire 28
instalment the Sellers shall furnish the Buyers with a 29
Bill of Sale duly attested and legalized, together with a 30
certificate setting out the registered encumbrances, if 31
any. On delivery of the Vessel the Sellers shall provide 32
for deletion of the Vessel from the Ship's Register and 33
deliver a certificate of deletion to the Buyers. 34
The Sellers shall, at the time of delivery, hand to the 35
Buyers all classification certificates (for hull, engines, 36
anchors, chains, etc.), as well as all plans which may 37
be in Sellers' possession. 38

The Wireless Installation and Nautical Instruments, 39
unless on hire, shall be included in the sale without any 40
extra payment. 41

The Vessel with everything belonging to her shall be at 42
Sellers' risk and expense until she is delivered to the 43
Buyers, subject to the conditions of this Contract and 44
the Vessel with everything belonging to her shall be 45
delivered and taken over as she is at the time of delivery, 46
after which the Sellers shall have no responsibility for 47
possible faults or deficiencies of any description. 48

The Buyers undertake to pay for the repatriation of the 49
Master, officers and other personnel if appointed by the 50
Sellers to the port where the Vessel entered the Bareboat 51
Charter as per Clause 3 (Part II) or to pay the equivalent 52
cost for their journey to any other place. 53

PART V
PROVISIONS TO APPLY FOR VESSELS REGISTERED IN A BAREBOAT CHARTER REGISTRY
(Optional, only to apply if expressly agreed and stated in Box 43)

1. Definitions 1
For the purpose of this PART V, the following terms shall 2
have the meanings hereby assigned to them: 3
"The Bareboat Charter Registry" shall mean the registry 4
of the State whose flag the Vessel will fly and in which 5
the Charterers are registered as the bareboat charterers 6
during the period of the Bareboat Charter. 7
"The Underlying Registry" shall mean the registry of the 8
State in which the Owners of the Vessel are registered 9
as Owners and to which jurisdiction and control of the 10
Vessel will revert upon termination of the Bareboat 11
Charter Registration. 12

2. Mortgage 13
The Vessel chartered under this Charter is financed by 14
a mortgage and the provisions of Clause 12(b) (Part II) 15
shall apply. 16

3. Termination of Charter by Default 17
If the Vessel chartered under this Charter is registered 18
in a Bareboat Charter Registry as stated in Box 44, and 19
if the Owners shall default in the payment of any amounts 20
due under the mortgage(s) specified in Box 28, the 21
Charterers shall, if so required by the mortgagee, direct 22
the Owners to re-register the Vessel in the Underlying 23
Registry as shown in Box 45. 24
In the event of the Vessel being deleted from the 25
Bareboat Charter Registry as stated in Box 44, due to a 26
default by the Owners in the payment of any amounts 27
due under the mortgage(s), the Charterers shall have 28
the right to terminate this Charter forthwith and without 29
prejudice to any other claim they may have against the 30
Owners under this Charter. 31

Bareboat charter-party (Barecon 2001)

operate the ship. For example, banking organisations may finance a newbuilding and charter it out to a ship operator.

In the same way, bareboat charters are favoured by persons or companies who have a particular requirement for a ship and the expertise with which to operate one but without the wish or ability to purchase. Typical of this category are shipping lines who may wish to take a ship on for a period of many years but who do not wish to make a large capital investment by buying one.

A ship hired out in this way is said to be **on bareboat charter**. This type of charter is also referred to as a **demise charter** or a **charter by demise**. The person or company who charters a ship in this way is the **bareboat charterer** and the contract document is called the **bareboat charter-party** or **bareboat charter**. This document contains the terms and conditions including the period of the charter, the rate of hire, the trading limits, if any, and all the rights and responsibilities of the two parties.

The Baltic and International Maritime Conference (BIMCO) publishes a standard bareboat charter-party, codenamed **Barecon 2001**, reproduced on pp. 6–16. This contract contains optional sections dealing with hire/purchase agreements and vessels registered in a bareboat charter registry. A **bareboat charter registry** is the country in which the charterer is registered. This is distinguished from the underlying registry, which is the country where the owners of the ship are registered.

BIMCO also publishes a standard barge bareboat charter party code named **Bargehire 94**.

Associated definition:
to bareboat charter to hire or lease a ship on bareboat charter

Associated terms:
to demise charter
to charter by demise

Berth

Place in a port alongside a quay where a ship loads (**loading berth**) or discharges (**discharging berth**) cargo or, in the case of a **lay-by berth**, waits until a loading or discharging berth is available. This term is also frequently used to signify a place alongside a quay, each of which is capable of accommodating only one ship at a time.

When a ship arrives at a port, the requirement for her to be **on the berth** or not is important in determining the commencement of laytime, that is, the time allowed for loading or discharging, as the case may be. In the case of a **berth charter-party**, a particular berth is nominated by the charterer; laytime does not commence until the ship reaches that specific berth. Conversely, a **port charter-party** stipulates that, once the ship has arrived at the port, laytime will

Berth

start to count whether or not the ship has reached a berth. There may be other factors affecting the commencement of laytime, notably the requirement in certain cases to tender notice of readiness; these will be provided for in the charter-party .

A **safe berth** is one at which it is physically safe for a vessel to remain. A frequent clause in voyage charter-parties places the responsibility onto cargo interests to order the chartered ship only to a safe berth, for the purpose of loading or discharging. This is expressed as **one safe berth** when it is further intended to restrict cargo interests to one berth only.

To stem a berth is to reserve a berth for a ship. This is routinely done at the port by the ship's agent with the appropriate terminal operator prior to the ship's arrival.

A **common berth** or **common user berth** is one whose use is not restricted to the ships of any one line or shipping company.

Associated abbreviations:
1sb one safe berth
osb one safe berth
sb safe berth
wibon whether in berth or not

Associated definition:
to berth (a ship) to moor a ship alongside a quay

See also:
Arrived ship
Laytime

Bill of Lading

Document issued by a shipowner to a shipper of goods. It serves three purposes: a receipt for the goods, evidence of the contract of carriage and document of title. It contains full details of the cargo (*see below*).

Depending on the particular requirements of cargo interests, a number of originals, often three, and a number of copies, which are non-negotiable, are issued. One **original bill of lading** is surrendered to the carrying ship at the discharge port or destination in exchange for the goods. Such a bill of lading is then said to be **accomplished**. Once this is done, any other original bills become non-negotiable. The **copy bills of lading** are retained for reference by various parties including the shipper and consignee.

Generally, all the information relating to the cargo, the origin and destination and the name of ship is contained in boxes on one side of the document. The contents on the reverse of the document depend on the nature of the contract itself.

Typical boxes are:

—Shipper: the person despatching the goods.
—Consignee: party designated to take delivery of the goods. This party could be the receiver of the goods or an agent.
—Notify party: person who should be notified by the shipping line of the arrival of the goods. This could be a customs broker or a sales agent for the exporter.
—Place of receipt: inland place where the goods are placed in the care of the shipping line.
—Vessel: the name of the carrying ocean vessel.
—Port of loading.
—Port of discharge.
—Place of delivery: inland place where the shipping line is contracted to deliver the goods.
—Marks and numbers.
—Number and kind of packages.
—Description of the goods.
—Gross weight.
—Measurement: total number of cubic metres for each item.
—Freight details and charges: this may be left off at the request of the shipper and with the agreement of the shipping line. This is done when the shipper does not want the receiver to know the amount of freight paid.
—Freight payable at: the place where freight is to be paid is shown, which will show whether freight is prepaid or payable at destination.
—Place and date of issue.
—Signature: the bill of lading is signed and dated, normally by the master or his agent. If signed by the agent, often the words **as agent only** will accompany the signature, indicating that the person signing does so as agent and not principal and has no rights or liabilities under the contract of carriage.

Bills of lading arise from both liner and charter shipments. *For charter shipments, see* **Charter-party bills of lading, waybills and cargo receipts**. In the case of liner shipments, the reverse of the bill contains all the terms and conditions of carriage, including any reference to statutory terms. Some shipping lines issue **short form bills of lading** which do not contain their terms and conditions but which contain a reference to the carrier's conditions, normally stating that a copy is available on request. A **common short form bill of lading** is a short form bill which may be used by any shipping line since neither the name of the line nor any conditions are printed on it; it too contains a reference to the carrier's conditions.

Liner bills of lading are normally issued by the ship's agent at the load port. In the past, the shipper or his forwarding agent would have a stock of bills for each shipping line used and would prepare the bill of lading for the line's agent to sign. Nowadays, the necessary computer software may be individual to the particular line and the bills of lading are printed out from data fed into a

Bill of Lading

Shipper (full style and address)	**BIMCO LINER BILL OF LADING** **CODE NAME: "CONLINEBILL 2000"**	
	Amended January 1950; August 1952; January 1973; July 1974; August 1976; January 1978; November 2000.	
Consignee (full style and address) or Order	B/L No.	Reference No.
	Vessel	
Notify Party (full style and address)	Port of loading	
	Port of discharge	

PARTICULARS DECLARED BY THE SHIPPER BUT NOT ACKNOWLEDGED BY THE CARRIER			
Container No./Seal No./Marks and Numbers	Number and kind of packages; description of cargo	Gross weight, kg	Measurement, m³

Draft Copy

SHIPPED on board in apparent good order and condition (unless otherwise stated herein) the total number of Containers/Packages or Units indicated in the Box opposite entitled "Total number of Containers/Packages or Units received by the Carrier" and the cargo as specified above, weight, measure, marks, numbers, quality, contents and value unknown, for carriage to the Port of discharge or so near thereunto as the vessel may safely get and lie always afloat, to be delivered in the like good order and condition at the Port of discharge unto the lawful holder of the Bill of Lading, on payment of freight as indicated to the right plus other charges incurred in accordance with the provisions contained in this Bill of Lading. In accepting this Bill of Lading the Merchant* expressly accepts and agrees to all its stipulations on both Page 1 and Page 2, whether written, printed, stamped or otherwise incorporated, as fully as if they were all signed by the Merchant. One original Bill of Lading must be surrendered duly endorsed in exchange for the cargo or delivery order, whereupon all other Bills of Lading to be void. IN WITNESS whereof the Carrier, Master or their Agent has signed the number of original Bills of Lading stated below right, all of this tenor and date.	Total number of Containers/Packages or Units received by the Carrier	
	Shipper's declared value	Declared value charge
	Freight details and charges	
Carrier's name/principal place of business	Date shipped on board	Place and date of issue
	Number of original Bills of Lading	
	Pre-carriage by**	
Signature .... Carrier or, for the Carrier .... as Master *(Master's name/signature)* .... as Agents *(Agent's name/signature)*	Place of receipt by pre-carrier**	
	Place of delivery by on-carrier**	

*As defined hereinafter (Cl. 1)
**Applicable only when pre-/on-carriage is arranged in accordance with Clause 8

Printed and sold by Fr. G. Knudtzons Bogtrykkeri A/S, Vallensbaekvej 61, DK-2625 Vallensbaek, Fax: +45 4366 070'

Liner bill of lading (Conlinebill)

BIMCO LINER BILL OF LADING

Code Name: "CONLINEBILL 2000"

1. Definition.
"Merchant" includes the shipper, the receiver, the consignor, the consignee, the holder of the Bill of Lading, the owner of the cargo and any person entitled to possession of the cargo.

2. Notification.
Any mention in this Bill of Lading of parties to be notified of the arrival of the cargo is solely for the information of the Carrier and failure to give such notification shall not involve the Carrier in any liability nor relieve the Merchant of any obligation hereunder.

3. Liability for Carriage Between Port of Loading and Port of Discharge.
(a) The International Convention for the Unification of Certain Rules of Law relating to Bills of Lading signed at Brussels on 25 August 1924 ("the Hague Rules") as amended by the Protocol signed at Brussels on 23 February 1968 ("the Hague-Visby Rules") and as enacted in the country of shipment shall apply to this Contract. When the Hague-Visby Rules are not enacted in the country of shipment, the corresponding legislation of the country of destination shall apply, irrespective of whether such legislation may only regulate outbound shipments.

When there is no enactment of the Hague-Visby Rules in either the country of shipment or in the country of destination, the Hague-Visby Rules shall apply to this Contract save where the Hague Rules as enacted in the country of shipment or, if no such enactment is in place, the Hague Rules as enacted in the country of destination apply compulsorily to this Contract.

The Protocol signed at Brussels on 21 December 1979 ("the SDR Protocol 1979") shall apply where the Hague-Visby Rules apply, whether mandatorily or by this Contract.

The Carrier shall in no case be responsible for loss of or damage to cargo arising prior to loading, after discharging, or with respect to deck cargo and live animals.

(b) If the Carrier is held liable in respect of delay, consequential loss or damage other than loss of or damage to the cargo, the liability of the Carrier shall be limited to the freight for the carriage covered by this Bill of Lading, or to the limitation amount as determined in sub-clause 3(a), whichever is the lesser.

(c) The aggregate liability of the Carrier and/or any of his servants, agents or independent contractors under this Contract shall, in no circumstances, exceed the limits of liability for the total loss of the cargo under sub-clause 3(a) or, if applicable, the Additional Clause.

4. Law and Jurisdiction.
Disputes arising out of or in connection with this Bill of Lading shall be exclusively determined by the courts and in accordance with the law of the place where the Carrier has his principal place of business, as stated on Page 1, except as provided elsewhere herein.

5. The Scope of Carriage.
The intended carriage shall not be limited to the direct route but shall be deemed to include any proceeding or returning to or stopping or slowing down at or off any ports or places for any reasonable purpose connected with the carriage including bunkering, loading, discharging, or other cargo operations and maintenance of Vessel and crew.

6. Substitution of Vessel.
The Carrier shall be at liberty to carry the cargo or part thereof to the Port of discharge by the said or other vessel or vessels either belonging to the Carrier or others, or by other means of transport, proceeding either directly or indirectly to such port.

7. Transhipment.
The Carrier shall be at liberty to tranship, lighter, land and store the cargo either on shore or afloat and reship and forward the same to the Port of discharge.

8. Liability for Pre- and On-Carriage.
When the Carrier arranges pre-carriage of the cargo from a place other than the Vessel's Port of loading or on-carriage of the cargo to a place other than the Vessel's Port of discharge, the Carrier shall contract as the Merchant's Agent only and the Carrier shall not be liable for any loss or damage arising during any part of the carriage other than between the Port of loading and the Port of discharge even though the freight for the whole carriage has been collected by him.

9. Loading and Discharging.
(a) Loading and discharging of the cargo shall be arranged by the Carrier or his Agent.

(b) The Merchant shall, at his risk and expense, handle and/or store the cargo before loading and after discharging.

(c) Loading and discharging may commence without prior notice.

(d) The Merchant or his Agent shall tender the cargo when the Vessel is ready to load and as fast as the Vessel can receive including, if required by the Carrier, outside ordinary working hours notwithstanding any custom of the port. If the Merchant or his Agent fails to tender the cargo when the Vessel is ready to load or fails to load as fast as the Vessel can receive the cargo, the Carrier shall be relieved of any obligation to load such cargo, the Vessel shall be entitled to leave the port without further notice and the Merchant shall be liable to the Carrier for deadfreight and/or any overtime charges, losses, costs and expenses incurred by the Carrier.

(e) The Merchant or his Agent shall take delivery of the cargo as fast as the Vessel can discharge including, if required by the Carrier, outside ordinary working hours notwithstanding any custom of the port. If the Merchant or his Agent fails to take delivery of the cargo the Carrier's discharging of the cargo shall be deemed fulfilment of the contract of carriage. Should the cargo not be applied for within a reasonable time, the Carrier may sell the same privately or by auction. If the Merchant or his Agent fails to take delivery of the cargo as fast as the Vessel can discharge, the Merchant shall be liable to the Carrier for any overtime charges, losses, costs and expenses incurred by the Carrier.

(f) The Merchant shall accept his reasonable proportion of unidentified loose cargo.

10. Freight, Charges, Costs, Expenses, Duties, Taxes and Fines.
(a) Freight, whether paid or not, shall be considered as fully earned upon loading and non-returnable in any event. Unless otherwise specified, freight and/or charges under this Contract are payable by the Merchant to the Carrier on demand. Interest at Libor (or its successor) plus 2 per cent. shall run from fourteen days after the date when freight and charges are payable.

(b) The Merchant shall be liable for all costs and expenses of fumigation, gathering and sorting loose cargo and weighing onboard, repairing damage to and replacing packing due to excepted causes, and any extra handling of the cargo for any of the aforementioned reasons.

(c) The Merchant shall be liable for any dues, duties, taxes and charges which under any denomination may be levied, *inter alia*, on the basis of freight, weight of cargo or tonnage of the Vessel.

(d) The Merchant shall be liable for all fines, penalties, costs, expenses and losses which the Carrier, Vessel or cargo may incur through non-observance of Customs House and/or import or export regulations.

(e) The Carrier is entitled in case of incorrect declaration of contents, weights, measurements or value of the cargo to claim double the amount of freight which would have been due if such declaration had been correctly given. For the purpose of ascertaining the actual facts, the Carrier shall have the right to obtain from the Merchant the original invoice and to have the cargo inspected and its contents, weight, measurement or value verified.

11. Lien.
The Carrier shall have a lien on all cargo for any amount due under this contract and the costs of recovering the same and shall be entitled to sell the cargo privately or by auction to satisfy any such claims.

12. General Average and Salvage.
General Average shall be adjusted, stated and settled in London according to the York-Antwerp Rules 1994, or any modification thereof, in respect of all cargo, whether carried on or under deck. In the event of accident, danger, damage or disaster before or after commencement of the voyage resulting from any cause whatsoever, whether due to negligence or not, for which or for the consequence of which the Carrier is not responsible by statute, contract or otherwise, the Merchant shall contribute with the Carrier in General Average to the payment of any sacrifice, losses or expenses of a General Average nature that may be made or incurred, and shall pay salvage and special charges incurred in respect of the cargo. If a salving vessel is owned or operated by the Carrier, salvage shall be paid for as fully as if the salving vessel or vessels belonged to strangers.

13. Both-to-Blame Collision Clause.
If the Vessel comes into collision with another vessel as a result of the negligence of the other vessel and any act, negligence or default of the Master, Mariner, Pilot or the servants of the Carrier in the navigation or in the management of the Vessel, the Merchant will indemnify the Carrier against all loss or liability to the other or non-carrying vessel or her Owner in so far as such loss or liability represents loss of or damage to or any claim whatsoever of the owner of the cargo paid or payable by the other or non-carrying vessel or her Owner to the owner of the cargo and set-off, recouped or recovered by the other or non-carrying vessel or her Owner as part of his claim against the carrying vessel or Carrier. The foregoing provisions shall also apply where the Owner, operator or those in charge of any vessel or vessels or objects other than, or in addition to, the colliding vessels or objects are at fault in respect of a collision or contact.

14. Government directions, War, Epidemics, Ice, Strikes, etc.
(a) The Master and the Carrier shall have liberty to comply with any order or directions or recommendations in connection with the carriage under this Contract given by any Government or Authority, or anybody acting or purporting to act on behalf of such Government or Authority, or having under the terms of the insurance on the Vessel the right to give such orders or directions or recommendations.

(b) Should it appear that the performance of the carriage would expose the Vessel or any cargo onboard to risk of seizure, damage or delay, in consequence of war, warlike operations, blockade, riots, civil commotions or piracy, or any person onboard to risk of loss of life or freedom, or that any such risk has increased, the Master may discharge the cargo at the Port of loading or any other safe and convenient port.

(c) Should it appear that epidemics; quarantine; ice; labour troubles, labour obstructions, strikes, lockouts (whether onboard or on shore); difficulties in loading or discharging would prevent the Vessel from leaving the Port of loading or reaching or entering the Port of discharge or there discharging in the usual manner and departing therefrom, all of which safely and without unreasonable delay, the Master may discharge the cargo at the Port of loading or any other safe and convenient port.

(d) The discharge, under the provisions of this Clause, of any cargo shall be deemed due fulfilment of the contract of carriage.

(e) If in connection with the exercise of any liberty under this Clause any extra expenses are incurred they shall be paid by the Merchant in addition to the freight, together with return freight, if any, and a reasonable compensation for any extra services rendered to the cargo.

15. Defences and Limits of Liability for the Carrier, Servants and Agents.
(a) It is hereby expressly agreed that no servant or agent of the Carrier (which for the purpose of this Clause includes every independent contractor from time to time employed by the Carrier) shall in any circumstances whatsoever be under any liability whatsoever to the Merchant under this Contract of carriage for any loss, damage or delay of whatsoever kind arising or resulting directly or indirectly from any act, neglect or default on his part while acting in the course of or in connection with his employment.

(b) Without prejudice to the generality of the foregoing provisions in this Clause, every exemption from liability, limitation, condition and liberty herein contained and every right, defence and immunity of whatsoever nature applicable to the Carrier or to which the Carrier is entitled, shall also be available and shall extend to protect every such servant and agent of the Carrier acting as aforesaid.

(c) The Merchant undertakes that no claim shall be made against any servant or agent of the Carrier and, if any claim should nevertheless be made, to indemnify the Carrier against all consequences thereof.

(d) For the purpose of all the foregoing provisions of this Clause the Carrier is or shall be deemed to be acting as agent or trustee on behalf of and for the benefit of all persons who might be his servants or agents from time to time and all such persons shall to this extent be or be deemed to be parties to this Contract of carriage.

16. Stowage.
(a) The Carrier shall have the right to stow cargo by means of containers, trailers, transportable tanks, flats, pallets, or similar articles of transport used to consolidate goods.

(b) The Carrier shall have the right to carry containers, trailers, transportable tanks and covered flats, whether stowed by the Carrier or received by him in a stowed condition from the Merchant, on or under deck without notice to the Merchant.

17. Shipper-Packed Containers, trailers, transportable tanks, flats and pallets.
(a) If a container has not been filled, packed or stowed by the Carrier, the Carrier shall not be liable for any loss of or damage to its contents and the Merchant shall cover any loss or expense incurred by the Carrier, if such loss, damage or expense has been caused by:

(i) negligent filling, packing or stowing of the container;

(ii) the contents being unsuitable for carriage in container; or

(iii) the unsuitability or defective condition of the container unless the container has been supplied by the Carrier and the unsuitability or defective condition would not have been apparent upon reasonable inspection at or prior to the time when the container was filled, packed or stowed.

(b) The provisions of sub-clause (i) of this Clause also apply with respect to trailers, transportable tanks, flats and pallets which have not been filled, packed or stowed by the Carrier.

(c) The Carrier does not accept liability for damage due to the unsuitability or defective condition of reefer equipment or trailers supplied by the Merchant.

18. Return of Containers.
(a) Containers, pallets or similar articles of transport supplied by or on behalf of the Carrier shall be returned to the Carrier in the same order and condition as handed over to the Merchant, normal wear and tear excepted, with interiors clean and within the time prescribed in the Carrier's tariff or elsewhere.

(b) The Merchant shall be liable to the Carrier for any loss, damage to, or delay, including demurrage and detention incurred by or sustained to containers, pallets or similar articles of transport during the period between handing over to the Merchant and return to the Carrier.

ADDITIONAL CLAUSE

U.S. Trade. Period of Responsibility.
(i) In case the Contract evidenced by this Bill of Lading is subject to the Carriage of Goods by Sea Act of the United States of America, 1936 (U.S. COGSA), then the provisions stated in said Act shall govern before loading and after discharge and throughout the entire time the cargo is in the Carrier's custody and in which event freight shall be payable on the cargo coming into the Carrier's custody.

(ii) If the U.S. COGSA applies, and unless the nature and value of the cargo has been declared by the shipper before the cargo has been handed over to the Carrier and inserted in this Bill of Lading, the Carrier shall in no event be or become liable for any loss or damage to the cargo in an amount exceeding USD 500 per package or customary freight unit.

Liner bill of lading (Conlinebill)

computer by the line's agent. Some larger forwarders may have access to the software and these companies continue to prepare the bills of lading for signature. Where the line's agent does the work, there may be a charge to the shipper called a **bill of lading charge**.

A **combined transport bill of lading** or **combined transport document** has all the functions of a liner bill but also reflects the fact that the contract of carriage involves at least two legs.

A **through bill of lading** is issued by a shipping line for a voyage requiring on-carriage, thus involving at least one transhipment.

A **groupage bill of lading** is issued to a forwarder by a shipping line and covers consignments from various shippers for the same destination which have been consolidated into one consignment by the forwarding agent. Each shipper receives a **house bill of lading** from the forwarding agent.

An example of a liner bill of lading is the **Conlinebill**, published by the Baltic and International Maritime Council (BIMCO), reproduced on pp. 20–21. BIMCO also publishes a **blank back liner bill of lading**. The contract for goods carried under this bill of lading is subject to the carrier's standard conditions of carriage, or, if the carrier does not have standard conditions, subject to the Conlinebill conditions.

Associated definitions:
bill common short form for bill of lading
to accomplish a bill of lading to surrender an original bill of lading at destination in exchange for the goods

Associated abbreviations:
b/l bill of lading
cbl combined transport bill of lading

See also:
Baltic and International Maritime Council (BIMCO)
Bill of lading as document of title
Bill of lading as evidence of contract of carriage
Bill of lading as receipt
Bill of lading—common clauses
Charter-party bills of lading, waybills and cargo receipts
Combined transport
Manifest

Bill of lading as document of title

One of the three functions of the bill of lading is that of document of title. In this capacity, it may be passed by the shipper to a third party, most often the buyer of the goods or the buyer's agent. This third party, once in possession of the bill of lading, is known as the **bearer** of the bill of lading.

He presents it to the ship at the place of delivery in the contract of carriage and may thus take delivery of the goods.

Depending on the particular requirements of cargo interests, a number of originals, often three, and a number of copies, which are non-negotiable, are issued. The originals might be sent by separate methods to maximise the chance of at least one arriving safely. Only one original bill of lading need be surrendered to the carrying ship at the discharge port or destination in order to take delivery of the goods. Such a bill of lading is then said to be **accomplished**. Once this is done, any other original bills become non-negotiable.

Copy bills of lading are used for administrative purposes only and are said to be **non-negotiable bills of lading**.

By virtue of the fact that an original bill of lading represents title to the goods, it is used by banks as collateral security. When a bank is involved, the bill is first sent to the bank and held by them until payment for the goods has been received. It then passes to the receiver so that it can be exchanged for the goods.

Bills of lading may be made out to a named third party, most commonly the buyer of the goods named in the bill. Alternatively, they may be made out **to bearer,** especially when the goods are expected to be sold, perhaps more than once, while they are on the high seas. When the goods change hands in this way, the bill of lading is endorsed by one party to another, that is, it is signed over.

A bill of lading may be made out **to order**; if made out to the consignee or order, the consignee may endorse it over to whomever he pleases. If it is simply made out to order, it is up to the shipper to endorse it to another party who then becomes entitled to the goods.

On occasion, the original bill of lading does not arrive at the discharge port in time for the vessel's arrival. In this situation, the shipper may instruct the master of the ship or the shipowner to release the goods to a named third party without production of an original bill of lading. The master or owner, if they agree to do this, may require a **letter of indemnity** from the shipper absolving them from the costs and consequences of complying should it turn out that the named party is not entitled to take delivery of the goods. It should be noted that, as a rule, any such letter which seeks to indemnify against an act which is intended to defraud an innocent third party is not enforceable in a court of law.

Associated definition:
bill common short form for bill of lading

Associated abbreviations:
b/l or **bol** bill of lading
loi letter of indemnity

See also:
Bill of lading
Bill of lading as evidence of contract of carriage

Bill of lading as evidence of contract of carriage

One of the three functions of the bill of lading is to act as evidence of the contract of carriage. It is not necessarily the contract itself which may be verbal or may be made up of protracted correspondence, however it is considered best evidence of the contract. When the bill of lading is transferred to a third party, it may become the contract. Many contracts are port to port and are between the shipowner or shipping line and the shipper of the cargo.

A **through bill of lading** is issued by a shipping line for a voyage requiring on-carriage, thus involving at least one transhipment. According to the particular contract, the issuer of the bill of lading may be responsible for the goods throughout the voyage or only for one leg, acting as agent for the on-carriage. Such a bill is often referred to simply as a **through bill**.

A **combined transport bill of lading** or **combined transport document** is similar to a liner bill but also reflects the fact that the contract of carriage involves at least two legs.

A **groupage bill of lading** is issued to a forwarder by a shipping line and covers consignments from various shippers for the same destination which have been consolidated into one consignment by the forwarding agent. Each shipper receives a **house bill of lading** from the forwarding agent who acts as carrier. There are consequently two contracts of carriage in respect of the same goods.

Some shipping lines issue **short form bills of lading** which do not contain their terms and conditions but which contain a reference to the carrier's conditions, normally stating that a copy is available on request. A **common short form bill of lading** is a short form bill which may be used by any shipping line since neither the name of the line nor any conditions are printed on it; it too contains a reference to the carrier's conditions.

A **charter-party bill of lading** may be issued for a shipment of cargo on a chartered ship when it is intended that the receiver be bound by the terms and conditions of the charter-party. A clause to this effect incorporating the place and date of the charter-party appears on the face of the bill.

A **charterer's bill of lading** is a bill of lading issued by a charterer and signed by him or his agent. Under certain circumstances, the charterer who signs his own bills of lading may be deemed to be the carrier, thus taking on all the responsibilities of a carrier.

Associated definition:
bill common short form for bill of lading

Associated abbreviation:
b/l bill of lading

See also:
Bill of lading
Bill of lading as document of title
Bill of lading as receipt

Bill of lading as receipt

In its role as receipt, a bill of lading is commonly issued when the goods have been loaded on board the carrying vessel. Such a bill of lading is known as a **shipped bill of lading** or **shipped on board bill of lading**. This type of bill is often a requirement of banks who advance money using the bill of lading as collateral security and who may wish to be satisfied that the goods are on board the ship. Accordingly, it has a clause on the face to this effect. Note that generally, banks require such bills to be clean (*see below*).

Alternatively, the bill may be issued when the goods have been received into the care of the carrier, but not yet loaded on board. Such a bill is termed a **received for shipment bill of lading**. It serves all the purposes of a shipped bill of lading but may not be acceptable to banks as collateral security.

As a receipt, the bill of lading contains the description and quantity of the goods. Should goods be packed in cases, crates or bundles or otherwise not be visible by virtue of their packaging, the master or carrier may be unaware of the nature or quantity of the contents and may therefore rely on the definition furnished by the shipper. In these circumstances, the term **said to contain** may precede the description or quantity on the bill of lading.

Should the master, first officer or protection and indemnity club surveyor find that the goods, when received into the care of the ship, are in apparent good order and condition, the bill is known as **clean**. If any defect is found to the cargo or its packing, termed an **exception**, a notation will be made on the bill of lading by means of a superimposed clause or clauses. Such a bill is known as **dirty**, **foul** or **unclean**. A **claused bill of lading** also contains superimposed clauses which may relate to defects or may be any comment of the master regarding the carriage of goods, for example that they are unprotected or shipped on deck at shipper's risk. Sometimes claused bills are used synonymously with unclean bills.

Associated definitions:
bill common short form for bill of lading

Associated abbreviations:
b/l bill of lading
m/r mate's receipt
stc said to contain

See also:
Bill of lading
Bill of lading as document of title
Bill of lading as evidence of contract of carriage

Bill of lading—common clauses

Most liner bills of lading are printed on both sides. On the face (front) are boxes or spaces into which are entered all the information necessary to identify the particular cargo, the journey, the names and addresses of cargo interests and, possibly, other details, such as freight. The back of charter-party bills of lading usually contains a reference to the charter-party together with a small number of the more important clauses such as the clause paramount and the general average clause (*for both of which, see below*).

Two clauses are often printed on the face of the bill: a clause with very much a standard wording to say that the goods have been shipped on board in apparent good order and condition. Such wording makes the bill a **shipped bill of lading**. This type of bill is often a requirement of banks who advance money using the bill of lading as collateral security and who wish to be satisfied that the goods are on board the ship.

Sometimes the shipper requires a bill of lading before the goods have been loaded on board. In such a case, the shipping line may issue a so-called **received for shipment bill of lading** indicating that the goods have been received into its care but not yet loaded on board. Such a bill is not usually acceptable to the banks.

The other clause to be found regularly on the face is one which states that only one original bill need be surrendered, or accomplished, in exchange for the goods at destination, the others then being null and void.

On the back of the bill of lading are to be found the liner company's standard terms and conditions. These are set out in clauses, normally numbered one and up, often also broken down into sections. Types of clause which are to be found in most bills of lading are shown below. The wording differs according to the particular company although there are standard forms, notably issued by BIMCO, the Baltic and International Maritime Council:

Clause paramount: Clause which stipulates that the contract of carriage is governed by the Hague Rules or Hague-Visby Rules or the enactment of these rules in the country having jurisdiction over the contract. Also referred to as the **paramount clause**.

Deck cargo clause: Clause which exempts the ship from liability for loss or damage to cargo carried on deck.

Demise clause: Clause stipulating that the contract of carriage is between the shipper or bill of lading holder and the shipowner, who is deemed to be the carrier. Bills of lading issued by charterers of a ship on behalf of the owner and master often contain this clause. The carrier is the party responsible for the care of the cargo under the contract of carriage and the performance of that contract. The inclusion of this clause is normally intended to identify the carrier as the shipowner, thus distinguishing him from the liner company who may have chartered the ship and may therefore not be legally responsible for the navigation of the ship and the care of the cargo. Also called the **identity of carrier clause**. There are some countries where such a clause may not be upheld.

Demurrage clause: Demurrage is associated more with charter-parties than with liner bills of lading but, in some liner trades, there is a provision for demurrage in the event that the ship is delayed in loading or discharging. Such delays can occur when cargo is slow in arriving at the load port or when receivers cannot clear the quay quickly enough at the discharge port to free up space for the ship to continue discharging. In such cases, all the cargo interests may be liable for a share of the specified demurrage.

Deviation clause: Clause allowing the shipping line or shipowner to deviate from the agreed route or normal trade route. This clause varies from contract to contract and may permit the ship to call at unscheduled ports for whatever reason, or simply to deviate to save life or property.

Exceptions clause: Clause which exonerates the carrying ship from responsibility for damage to cargo from certain named causes such as an Act of God or negligence of the master.

Freight clause: Clause which sets out the time when freight is due, normally prepaid, and may provide for cargo interests to pay for any unspecified charges, such as duties and taxes, which may arise.

General average clause: A standard clause incorporating the York-Antwerp Rules into the contract. The clause also stipulates in what country or place general average is to be adjusted.

Lien clause: This clause allows the ship to retain control of the cargo until freight and any other charges due are paid.

Litigation clause: Clause in a bill of lading or charter-party which stipulates that any dispute between the parties arising from the contract be resolved in a court of law, as opposed to arbitration. It also specifies which country has jurisdiction, that is, the authority to administer justice. Also known as the **jurisdiction clause** although jurisdiction is also used to describe the prevailing law.

New Jason clause: Protective clause which provides that the shipowner is entitled to recover in general average even when the loss is caused by negligent navigation. The need for such a clause arises from the decision of an American court that, while American law exempted a shipowner from liability for loss or damage to cargo resulting from negligent navigation, this did not entitle the shipowner to recover in general average for such a loss.

Optional cargo clause: **Optional cargo** is cargo which is destined for one of the ship's discharge ports, the exact one not being known when the goods are loaded. It must therefore be stowed in such a position that it can be removed at any of the selected ports which are known as **optional ports**, without disturbing other cargo. The clause stipulates the amount of notice prior to arrival at one of the optional ports which the shipping line requires in order to discharge the cargo at that port. It specifies the options open to the ship when such notice is not given, or not given in time.

Scope of the voyage: Depending on the individual clause, this may give the ship certain freedoms, such as allowing her to call at any port on or off the route for specific reasons, such as taking on bunkers, or to call at ports in or out of geographical rotation.

War, strikes, ice clause: This clause sets out the course of action open to the master of the ship in the event that the ship or her crew would be put at risk of harm or delay should one of these situations arise during the voyage. Possible actions, depending on the particular clause, include sailing before completing cargo operations, or proceeding to a different port to the one named in the contract.

Associated abbreviations:
b/l bill of lading
ga general average

BIMCO (Baltic and International Maritime Council)

Founded in 1905 as the Baltic and White Sea Conference, the Baltic and International Maritime Council (BIMCO) is now the world's largest private shipping organisation with 2,650 members worldwide.

From its origin as a Northern European owners' organisation, BIMCO today has members in more than 100 countries. The membership is divided into four categories:

- —Owner-members, companies which own or manage ships, operate ships on bareboat charter, operate ships on time charter or operate scheduled liner services with chartered ships; owner-members number nearly 1,000 and control a worldwide fleet of 451 million deadweight—about 60 per cent of the world merchant fleet;
- —Broker-members, companies operating as **shipbrokers**, **ship agents** or **chartering agents**; these account for 1,600 members;
- —Club-members include **Protection and Indemnity Associations**, Freight, Demurrage and Defence Associations and other mutual associations of shipowners as well as national associations of shipowners and shipbrokers;
- —Associate-members are those companies having a demonstrable interest in shipping, including leading **classification societies**, maritime law firms, banks and insurance companies.

Given BIMCO's broad membership, it is ideally placed to represent the interests of the entire shipping community when participating in deliberations of any international or national organisation.

BIMCO is represented in most committees and working groups of the International Maritime Organization (IMO) where it has had consultative status for over 25 years. In addition, BIMCO, together with the International Shipping Federation, has undertaken detailed studies of the demand and supply of qualified seafarers, published in 1990 as the Manpower Report. The report concluded that unless urgent measures were taken to recruit and train more

cadets and ratings, the industry would face a serious shortage of qualified seafarers before the turn of the millennium.

Another major BIMCO activity is the development of standard charter-parties
and other documents for use throughout the industry. The endorsement of
charterers is normally secured by inviting their comments during the drafting
process. Drafted documents are presented to BIMCO's Documentary Committee,
composed of shipowners and club representatives with formidable expertise in
documentary and practical shipping matters for debate and possible approval.

BIMCO's knowledge is continuously available to members who desire
assistance and guidance in their daily undertakings. The services available to
members include information and advice on matters pertaining to ports,
guidance and opinions on documentary matters, information on freight taxes,
assistance on security matters and technical support. In this regard, BIMCO
responds to more than 12,000 requests for information and assistance each year.

Through close co-operation with Customs authorities in the US and various
European countries, BIMCO has secured the support of its owner-members in
combating illegal drug trafficking on merchant ships. Members are invited to
sign voluntary agreements with the Customs authorities to implement strict
security measures aimed at reducing opportunities for drug smuggling. In
return, those participating in these programmes receive fair and correct treatment
should drugs be discovered in the cargo despite agreed security measures.
This may allow the ship to sail from port without, or with a minimum of delay,
avoiding detention or arrest and exposure to heavy penalties.

In addition to the many services which are available to members free of charge,
all members receive weekly newsletters, specialised bulletins and other shipping
publications. Two BIMCO subsidiaries offer professional shipping software and a
range of manuals on practical shipping matters to both members and non-members. BIMCO also organises vocational training courses and specialised
seminars, drawing on its vast repository of shipping information and expertise.

Associated abbreviation:
BIMCO Baltic and International Maritime Council

See also:
BIMCO sundry documents
BIMCO time charter-parties
BIMCO voyage charter-parties

BIMCO sundry documents

The Baltic and International Maritime Council (BIMCO) publishes a number
of standard forms for use in a variety of situations. These are listed here:

—Bill of sale (*see under* **Sale and purchase**).
—BIMCO Blank back (form of) liner bill of lading (*see under* **Bill of lading**).

BIMCO sundry documents

—Dangerous Goods Container/Trailer Packing Certificate (*see under* **Dangerous goods**).

—Dangerous Goods Declaration (*see under* **Dangerous goods**).

—FONASBA General Agency Agreement.

—FONASBA International Broker's Commission Contract.

—FONASBA Standard Liner Agency Agreement.

—International Ocean Towage Agreement (daily hire).

—International Ocean Towage Agreement (lump sum).

—International Wreck Removal and Marine Services Agreement (daily hire).

—International Wreck Removal and Marine Services Agreement (lump sum).

—Liner Booking Note code named "CONLINEBOOKING" (*see under* **Bookings**).

—Memorandum of Agreement (*see under* **Sale and purchase**).

—Standard Bareboat Charter (*see under* **Bareboat charter**).

—Standard Barge Bareboat Charter Party (*see under* **Bareboat charter**).

—Standard Contract for the Sale of Vessels for Demolition (*see under* **Sale and purchase**).

—Standard Crew Management Agreement.

—Standard Disbursements Account (*see under* **Disbursements**).

—Standard Marine Fuels Purchasing Contract (*see under* **Bunkers**).

—Standard Ship Management Agreement.

—Standard Slot Charter Charter Party (*see under* **Liner shipping**).

—Standard Statement of Facts (Short Form) (*see under* **Laytime—calculation**).

—Standard Statement of Facts (Long Form) (*see under* **Laytime—calculation**).

—Standard Time Sheet (Short Form) (*see under* **Laytime—calculation**).

—Standard Time Sheet (Long Form) (*see under* **Laytime—calculation**).

—Standard Statement of Facts (Oil and Chemical Tank Vessels) (Long Form) (*see under* **Laytime—calculation**).

—Standard Statement of Facts (Oil and Chemical Tank Vessels) (Short Form) (*see under* **Laytime—calculation**).

—Standard Transportation Contract for Heavy and Voluminous Cargoes.

—Standard Volume Contract for Contracts of Affreightment (*see under* **Chartering**).

—Voyage Charterparty Laytime Interpretation Rules 1993, code named VOYLAYRULES; issued jointly by BIMCO, CMI, FONASBA and INTERCARGO.

See also:
BIMCO (Baltic and International Maritime Council)

BIMCO time charter-parties

The Baltic and International Maritime Council (BIMCO) publishes a number of standard time charter-parties covering a wide variety of situations. These are listed here:

—The Baltic and International Maritime Conference Uniform Time-Charter (Box Layout 1974). Code name **Baltime 1939**.

—The Baltic and International Maritime Conference Deep Sea Time Charter (Box Layout 1974). Code name **Linertime**.

—Uniform Time Charter Party for Offshore Service Vessels. Code name **Supplytime 89**.

—Uniform Time Charter Party for Container Vessels. Code name **Boxtime**.

—The Baltic and International Maritime Conference Uniform Time Charter Party for Vessels Carrying Liquified Gas. Code name **Gastime**.

—International Association of Independent Tanker Owners Tanker Time Charter Party, issued by INTERTANKO. Code name **Intertanktime 80**.

—The Baltic and International Maritime Conference Uniform Time Charter Party for Vessels Carrying Chemicals in Bulk. Code name **Bimchemtime**.

—New York Produce Exchange Form Time Charter, issued by the Association of Ship Brokers and Agents (U.S.A.), Inc. Code name **NYPE 93**, reproduced on pp. 32–46.

Note that BIMCO's previous name is incorporated into the title of some of these charter-parties.

See also:
BIMCO (Baltic and International Maritime Council)
International Association of Independent Tanker Owners (INTERTANKO)

BIMCO voyage charter-parties

The Baltic and International Maritime Council (BIMCO) publishes a number of standard voyage charter-parties covering a wide variety of commodities and situations. These are listed here. The reason for developing standard charter-parties for different commodities is to provide for specific properties of handling and carriage. In some cases, BIMCO publishes a bill of lading to be used with the charter-party. These are also listed.

Cement

Standard Voyage Charter Party for the Transportation of Bulk Cement and Cement Clinker in Bulk: Code name **Cementvoy**. Because of the problems of dust which occur with cement, this document has lengthy clauses covering options for loading and discharging, which are open to negotiation between the two parties. Alternative cargo handling methods which minimise dust, and the apportionment of the associated costs, are set out. The corresponding bill of lading is code named **Cementvoybill**.

Coal

The Baltic and International Maritime Conference Coal Voyage Charter 1971 (revised 1976). Code name **Polcoalvoy**. This charter-party is used for shipments

B 1.8

Code Name: "NYPE 93"
Recommended by:
The Baltic and International Maritime Council (BIMCO)
The Federation of National Associations of
Ship Brokers and Agents (FONASBA)

TIME CHARTER©
New York Produce Exchange Form
Issued by the Association of Ship Brokers and Agents (U.S.A.), Inc.

November 6th, 1913 - Amended October 20th, 1921; August 6th, 1931; October 3rd, 1946;
Revised June 12th, 1981; September 14th 1993.

THIS CHARTER PARTY, made and concluded in 1

this ....day of............................19.. 2

Between... 3

.... 4

Owners of the Vessel described below, and.. 5

.... 6

.... 7

Charterers. 8

Description of Vessel
9

Name .... Flag .... Built ....(year). 10
Port and number of Registry 11
Classed..in... 12
Deadweight......................................long*/metric* tons (cargo and bunkers, including freshwater and 13
stores not exceeding .... long*/metric* tons) on a salt water draft of 14
on summer freeboard. 15
Capacity .... cubic feet grain.................................cubic feet bale space. 16
Tonnage.. GT/GRT. 17
Speed about .... knots, fully laden, in good weather conditions up to and including maximum 18
Force .... on the Beaufort wind scale, on a consumption of about .... long*/metric* 19
tons of...................................... 20

* Delete as appropriate. 21
For further description see Appendix "A" (if applicable) 22

1. Duration
23

The Owners agree to let and the Charterers agree to hire the Vessel from the time of delivery for a period 24
of.. 25
.... 26
.... 27
....within below mentioned trading limits. 28

Printed and sold by Fr. G. Knudtzon A/S with permission
of ASBA, NY. TEL +45 33 14 11 83 FAX +45 33 93 11 84

NYPE 93

2.   Delivery   29

The Vessel shall be placed at the disposal of the Charterers at 30
.... 31
.... 32
.... The Vessel on her delivery 33
shall be ready to receive cargo with clean-swept holds and tight, staunch, strong and in every way fitted 34
for ordinary cargo service, having water ballast and with sufficient power to operate all cargo-handling gear 35
simultaneously.   36

The Owners shall give the Charterers not less than ....days notice of expected date of 37
delivery.   38

3.   On-Off Hire Survey   39

Prior to delivery and redelivery the parties shall, unless otherwise agreed, each appoint surveyors, for their 40
respective accounts, who shall not later than at first loading port/last discharging port respectively, conduct 41
joint on-hire/off-hire surveys, for the purpose of ascertaining quantity of bunkers on board and the condition 42
of the Vessel. A single report shall be prepared on each occasion and signed by each surveyor, without 43
prejudice to his right to file a separate report setting forth items upon which the surveyors cannot agree. 44
If either party fails to have a representative attend the survey and sign the joint survey report, such party 45
shall nevertheless be bound for all purposes by the findings in any report prepared by the other party. 46
On-hire survey shall be on Charterers' time and off-hire survey on Owners' time.   47

4.   Dangerous Cargo/Cargo Exclusions   48

(a) The Vessel shall be employed in carrying lawful merchandise excluding any goods of a dangerous, 49
injurious, flammable or corrosive nature unless carried in accordance with the requirements or 50
recommendations of the competent authorities of the country of the Vessel's registry and of ports of 51
shipment and discharge and of any intermediate countries or ports through whose waters the Vessel must 52
pass. Without prejudice to the generality of the foregoing, in addition the following are specifically 53
excluded: livestock of any description, arms, ammunition, explosives, nuclear and radioactive materials, 54
.... 55
.... 56
.... 57
.... 58
.... 59
.... 60
.... 61
.... 62
.... 63
.... 64

(b) If IMO-classified cargo is agreed to be carried, the amount of such cargo shall be limited to 65
.... tons and the Charterers shall provide the Master with any evidence he may 66
reasonably require to show that the cargo is packaged, labelled, loaded and stowed in accordance with IMO 67
regulations, failing which the Master is entitled to refuse such cargo or, if already loaded, to unload it at 68
the Charterers' risk and expense.   69

NYPE 93

BIMCO voyage charter-parties

5.   Trading Limits   70

The Vessel shall be employed in such lawful trades between safe ports and safe places   71
within..   72
....excluding   73
....   74
....   75
....as the Charterers shall direct.   76

6.   Owners to Provide   77

The Owners shall provide and pay for the insurance of the Vessel, except as otherwise provided, and for   78
all provisions, cabin, deck, engine-room and other necessary stores, including boiler water; shall pay for   79
wages, consular shipping and discharging fees of the crew and charges for port services pertaining to the   80
crew; shall maintain the Vessel's class and keep her in a thoroughly efficient state in hull, machinery and   81
equipment for and during the service, and have a full complement of officers and crew.   82

7.   Charterers to Provide   83

The Charterers, while the Vessel is on hire, shall provide and pay for all the bunkers except as otherwise   84
agreed; shall pay for port charges (including compulsory watchmen and cargo watchmen and compulsory   85
garbage disposal), all communication expenses pertaining to the Charterers' business at cost, pilotages,   86
towages, agencies, commissions, consular charges (except those pertaining to individual crew members   87
or flag of the Vessel), and all other usual expenses except those stated in Clause 6, but when the Vessel   88
puts into a port for causes for which the Vessel is responsible (other than by stress of weather), then all   89
such charges incurred shall be paid by the Owners. Fumigations ordered because of illness of the crew   90
shall be for the Owners' account. Fumigations ordered because of cargoes carried or ports visited while   91
the Vessel is employed under this Charter Party shall be for the Charterers' account. All other fumigations   92
shall be for the Charterers'account after the Vessel has been on charter for a continuous period of six   93
months or more.   94

The Charterers shall provide and pay for necessary dunnage and also any extra fittings requisite for a   95
special trade or unusual cargo, but the Owners shall allow them the use of any dunnage already aboard   96
the Vessel. Prior to redelivery the Charterers shall remove their dunnage and fittings at their cost and in   97
their time.   98

8.   Performance of Voyages   99

(a) The Master shall perform the voyages with due despatch, and shall render all customary assistance   100
with the Vessel's crew. The Master shall be conversant with the English language and (although   101
appointed by the Owners) shall be under the orders and directions of the Charterers as regards   102
employment and agency; and the Charterers shall perform all cargo handling, including but not limited to   103
loading, stowing, trimming, lashing, securing, dunnaging, unlashing, discharging, and tallying, at their risk   104
and expense, under the supervision of the Master.   105

(b) If the Charterers shall have reasonable cause to be dissatisfied with the conduct of the Master or   106
officers, the Owners shall, on receiving particulars of the complaint, investigate the same, and, if   107
necessary, make a change in the appointments.   108

NYPE 93

34

9.   **Bunkers**   109

(a) The Charterers on delivery, and the Owners on redelivery, shall take over and pay for all fuel and   110
diesel oil remaining on board the Vessel as hereunder.   The Vessel shall be delivered with: 111
.... long*/metric* tons of fuel oil at the price of .... per ton;   112
....tons of diesel oil at the price of .... per ton. The vessel shall   113
be redelivered with: .... tons of fuel oil at the price of.................................... per ton;   114
.... tons of diesel oil at the price of .... per ton.   115

* *Same tons apply throughout this clause.*   116

(b) The Charterers shall supply bunkers of a quality suitable for burning in the Vessel's engines and   117
auxiliaries and which conform to the specification(s) as set out in Appendix A.   118

The Owners reserve their right to make a claim against the Charterers for any damage to the main engines   119
or the auxiliaries caused by the use of unsuitable fuels or fuels not complying with the agreed   120
specification(s). Additionally, if bunker fuels supplied do not conform with the mutually agreed   121
specification(s) or otherwise prove unsuitable for burning in the Vessel's engines or auxiliaries, the Owners   122
shall not be held responsible for any reduction in the Vessel's speed performance and/or increased bunker   123
consumption, nor for any time lost and any other consequences.   124

10.   **Rate of Hire/Redelivery Areas and Notices**   125

The Charterers shall pay for the use and hire of the said Vessel at the rate of $.....................................   126
U.S. currency, daily, or $.................................. U.S. currency per ton on the Vessel's total deadweight   127
carrying capacity, including bunkers and stores, on .... summer freeboard, per 30 days,   128
commencing on and from the day of her delivery, as aforesaid, and at and after the same rate for any part   129
of a month; hire shall continue until the hour of the day of her redelivery in like good order and condition,   130
ordinary wear and tear excepted, to the Owners (unless Vessel lost) at....................................   131
....   132
....   133
.... unless otherwise mutually agreed.   134

The Charterers shall give the Owners not less than .... days notice of the Vessel's   135
expected date and probable port of redelivery.   136

For the purpose of hire calculations, the times of delivery, redelivery or termination of charter shall be   137
adjusted to GMT.   138

11.   **Hire Payment**   139

(a)   *Payment*   140

Payment of Hire shall be made so as to be received by the Owners or their designated payee in   141
...., viz...   142
....   143
....   144
....in   145

NYPE 93

.... currency, or in United States Currency, in funds available to the 146
Owners on the due date, 15 days in advance, and for the last month or part of same the approximate 147
amount of hire, and should same not cover the actual time, hire shall be paid for the balance day by day 148
as it becomes due, if so required by the Owners. Failing the punctual and regular payment of the hire, 149
or on any fundamental breach whatsoever of this Charter Party, the Owners shall be at liberty to 150
withdraw the Vessel from the service of the Charterers without prejudice to any claims they (the Owners) 151
may otherwise have on the Charterers. 152

At any time after the expiry of the grace period provided in Sub-clause 11 (b) hereunder and while the 153
hire is outstanding, the Owners shall, without prejudice to the liberty to withdraw, be entitled to withhold 154
the performance of any and all of their obligations hereunder and shall have no responsibility whatsoever 155
for any consequences thereof, in respect of which the Charterers hereby indemnify the Owners, and hire 156
shall continue to accrue and any extra expenses resulting from such withholding shall be for the 157
Charterers' account. 158

(b) *Grace Period* 159

Where there is failure to make punctual and regular payment of hire due to oversight, negligence, errors 160
or omissions on the part of the Charterers or their bankers, the Charterers shall be given by the Owners 161
.... clear banking days (as recognized at the agreed place of payment) written notice to rectify the 162
failure, and when so rectified within those .... days following the Owners' notice, the payment shall 163
stand as regular and punctual. 164

Failure by the Charterers to pay the hire within .... days of their receiving the Owners' notice as 165
provided herein, shall entitle the Owners to withdraw as set forth in Sub-clause 11 (a) above. 166

(c) *Last Hire Payment* 167

Should the Vessel be on her voyage towards port of redelivery at the time the last and/or the penultimate 168
payment of hire is/are due, said payment(s) is/are to be made for such length of time as the Owners and 169
the Charterers may agree upon as being the estimated time necessary to complete the voyage, and taking 170
into account bunkers actually on board, to be taken over by the Owners and estimated disbursements for 171
the Owners' account before redelivery. Should same not cover the actual time, hire is to be paid for the 172
balance, day by day, as it becomes due. When the Vessel has been redelivered, any difference is to be 173
refunded by the Owners or paid by the Charterers, as the case may be. 174

(d) *Cash Advances* 175

Cash for the Vessel's ordinary disbursements at any port may be advanced by the Charterers, as required 176
by the Owners, subject to 2½ percent commission and such advances shall be deducted from the hire. 177
The Charterers, however, shall in no way be responsible for the application of such advances. 178

12. **Berths** 179

The Vessel shall be loaded and discharged in any safe dock or at any safe berth or safe place that 180
Charterers or their agents may direct, provided the Vessel can safely enter, lie and depart always afloat 181
at any time of tide. 182

NYPE 93

36

13. **Spaces Available** 183

(a) The whole reach of the Vessel's holds, decks, and other cargo spaces (not more than she can 184
reasonably and safely stow and carry), also accommodations for supercargo, if carried, shall be at the 185
Charterers' disposal, reserving only proper and sufficient space for the Vessel's officers, crew, tackle, 186
apparel, furniture, provisions, stores and fuel. 187

(b) In the event of deck cargo being carried, the Owners are to be and are hereby indemnified by the 188
Charterers for any loss and/or damage and/or liability of whatsoever nature caused to the Vessel as a 189
result of the carriage of deck cargo and which would not have arisen had deck cargo not been loaded. 190

14. **Supercargo and Meals** 191

The Charterers are entitled to appoint a supercargo, who shall accompany the Vessel at the Charterers' 192
risk and see that voyages are performed with due despatch. He is to be furnished with free 193
accommodation and same fare as provided for the Master's table, the Charterers paying at the rate of 194
.... per day. The Owners shall victual pilots and customs officers, and also, when 195
authorized by the Charterers or their agents, shall victual tally clerks, stevedore's foreman, etc., 196
Charterers paying at the rate of .... per meal for all such victualling. 197

15. **Sailing Orders and Logs** 198

The Charterers shall furnish the Master from time to time with all requisite instructions and sailing 199
directions, in writing, in the English language, and the Master shall keep full and correct deck and engine 200
logs of the voyage or voyages, which are to be patent to the Charterers or their agents, and furnish the 201
Charterers, their agents or supercargo, when required, with a true copy of such deck and engine logs, 202
showing the course of the Vessel, distance run and the consumption of bunkers. Any log extracts 203
required by the Charterers shall be in the English language. 204

16. **Delivery/Cancelling** 205

If required by the Charterers, time shall not commence before .... and should the 206
Vessel not be ready for delivery on or before...but not later than...........hours, 207
the Charterers shall have the option of cancelling this Charter Party. 208

Extension of Cancelling 209

If the Owners warrant that, despite the exercise of due diligence by them, the Vessel will not be ready 210
for delivery by the cancelling date, and provided the Owners are able to state with reasonable certainty 211
the date on which the Vessel will be ready, they may, at the earliest seven days before the Vessel is 212
expected to sail for the port or place of delivery, require the Charterers to declare whether or not they will 213
cancel the Charter Party. Should the Charterers elect not to cancel, or should they fail to reply within two 214
days or by the cancelling date, whichever shall first occur, then the seventh day after the expected date 215
of readiness for delivery as notified by the Owners shall replace the original cancelling date. Should the 216
Vessel be further delayed, the Owners shall be entitled to require further declarations of the Charterers 217
in accordance with this Clause. 218

NYPE 93

BIMCO voyage charter-parties

17. Off Hire
219

In the event of loss of time from deficiency and/or default and/or strike of officers or crew, or deficiency 220
of stores, fire, breakdown of, or damages to hull, machinery or equipment, grounding, detention by the 221
arrest of the Vessel, (unless such arrest is caused by events for which the Charterers, their servants, 222
agents or subcontractors are responsible), or detention by average accidents to the Vessel or cargo unless 223
resulting from inherent vice, quality or defect of the cargo, drydocking for the purpose of examination or 224
painting bottom, or by any other similar cause preventing the full working of the Vessel, the payment of 225
hire and overtime, if any, shall cease for the time thereby lost. Should the Vessel deviate or put back 226
during a voyage, contrary to the orders or directions of the Charterers, for any reason other than accident 227
to the cargo or where permitted in lines 257 to 258 hereunder, the hire is to be suspended from the time 228
of her deviating or putting back until she is again in the same or equidistant position from the destination 229
and the voyage resumed therefrom. All bunkers used by the Vessel while off hire shall be for the Owners' 230
account. In the event of the Vessel being driven into port or to anchorage through stress of weather, 231
trading to shallow harbors or to rivers or ports with bars, any detention of the Vessel and/or expenses 232
resulting from such detention shall be for the Charterers' account. If upon the voyage the speed be 233
reduced by defect in, or breakdown of, any part of her hull, machinery or equipment, the time so lost, and 234
the cost of any extra bunkers consumed in consequence thereof, and all extra proven expenses may be 235
deducted from the hire. 236

18. Sublet
237

Unless otherwise agreed, the Charterers shall have the liberty to sublet the Vessel for all or any part of 238
the time covered by this Charter Party, but the Charterers remain responsible for the fulfillment of this 239
Charter Party. 240

19. Drydocking
241

The Vessel was last drydocked 242

*(a) The Owners shall have the option to place the Vessel in drydock during the currency of this Charter 243
at a convenient time and place, to be mutually agreed upon between the Owners and the Charterers, for 244
bottom cleaning and painting and/or repair as required by class or dictated by circumstances. 245

*(b) Except in case of emergency no drydocking shall take place during the currency of this Charter 246
Party. 247

* Delete as appropriate 248

20. Total Loss
249

Should the Vessel be lost, money paid in advance and not earned (reckoning from the date of loss or 250
being last heard of) shall be returned to the Charterers at once. 251

21. Exceptions
252

The act of God, enemies, fire, restraint of princes, rulers and people, and all dangers and accidents of the 253
seas, rivers, machinery, boilers, and navigation, and errors of navigation throughout this Charter, always 254
mutually excepted. 255

NYPE 93

22. <u>Liberties</u>   256

The Vessel shall have the liberty to sail with or without pilots, to tow and to be towed, to assist vessels   257
in distress, and to deviate for the purpose of saving life and property.   258

23. <u>Liens</u>   259

The Owners shall have a lien upon all cargoes and all sub-freights and/or sub-hire for any amounts due   260
under this Charter Party, including general average contributions, and the Charterers shall have a lien on   261
the Vessel for all monies paid in advance and not earned, and any overpaid hire or excess deposit to be   262
returned at once.   263

The Charterers will not directly or indirectly suffer, nor permit to be continued, any lien or encumbrance,   264
which might have priority over the title and interest of the Owners in the Vessel.   The Charterers   265
undertake that during the period of this Charter Party, they will not procure any supplies or necessaries   266
or services, including any port expenses and bunkers, on the credit of the Owners or in the Owners' time.   267

24. <u>Salvage</u>   268

All derelicts and salvage shall be for the Owners' and the Charterers' equal benefit after deducting   269
Owners' and Charterers' expenses and crew's proportion.   270

25. <u>General Average</u>   271

General average shall be adjusted according to York-Antwerp Rules 1974, as amended 1990, or any   272
subsequent modification thereof, in .... and settled in   273
currency.   274

The Charterers shall procure that all bills of lading issued during the currency of the Charter Party will   275
contain a provision to the effect that general average shall be adjusted according to York-Antwerp Rules   276
1974, as amended 1990, or any subsequent modification thereof and will include the "New Jason   277
Clause" as per Clause 31.   278

Time charter hire shall not contribute to general average.   279

26. <u>Navigation</u>   280

Nothing herein stated is to be construed as a demise of the Vessel to the Time Charterers. The Owners   281
shall remain responsible for the navigation of the Vessel, acts of pilots and tug boats, insurance, crew,   282
and all other matters, same as when trading for their own account.   283

27. <u>Cargo Claims</u>   284

Cargo claims as between the Owners and the Charterers shall be settled in accordance with the Inter-Club   285
New York Produce Exchange Agreement of February 1970, as amended May, 1984, or any subsequent   286
modification or replacement thereof.   287

NYPE 93

28.   Cargo Gear and Lights   288

The Owners shall maintain the cargo handling gear of the Vessel which is as follows:.......................... 289
.... 290
.... 291
.... 292
providing gear (for all derricks or cranes) capable of lifting capacity as described. The Owners shall also   293
provide on the Vessel for night work lights as on board, but all additional lights over those on board shall   294
be at the Charterers' expense. The Charterers shall have the use of any gear on board the Vessel. If   295
required by the Charterers, the Vessel shall work night and day and all cargo handling gear shall be at the   296
Charterers' disposal during loading and discharging. In the event of disabled cargo handling gear, or   297
insufficient power to operate the same, the Vessel is to be considered to be off hire to the extent that   298
time is actually lost to the Charterers and the Owners to pay stevedore stand-by charges occasioned   299
thereby, unless such disablement or insufficiency of power is caused by the Charterers' stevedores. If   300
required by the Charterers, the Owners shall bear the cost of hiring shore gear in lieu thereof, in which   301
case the Vessel shall remain on hire.   302

29.   Crew Overtime   303

In lieu of any overtime payments to officers and crew for work ordered by the Charterers or their agents,   304
the Charterers shall pay the Owners, concurrently with the hire ....per month   305
or pro rata.   306

30.   Bills of Lading   307

(a) The Master shall sign the bills of lading or waybills for cargo as presented in conformity with mates   308
or tally clerk's receipts. However, the Charterers may sign bills of lading or waybills on behalf of the   309
Master, with the Owner's prior written authority, always in conformity with mates or tally clerk's receipts.   310

(b) All bills of lading or waybills shall be without prejudice to this Charter Party and the Charterers shall   311
indemnify the Owners against all consequences or liabilities which may arise from any inconsistency   312
between this Charter Party and any bills of lading or waybills signed by the Charterers or by the Master   313
at their request.   314

(c) Bills of lading covering deck cargo shall be claused: "Shipped on deck at Charterers', Shippers' and   315
Receivers' risk, expense and responsibility, without liability on the part of the Vessel, or her Owners for   316
any loss, damage, expense or delay howsoever caused."   317

31.   Protective Clauses   318

This Charter Party is subject to the following clauses all of which are also to be included in all bills of   319
lading or waybills issued hereunder: 320

(a)   CLAUSE PARAMOUNT   321
"This bill of lading shall have effect subject to the provisions of the Carriage of Goods by Sea Act of the   322
United States, the Hague Rules, or the Hague-Visby Rules, as applicable, or such other similar national   323
legislation as may mandatorily apply by virtue of origin or destination of the bills of lading, which shall   324
be deemed to be incorporated herein and nothing herein contained shall be deemed a surrender by the   325

NYPE 93

carrier of any of its rights or immunities or an increase of any of its responsibilities or liabilities under said   326
applicable Act. If any term of this bill of lading be repugnant to said applicable Act to any extent, such   327
term shall be void to that extent, but no further."   328

and   329

(b)   BOTH-TO-BLAME COLLISION CLAUSE   330
"If the ship comes into collision with another ship as a result of the negligence of the other ship and any   331
act, neglect or default of the master, mariner, pilot or the servants of the carrier in the navigation or in   332
the management of the ship, the owners of the goods carried hereunder will indemnify the carrier against   333
all loss or liability to the other or non-carrying ship or her owners insofar as such loss or liability represents   334
loss of, or damage to, or any claim whatsoever of the owners of said goods, paid or payable by the other   335
or non-carrying ship or her owners to the owners of said goods and set off, recouped or recovered by the   336
other or non-carrying ship or her owners as part of their claim against the carrying ship or carrier.   337

The foregoing provisions shall also apply where the owners, operators or those in charge of any ships or   338
objects other than, or in addition to, the colliding ships or objects are at fault in respect to a collision or   339
contact."   340

and   341

(c)   NEW JASON CLAUSE   342
"In the event of accident, danger, damage or disaster before or after the commencement of the voyage   343
resulting from any cause whatsoever, whether due to negligence or not, for which, or for the   344
consequences of which, the carrier is not responsible, by statute, contract, or otherwise, the goods,   345
shippers, consignees, or owners of the goods shall contribute with the carrier in general average to the   346
payment of any sacrifices, losses, or expenses of a general average nature that may be made or incurred,   347
and shall pay salvage and special charges incurred in respect of the goods.   348

If a salving ship is owned or operated by the carrier, salvage shall be paid for as fully as if salving ship   349
or ships belonged to strangers. Such deposit as the carrier or his agents may deem sufficient to cover   350
the estimated contribution of the goods and any salvage and special charges thereon shall, if required,   351
be made by the goods, shippers, consignees or owners of the goods to the carrier before delivery."   352

and   353

(d)   U.S. TRADE - DRUG CLAUSE   354
"In pursuance of the provisions of the U.S. Anti Drug Abuse Act 1986 or any re-enactment thereof, the   355
Charterers warrant to exercise the highest degree of care and diligence in preventing unmanifested   356
narcotic drugs and marijuana to be loaded or concealed on board the Vessel.   357

Non-compliance with the provisions of this clause shall amount to breach of warranty for consequences   358
of which the Charterers shall be liable and shall hold the Owners, the Master and the crew of the Vessel   359
harmless and shall keep them indemnified against all claims whatsoever which may arise and be made   360
against them individually or jointly. Furthermore, all time lost and all expenses incurred, including fines,   361
as a result of the Charterers' breach of the provisions of this clause shall be for the Charterer's account   362
and the Vessel shall remain on hire.   363

NYPE 93

Should the Vessel be arrested as a result of the Charterers' non-compliance with the provisions of this 364
clause, the Charterers shall at their expense take all reasonable steps to secure that within a reasonable 365
time the Vessel is released and at their expense put up the bails to secure release of the Vessel. 366

The Owners shall remain responsible for all time lost and all expenses incurred, including fines, in the 367
event that unmanifested narcotic drugs and marijuana are found in the possession or effects of the 368
Vessel's personnel." 369

and 370

(e)   WAR CLAUSES 371
"(i) No contraband of war shall be shipped. The Vessel shall not be required, without the consent of the 372
Owners, which shall not be unreasonably withheld, to enter any port or zone which is involved in a state 373
of war, warlike operations, or hostilities, civil strife, insurrection or piracy whether there be a declaration 374
of war or not, where the Vessel, cargo or crew might reasonably be expected to be subject to capture, 375
seizure or arrest, or to a hostile act by a belligerent power (the term "power" meaning any de jure or de 376
facto authority or any purported governmental organization maintaining naval, military or air forces). 377

(ii) If such consent is given by the Owners, the Charterers will pay the provable additional cost of insuring 378
the Vessel against hull war risks in an amount equal to the value under her ordinary hull policy but not 379
exceeding a valuation of... In addition, the Owners may purchase and the 380
Charterers will pay for war risk insurance on ancillary risks such as loss of hire, freight disbursements, 381
total loss, blocking and trapping, etc. If such insurance is not obtainable commercially or through a 382
government program, the Vessel shall not be required to enter or remain at any such port or zone. 383

(iii) In the event of the existence of the conditions described in (i) subsequent to the date of this Charter, 384
or while the Vessel is on hire under this Charter, the Charterers shall, in respect of voyages to any such 385
port or zone assume the provable additional cost of wages and insurance properly incurred in connection 386
with master, officers and crew as a consequence of such war, warlike operations or hostilities. 387

(iv) Any war bonus to officers and crew due to the Vessel's trading or cargo carried shall be for the 388
Charterers' account." 389

32.   War Cancellation 390

In the event of the outbreak of war (whether there be a declaration of war or not) between any two or 391
more of the following countries:.. 392
.... 393
.... 394
.... 395
either the Owners or the Charterers may cancel this Charter Party. Whereupon, the Charterers shall 396
redeliver the Vessel to the Owners in accordance with Clause 10; if she has cargo on board, after 397
discharge thereof at destination, or, if debarred under this Clause from reaching or entering it, at a near 398
open and safe port as directed by the Owners; or, if she has no cargo on board, at the port at which she 399
then is; or, if at sea, at a near open and safe port as directed by the Owners. In all cases hire shall 400
continue to be paid in accordance with Clause 11 and except as aforesaid all other provisions of this 401
Charter Party shall apply until redelivery. 402

NYPE 93

33. **Ice** 403

The Vessel shall not be required to enter or remain in any icebound port or area, nor any port or area 404
where lights or lightships have been or are about to be withdrawn by reason of ice, nor where there is 405
risk that in the ordinary course of things the Vessel will not be able on account of ice to safely enter and 406
remain in the port or area or to get out after having completed loading or discharging. Subject to the 407
Owners' prior approval the Vessel is to follow ice-breakers when reasonably required with regard to her 408
size, construction and ice class. 409

34. **Requisition** 410

Should the Vessel be requisitioned by the government of the Vessel's flag during the period of this Charter 411
Party, the Vessel shall be deemed to be off hire during the period of such requisition, and any hire paid 412
by the said government in respect of such requisition period shall be retained by the Owners. The period 413
during which the Vessel is on requisition to the said government shall count as part of the period provided 414
for in this Charter Party. 415

If the period of requisition exceeds .... months, either party shall have the option 416
of cancelling this Charter Party and no consequential claim may be made by either party. 417

35. **Stevedore Damage** 418

Notwithstanding anything contained herein to the contrary, the Charterers shall pay for any and all 419
damage to the Vessel caused by stevedores provided the Master has notified the Charterers and/or their 420
agents in writing as soon as practical but not later than 48 hours after any damage is discovered. Such 421
notice to specify the damage in detail and to invite Charterers to appoint a surveyor to assess the extent 422
of such damage. 423

(a) In case of any and all damage(s) affecting the Vessel's seaworthiness and/or the safety of the crew 424
and/or affecting the trading capabilities of the Vessel, the Charterers shall immediately arrange for repairs 425
of such damage(s) at their expense and the Vessel is to remain on hire until such repairs are completed 426
and if required passed by the Vessel's classification society. 427

(b) Any and all damage(s) not described under point (a) above shall be repaired at the Charterers' option, 428
before or after redelivery concurrently with the Owners' work. In such case no hire and/or expenses will 429
be paid to the Owners except and insofar as the time and/or the expenses required for the repairs for 430
which the Charterers are responsible, exceed the time and/or expenses necessary to carry out the 431
Owners' work. 432

36. **Cleaning of Holds** 433

The Charterers shall provide and pay extra for sweeping and/or washing and/or cleaning of holds between 434
voyages and/or between cargoes provided such work can be undertaken by the crew and is permitted by 435
local regulations, at the rate of................................ per hold. 436

In connection with any such operation, the Owners shall not be responsible if the Vessel's holds are not 437
accepted or passed by the port or any other authority. The Charterers shall have the option to re-deliver 438
the Vessel with unclean/unswept holds against a lumpsum payment of.......................in lieu of cleaning. 439

NYPE 93

43

37. **Taxes**   440

Charterers to pay all local, State, National taxes and/or dues assessed on the Vessel or the Owners   441
resulting from the Charterers' orders herein, whether assessed during or after the currency of this Charter   442
Party including any taxes and/or dues on cargo and/or freights and/or sub-freights and/or hire (excluding   443
taxes levied by the country of the flag of the Vessel or the Owners).   444

38. **Charterers' Colors**   445

The Charterers shall have the privilege of flying their own house flag and painting the Vessel with their   446
own markings. The Vessel shall be repainted in the Owners' colors before termination of the Charter   447
Party. Cost and time of painting, maintaining and repainting those changes effected by the Charterers   448
shall be for the Charterers' account.   449

39. **Laid Up Returns**   450

The Charterers shall have the benefit of any return insurance premium receivable by the Owners from their   451
underwriters as and when received from underwriters by reason of the Vessel being in port for a minimum   452
period of 30 days if on full hire for this period or pro rata for the time actually on hire.   453

40. **Documentation**   454

The Owners shall provide any documentation relating to the Vessel that may be required to permit the   455
Vessel to trade within the agreed trade limits, including, but not limited to certificates of financial   456
responsibility for oil pollution, provided such oil pollution certificates are obtainable from the Owners'   457
P & I club, valid international tonnage certificate, Suez and Panama tonnage certificates, valid certificate   458
of registry and certificates relating to the strength and/or serviceability of the Vessel's gear.   459

41. **Stowaways**   460

(a)   (i) The Charterers warrant to exercise due care and diligence in preventing stowaways in gaining   461
access to the Vessel by means of secreting away in the goods and/or containers shipped by the   462
Charterers.   463

(ii) If, despite the exercise of due care and diligence by the Charterers, stowaways have gained   464
access to the Vessel by means of secreting away in the goods and/or containers shipped by the   465
Charterers, this shall amount to breach of charter for the consequences of which the Charterers   466
shall be liable and shall hold the Owners harmless and shall keep them indemnified against all   467
claims whatsoever which may arise and be made against them. Furthermore, all time lost and all   468
expenses whatsoever and howsoever incurred, including fines, shall be for the Charterers' account   469
and the Vessel shall remain on hire.   470

(iii) Should the Vessel be arrested as a result of the Charterers' breach of charter according to   471
sub-clause (a)(ii) above, the Charterers shall take all reasonable steps to secure that, within a   472
reasonable time, the Vessel is released and at their expense put up bail to secure release of the   473
Vessel.   474

(b)   (i) If, despite the exercise of due care and diligence by the Owners, stowaways have gained   475
access to the Vessel by means other than secreting away in the goods and/or containers shipped   476
by the Charterers, all time lost and all expenses whatsoever and howsoever incurred, including   477
fines, shall be for the Owners' account and the Vessel shall be off hire.   478

    (ii) Should the Vessel be arrested as a result of stowaways having gained access to the Vessel   479
by means other than secreting away in the goods and/or containers shipped by the Charterers,   480
the Owners shall take all reasonable steps to secure that, within a reasonable time, the Vessel   481
is released and at their expense put up bail to secure release of the Vessel.   482

42.   Smuggling   483

In the event of smuggling by the Master, Officers and/or crew, the Owners shall bear the cost of any   484
fines, taxes, or imposts levied and the Vessel shall be off hire for any time lost as a result thereof.   485

43.   Commissions   486

A commission of........................ percent is payable by the Vessel and the Owners to..........................   487
....   488
....   489
....   490
on hire earned and paid under this Charter, and also upon any continuation or extension of this Charter.   491

44.   Address Commission   492

An address commission of .... percent is payable to...   493
....   494
....   495
....on hire earned and paid under this Charter.   496

45.   Arbitration   497

(a)   NEW YORK   498
All disputes arising out of this contract shall be arbitrated at New York in the following manner, and   499
subject to U.S. Law: 500

One Arbitrator is to be appointed by each of the parties hereto and a third by the two so chosen. Their   501
decision or that of any two of them shall be final, and for the purpose of enforcing any award, this   502
agreement may be made a rule of the court. The Arbitrators shall be commercial men, conversant with   503
shipping matters. Such Arbitration is to be conducted in accordance with the rules of the Society of   504
Maritime Arbitrators Inc.   505

For disputes where the total amount claimed by either party does not exceed US $ ....**   506
the arbitration shall be conducted in accordance with the Shortened Arbitration Procedure of the Society   507
of Maritime Arbitrators Inc.   508

NYPE 93

BIMCO voyage charter-parties

(b) LONDON 509

All disputes arising out of this contract shall be arbitrated at London and, unless the parties agree 510
forthwith on a single Arbitrator, be referred to the final arbitrament of two Arbitrators carrying on business 511
in London who shall be members of the Baltic Mercantile & Shipping Exchange and engaged in Shipping, 512
one to be appointed by each of the parties, with power to such Arbitrators to appoint an Umpire. No 513
award shall be questioned or invalidated on the ground that any of the Arbitrators is not qualified as 514
above, unless objection to his action be taken before the award is made. Any dispute arising hereunder 515
shall be governed by English Law. 516

For disputes where the total amount claimed by either party does not exceed US $ ....** 517
the arbitration shall be conducted in accordance with the Small Claims Procedure of the London Maritime 518
Arbitrators Association. 519

* *Delete para (a) or (b) as appropriate* 520

** *Where no figure is supplied in the blank space this provision only shall be void but the other provisions* 521
of this clause shall have full force and remain in effect. 522

If mutually agreed, clauses .... to ...., both inclusive, as attached hereto are fully 523
incorporated in this Charter Party. 524

APPENDIX "A" 525

To Charter Party dated 526

Between...Owners 527

and .... Charterers 528

Further details of the Vessel: 529

530

NYPE 93

46

of coal from Poland. It provides information specific to the loading ports and berths used in this trade, including draughts, notices and laytime. Note that BIMCO's previous name is incorporated into the title of this charter-party. In 1988, BIMCO produced the **Polcoalvoy-Atic** Terms which introduced amendments to the standard charter-party and some new terms. In 1990, the **Polcoalvoy Rider Clauses** were introduced and, in 1995, the **Polcoalvoy Slip**, containing loading and demurrage scales. The corresponding bill of lading is code named **Polcoalbill**.

Soviet Coal Charter 1962 (Amended 1971, 1981 and 1987)—for Coal, Coke and Coaltarpitch from the USSR (Layout 1971). Specifically, this document is used for shipments from named Baltic, Black Sea and Azov Sea ports. Code name **Sovcoal**. The **Sovcoal-Atic** Terms—amendments to the standard charter-party including a scale of daily discharging rates at named French ports—were introduced in 1988. The corresponding bill of lading is code named **Sovcoalbill**.

The Documentary Committee of the Japan Shipping Exchange, Inc. Coal Charter Party. Code name **Nipponcoal**.

Americanised Welsh Coal Charter issued by the Association of Ship Brokers and Agents (USA) Inc. (revised 1993). Code name **Amwelsh 93**. This charter-party is reproduced on pp. 48–58.

Fertilisers

Chamber of Shipping Fertilisers Charter 1942. Code name **Ferticon**.

North American Fertilizer Charter Party 1978/88. Code name **Fertivoy 88**.

Hydrocharter Voyage Charter Party (Amended 1975). Code name **Hydrocharter**. This charter-party is used by Norsk Hydro a.s. of Oslo as charterers. It contains specific notice and laytime provisions. BIMCO publishes a bill of lading to be used with this charter-party.

Soviet Fertiliser Charter Party, used for shipments of fertilisers including muriate of potash and urea from USSR ports. Code name **Fertisov**. The corresponding bill of lading is code named **Fertisovbill**.

Fertiliser Voyage Charter Party, used by the Qatar Fertiliser Company (S.A.Q.) as charterers for cargoes loaded at the ports of Umm Said and Qatar. Code name **Qafcharter**. The corresponding bill of lading is code named **Qafcobill**.

Gas

Gas Voyage Charter Party to be used in the LPG ammonia and liquified petrochemical gas trades. Code name **Gasvoy 2005**. This document includes boxes to be completed which are specific to this type of cargo, for example, the cargo tank volume in cubic metres, the lowest temperature permissible in the tanks and the specific gravity of the cargo at a temperature of 15 degrees Celsius. The body of the charter-party contains a clause setting out the responsibilities of the owner in respect of cleaning and purging of the tanks prior to loading and the temperature of the cargo during the voyage.

BIMCO voyage charter-parties

Code Name: "AMWELSH 93"
Recommended by
The Baltic and International Maritime Council (BIMCO)
The Federation of National Associations of
Ship Brokers and Agents (FONASBA)

AMERICANIZED WELSH COAL CHARTER©
Issued by the Association of Ship Brokers and Agents (U.S.A), Inc.
New York - 1953; Amended 1979; Revised 1993

THIS CHARTER PARTY, made and concluded in.. 1

this..day of...19.............................. 2

Between... 3

.... 4

Owners of the...(flag) Vessel.. 5

of.., built.............................(year) at.................................(where) 6

of................................tons of 1000 kilos total deadweight on summer freeboard, inclusive of bunkers, 7

classed...in..and registered 8

at...under No...............................The Vessel's length overall is 9

.... and beam is.......................................The Vessel's fully laden draft on summer 10

freeboard is................................now..and 11

.... 12

Charterers.. 13

of the city of.. 14

1. Loading Port(s)/Discharging Port(s) 15

That the said Vessel being tight, staunch and strong, and in every way fit for the voyage, shall, with all 16

convenient speed, proceed to 17

.... 18

....and there load, always afloat, and in the 19

customary manner from the Charterers, in such safe berth as they shall direct, a full and complete cargo 20

of coal...........................tons of 2240 lbs/1000 kilos*.......................% more or less in the Owners' 21

option; and being so loaded, shall therefrom proceed, with all convenient speed, to 22

..................................or so near thereunto as she can safely get, and there deliver her cargo, as ordered 23

by the Charterers, where she can safely deliver it, always afloat, on having been paid freight at the rate of 24

.... US $ per ton of 2240 lbs/1000 kilos* on bill of lading quantity. 25

*) Delete as appropriate 26

2. Freight Payment 27

The FREIGHT shall be paid in 28

.... 29

.... 30

Amwelsh 93

3.   <u>Notices & Loading Port Orders</u>   31

The Master shall give the Charterers (telegraphic address "...",   32
Telex No..........................., Fax No.............................) and .... days notice of the date of the   33
Vessel's expected readiness to load, and approximate quantity of cargo required with the....................   34
day notice. The Charterers shall be kept advised by any form of telecommunication of any alterations in   35
that date, as and when known. The Charterers shall declare first or sole loading port on receipt of the   36
Master's.....................day notice, unless declared earlier.   37

4.   <u>Discharging Port Orders</u>   38

The Master shall apply to the Charterers by any form of telecommunication for declaration of the first or   39
sole discharging port 96 hours before the Vessel is due off/at...   40
......................................and they are to declare same to the Master not later than 48 hours following   41
receipt of the Master's application.   42

5.   <u>Laydays/Cancelling</u>   43

Laytime for loading shall not commence before 0800 on the........................day of............................   44
Should the Vessel's notice of readiness not have been tendered in accordance with Clause 6, before 1700   45
on the........................day of..........................., the Charterers shall have the option of cancelling this   46
Charter Party, not later than one hour after the said notice has been tendered. The said cancelling date shall   47
be extended by as many days (rounded to the nearest day) as the Charterers shall have failed to give load   48
ing port orders as provided in Clause 3 hereabove, without prejudice to the Owners' claim for detention.   49

If the Owners warrant that, despite the exercise of due diligence by the Owners, the Vessel will not be   50
ready to tender notice of readiness by the cancelling date, and provided the Owners are able to state with   51
reasonable certainty the date on which the Vessel will be ready, they may, at the earliest seven days before   52
the Vessel is expected to sail for the port or place of loading, require the Charterers to declare whether or   53
not they will cancel the Charter. Should the Charterers elect not to cancel, or should they fail to reply with-   54
in seven days or by the cancelling date, whichever shall first occur, then the seventh day after the expected   55
date of readiness for loading as notified by the Owners shall replace the original cancelling date. Should   56
the Vessel be further delayed, the Owners shall be entitled to require further declarations of the Charterers   57
in accordance with this Clause.   58

6.   <u>Time Counting</u>   59

(a)   Notice of the Vessel's readiness to load and discharge at the first or sole port shall be tendered in   60
        writing to the Charterers between 0800 and 1700 on Mondays to Fridays and between 0800 and   61
        1200 on Saturdays. Following tender of notice of readiness, laytime shall commence 12 hours   62
        thereafter, unless the Vessel's loading or discharging has sooner commenced.   63

        Such notice of readiness shall be tendered when the Vessel is in the loading or discharging berth,   64
        if available, and is in all respects ready to load or discharge the cargo, unless the berth is not   65
        available on the Vessel's arrival, whereupon the Master may tender the said notice from a lay berth   66
        or anchorage within the port limits.   67

Amwelsh 93

BIMCO voyage charter-parties

(b)   If the Vessel is prevented from entering the port limits because the first or sole loading or 68
discharging berth, or a lay berth or anchorage is not available, or on the order of the Charterers or 69
any competent official body or authority, and the Master warrants that the Vessel is physically 70
ready in all respects to load or discharge, he may tender notice, by radio, if desired, from the usual 71
anchorage outside the port limits, whether in free pratique or not, and/or whether customs cleared 72
or not. If after entering the port limits the Vessel is found not to be ready, the time lost from the 73
discovery thereof, until she is ready, shall not count as laytime, or time on demurrage. 74

(c)   Once the loading or discharging berth becomes available laytime or time on demurrage shall cease 75
until the Vessel is in the berth, and shifting expenses shall be for the Owners'account. 76

(d)   *Subsequent Ports* - At second or subsequent ports of loading and/or discharging, laytime or time 77
on demurrage shall resume counting from the Vessel's arrival in loading or discharging berth, if 78
available, or if unavailable, from the arrival time within or outside the port limits, as provided in 79
paragraph (a) supra. 80

7.   Laytime 81

(a)   The Vessel shall be loaded at the average rate of.....................tons of 1000 kilos per day, or 82
pro-rata for any part of a day, or within..................... running days, both of twenty-four 83
consecutive hours, weather permitting, Sundays and Holidays excepted/included*, and discharged 84
at the average rate of ....tons of 1000 kilos per day, or pro-rata for any part of a day, or 85
within..........................running days, both of twenty four consecutive hours, weather permitting, 86
Sundays and Holidays excepted/included*. 87

    Days Purposes 88

(b)   Vessel shall be loaded and discharged within...............days of twenty-four consecutive hours, 89
weather permitting, Sundays and Holidays excepted/included* at loading, and excepted/included* 90
at discharge. 91

(c)   Time used in loading and discharging during excepted periods, if any, shall count as laytime. 92

    Non-reversible laytime 93

(d)   In cases of separate laytime for loading and discharging, laytime shall be non-reversible. 94

*) *Delete as appropriate* 95

8.   Exceptions 96

The Owners shall be bound before and at the beginning of the voyage to exercise due diligence to make 97
the Vessel seaworthy, and to have her properly manned, equipped and supplied, and neither the Vessel, 98
nor the Master, or Owners shall be, or shall be held liable for any loss of, or damage, or delay to the cargo 99
for causes excepted by the Hague Rules, or the Hague-Visby Rules, where applicable. 100

Amwelsh 93

BIMCO voyage charter-parties

Neither the Vessel, her Master or Owners, nor the Charterers shall, unless otherwise expressly provided 101
in this Charter Party, be responsible for loss or damage to, or failure to supply, load, discharge or deliver 102
the cargo resulting from: Act of God, act of war, act of public enemies, pirates or assailing thieves; 103
arrest or restraint of princes, rulers or people; embargoes; seizure under legal process, provided bond is 104
promptly furnished to release vessel or cargo; floods; frosts; fogs; fires; blockades; riots; insurrections; 105
civil commotions; earthquakes; explosions; collisions; strandings and accidents of navigation; accidents 106
at the mines or to machinery or to loading equipment; or any other causes beyond the Owners' or the 107
Charterers' control; always provided that such events directly affect the loading and/or discharging 108
process of the Vessel, and its performance under this Charter Party. 109

9. **Strikes** 110

In the event of loss of time to the Vessel directly affecting the loading or discharging of this cargo, caused 111
by a strike or lockout of any personnel connected with the production, mining, or any essential inland 112
transport of the cargo to be loaded or discharged into/from this Vessel from point of origin, up to, and 113
including the actual loading and discharging operations, or by any personnel essential to the actual loading 114
and discharging of the cargo, half the laytime shall count during such periods, provided always that none 115
of the aforementioned events did exist at the date of the charter party. If at any time during the 116
continuance of such strikes or lockouts the Vessel goes on demurrage, said demurrage shall be paid at 117
half the rate specified in Clause 10, hereunder, until such time as the strike or lockout terminates; thence 118
full demurrage unless the Vessel was already on demurrage before the strike broke out, in which case full 119
demurrage shall be paid for its entire period. 120

10. **Demurrage/Despatch** 121

Demurrage, if incurred, at loading and/or discharging port(s), shall be paid by the Charterers to the 122
Owners at the rate of.......................... per day, or pro-rata for part of a day. Despatch money shall be 123
paid by the Owners to the Charterers at half the demurrage rate for all laytime saved. 124

11. **Cost of Loading and Discharging** 125

The cargo shall be loaded, dumped, spout trimmed, and discharged by Charterers'*/Receivers'* 126
stevedores free of risk and expense to the Vessel, under the supervision of the Master. Should the 127
stevedores refuse to follow his instructions, the Master shall protest to them in writing and shall advise 128
the Charterers immediately thereof. 129

12. **Overtime** 130

(a) *Expenses* 131

   (i)   All overtime expenses at loading and discharging ports shall be for account of the party 132
         ordering same. 133

   (ii) If overtime is ordered by port authorities or the party controlling the loading and/or 134
         discharging terminal or facility all overtime expenses shall be equally shared between the 135
         Owners and the Charterers*/Receivers*. 136

Amwelsh 93

(iii)   Overtime expenses for the Vessel's officers and crew shall always be for the Owners'   137
account.   138

(b)   *Time Counting*   139

If overtime work ordered by the Owners be performed during periods excepted from laytime the   140
actual time used shall count; if ordered by the Charterers/Receivers, the actual time used shall not   141
count; if ordered by port authorities or the party controlling the loading and/or discharging terminal   142
or facility half the actual time used shall count.   143

*) Delete as appropriate   144

13.   Opening & Closing Hatches   145

Opening and closing of hatches at commencement and completion of loading and discharging shall be for   146
the Owners' account and time so used is not to count. All other opening and closing of hatches shall be   147
for the Charterers' account and time so used shall count.   148

14.   Seaworthy Trim   149

Charterers shall leave the Vessel in seaworthy trim and with cargo on board safely stowed to Master's   150
satisfaction between loading berths/ports and between discharging berths/ports, respectively; any   151
expenses resulting therefrom shall be for Charterers' account and any time used shall count.   152

15.   Shifting   153

If more than one berth of loading and discharging has been agreed, and used, costs of shifting, including   154
cost of bunkers used, shall be for the Charterers' account, time counting.   155

16.   Lighterage   156

Should the Vessel be ordered to discharge at a place where there is insufficient water for the Vessel to   157
reach it in the first tide after her arrival there, without lightening and lie always afloat, laytime shall count   158
as per Clause 6 at a safe anchorage or lightening place for similar size vessels bound for such a place,   159
and any lighterage expenses incurred to enable her to reach the place of discharge shall be for the   160
Charterers' account, any custom of the port to the contrary notwithstanding. Time occupied in   161
proceeding from the lightening place to the discharging berth shall not count as laytime or time on   162
demurrage.   163

17.   Agents   164

The Vessel shall be consigned to...agents at port(s) of loading, and to   165
....agents at port(s) of discharge.   166

18.   **Extra Insurance on Cargo**   167

Any extra insurance on cargo, incurred owing to Vessel's age, class, flag, or ownership to be for Owners'   168
account up to a maximum of............................. and may be deducted from the freight in the   169
Charterers' option. The Charterers shall furnish evidence of payment supporting such deduction.   170

19.   **Stevedore Damage**   171

(a)   Any damage caused by stevedores shall be settled directly between the Owners and the   172
        stevedores.   173

(b)   *In case the Owners are unsuccessful in obtaining compensation from the stevedores for damage   174
        for which they are legally liable, then the Charterers shall indemnify the Owners for any sums so   175
        due and unpaid.   176

*) Sub-clause (b) is optional and shall apply unless deleted.   177

20.   **Deviation**   178

Should the Vessel deviate to save or attempt to save life or property at sea, or make any reasonable   179
deviation, the said deviation shall not be deemed to be an infringement or breach of this Charter Party,   180
and the Owners shall not be liable for any loss or damage resulting therefrom provided, however, that if   181
the deviation is for the purpose of loading or unloading cargo or passengers, it shall "prima facie", be   182
regarded as unreasonable.   183

21.   **Lien and Cesser**   184

The Charterers' liability under this Charter Party shall cease on cargo being shipped, except for payment   185
of freight, deadfreight and demurrage, and except for all other matters provided for in this Charter Party   186
where the Charterers' responsibility is specified. The Owners shall have a lien on the cargo for freight,   187
deadfreight, demurrage and general average contribution due to them under this Charter Party.   188

22.   **Bills of Lading**   189

The bills of lading shall be prepared in accordance with the dock or railway weight and shall be endorsed   190
by the Master, agent or Owners, weight unknown, freight and all conditions as per this Charter, such bills   191
of lading to be signed at the Charterers' or shippers' office within twenty four hours after the Vessel is   192
loaded. The Master shall sign a certificate stating that the weight of the cargo loaded is in accordance   193
with railway weight certificate. The Charterers are to hold the Owners harmless should any shortage   194
occur.   195

23.   **Grab Discharge**   196

No cargo shall be loaded in any cargo compartment inaccessible to reach by grabs.   197

Amwelsh 93

BIMCO voyage charter-parties

24.   **Protective Clauses**   198

This Charter Party is subject to the following clauses all of which are also to be included in all bills of   199
lading issued hereunder: 200

(a)   "CLAUSE PARAMOUNT: This bill of lading shall have effect subject to the provisions of the   201
       Carriage of Goods by Sea Act of the United States, the Hague Rules, or the Hague-Visby Rules,   202
       as applicable, or such other similar national legislation as may mandatorily apply by virtue of origin   203
       or destination of the bills of lading, which shall be deemed to be incorporated herein and nothing   204
       herein contained shall be deemed a surrender by the carrier of any of its rights or immunities or   205
       an increase of any of its responsibilities or liabilities under said applicable Act. If any term of this 206
       bill of lading be repugnant to said applicable Act to any extent, such term shall be void to that   207
       extent, but no further."   208

and   209

(b)   "NEW BOTH-TO-BLAME COLLISION CLAUSE: If the ship comes into collision with another ship   210
       as a result of the negligence of the other ship and any act, neglect or default of the master,   211
       mariner, pilot or the servants of the carrier in the navigation or in the management of the ship,   212
       the owners of the goods carried hereunder will indemnify the carrier against all loss or liability to   213
       the other or non-carrying ship or her owners in so far as such loss or liability represents loss of,   214
       or damage to, or any claim whatsoever of the owners of said goods, paid or payable by the other   215
       or non-carrying ship or her owners to the owners of said goods and set off, recouped or recovered   216
       by the other or non-carrying ship or her owners as part of their claim against the carrying ship or   217
       carrier.   218

       The foregoing provisions shall also apply where the owners, operators or those in charge of any   219
       ship or ships or objects other than, or in addition to, the colliding ships or objects are at fault in   220
       respect to a collision or contact."   221

and   222

(c)   "NEW JASON CLAUSE: In the event of accident, danger, damage or disaster before or after   223
       commencement of the voyage, resulting from any cause whatsoever, whether due to negligence   224
       or not, for which, or for the consequences of which, the carrier is not responsible, by statute,   225
       contract or otherwise, the goods, shippers, consignees or owners of the goods shall contribute   226
       with the carrier in general average to the payment of any sacrifices, losses or expenses of a   227
       general average nature that may be made or incurred, and shall pay salvage and special charges   228
       incurred in respect of the goods.   229

       If a salving ship is owned or operated by the carrier, salvage shall be paid for as fully as if such   230
       salving ship or ships belonged to strangers. Such deposit as the carrier or his agents may deem   231
       sufficient to cover the estimated contribution of the goods, and any salvage and special charges   232
       thereon shall, if required, be made by the goods, shippers, consignees or owners of the goods to   233
       the carrier before delivery."   234

and   235

(d) "PROTECTION AND INDEMNITY BUNKERING CLAUSE: The Vessel in addition to all other 236
liberties shall have liberty as part of the contract voyage and at any stage thereof to proceed to 237
any port or ports whatsoever whether such ports are on or off the direct and/or customary route 238
or routes to the ports of loading or discharge named in this Charter and there take oil bunkers in 239
any quantity in the discretion of the Owners even to the full capacity of fuel tanks, deep tanks 240
and any other compartment in which oil can be carried whether such amount is or is not required 241
for the chartered voyage." 242

25. Ice Clause 243

Loading Port 244

(a) If the Vessel cannot reach the loading port by reason of ice when she is ready to proceed from 245
her last port, or at any time during the voyage, or on her arrival, or if frost sets in after her arrival, 246
the Master - for fear of the Vessel being frozen in - is at liberty to leave without cargo; in such 247
cases this Charter Party shall be null and void. 248

(b) If during loading, the Master, for fear of the Vessel being frozen in, deems it advisable to leave, 249
he has the liberty to do so with what cargo he has on board and to proceed to any other port with 250
option of completing cargo for the Owners' own account to any port or ports including the port 251
of discharge. Any part cargo thus loaded under this Charter Party to be forwarded to destination 252
at the Vessel's expense against payment of the agreed freight, provided that no extra expenses 253
be thereby caused to the Consignees, freight being paid on quantity delivered (in proportion if 254
lump sum), all other conditions as per Charter Party. 255

(c) In case of more than one loading port, and if one or more of the ports are closed by ice, the 256
Master or Owners to be at liberty either to load the part cargo at the open port and fill up 257
elsewhere for the Owners' own account as under sub-clause (b) or to declare the Charter Party 258
null and void unless the Charterers agree to load full cargo at the open port. 259

Voyage and Discharging Port 260

(d) Should ice prevent the Vessel from reaching the port of discharge, the Charterers/Receivers shall 261
have the option of keeping the Vessel waiting until the re-opening of navigation and paying 262
demurrage or of ordering the Vessel to a safe and immediately accessible port where she can 263
safely discharge without risk of detention by ice. Such orders to be given within 48 hours after 264
the Owners or Master have given notice to the Charterers/Receivers of impossibility of reaching 265
port of destination. 266

(e) If during discharging, the Master, for fear of the Vessel being frozen in, deems it advisable to 267
leave, he has liberty to do so with what cargo he has on board and to proceed to the nearest safe 268
and accessible port. Such port to be nominated by the Charterers/Receivers as soon as possible, 269
but not later than 24 running hours, Sundays and holidays excluded, of receipt of the Owners' 270
request for nomination of a substitute discharging port, failing which the Master will himself 271
choose such port. 272

Amwelsh 93

(f)   On delivery of the cargo at such port, all conditions of the Bill of Lading shall apply and the   273
Owners shall receive the same freight as if the Vessel had discharged at the original port of   274
destination, except that if the distance to the substitute port exceeds 100 nautical miles the   275
freight on the cargo delivered at that port to be increased in proportion.   276

26.   **General Average**   277

General average shall be adjusted according to York-Antwerp Rules 1974, as amended 1990, or any   278
subsequent modification thereof, in............................., and settled in...   279
currency.   280

27.   **War Risks**   281

1.   The Master shall not be required or bound to sign Bills of Lading for any blockaded port or for any   282
port which the Master or Owners in his or their discretion consider dangerous or impossible to   283
enter or reach.   284

2.   (A)   If any port of loading or of discharge named in this Charter Party or to which the Vessel   285
may properly be ordered pursuant to the terms of the Bills of Lading be blockaded, or   286

       (B)   If owing to any war, hostilities, warlike operations, civil war, civil commotions, revolutions,   287
or the operation of international law (a) entry to any such port of loading or of discharge or the   288
loading or discharge of cargo at any such port be considered by the Master or Owners in his or   289
their discretion dangerous or (b) it be considered by the Master or Owners in his or their discretion   290
dangerous or impossible for the Vessel to reach any such port of loading or of discharge - the   291
Charterers shall have the right to order the cargo or such part of it as may be affected to be   292
loaded or discharged at any other safe port of loading or of discharge within the range of loading   293
or discharging ports respectively established under the provisions of the Charter Party (provided   294
such other port is not blockaded or that entry thereto or loading or discharge of cargo thereat is   295
not in the Master's or Owners' discretion dangerous or prohibited). If in respect of a port of   296
discharge no orders be received from the Charterers within 48 hours after they or their agents   297
have received from the Owners a request for the nomination of a substitute port, the Owners shall   298
then be at liberty to discharge the cargo at any safe port which they or the Master may in their   299
or his discretion decide on (whether within the range of discharging ports established under the   300
provisions of the Charter Party or not) and such discharge shall be deemed to be due fulfilment   301
of the contract or contracts of affreightment so far as cargo so discharged is concerned. In the   302
event of the cargo being loaded or discharged at any such other port within the respective range   303
of loading or discharging ports established under the provisions of the Charter Party, the Charter   304
Party shall be read in respect of the freight and all other conditions whatsoever as if the voyage   305
performed were that originally designated. In the event, however, that the Vessel discharges the   306
cargo at a port outside the range of discharging ports established under the provisions of the   307
Charter Party, freight shall be paid for as for the voyage originally designated and all extra   308
expenses involved in reaching the actual port of discharge and/or discharging the cargo thereat   309
shall be paid by the Charterers or cargo owners. In this latter event the Owners shall have a lien   310
on the cargo for all such extra expenses.   311

3.   The Vessel shall have liberty to comply with any directions or recommendations as to departure,   312
arrival, routes, ports of call, stoppages, destinations, zones, waters, delivery or in any other wise   313
whatsoever given by the government of the nation under whose flag the Vessel sails or any other   314
government or local authority including any de facto government or local authority or by any   315
person or body acting or purporting to act as or with the authority of any such government or   316
authority or by any committee or person having under the terms of the war risks insurance on the   317
Vessel the right to give any such directions or recommendations. If by reason of or in compliance   318
with any such directions or recommendations, anything is done or is not done such shall not be   319
deemed a deviation.   320

If by reason of or in compliance with any such directions or recommendations the Vessel does   321
not proceed to the port or ports of discharge originally designated or to which she may have been   322
ordered pursuant to the terms of the Bills of Lading, the Vessel may proceed to any safe port of   323
discharge which the Master or Owners in his or their discretion may decide on and there discharge   324
the cargo. Such discharge shall be deemed to be due fulfilment of the contract or contracts of   325
affreightment and the Owners shall be entitled to freight as if discharge has been effected at the   326
port or ports originally designated or to which the Vessel may have been ordered pursuant to the   327
terms of the Bill of Lading. All extra expenses involved in reaching and discharging the cargo at   328
any such other port of discharge shall be paid by the Charterers and/or cargo owners and the   329
Owners shall have a lien on the cargo for freight and all such expenses.   330

28.   **Dues and/or Taxes**   331

....   332
....   333
....   334

29.   **Transfer**   335

The Charterers shall have the privilege of transferring part or whole of the Charter Party to others,   336
guaranteeing to the Owners due fulfillment of this Charter Party.   337

30.   **Address Commission**   338

An address commission of..................% on gross freight, deadfreight, and demurrage is due to the   339
Charterers at the time these are paid, Vessel lost or not lost. The Charterers shall have the right to   340
deduct such commissions from such payments.   341

31.   **Brokerage Commission**   342

A brokerage commission of..................% on gross freight, deadfreight and demurrage is payable by the   343
Owners to..   344
....   345
....at the time of the Owners receiving these payments.   346

Amwelsh 93

57

BIMCO voyage charter-parties

| 32. | **Arbitration** | 347 |

| (a) | *NEW YORK | 348 |

All disputes arising out of this contract shall be arbitrated at New York in the following manner, 349
and subject to U.S. Law: 350

One Arbitrator is to be appointed by each of the parties hereto and a third by the two so chosen. 351
Their decision or that of any two of them shall be final, and for the purpose of enforcing any 352
award, this agreement may be made a rule of court. The Arbitrators shall be commercial men, 353
conversant with shipping matters. Such Arbitration is to be conducted in accordance with the 354
rules of the Society of Maritime Arbitrators Inc. 355

For disputes where the total amount claimed by either party does not exceed US 356
$.............................** the arbitration shall be conducted in accordance with the Shortened 357
Arbitration Procedure of the Society of Maritime Arbitrators Inc. 358

| (b) | *LONDON | 359 |

All disputes arising out of this contract shall be arbitrated at London and, unless the parties agree 360
forthwith on a single Arbitrator, be referred to the final arbitrament of two Arbitrators carrying on 361
business in London who shall be members of the Baltic Mercantile & Shipping Exchange and 362
engaged in Shipping, one to be appointed by each of the parties, with power to such Arbitrators 363
to appoint an Umpire. No award shall be questioned or invalidated on the ground that any of the 364
Arbitrators is not qualified as above, unless objection to his action be taken before the award is 365
made. Any dispute arising hereunder shall be governed by English Law. 366

For disputes where the total amount claimed by either party does not exceed US $................. 367
...........** the arbitration shall be conducted in accordance with the Small Claims Procedure of 368
the London Maritime Arbitrators Association. 369

Delete (a) or (b) as appropriate 370

** *Where no figure is supplied in the blank space this provision only shall be void but the other provisions* 371
of this clause shall have full force and remain in effect. 372

Amwelsh 93

General

The Baltic and International Maritime Council Uniform General Charter (as revised 1922, 1974, 1976 and 1994). Code name **Gencon** (*See separate entry under* **Voyage charter**, *where the form is reproduced at pp. 294-296*). The corresponding bill of lading is code named **Congenbill**.

The Baltic and International Maritime Council Scandinavian Voyage Charter 1956 (amended 1962 and 1993). This charter-party is to be used for fixtures with Scandinavian charterers for trades for which no other approved form specially drafted for the trade in question is in force. Code name **Scancon**. The corresponding bill of lading is code named **Scanconbill**.

Universal Voyage Charter 1984 (revised Voyage Charter Party 1964) published by Polish Chamber of Foreign Trade, Gdynia. Code name **Nuvoy-84**. The corresponding bill of lading is code named **Nuvoybill-84**.

The World Food Programme Voyage Charter Party. This charter-party is used by the World Food Programme in Rome as charterers. Code name **Worldfood**. A non-negotiable Cargo Receipt is published for use with this charter-party code named **Worldfoodreceipt**.

Grain

BIMCO grain voyage charter-party. Code name **Graincon**. Standard grain voyage charter-party created in 2001.

Australian Wheat Charter 1990 (Amended 1991). Code name **Austwheat**. This charter-party is used by the Australian Wheat Board of Melbourne as shippers, for the shipment from named Australian ports of wheat in bulk ex silo. It has specific provisions for notices and loading rates. The corresponding bill of lading is code named **Austwheat Bill**.

Continent Grain Charter Party. Code name **Synacomex 90**. This charter-party is by the Syndicat National du Commerce Extérieur des Céréales (amended 1960, 1974 and 1990) in agreement with Comité Central des Armateurs de France in cooperation with the French Chartering and S. & P. Brokers' Association.

North American Grain Charterparty 1973, issued by the Association of Ship Brokers and Agents (USA) Inc. in 1973 and amended in 1989. Code name **Norgrain 89**. The corresponding bill of lading is called the North American Grain Bill of Lading.

Grain Voyage Charter Party 1966 (revised and recommended 1974). Code name **Grainvoy**. The corresponding bill of lading is code named **Grainvoybill**.

Ore

Soviet Ore Charter Party for Ores and Ore Concentrates from USSR Ports (Amended 1987). Code name **Sovorecon**. The corresponding bill of lading is code named **Sovoreconbill**.

Apatite Charter Party for Shipments of Apatite Ore and Apatite Concentrate from Murmansk (amended 1987). Code name **Murmapatit**. The corresponding bill of lading is code named **Murmapatitbill**.

BIMCO voyage charter-parties

The Japan Shipping Exchange, Inc. Iron Ore Charter Party. Code name **Nipponore**.

The Baltic and International Maritime Conference Standard Ore Charter Party. Code name **Orevoy**. This charter-party has been revised and renamed **Coal-Orevoy** to reflect the broadening of the scope of application of this document which can be used for shipments of coal as well as iron ore. The corresponding bill of lading is called **Coal-Orevoybill**.

Stone

Chamber of Shipping Stone Charter-Party, 1920 (amended 1925, 1959, 1974 and 1995). This charter-party is suitable for all ports in the UK and Eire, Channel Islands, and Continent between Elbe and Brest. Code name **Panstone**.

Tank

International Association of Independent Tanker Owners Tanker Voyage Charter Party. Code name **Tankervoy 87**. Spaces for the vessel's description include tank heating details and tank coatings.

Tanker Consecutive Voyage Clauses, issued by **INTERTANKO**, the International Association of Independent Tanker Owners. Code name **Interconsec 76**.

The Baltic and International Maritime Council Standard Voyage Charter Party for Vegetable/Animal Oils and Fats. Code name **Biscoilvoy 86**. The corresponding bill of lading is code named **Biscoilvoybill**.

Standard Voyage Charter Party for the Transportation of Chemicals in Tank Vessels. Code name **Chemtankvoy**. The corresponding bill of lading is code named **Chemtankvoybill**. A non-negotiable chemical tank waybill is also published by BIMCO, code named **Chemtankwaybill 85**.

Tanker Contract of Affreightment, issued by INTERTANKO, the International Association of Independent Tanker Owners. Code name **Intercoa 80**.

Wood (including pitwood, propos, pulpwood, roundwood and logs)

Black Sea Timber Charter Party for Timber from USSR and Romanian Black Sea and Danube Ports. Code name **Blackseawood**. The corresponding bill of lading is code named **Blackseawoodbill**.

Chamber of Shipping Baltic Wood Charter Party 1973 (Baltic and Norway to the United Kingdom and to the Republic of Ireland). Code name **Nubaltwood**. The corresponding bill of lading is code named **Nubaltwoodbill**.

Russian Wood Charter Party 1961 (Revised 1995). This charter-party is to be used from Russian Baltic, White Sea, Barents Sea and Kara Sea Ports to the United Kingdom, the Republic of Ireland and other countries. Code name **Ruswood**. BIMCO publishes a bill lading to be used with this charter-party code named **Ruswoodbill**.

The Baltic and International Maritime Conference Soviet Roundwood Charter Party for Pulpwood, Pitwood, Roundwood and Logs from Baltic and

White Sea Ports of the USSR. Code name **Sovconround**. The corresponding bill of lading is code named **Sovconroundbill**.

The Japan Shipping Exchange, Inc. Charter Party for Logs 1967. Code name **Nanyozai 1967**.

See also:
BIMCO (Baltic and International Maritime Council)
International Association of Independent Tanker Owners (INTERTANKO)

Bookings

Reservations made by a shipper or his agent with a carrier for the carriage of certain defined goods from a place of loading to a place of discharging. To reserve space in this way is **to book space**. The document containing the terms and conditions of the contract between a shipper and a shipping line is called the **booking note** or **liner booking note**; this document is superseded by the bill of lading when this is established. An example of a liner booking note is the **Conlinebooking**, published by the Baltic and International Maritime Council (BIMCO). It is signed by both principals to the contract and contains:

—the names of the parties, that is, the carrier and his agents and the party representing cargo interests;
—the vessel's name and approximate time for shipment;
—the loading and discharging ports;
—the description of the cargo;
—the freight rate and where/when freight is payable;
—the rate of demurrage if applicable; and
—any special terms.

On the reverse of the Conlinebooking are the terms of the applicable bill of lading, the Conlinebill (*see* **Bill of lading**).

BIMCO also publishes a blank back form of liner booking note. The difference between this and the Conlinebooking is that the blank back form is deemed to contain the carrier's standard conditions of carriage.

All the bookings for a particular sailing are listed together onto a **booking list**. This is compiled from lists supplied by each of the line's agents responsible for taking bookings for the various loading ports on the ship's itinerary.

Associated abbreviations:
b/l bill of lading
b/n booking note

See also:
BIMCO (Baltic and International Maritime Council)

Both to blame collision clause

Clause in a bill of lading or charter-party which stipulates that, in the event of a collision between two ships where both are at fault, the owners of the cargo must indemnify the carrying ship against any amount paid by the carrying ship to the non-carrying ship for damage to that cargo. This clause arises because, under American law, a cargo owner is not able to make any recovery from the carrier for damage resulting from negligent navigation but may instead sue the non-carrying ship which in turn seeks recovery from the carrying ship in proportion to its fault. This would render a carrier indirectly liable for a loss for which he is not directly liable to the cargo owner. The clause has, however, been held to be invalid in the American courts when incorporated into a contract with a common carrier.

The clause in BIMCO's **Gencon** charter-party reads as follows:

"If the Vessel comes into collision with another vessel as a result of the negligence of the other vessel and any act, neglect or default of the Master, Mariner, Pilot or the servants of the Owners in the navigation or in the management of the Vessel, the owners of the cargo carried hereunder indemnify the Owners against all loss or liability to the other or non-carrying vessel or her owners in so far as such loss or liability represents loss of, or damage to, or any claim whatsoever of the owners of said cargo, paid or payable by the other or non-carrying vessel or her owners to the owners of said cargo and set-off, recouped or recovered by the other or non-carrying vessel or her owners as part of their claim against the carrying Vessel or the Owners. The foregoing provisions shall also apply where the owners, operators or those in charge of any vessel or vessels or objects other than, or in addition to, the colliding vessels or objects are at fault in respect of a collision or contact."

Breakbulk liner ancillary charges

In this category fall the extra charges levied by shipping lines and liner conferences which do not come under the headings of temporary surcharges. They are many and varied and reflect, for example, the chosen voyage, the type of cargo and cargo handling. Conventional cargoes come in many different shapes and sizes and shipping lines often make an **additional charge**, known simply as an **additional**, when a piece of cargo exceeds a certain weight or length.

Most shipping lines charge an additional sum when carrying heavy pieces, the reason being that extra handling costs are incurred, such as the hire of a mobile crane. This additional charge is known as the **heavy lift additional**, **heavy weight additional** or **heavy lift cargo additional**. It is an amount per tonne (1000 kilogrammes) on a sliding scale which increases as the weight increases. The amount is added to the freight rate, and like the freight rate, is normally subject to any currency adjustment surcharge in force at the time of shipment. It may not be subject to any bunker surcharge, though, depending on the particular tariff. What constitutes a heavy piece is often dictated by the particular trade, the commodities regularly carried, port equipment and the vessels' lifting gear. In some trades, the extra charge applies to any piece, package or bundle weighing over 5,000 kilogrammes. In others, the dividing line is 10,000 kilogrammes. Although a heavy lift additional might apply to pieces over, say, 10,000 kilogrammes, the charge is levied on the entire weight of the piece, normally the gross weight, not just on the excess over 10,000 kilogrammes.

While some pieces are unusually heavy, others are exceptionally long and also require special handling, such as the use of spreader bars. Such pieces may also take longer to load and discharge. This involves extra costs which are passed on to the shipper as an additional charge known as a **long length additional**. It is an amount per 1000 kilogrammes or per cubic metre which increases on a sliding scale as the length increases. This is added to the freight rate and is subject to any currency surcharge (and bunker surcharge depending on the particular tariff). As with heavy lift charges, different tariffs have different starting points for the long length additional although many start around the 40 foot mark, either at exactly 40 feet or 12.2 metres or 12.25 metres. In some cases, the additional charge is an amount per tonne for each foot or part of a foot over whichever length is the starting point for this charge.

When a shipper has a large enough cargo to **induce** (attract) a ship to a (smaller) port not normally called at, the shipping line may charge a **direct additional**. Such a cargo is termed **inducement cargo**.

If the cargo is to taken to the port of loading by another ship, known as a **feeder ship**, a **feeder additional** or **transhipment additional** is usually charged.

Additional freight is an extra charge imposed in accordance with the contract of carriage by a shipping line on the shipper, receiver or bill of lading holder, as the case may be, for additional expenses incurred in discharging the cargo. This charge generally applies when the port stipulated in the contract is inaccessible or when to discharge there would result in an unreasonable delay to the ship: under these circumstances, the shipping line may have an option under the contract of carriage to proceed to another port to discharge the cargo where extra costs may be incurred.

The elements which make up the freight rates do not take account of the cost of bringing the goods to the ship (apart from some through transport or combined transport rates). In the case of conventional cargo, a separate charge exists for:

- receiving the goods into the port;
- storing them on the ground or in a warehouse, as appropriate, pending the arrival of the ship;
- delivery from store to the ship; and lifting to the ship.

Together, these make the **FOB charges** or simply **FOBs**. They are normally an amount per 1000 kilogrammes of cargo and vary according to the commodity. Generally in the liner trade, FOBs are paid by the shipper to the shipping line's agent who collects on behalf of the line. The money is then remitted to the port authority. Large volume shippers, particularly those who ship bulk cargoes, often pay the port authority direct. FOB charges are generally quoted and paid in the currency of the country of shipment. With liner shipments effected on full liner terms, there are no other cargo handling charges to pay apart from the FOBs since the freight rate includes stowage and securing. If, on the other hand, the freight rate is free in, cargo interests will have stowage and securing charges to pay as well as the FOBs.

In some parts of Europe, FOB charges are referred to as **Port Liner Term Charges**. They may vary depending on the method used for delivering to the port, i.e. by road, rail or barge.

A liner terms freight rate is defined as including some or all of the elements of loading, stowing and discharging, or indeed none of these, according to the custom of the particular port; whatever is not included at the discharge port is paid for by the consignee. In some ports, however, it is the practice to make a separate identifiable charge, called **landing, storage and delivery**, for:

- landing of the cargo to the quay;
- short term storage awaiting collection;
- delivery from store to the consignee's vehicle.

This charge, known widely in its abbreviated form LS&D, is an amount per freight ton, shown on the freight account and consequently paid by the shipper and not, as one might expect, by the consignee.

Alternative spellings:
Transshipment, trans-shipment

Associated abbreviations:
fob's free on board charges
hla heavy lift additional
lla long length additional
ls&d landing, storage and delivery charges
pltc's port liner term charges

See also:
Conventional freight and the export contract
Liner surcharges

British International Freight Association (BIFA)

BIFA is the trade organisation for companies engaged in the international movement of freight to and from the United Kingdom by all modes of transport, road, rail, sea and air. It incorporates the **Institute of Freight Professionals (IFP)** (formerly the **Institute of Freight Forwarders—IFF**), the professional organisation for individuals engaged in the international trade and transport sector of industry.

British International Freight Association (BIFA)

BIFA members comprise some 1,100 companies together with over 5,000 individuals in the Institute of Freight Professionals. Trading members are located throughout the UK, and the industry provides employment for over 70,000 individuals. A recent survey showed that BIFA members operate over 25,000 vehicles in the UK. Members also provide international rail freight services via the Channel Tunnel, and a number operate all-cargo aircraft on international routes.

BIFA members provide one or more of the following services:

—European road and rail distribution.
—Maritime **intermodal** services.
—Air freight consolidation and forwarding.
—Trade facilitation, Customs broking and consultancy.
—Logistics and supply chain management.

European road and rail distribution

A principal activity of BIFA members, European distribution includes **door to door** movement of full loads of freight, and the **consolidation** of small consignments into full loads for warehouse to warehouse trucking, thence final delivery to consignee. The opening of the Channel Tunnel in 1994 has led to the increasing use of rail for the long distance transport of goods between rail connected distribution centres.

Maritime intermodal services

The widespread introduction in the 1970s of these services provided freight forwarders with the opportunity to develop door to door and **warehouse to warehouse** services worldwide for **full container load** (FCL) cargo, and **less than container load** (LCL) shipments. BIFA members today provide such services to virtually every port and major industrial centre worldwide.

Air freight consolidation and forwarding

The use of scheduled airlines for the movement of freight increased considerably following the introduction of wide-bodied aircraft. Concentrated around the major international airports, BIFA members handle some 85 per cent of the UK's imports and exports by air, and provide a worldwide high quality range of services for urgent and high value freight. BIFA members provide airport handling and distribution services, and act as general sales agents.

Trade facilitation customs broking and consultancy

Many countries in Europe and elsewhere still maintain complex Customs procedures. Members hold up-to-date information on national requirements worldwide, enabling fast and reliable delivery of goods to final destination. Most imports into the UK are cleared by BIFA members, using electronic communication systems developed in conjunction with HM Customs. The facilitation of

British International Freight Association (BIFA)

import freight to final destination is an important aspect of the work of most BIFA members as is provision of a high level of consultancy in customs matters.

Corporate membership of BIFA is not automatic, and applicants undergo a vetting process and subsequently are required to adhere to a number of criteria, including:

—Adoption of the 1989 Standard Trading Conditions.
—Adequate liability insurance cover.
—BIFA Code of Conduct.
—Employment of minimum number of professionally qualified staff.

The Association operates through a structure of Management Committees each representing a sector of the trading membership and the professional membership. Additionally there are a number of Working Groups, responsible, for example, for:

—International Relations.
—Training and Education.
—Public Relations & Publicity.
—Political Matters.

The governing body is the Executive Board which meets six times a year and is comprised mainly of the chairmen of the Management Committees and Working Groups.

An Advisory Council meets twice a year and includes senior executives drawn from outside the Membership.

Policies

The role of the Association includes support for the principle of free trade worldwide and the development and maintenance of a healthy international freight services industry within the European Union by all modes of transport.

Lobbying and representation

BIFA seeks to influence the decision-making process of the national Government and the European Commission in Brussels. As appropriate BIF A operates independently or in conjunction with other associations and representative bodies, such as:

—British Shippers' Council
—Institute of Export.
—Transport & Distribution Liaison Group.
—Chambers of Commerce.
—Confederation of British Industry.
—SITPRO.

Training and education

Both as a professional institute and trade association, BIFA is heavily involved in the provision of training and education services and in bringing to the attention of its members relevant services provided by third party training organisations and academic institutions.

The BIFA *Directory of Education Training and Development* is distributed annually to trading members.

Individuals working in the freight services are encouraged to improve their expertise through training and further education and thus to qualify for higher grades of membership in the IFP. Depending on qualifications and experience, individuals may become:

—Affiliate.
—Associate.
—Member.
—Fellow.

The Code of Conduct for Trading Members is reproduced on p. 70. Also reproduced, on pp. 68–69, are the Standard Trading Conditions (2005 edition). It should be noted that the use of these conditions is restricted to members of the Association.

BIFA also publish a standard agreement between freight forwarders, known as an **agency agreement**. This is used in different situations: when a forwarder requires a counterpart in a foreign country to handle a particular piece of business, or, alternatively, when a forwarder is looking for a long term arrangement with another forwarder. The agreement is reproduced under Forwarding agent together with BIFA's explanatory guide.

Associated abbreviations:
BIFA British International Freight Association
fcl full container load
IFF Institute of Freight Forwarders
IFP Institute of Freight Professionals
lcl less than container load

British International Freight Association (BIFA)

BRITISH INTERNATIONAL FREIGHT ASSOCIATION (BIFA) – STANDARD TRADING CONDITIONS 2005 EDITION

The Customer's attention is drawn to specific Clauses hereof which exclude or limit the Company's liability and those which require the customer to indemnify the company in certain circumstances and those which limit time being Clauses 8, 10, 12-14 inclusive, 18-20 inclusive, and 24-27 inclusive

Insurance may only be effected by the Company under clause 11(A) if so authorised by the Financial Services Authority or its successor

All headings are indicative and do not form part of these conditions

DEFINITIONS AND APPLICATION

1 In these conditions the following words shall have the following meanings:-

"Company"	the BIFA member trading under these conditions
"Consignee"	the Person to whom the goods are consigned
"Customer"	any Person at whose request or on whose behalf the Company undertakes any business or provides advice, information or services
"Direct Representative"	the Company acting in the name of and on behalf of the Customer and/or Owner with H.M. Revenue and Customs ("HMRC") as defined by Council Regulation 2193/92 or as amended
"Goods"	the cargo to which any business under these conditions relates
"Person"	natural person(s) or any body or bodies corporate
"SDR"	are Special Drawing Rights as defined by the International Monetary Fund
"Transport Unit"	packing case, pallets, container, trailer, tanker, or any other device used whatsoever for and in connection with the carriage of Goods by land, sea or air
"Owner"	the Owner of the Goods or Transport Unit and any other Person who is or may become interested in them

2(A) Subject to sub-paragraph (B) below, all and any activities of the Company in the course of business, whether gratuitous or not, are undertaken subject to these conditions.

(B) If any legislation, to include regulations and directives, is compulsorily applicable to any business undertaken, these conditions shall, as regards such business, be read as subject to such legislation, and nothing in these conditions shall be construed as a surrender by the Company of any of its rights or immunities or as an increase of any of its responsibilities or liabilities under such legislation, and if any part of these conditions be repugnant to such legislation to any extent, such part shall as regards such business be overridden to that extent and no further.

3 The Customer warrants that he is either the Owner, or the authorised agent of the Owner and, also, that he is accepting these conditions not only for himself, but also as agent for and on behalf of the Owner.

THE COMPANY

4(A) Subject to clauses 11 and 12 below, the Company shall be entitled to procure any or all of the services as an agent, or, to provide those services as a principal.

(B) The Company reserves to itself full liberty as to the means, route and procedure to be followed in the performance of any service provided in the course of business undertaken subject to these conditions.

5 When the Company contracts as a principal for any services, it shall have full liberty to perform such services itself, or, to subcontract on any terms whatsoever, the whole or any part of such services.

6(A) When the Company acts as an agent on behalf of the Customer, the Company shall be entitled, and the Customer hereby expressly authorises the Company, to enter into all and any contracts on behalf of the Customer as may be necessary or desirable to fulfil the Customer's instructions, and whether such contracts are subject to the trading conditions of the parties with whom such contracts are made, or otherwise.

(B) The Company shall, on demand by the Customer, provide evidence of any contract entered into as agent for the Customer. Insofar as the Company may be in default of the obligation to provide such evidence, it shall be deemed to have contracted with the Customer as a principal for the performance of the Customer's instructions.

7 In all and any dealings with HMRC for and on behalf of the Customer and/or Owner, the Company is deemed to be appointed, and acts as, Direct Representative only.

8(A) Subject to sub-clause (B) below, the Company:

(i) has a general lien on all Goods and documents relating to Goods in its possession, custody or control for all sums due at any time to the Company from the Customer and/or Owner on any account whatsoever, whether relating to Goods belonging to, or services provided by or on behalf of the Company to the Customer or Owner. Storage charges shall continue to accrue on any Goods detained under lien;

(ii) shall be entitled, on at least 28 days notice in writing to the Customer, to sell or dispose of or deal with such Goods or documents as agent for, and at the expense of, the Customer and apply the proceeds in or towards the payment of such sums;

(iii) shall, upon accounting to the Customer for any balance remaining after payment of any sum due to the Company, and for the cost of sale and/or disposal and/or dealing, be discharged of any liability whatsoever in respect of the Goods or documents.

(B) When the Goods are liable to perish or deteriorate, the Company's right to sell or dispose of or deal with the Goods shall arise immediately upon any sum becoming due to the Company, subject only to the Company taking reasonable steps to bring to the Customer's attention its intention to sell or dispose of the Goods before doing so.

9 The Company shall be entitled to retain and be paid all brokerages, commissions, allowances and other remunerations customarily retained by, or paid to, freight forwarders.

10(A) Should the Customer, Consignee or Owner of the Goods fail to take delivery at the appointed time and place when and where the company is entitled to deliver, the Company shall be entitled to store the Goods, or any part thereof, at the sole risk of the Customer or Consignee or Owner, whereupon the Company's liability in respect of the Goods, or that part thereof, stored as aforesaid, shall wholly cease. The Company's liability, if any, in relation to such storage, shall be governed by these conditions. All costs incurred by the Company as a result of the failure to take delivery shall be deemed as freight earned, and such costs shall, upon demand, be paid by the Customer.

(B) The Company shall be entitled at the expense of the Customer to dispose of or deal with (by sale or otherwise as may be reasonable in all the circumstances):-

(i) after at least 28 days notice in writing to the Customer, or (where the Customer cannot be traced and reasonable efforts have been made to contact any parties who may reasonably be supposed by the Company to have any interest in the Goods) without notice, any Goods which have been held by the Company for 90 days and which cannot be delivered as instructed; and

(ii) without prior notice, any Goods which have perished, deteriorated, or altered, or are in immediate prospect of doing so in a manner which has caused or may reasonably be expected to cause loss or damage to the Company, or third parties, or to contravene any applicable laws or regulations.

11(A) No insurance will be effected except upon express instructions given in writing by the Customer and accepted in writing by the Company, and all insurances effected by the Company are subject to the usual exceptions and conditions of the policies of the insurers or underwriters taking the risk. Unless otherwise agreed in writing, the Company shall not be under any obligation to effect a separate insurance on the goods, but may declare it on any open or general policy held by the Company.

(B) Insofar as the Company agrees to effect insurance, the Company acts solely as agent for the Customer, and the limits of liability under clause 26(A) (ii) of these conditions shall not apply to the Company's obligations under clause 11.

12(A) Except under special arrangements previously made in writing by an officer of the Company so authorised, or made pursuant to or under the terms of a printed document signed by the Company, any instructions relating to the delivery or release of the Goods in specified circumstances (such as, but not limited to, against payment or against surrender of a particular document) are accepted by the Company, where the Company has to engage third parties to effect compliance with the instructions, only as agents for the Customer.

(B) Despite the acceptance by the Company of instructions from the Customer to collect freight, duties, charges, dues, or other expenses from the Consignee, or any other Person, on receipt of evidence of proper demand by the Company, and, in the absence of evidence of payment (for whatever reason) by such Consignee, or other Person, the Customer shall remain responsible for such freight, duties, charges, dues, or other expenses.

(C) The Company shall not be under any liability in respect of such arrangements as are referred to under sub-clause (A) and (B) hereof save where such arrangements are made in writing, and in any event, the Company's liability in respect of the performance of, or arranging the performance of, such instructions shall not exceed the limits set out in clause 26(A) (ii) of these conditions.

13 Advice and information, in whatever form it may be given, is provided by the Company for the Customer only. The Customer shall indemnify the Company against all loss and damage suffered as a consequence of passing such advice or information on to any third party.

14 Without prior agreement in writing by an officer of the Company so authorised, the Company will not accept or deal with Goods that require special handling regarding carriage, handling, or security whether owing to their thief attractive nature or otherwise including, but not limited to, bullion, coin, precious stones, jewellery, valuables, antiques, pictures, human remains, livestock, pets, plants. Should any Customer nevertheless deliver any such goods to the Company, or cause the Company to handle or deal

BIFA Standard Trading Conditions

68

with any such goods, otherwise than under such prior agreement, the Company shall have no liability whatsoever for or in connection with the goods, howsoever arising.

15 Except pursuant to instructions previously received in writing and accepted in writing by the Company, the Company will not accept or deal with Goods of a dangerous or damaging nature, nor with Goods likely to harbour or encourage vermin or other pests, nor with Goods liable to taint or affect other Goods. If such Goods are accepted pursuant to a special arrangement, but, thereafter, and in the opinion of the Company, constitute a risk to other goods, property, life or health, the Company shall, where reasonably practicable, contact the Customer in order to require him to remove or otherwise deal with the goods, but reserves the right, in any event, to do so at the expense of the Customer.

16 Where there is a choice of rates according to the extent or degree of the liability assumed by the Company and/or third parties, no declaration of value will be made and/or treated as having been made except under special arrangements previously made in writing by an officer of the Company so authorised as referred to in clause 26(D).

THE CUSTOMER

17(A) The Customer warrants:

(i) that the description and particulars of any Goods or information furnished, or services required, by or on behalf of the Customer are full and accurate, and

(ii) that any Transport Unit and/or equipment supplied by the Customer in relation to the performance of any requested service is fit for purpose, and

(B) that all Goods have been properly and sufficiently prepared, packed, stowed, labelled and/or marked, and that the preparation, packing, stowage, labelling and marking are appropriate to any operations or transactions affecting the Goods and the characteristics of the Goods.

(C) that where the Company receives the Goods from the Customer already stowed in or on a Transport Unit, the Transport Unit is in good condition, and is suitable for the carriage to the intended destination of the Goods loaded therein, or thereon, and

(D) that where the Company provides the Transport Unit, on loading by the Customer, the Transport Unit is in good condition, and is suitable for the carriage to the intended destination of the Goods loaded therein, or thereon.

18 Without prejudice to any rights under clause 15, where the Customer delivers to the Company, or causes the Company to deal with or handle Goods of a dangerous or damaging nature, or Goods likely to harbour or encourage vermin or other pests, or Goods liable to taint or affect other goods, whether declared to the Company or not, he shall be liable for all loss or damage arising in connection with such Goods, and shall indemnify the Company against all penalties, claims, damages, costs and expenses whatsoever arising in connection therewith, and the Goods may be dealt with in such manner as the Company, or any other person in whose custody they may be at any relevant time, shall think fit.

19 The Customer undertakes that no claim shall be made against any director, servant, or employee of the Company which imposes, or attempts to impose, upon them any liability in connection with any services which are the subject of these conditions, and, if any such claim should nevertheless be made, to indemnify the Company against all consequences thereof.

20 The Customer shall save harmless and keep the Company indemnified from and against:-

(A) all liability, loss, damage, costs and expenses whatsoever (including, without prejudice to the generality of the foregoing, all duties, taxes, imposts, levies, deposits and outlays of whatsoever nature levied by any authority in relation to the Goods) arising out of the Company acting in accordance with the Customer's instructions, or arising from any breach by the Customer of any warranty contained in these conditions, or from the negligence of the Customer, and

(B) without derogation from sub-clause (A) above, any liability assumed, or incurred by the Company when, by reason of carrying out the Customer's instructions, the Company has become liable to any other party, and

(C) all claims, costs and demands whatsoever and by whomsoever made or preferred, in excess of the liability of the Company under the terms of these conditions, regardless of whether such claims, costs and/or demands arise from, or in connection with, the breach of contract, negligence or breach of duty of the Company, its servants, sub-contractors or agents, and

(D) any claims of a general average nature which may be made on the Company.

21(A) The Customer shall pay to the Company in cash, or as otherwise agreed, all sums when due, immediately and without reduction or deferment on account of any claim, counterclaim or set-off.

(B) The Late Payment of Commercial Debts (Interest) Act 1998, as amended, shall apply to all sums due from the Customer.

22 Where liability arises in respect of claims of a general average nature in connection with the Goods, the Customer shall promptly provide security to the Company, or to any other party designated by the Company, in a form acceptable to the Company.

LIABILITY AND LIMITATION

23 The Company shall perform its duties with a reasonable degree of care, diligence, skill and judgment.

24 The Company shall be relieved of liability for any loss or damage if, and to the extent that, such loss or damage is caused by:-

(A) strike, lock-out, stoppage or restraint of labour, the consequences of which the Company is unable to avoid by the exercise of reasonable diligence; or

(B) any cause or event which the Company is unable to avoid, and the consequences of which the company is unable to prevent by the exercise of reasonable diligence.

25 Except under special arrangements previously made in writing by an officer of the Company so authorised, the Company accepts no responsibility with regard to any failure to adhere to agreed departure or arrival dates of Goods.

26(A) Subject to clause 2(B) and 11(B) above and sub-clause (D) below, the Company's liability howsoever arising and, notwithstanding that the cause of loss or damage be unexplained, shall not exceed

(i) in the case of claims for loss or damage to Goods:

(a) the value of any loss or damage, or

(b) a sum at the rate of 2 SDR per kilo of the gross weight of any Goods lost or damaged

whichever shall be the lower.

(ii) subject to (iii) below, in the case of all other claims:

(a) the value of the subject Goods of the relevant transaction between the Company and its Customer, or

(b) where the weight can be defined, a sum calculated at the rate of two SDR per kilo of the gross weight of the subject Goods of the said transaction, or

(c) 75,000 SDR in respect of any one transaction,

whichever shall be the least.

(iii) in the case of an error and/or omission, or a series of errors and/or omissions which are repetitions of or represent the continuation of an original error, and/or omission

(a) the loss incurred, or

(b) 75,000 SDR in the aggregate of any one trading year commencing from the time of the making of the original error, and/or omission,

whichever shall be the lower.

For the purposes of clause 26(A), the value of the Goods shall be their value when they were, or should have been, shipped. The value of SDR shall be calculated as at the date when the claim is received by the Company in writing.

(B) Subject to clause 2(B) above and sub-clause (D) below, the Company's liability for loss or damage as a result of failure to deliver, or arrange delivery of goods, in a reasonable time, or (where there is a special arrangement under Clause 25) to adhere to agreed departure or arrival dates, shall not in any circumstances whatever exceed a sum equal to twice the amount of the Company's charges in respect of the relevant contract.

(C) Save in respect of such loss or damage as is referred to at sub-clause (B), and subject to clause 2(B) above and Sub-Clause (D) below, the Company shall not in any circumstances whatsoever be liable for indirect or consequential loss such as (but not limited to) loss of profit, loss of market, or the consequences of delay or deviation, however caused.

(D) On express instructions in writing declaring the commodity and its value, received from the Customer and accepted by the Company, the Company may accept liability in excess of the limits set out in sub-clauses (A) to (C) above upon the Customer agreeing to pay the Company's additional charges for accepting such increased liability. Details of the Company's additional charges will be provided upon request.

27(A) Any claim by the Customer against the Company arising in respect of any service provided for the Customer, or which the Company has undertaken to provide, shall be made in writing and notified to the Company within 14 days of the date upon which the Customer became, or ought reasonably to have become, aware of any event or occurrence alleged to give rise to such claim, and any claim not made and notified as aforesaid shall be deemed to be waived and absolutely barred, except where the Customer can show that it was impossible for him to comply with this time limit, and that he has made the claim as soon as it was reasonably possible for him to do so.

(B) Notwithstanding the provisions of sub-paragraph (A) above, the Company shall in any event be discharged of all liability whatsoever and howsoever arising in respect of any service provided for the Customer, or which the Company has undertaken to provide, unless suit be brought and written notice thereof given to the Company within nine months from the date of the event or occurrence alleged to give rise to a cause of action against the Company.

JURISDICTION AND LAW

28 These conditions and any act or contract to which they apply shall be governed by English law and any dispute arising out of any act or contract to which these Conditions apply shall be subject to the exclusive jurisdiction of the English courts.

BIFA Standard Trading Conditions

Code of Conduct
for Trading Members of the

British International Freight Association (BIFA)

Every member shall comply with the Association's code of conduct as set out below -

1   Objects

The objects of the Association and the intentions of the Association's Code of Conduct are to:

a)   Ensure fair business relationships between Members and their clients, and between Members.

b)   Maintain the reputation, standing and good name of the Association and its Members.

c)   Generally watch over, promote and safeguard the interests of the general public by establishing and maintaining a high standard of professional behaviour with the object that membership of the Association shall denote integrity and a high quality of service.

d)   Generally promote public confidence in the profession particularly through prevention or correction of any abuses which might undermine this confidence.

e)   Promote and develop the general interests of all Members of the Association in their relations with clients, with operators of all forms of transport and with one another.

f)   Promote the interests and welfare of freight forwarders, improve their professional status, and secure high standards of professional conduct and practice.

2   Conduct

a)   At all times, within the law, Members undertake to provide confidential and competent service in the interests of their clients.

b)   Members undertake not intentionally to mislead the public.

c)   In their dealings with third parties in the performance of their service to clients, Members undertake that any information they provide shall be accurate so far as it is known to them.

3   Enforcement

a)   The Council of the Association will appoint a Policy Group Membership.

b)   The Policy Group Membership is empowered to consider any complaint against any member of the Association whether made by a member of the public or by another Member. Upon request from the Policy Group Membership, the Member against whom a complaint has been made shall provide such further information or document(s) and within such period as may be reasonably required by the Policy Group Membership. The Policy Group Membership will not apply or recommend the application of any sanction against the said Member without giving the said Member reasonable opportunity to make representations (in writing or in person) in connection with the said complaint.

c)   The Council of the Association is empowered under the Association's Regulations to

    i)   issue such cautions, warnings or reprimands as it may consider necessary, and/or

    ii)   require from such Member any specific or general undertaking as to such Member's future conduct, *and/or*

    iii)   terminate the membership of any such Member.

The Council is further empowered to delegate, and has so delegated, its disciplinary powers under sub-paragraph (I) and (ii) above to the Policy Group Membership.

d)   Not withstanding the foregoing, any Member whose membership has been terminated by the Policy Group Membership shall have the right to appeal to the Council within 21 days of such termination being announced.

British Shippers' Council (BSC)

Since 1955 the British Shippers' Council has represented the interests of British importers and exporters in relation to deep sea shipping, air transport, and customs and procedural matters. It was the first shippers' council to be formed; there are now councils in most industrialised countries.

BSC representatives have always played a leading role in the international arena. The growing importance of political lobbying has been reflected in the evolution of BSC's role from a body primarily concerned with consultation and negotiation with liner conferences. Whilst this negotiating role remains vitally important, the changes in maritime markets of a structural and political nature in recent years and the growing importance of air transport mean that much time and effort is now concentrated in monitoring and influencing events in Westminster, Brussels and Geneva—and places as far away as Washington, Ottawa and Canberra.

BSC is changing the face of the maritime transport scene both commercially and politically. On the commercial side, BSC has led the way in encouraging more aggressive action against conference increases, inland haulage restrictions and the imposition of surcharges. On the political front, BSC has been active in influencing both the Government and EC authorities to recognise the vital needs of international trade as distinct from the sectoral interests of shipowners, and the importance of competition and choice in both price and service levels.

BSC was a founder member of the European Air Shippers' Council and provides its secretariat. Its work on behalf of air freight users ranges from commercial discussions between airlines and shippers to lobbying for liberalisation in EC air freight policy at national and Community levels. In the important area of trade facilitation, BSC has been active for many years in raising political awareness of the need to eliminate barriers to trade, and is extensively involved at both political and practical levels in the progress towards the Single European Market.

The British Shippers' Council therefore has a role to play that is both vital and unique—in representing, at all levels and both domestically and internationally, the interests of the UK's international trading community in relation to the movement of its goods. The support of British importers and exporters is vital in order to achieve this end.

Associated abbreviation:
BSC British Shippers' Council

See also:
European Shippers' Councils (ESC)

Bulk carriers

Single deck ships designed to carry homogeneous unpacked dry cargoes such as sugar or cereals. Such ships have large hatchways to facilitate cargo handling, hopper sides and wing tanks. The latter are used either for the carriage of grain, other bulk cargoes or water ballast. Bulk carriers, or bulkers as they are sometimes called, are built in a wide range of sizes and are generally gearless, although smaller vessels may have their own gear.

A variety of specialised types of bulk carrier have evolved, and a number are mentioned here.

Alumina carrier: typically having four holds, she is fully enclosed because of the amount of alumina dust generated by conventional systems. Loading is effected by means of a chute lowered into the holds. Self-discharging is achieved by opening gates in the floor of the holds which allow the cargo to drop on to conveyor belts leading to one end where mechanical or pneumatic equipment elevates it to deck level.

Bulk-ore carrier: having wide hatchways and a high centre of gravity, this ship has self-trimming holds, that is, she is shaped in such a way that the cargo levels itself. This makes such ships suitable for the carriage of grain.

Capesize vessel: category of bulk carrier so called because she is too large to negotiate the Suez and Panama Canals. Vessels of over 150,000 tonnes deadweight fall into this category.

Cement carrier: a self-unloading ship, she has one or more conveyor belts running fore and aft which carry the cargo to the stern where one of several means of elevating brings the cargo to deck level from which it is transferred to a boom for discharging. Because of the problems with dust, special terminal facilities are required.

Collier: normally with three, four or five holds, she has large hatchways to give rapid discharge by allowing the grabs easy access to all parts of the holds. Loading is effected by gravity from chutes. Some colliers have conveyor belts for discharging, in which case they are said to be self-unloaders.

Handymax: bulk carrier of about 25,000 tonnes deadweight, so called because it is suitable for many different trades.

Handy-sized bulker: ship at the smaller end of the range of sizes of bulk carriers, typically up to 30,000/35,000 tonnes deadweight. Within this category are ships which are intended to trade into the Great Lakes of North America; their dimensions are within the constraints of the St Lawrence Seaway which is the limiting factor in this trade.

Ice-breaking bulk carrier: bulk carrier whose hull is strengthened to enable her to navigate in conditions of ice, particularly in the ore trade carried on in the Canadian Arctic.

Laker: ship specially designed to trade in the North American Great Lakes system. Lakers are normally geared and possess an unusually large number of hatches. Some lakers never leave the Lakes and indeed a few are too large to negotiate the St Lawrence Seaway's locks which lead to the St Lawrence River and thence to the Atlantic. Others trade worldwide to avoid being laid up in the Lakes during the winter when the Seaway closes. Lakers are used principally to carry iron ore from the St Lawrence and from ore terminals within the Lakes to steel mills in the US mid-West and grain from the western Lakes to the St Lawrence.

Log carrier: any bulk carrier used for carrying logs; this ship requires a high cubic capacity because of the stowage factor of this cargo.

Mini-bulker: vessel of about 3,000 tonnes deadweight which has the constructional features of a bulk carrier, having a single deck, hoppered holds and wing tanks, but which is smaller. As with the larger bulk carriers, the mini-bulk carrier may be geared or gearless. Equally, she may have hatch covers capable of taking timber deck cargo or shipping containers.

Ore carrier: large ship, generally gearless and with large hatchways, designed to be used for the carriage of various types of ore. Because of the high density of ore, ore carriers have a relatively high centre of gravity to prevent them being stiff when at sea, that is, rolling heavily with possible stress to the hull. This high centre of gravity is achieved by having relatively small cargo holds (small because the cargo takes up relatively little space) built over deep double-bottoms.

Ore pellet carrier: ship which must be equipped with suitable fire-fighting equipment since this type of cargo is prone to spontaneous combustion.

Open hatch bulk carrier: type of bulk carrier whose hatch openings correspond in size to the floor of the hold. This allows the crane to position cargo for stowage directly into its location for the voyage and enables it to be lifted out without first being moved sideways. This configuration speeds up cargo handling and reduces damage. Such vessels are widely used for the carriage of paper rolls.

Self-trimming ship or self-trimmer: ship whose holds are shaped in such a way that a bulk cargo loaded into her will level itself.

Self-unloader: ship equipped with gear to enable her to discharge without using shore equipment. Vessels of this type are used in the iron ore and coal trades. Typical gear is a boom conveyor which is capable of a high rate of discharging from ship to shore or from ship to ship. Often, this is fed by opening gates on the floor of the holds, thus allowing the cargo to drop onto conveyor belts. It is then taken to one end where it is elevated to deck level by mechanical or pneumatic means.

Bulk carriers

Timber carrier: ship which is usually geared and with large hatchways. Sometimes referred to as a **forest products carrier**.

Universal bulk carrier: early bulk carrier designed to carry a wide range of bulk cargoes (but only one at a time). She has separate upper holds which could be used for ballast or for dense cargoes such as iron ore, while the main holds carry less dense cargoes.

Woodchip carrier: vessel designed to carry woodchips in bulk. Normally in the size range 20,000 to 60,000 tonnes deadweight, such vessels have a high cubic capacity because of the high stowage factor of this commodity which enables them to be loaded to their marks. Discharging is effected in one of various ways, for example pneumatic conveyor belts or buckets. The advantage of woodchips over other timber products, as far as shipping is concerned, is that they are quicker to handle and are consequently more economic to transport.

Woodpulp carrier: ship whose holds are box-shaped, that is, with vertical sides and having no obstructions, so as to allow the cargo, which is presented in large blocks, to be stowed efficiently. Some ships have side doors to allow loading of these blocks of wood pulp when they are palletised. If the ship is also used to carry paper rolls, she must have adequate dehumidifying equipment.

Associated abbreviations:
ohbc open hatch bulk carrier
ubc universal bulk carrier

See also:
Ship types

Bunker surcharge

The bunker surcharge is also termed **bunker adjustment factor**, **fuel oil surcharge**, **fuel adjustment factor** and **interim fuel participation**. The need for this surcharge arose suddenly in 1974 when oil prices quadrupled. Fuel then became a significant element in the shipowner's costs (to a lesser extent it still is although, because of the high prices reached by bunker prices, shipowners have striven to find ways of reducing consumption).

The data needed by a shipowner in order to calculate the bunker surcharge are as follows:

- base date for fuel prices—like the currency adjustment factor, a starting date is necessary. At this point the bunker surcharge stands at zero (or has been reduced following a partial incorporation into the tariff rates—see "rolling in" below);

- fuel prices on the base date—fuel oil and/or diesel oil according to the type of engines used;
- current fuel prices—prices prevailing at the date when the bunker surcharge is to be introduced or changed;
- percentage increase or decrease in fuel prices between the base date and the date when the B/S is calculated;
- weighting factors—the percentage of the total costs represented by fuel;
- weighted percentage change—the percentage bunker surcharge arrived at by multiplying the weighting factor by the percentage increase or decrease in the prices. The surcharge is generally translated into a monetary amount per freight ton although sometimes left as a percentage of the freight. Shown above is a method of calculating the bunker surcharge using actual costs. Occasionally this method cannot be used because, for example, of secrecy existing between the various members of a liner conference or because a shipping line may operate to two areas or countries each of which comes under a separate conference. In this case, it is difficult to make individual calculations. Often in this situation, a conference will calculate the bunker surcharge using the following elements;
- posted prices—the current prices of fuel as advertised by the oil companies at a port relevant to the trade in question;
- bunkering port (port where fuel is taken) frequently used by the member lines;
- grade of fuel commonly used by their vessels.

Less frequently the bunker surcharge is calculated by means of movements in bunker prices ascertained from published indices.

Worldwide, fuel is quoted and purchased in US Dollars and when a tariff currency is also the US Dollar, the bunker surcharge can neatly be expressed in that currency. It should be noted, however, that any fluctuation in the value of the Dollar in relation to the cost currencies should be allowed for in the currency adjustment factor. The bunker surcharge should therefore only change when fuel prices fluctuate.

As with the currency adjustment factor, the bunker surcharge can be negative as well as positive since fuel prices can fall as well as rise.

So that minor fluctuations in the prices of fuel do not in turn mean constant alterations to the bunker surcharge, most shipping lines and liner conferences will only change the level of the surcharge when the price changes by a certain minimum percentage, known as a **trigger point**. The percentage varies from case to case.

Many liner conferences tend to incorporate or roll in some or all of the bunker surcharge at the time of a general rate increase. This has the effect of keeping the level of the surcharge relatively small.

Some liner conferences combine the currency adjustment factor and the bunker surcharge into one surcharge. In their internal calculations, the lines calculate the two elements separately then add them together and express as a

Bunker surcharge

single percentage of the freight. This combined surcharge is known as a **currency and bunker adjustment factor**. Since the two constituent elements of this surcharge can be negative, or their combined result negative, the surcharge itself can therefore be negative. Trigger points exist for this surcharge in the same way as they do for the surcharges when quoted and used separately. The difference is that the currency and bunker adjustment factor will only change when the combined effect of the movements in the two reaches the minimum level required to trigger an increase.

It is not unusual to find a bunker surcharge provided for in a voyage charter for several consecutive voyages since the duration of the charter is relatively long and the shipowner is thus protected against fluctuations in fuel prices over that period (in the case of time charters, it is the charterer who pays for fuel, not the shipowner so there is no need for the owner to protect himself with a bunker surcharge clause).

Associated abbreviations:
baf bunker adjustment factor
b/s bunker surcharge
cabaf currency and bunker adjustment factor
faf fuel adjustment factor
fos fuel oil surcharge
ifp interim fuel participation
pp posted price

See also:
Currency adjustment factor
Liner surcharges

Bunkers

Ship's fuel. The amount of fuel burned by a ship, the prices paid and changes in price are important in a number of contexts: in time charters, voyage charters and liner contracts.

In a time charter, the shipowner calculates the amount of bunkers, fuel and diesel, which will be on board at the time of delivery, and he and the charterer agree prices for these. The charterer pays the shipowner accordingly when he takes delivery of the ship. When the ship is re-delivered to the owner at the end of the period of the charter, the exercise is done in reverse, with the owner paying the charterer at agreed prices for bunkers remaining on board.

The price of bunkers and the ship's consumptions are big factors in the estimates done by a prospective time charterer when examining voyages and comparing possible ships. Once the ship is fixed, the time charterer may have options open to him should he need to take on fuel during the voyage: where he bunkers the ship, which supplier he uses, and what quantities to take, bearing in mind the voyage to be undertaken and the requirement to leave a certain quantity of bunkers remaining on board on re-delivery.

In voyage charters, bunkers are the responsibility of the shipowner, and paid for by him, but charter-parties may include clauses referring to bunkers: the **bunker deviation clause** is a clause permitting the shipowner to proceed to any port on or off the route to take on bunkers. The **bunker escalation clause** states that, although the charter has been concluded on the basis of a particular price for bunkers, if a higher price is paid during the contracted voyage, the shipowner is to be reimbursed for the extra cost by the charterer.

Shipping lines and liner conferences may set their freight rates for long periods, typically for a year, and are therefore vulnerable to changes in the prices of bunkers. For this reason, they may apply a surcharge, known variously as a **bunker surcharge**, **bunker adjustment factor**, **fuel oil surcharge**, **fuel adjustment factor** or **interim fuel participation**, to reflect fluctuations in prices. This surcharge is expressed in different ways: as an amount per container, per freight ton or as a percentage of the freight.

A **bunkering port** is a port at which a ship calls to take on bunkers. It is not a port where cargo is normally loaded or discharged, particularly if the bunkers are taken on at an anchorage rather than on the berth. Sometimes, shipping lines will try to take advantage of the fact that the ship is making a call at the port and will canvass for a cargo to load or discharge there, if necessary to or from barges.

The Baltic and International Maritime Council (BIMCO) publishes a standard marine fuels purchasing contract, codenamed **Fuelcon**. This document contains all the terms and conditions relating to the purchase of bunkers, including place, time and method of delivery, that is whether by truck or barge, quality, price and payment terms. The contract also includes a provision for samples of the fuel to be taken, which can be used later in the event of a dispute regarding quality. When a ship's master is in disagreement with a supplier of bunkers as to the quantity taken on board, or the quality, he may detail his reservations on a receipt to be given to the bunker suppliers. Alternatively he may **note protest** before sailing, that is, put in writing his reservations on a separate document. This document would be important in any subsequent dispute. The receipt should bear a reference to the existence of the **letter of protest**.

Shipowners and ship operators often use intermediaries, known as **bunker brokers**, when buying bunkers from oil companies. These are specialists in matters of price, availability and quality.

Associated abbreviations:
baf bunker adjustment factor
bs bunker surcharge
faf fuel adjustment factor
fos fuel oil surcharge
ifp interim fuel participation
rob remaining on board

Bunkers

Associated definition:
to bunker to take on fuel

Cancellation of a charter

Repudiation of the contract, most often by the voyage charterer or time charterer when the ship **misses her cancelling date**, or by the time charterer when the ship is off hire for longer than the period stipulated in the charter-party.

Every charter has a date by which the shipowner must tender notice of readiness to the charterer that the ship has arrived at the port of loading and is ready to load. This date is known as the **cancelling date**. The charterer may have the option of cancelling the charter if the ship arrives after this date. It may be the second of two dates which comprise the **laydays cancelling**, for example laydays 25 March cancelling 2 April or, when abbreviated to **laycan**, laycan 25 March/2 April. The charterer is not obliged to commence loading until the first of these dates if the ship arrives earlier.

If a ship is likely to be delayed in reaching the load port (in the case of a voyage charter) or the place of delivery (in the case of a time charter), the shipowner may ask the charterer to extend the cancelling date. If the charterer agrees, the contract is amended accordingly. If not, the charterer may have the option to cancel the charter either before the cancelling date by mutual agreement or after the cancelling date within a time specified in the charter-party. Alternatively, the shipowner may be obliged to present his ship at the load port, however late.

The cancelling date may be contained in a **cancellation clause** or **cancelling clause**. Alternatively, it may be shown separately, such as in a box on the face of the charter-party. In this case, the cancelling clause merely contains the definition. This latter is how Gencon, BIMCO's general purpose voyage charter-party, deals with cancellation:

"Should the vessel not be ready to load (whether in berth or not) on or before the date indicated in Box 19, Charterers have the option of cancelling this contract, such option to be declared, if demanded, at least 48 hours before the vessel's expected arrival at the port of loading. Should the vessel be delayed on account of average or otherwise, Charterers to be informed as soon as possible, and if the vessel is delayed for more than 10 days after the day she is stated to be expected ready to load, Charterers have the option of cancelling this contract, unless a cancelling date has been agreed upon."

Associated abbreviation:
l/c laycan

Associated definition:
extension to the cancelling date Agreement by the charterer to a date later than the one agreed in the charter-party by which a ship must tender notice of readiness to the charterer that she has arrived and is ready to load

See also:
Laytime—commencement

Cargo handling charges

Shipowners and shipping lines have a number of standard types of charges which they levy on cargo interests to reflect the cost of cargo handling at the load port and the discharge port. These are levied in addition to the freight. Generally they are known as **pre-shipment charges**. The way they are charged depends on whether the cargo is conventional or containerised.

Conventional cargoes

The principal example of a charge at the load port is **fob charges**, representing loading charges, sometimes referred to as **port liner term charges**. If the cargo is above a certain length, or over a certain piece weight, as defined in the tariff, the shipping line may impose a **long length additional** or **heavy lift additional** respectively. These charges are normally expressed as an amount of money per tonne; in the case of the long length additional, this is for each unit of length, for example for each metre, or part of a metre, over a specified length.

In some trades, there is a **landing charge** or **landing, storage and delivery charge**. The landing charge is for putting the cargo onto the quay. The landing, storage and delivery charge is not only for putting the cargo onto the quay but also for storing it and subsequently delivering it ex store onto the consignee's vehicles.

Containerised cargoes

Container shipping lines have charges unique to them, some more widely applicable than others.

The **terminal handling charge** is a charge payable to a shipping line either for receiving a full container load at the container terminal, storing it and delivering it to the ship at the load port or for receiving it from the ship at the discharge port, storing it and delivering it to the consignee.

A **lift-on/lift-off charge** originally applied in situations where the shipping line arranged loading or unloading of the shipper's own haulage. Now this charge also applies in certain trades to the charge for loading and unloading carrier haulage.

A **delivered in charge** applies in some trades for taking containers away from the port terminal to an inland depot, e.g. Manchester cfs for clearance.

Associated abbreviations:
cfs container freight station
dic delivered in charge
fob's free on board charges
lla long length additional
ls&d landing, storage and delivery charges
pltc's port liner term charges
thc terminal handling charges

Associated terms:
Long length extra Long length additional

Cargo handling charges

Heavy lift extra or **heavy lift surcharge** Heavy lift additional

See also:
Breakbulk liner ancillary charges
Liner surcharges

Cargo types

Cargoes fall into two basic categories: liquid and non-liquid, termed wet cargoes and dry cargoes. Each type is carried in different ways for different reasons.

Dry cargoes fall into three main categories: conventional, containerised and roll-on/roll-off. A **conventional cargo**, sometimes referred to as **breakbulk cargo**, is one which is lifted on and off a ship one piece, or bundle, at a time by means of cranes or derricks, but not shipped on trailers or in shipping containers. Such cargoes are carried in **conventional ships** which, if operated on a regular basis between advertised ports, provide a **conventional service**. These ships are often of the tween deck or multideck type which not only allows them to carry safely cargoes having many different stowage requirements but also facilitates distribution in the ship of cargo for several ports of discharge. Conventional cargo is cargo which very often does not fit into or onto any of the standard shipping containers by virtue of its length, width or height. Such cargoes are termed **uncontainerable** or **uncontainerisable**.

Containerised cargoes are cargoes carried in shipping containers. There are a number of standard sizes of container permitting their use in different transport modes worldwide. Ocean transport is generally effected in specialised ships which have cells into which the containers are lowered and where they are held in place by uprights known as cell guides. These ships are known as cellular containerships. Container barges, also known as cellular barges, are barges similarly constructed and used for river transport of containers. Containers can also be carried on conventional ships, often on deck, held down by means of special container deck fittings.

Roll-on/roll-off ships are of various types, from ferries to car carriers, but all have a loading and discharging ramp, connecting the ship with the quay. Inside the ship are vehicle decks, often many. Vehicles are driven on and off the ship over these ramps and are stowed on the decks. Other types of cargo, ranging from rolls of paper to heavy machinery, are towed on and off the ship on specialised trailers which are secured to the deck. A variation is the sto-ro system where cargo is towed onto the ship on trailers but then lifted off the trailers and stowed directly on the deck, enabling the specialised trailers to be retained at the loading terminal. All cargo which is on wheels and which can be driven or towed on to roll-on/roll-off ships is known as **rolling cargo** or **wheeled cargo**.

General cargo, or **generals**, is cargo consisting of goods unpacked or packed, for example in cartons, crates, bags or bales, often palletised, but specifically not cargo shipped in bulk (*see below*), on trailers or in shipping containers although the term general cargo is also used to describe all dry cargo other than bulk, taking in containerised goods.

General cargo is presented in different ways. Increasingly, such goods are **unitised,** that is, grouped into units of regular size, known as **unit loads,** to facilitate handling. As there are fewer lifts, unitisation increases the rate of loading and discharging of a ship. Goods shipped on pallets are examples of **unitisation.** Containerisation itself is sometimes said to be a form of unitisation in that the shipping container is a perfect example of a uniform shape.

Some importing countries require goods to be **pre-slung,** that is, to have the slings which were used to load them onto the ship left around them to simplify and speed up the discharge. This is another form of unit load.

A **bulk cargo** is a homogeneous unpacked cargo such as grain, iron ore or coal, very often carried as a full cargo on a bulk carrier. Any commodity shipped in this way is said to be **in bulk.**

Wet cargoes may be divided into black products and white products. **Black products** are crude oils, such as heavy fuel oils. These are also referred to as **dirty products** or **dirty petroleum products.** White products are refined products such as aviation spirit, motor spirit and kerosene. These are also referred to as **clean products** or **clean petroleum products.**

Associated abbreviations:
b/b breakbulk
cpp clean petroleum products
dpp dirty petroleum products
ro-ro roll-on/roll-off
uncon uncontainerable, uncontainerisable

Associated definition:
Palletised said of goods loaded onto pallets

Associated term:
To pre-sling

See also:
Containers and associated ancillary charges

Carrier

Party who enters into a contract with a charterer or shipper, as the case may be, for the carriage of cargo.

The carrier's principal responsibilities, subject to the terms of the contract, are for the delivery of the cargo to its destination and for the care of that cargo while it is under his control. He is responsible to the charterer or shipper in the first instance and possibly later on to other cargo interests, for example, when the bill of lading, which is a document of title to the cargo and evidence of the contract of carriage, is transferred to a third party.

Contracts of carriage arise in different circumstances, each of which determines the identity of the carrier.

The most straightforward situations arise when the contract of carriage is between the owner of a ship and the charterer, shipper or receiver, as the case may be, covering the carriage of goods by sea: when a vessel is chartered by its owner to a charterer to carry a cargo, the charter-party provides the contract of carriage between the owner as carrier and the charterer; if it is intended that the receiver be bound by the contract, the owner issues a charter-party bill of lading and he is thereby responsible as carrier to the receiver from the time when the bill of lading is transferred to the receiver.

Likewise, a shipping line, using one of its own vessels, when it contracts with a shipper to carry a cargo, becomes carrier, the contract being most often evidenced by a liner bill of lading. As with the charter-party bill of lading, transfer of the liner bill of lading to a third party means that the shipping line's responsibility as carrier is to that third party.

The position is not so clear when the carrying ship is not owned by either of the parties to the contract of carriage. A **disponent owner**, or **head charterer**, is a person or company who does not own the ship but, having chartered it, may control its commercial operation. Such a person or company may sub-charter the vessel and enter into a contract of carriage with a sub-charterer by means of a charter-party. Alternatively, in the case of a shipping line, the disponent owner may operate it as a liner ship, issuing a liner bill of lading. Disponent owners sometimes endeavour to restrict their liability under the charter-party or bill of lading by inserting a clause, known as a **demise clause** or **identity of carrier clause**, which seeks to identify the actual owner of the ship as the carrier. The purpose of such clauses is to refer cargo interests, when they have a claim for damage or shortage, to the actual owner. This is because it is the actual owner who may be controlling the navigation of the ship and the care of the cargo, particularly when it is on board the ship. There are, however, countries where such clauses are not upheld.

A **combined transport operator** or **multimodal transport operator** enters into a contract with a shipper for the carriage of goods on a voyage involving at least two legs. Normally the issuer of this document is responsible for the goods as carrier from the time they are received into his care until the time they are delivered at destination. A through bill of lading is similar but, depending on the individual contract, the issuer may only be responsible as carrier for the sea leg, acting purely as agent for the on-carriage.

A **non vessel owning common carrier**, also referred to as **non vessel operating carrier** or **non vessel owning carrier**, is a person or company, often a forwarding agent, who does not own or even operate the carrying ship. He advertises his service based on one or more regular shipping lines with whom he may have long term contracts. By combining many small shipments, he can cater for shippers who may be too small to deal directly or effectively with the shipping lines. He contracts with these shippers for the carriage of their cargo, normally not only for the sea leg but also to inland destinations. He issues a house bill of lading to the shipper. Whether he is a carrier by law depends on the particular terms and conditions under which he trades.

An **on-carrier** contracts to transport cargo from the port or place of discharge of a sea-going or ocean-going ship to another, often inland, destination by a different means of transport such as truck, train or barge.

A **common carrier** is anyone who advertises a service involving the carriage of goods to and from ports on a particular route. Such a carrier is required by law to accept all cargoes offered, except dangerous ones, and to make a reasonable charge for their carriage.

Associated term:
to on-carry

Associated abbreviations:
nvo, nvoc, nvocc Non vessel owning common carrier, non vessel operating carrier, non vessel owning carrier

Chamber of Shipping

The Chamber of Shipping of the UK is the trade association and employers' association for British **shipowners** and **shipmanagers**. It promotes and protects the interests of its member companies, both nationally and internationally. It represents British shipping to the Government, Parliament, international organisations, unions and the general public. It covers all issues which have a bearing on British shipping, ranging from fiscal policy and freedom to trade, through to recruitment and training, maritime safety and the environment, navigational aids and pilotage.

The Chamber represents six very different commercial sectors trading at sea: deep-sea bulk, short-sea bulk, deep-sea liner, ferry, cruise and off-shore support.

The Chamber has a number of section committees and policy and related functional committees. There are section committees for deep-sea bulk, deep-sea liner (including a container panel), ferry and passenger ship, offshore support vessel and short sea.

Policy committees include:

—International Shipping Policy Committee which has a Competition Issues Panel. The role of this committee is to advise on all international economic and trade issues, with a particular focus on relations with international organisations including the European Union institutions.
—Marine Policy Committee: advises on, and monitors, safety policy issues regarding vessel operations under discussion internationally, regionally and nationally through, for example, the International Maritime Organization

(IMO), the European Union and the Marine Safety Agency (MSA). This committee has a number of panels:

- Carriage of Dangerous Goods Panel: monitors all issues relative to packaged dangerous goods, especially the International Maritime Dangerous Goods (IMDG) Code and the UN recommendations on the Transport of Dangerous Goods.
- Chemical Carriers Panel: covers chemical carrier issues, in particular MARPOL, ANNEX 2 and the IBC and BCH codes.
- Communications/Electronics Committee: advises on, and monitors, developments in the IMO Sub-Committee on Radiocommunications, Department of Trade and Industry, Marine Safety Agency and British Telecom on maritime radiocommunications and their technical, operational and financial implications.
- Construction Committee: advises on, and monitors, developments in IMO Sub-Committees (Ship Design and Equipment (DE), Stability and Load Lines (SLF) and Fire Protection (FP)) and the implementation of UK and European legislation concerning all aspects of ship construction and design, stability, fire protection, loadline, tonnage measurement, strength and safety.
- Gas Carriers Panel: monitors issues related to the operation of liquefied petroleum gas and liquefied natural gas carriers, the Gas Carrier (GC) and International Gas Carrier (IGC) codes and the IMO Bulk Liquids and Gas (BLG) Sub-Committee.
- Marine Environment Committee: advises on, and monitors, the work of the IMO Marine Environmental Protection Committee (MEPC), the IMO Sub-Committee on Bulk Liquids and Gases (BLG) and marine environmental matters under discussion regionally and nationally through the European Union and the Marine Safety Agency.
- Nautical Committee: advises on, and monitors, safety of navigation issues and related matters.

—Maritime Law Policy: monitors and comments on legal policy developments at IMO and national legislation concerning shipping, together with any other legal issues affecting members' interests.

—Insurance Panel: encourages cost effective insurance as it affects the shipping industry.

—Documentary Committee: provides Chamber input on documentary matters.

—Trade Procedures Committee: covers developments in official and commercial documentation and procedures, relating to the movement of ships, goods and persons, and pursues simplification, rationalisation and standardisation.

—Ports & Pilotage Policy Committee: protects members' interests in all matters relating to Ports, Pilotage and Lights; provides official Chamber representation to the Lights Advisory Committee.

—Taxation Panel: exchanges views and comments on Chamber policy on taxation matters affecting shipping, first, on all Corporate taxation issues and, secondly, on Indirect Taxation.

Change of destination

It happens sometimes that the merchant is required to change the destination of a consignment after the bill of lading has been prepared and the ship is on the high seas. Often this is so because a customer decides that the goods are needed at a different location, perhaps another of several processing plants, to the one agreed at the time of placing the order. Alternatively, goods may be sold while on the high seas to an end user in a different location to the original customer. Such a change of plans would only be viable if the new destination is one of the ports on the vessel's itinerary at which she has not yet arrived or a place inland from one of the ports on the vessel's itinerary at which she has not yet arrived. From the ship's point of view, there are two factors involved in a **change of destination**: flexibility and cost.

In the case of LCL goods, since the concept of shipping LCL is that goods from several suppliers/shippers are grouped into a container for delivery to the same destination, it follows that a change in that destination for one part of the cargo is ruled out.

With FCL goods, the contract of carriage normally specifies the places where the carrier's responsibility starts and finishes and so any variation requested by the merchant is at the carrier's discretion. Liner tariffs generally call for a few days' notice to be able to effect a change. Such a change will also depend on the container being in the right place for discharge at the newly requested terminal. If it has other containers on top of it, it would be impractical, time-consuming and costly to take these off the ship and reload them afterwards. Assuming that the container is accessible and the carrier agrees, the merchant will be subject to the following extra charges:

- extra freight if the new port of discharge attracts a higher freight;
- extra actual costs incurred at the new terminal, if any. In any event, the carrier will want payment for the administration and operational costs of altering the destination and the merchant will therefore pay the extra actual costs or a minimum charge whichever is the greater. This charge is normally an amount per container, higher for a 40-foot container than for a 20-footer;
- additional inland freight, if any, for delivery to a different container yard;
- additional zone haulage, if any, for delivery to a different inland place of delivery.

A similar picture arises for breakbulk goods as for FCL goods: a change of destination requested by the merchant is at the discretion of the carrier; a few days' notice of the new destination is required; for the goods to be discharged at a different port, they must be accessible and should not be overstowed, that is, there must be no goods for other, later, ports on top of them; and additional freight is payable if the new port attracts a higher freight.

The change of destination just referred to occurs after the ship has loaded and is on her way. If the shipper is in doubt about the exact place of delivery at the time of booking space on the ship, he may ask the shipping line for an option to

Change of destination

deliver the cargo at one of two or more places. As with the change of destination, agreement by the carrying line is at its discretion. Goods so shipped become known as **optional cargo** which, whether containerised or breakbulk, require an **optional stow**: this means that they are placed on board the ship in such a way that they can be taken off at any of the **optional ports** without the need to disturb cargo for later ports. Shipping lines usually charge a fee for this service which consists of an amount per freight ton for breakbulk cargo or an amount per container (higher for a 40-foot container than for a 20-footer) if goods are shipped FCL. This facility is not available for goods shipped LCL in the same way that a change of destination is not possible since the container has several consignments for the same, single destination. The merchant is required to give the shipping line an agreed number of days' notice before arrival at the first of the optional ports as to which of the ports he is selecting for discharge of his cargo.

Associated abbreviations:
FCL full container load
LCL less than container load

Charter documentation

This section examines the documentation associated with charters from the perspective of the charterer. There are significant differences between time charters and voyage charters in respect of the functions of the charterer and hence of some of the documents involved.

Both voyage and time charters

The ship's agent at the loading and discharging ports prepares a **statement of facts**, detailing the dates and times of arrival of the ship and the commencement and completion of loading and discharging. This statement also details:

—the quantity of cargo loaded or discharged each day;
—normal working hours at the port;
—the hours worked and the hours stopped with the reasons for the stoppages, such as bad weather, a strike or breakdown of equipment;
—the number of gangs;
—any relevant remarks.

This document is sometimes referred to as a **port log**.

Voyage charters

In certain voyage charters, it is agreed that the charterer can appoint his own port agents (*see* **Ship's agent**). In these circumstances, he needs to appoint an agent at each of the ports of the voyage. The first of these is appointed before the voyage commences, the others either at the same time or, at least, well before the ship arrives at the respective port.

The **time sheet** is a statement drawn up by the ship's agent at the loading and discharging ports, which details the time worked in loading or discharging the cargo together with the amount of laytime used. This latter figure, when compared with the time allowed in the charter-party, is used by the shipowner and charterer to calculate demurrage or despatch, as the case may be. BIMCO publishes a Standard Time Sheet in two formats: short form and long form, the latter being where cargo handling operations take place over an extended period.

Time charters

Time charterers always appoint their own port agents. Before the charter is agreed, the charterer contacts prospective agents at each of the ports he intends the vessel to call at during the period of the charter. He advises the prospective agent of the intended call and asks the agent for a **pro forma disbursements account**, that is, a statement of the expenses which are likely to be incurred, including port charges, pilotage, towage and the agent's fee. This account is used to help the charterer calculate in advance the viability of the voyage. It also serves as a basis for a request for funds by the agent when he is appointed, such funds to be made available prior to the ship's arrival.

Before the voyage commences, or at least well before the vessel arrives at each respective port, the charterer appoints the port agents. Terms are agreed, usually in writing, with the agent, including the agency fee and the duties required. Once this is done, the charterer sends each agent a set of instructions relating to the intended voyage, setting out details of the cargo, requirements such as the frequency of notices to be sent, and contact details for the other agents concerned with the voyage.

An **on hire survey**, or **on hire condition survey**, is carried out and the results typed up by the surveyor(s) for the owner and charterer. This survey is carried out at the time the ship is delivered at the beginning of the period of the charter. It is carried out to determine the condition of the ship which may subsequently be compared with her condition at the end of the charter. The quantity of bunkers is ascertained for comparison with the amounts specified in the charter-party. By agreement, the ship is inspected by one surveyor only or one surveyor for each of the two parties. Which party pays for the survey and whether the time taken counts for the purpose of calculating hire money are matters agreed in the charter-party.

A **delivery certificate** is issued and signed by both charterer and owner, certifying the time, date and place of delivery of the ship, together with any notations by the charterer concerning the failure of the ship to comply in any respect with the terms of the charter-party.

As soon as possible after the contract is agreed, the charterer sends his **instructions to the master**. These contain details of the cargo, the voyage(s), names, addresses, phone numbers etc. of all the port agents and bunkering plans.

After the ship completes at each of the ports, the agent sends the charterer a **disbursements account**. This is an account of all sums paid out in respect of

Charter documentation

mb: _____   T/C Rate: US$12,000/day

Port: _____

Duration: From: 06/12/05 @ 07:20 Local
                To: 07/12/05 @ 13:50 Local

Total off-hire: 30 hrs 30 minutes (1.271 days)

Fuel consumed during off-hire period

HFO (2.75 MT @ US$90/MT) + MDO (2.15 MT @ US$295/MT)

Compensation Due to Charterer:

Refund of hire:	US$12,000 x 1.271 days	= US$15,252.00
Fuel (HFO):	US$90 x 2.75	= US$ 247.50
(MDO):	US$295 x 2.15	= US$ 634.25
		US$16,133.75

Typical off hire statement

the ship's call at the port such as pilotage, towage, port charges, any cash advanced to the master, supply of provisions and stores and the agency fee. The account is supported by receipts known as **vouchers**.

If during the charter the ship or an important piece of equipment breaks down, the ship is taken **off hire** by the charterer. Hire money is temporarily suspended until the breakdown is repaired. In practice, hire money may continue to be paid by the charterer, and refunded after the ship comes back **on hire**, together with a refund covering the amount of bunkers consumed during this period. The document detailing the off hire period is called the **off hire statement** (*see example*, p. 88).

At the end of the charter when the ship is redelivered to the owner, an **off hire survey**, or **off hire condition survey**, is carried out. This inspection is carried out in order to determine whether, or to what extent, the ship is in the same condition, wear and tear excepted, as on delivery. The quantity of bunkers is ascertained for comparison with the amounts specified in the charter-party. The results of the survey are typed up and sent to the owner and the charterer. A **redelivery certificate** is drawn up and signed by or on behalf of the shipowner and the charterer certifying the time, date and place of redelivery of the ship.

Alternative spelling:
off-hire

Associated abbreviations:
dly delivery
redly redelivery

See also:
Chartering
Charter-party
Time charter
Voyage charter

Charter freight terms

Voyage charter freight, more often than not, consists of the ocean freight or sea freight only. This is because cargoes of sufficient size to warrant chartering a ship (**charterable quantity**) are larger than liner cargoes, normally sufficient to fill the ship; the loading and discharging berths are very often controlled by cargo owners or used frequently by them. Freight on this basis is said to be on a free in and out basis.

Free in and out

While liner terms is the mainstay of the freight rates used in the liner trade, **free in and out**, normally abbreviated to fio, together with its variations, is the backbone of the voyage chartering business. To understand the meaning of this term,

Charter freight terms

it is helpful to break it down into its constituent parts. This will also assist in understanding the variations:

- free—the cost of cargo handling is free to the shipowner, that is to say, it is paid for by some other party
- in—at the port of loading
- out—at the port of discharging.

Variations of fio

The variations of the fio rate all define the precise responsibilities of the charterer or shipper at the port of loading. More exactly, they spell out those elements for which the shipowner is not responsible. There is a school of thought that if an fio rate is not qualified, as it is in the under-mentioned examples, the shipowner is liable for the cost of, for example, stowing and trimming. To avoid any ambiguity, and possible dispute, it is therefore worthwhile using these terms:

- **free in and out and stowed**—the charterer or shipper is responsible for the cost of stowage, that is, the placing of cargo in the ship in the position which it will occupy during the voyage;
- **free in and out and stowed, lashed, secured and dunnaged**—this goes a step further than the fios rate in specifying that the costs of lashing, securing and dunnage are to be borne by the charterer or shipper (i.e. not the shipowner);
- **free in and out and trimmed**—bulk cargoes such as grain or coal which are tipped into the hold of a ship require levelling or, as it is known, trimming. This is done for reasons of ship stability. When this task is necessary, it is performed either manually or by means of bulldozers. The fiot rate makes it clear that the charterer or shipper is required to pay for it.

Gross terms

If the shipowner does pay for loading and discharging, the contract is said to be on **gross terms**.

Basis of freight

In a voyage-charter, the charterer may pay the shipowner either an fio freight, that is, the pure carriage only or some cargo handling may be included. In either case, the freight may be payable as a lump sum or per tonne. The former occurs in a **lump sum charter**. The charterer tells the shipowner the stowage factor of the cargo (the ratio of the cargo's measurement to its weight). The shipowner responds by stipulating the minimum quantity which the ship can lift. The whole of the ship's carrying capacity is made available to the charterer who pays a **lump sum freight**. When charter freight is paid per tonne, similar discussions will take place between shipowner and charterer as to the stowage factor of the cargo since this affects the ship's ability to carry the intended cargo and a ship with insufficient grain or bale capacity may have to be forgone. If the ship is suitable, however, agreement has to be reached as to the contractual quantity, and hence the basis of payment of freight:

- **min/max quantity**—the shipowner stipulates an exact quantity which cannot be varied: this is the quantity on which freight is payable;
- a quantity with a tolerance—the quantity is specified but in this case there is an option to declare the final quantity within an agreed percentage. The option could belong to the shipowner (via the master) or to the charterer. The percentage varies from contract to contract and can be "more" than the specified quantity or "more or less". A charter-party with such a provision might read: "100000 tonnes, 5 per cent **more or less in owner's option**". More or less is often abbreviated to "MOL", particularly in telex negotiations. "Owner's option" becomes OO and "charterer's option" CHOP. Hence the acronyms MOLOO and MOLCHOP;
- a minimum quantity with the charterer having the option to fill the ship to capacity. A contract might stipulate 15000 tonnes minimum, charterer having the right to provide a **full and complete cargo** (popularly shortened to F&CC);
- **delivered weight**—this is perhaps the most frequent method of paying freight, based on weighing the cargo on discharge. The delivered or **outturn weight** will often be lower than the loaded weight because of loss of cargo caused, for example, by windage: small amounts of fine cargo, such as grain and some types of coal, are literally blown away while being handled;
- **bill of lading weight** with option on delivered weight—some charter-parties allow the merchant to pay freight on the bill of lading weight or to declare prior to breaking bulk (commencement of discharge) that he wishes to pay on the delivered weight;
- **discount in lieu of weighing**—some contracts which call for the cargo to be weighed on discharge at the ship's expense allow the merchant a discount if weighing can be dispensed with, thus saving time and money. In this case, the parties will use the bill of lading weight. The discount varies but typically could be 1 or 2 per cent.

Associated abbreviations:
f&cc full and complete cargo
fio free in and out
fios free in and out and stowed
fiot free in and out and trimmed
gt gross terms
ls lump sum
min/max minimum/maximum
molchop more or less in charterer's option
moloo more or less in owner's option

See also:
Chartering

Chartering

Ships may be operated commercially by their owners or they may be hired out. This hiring out is called **chartering** and it takes various forms, depending on the particular trade. Ships are **chartered (in)**, that is, hired from their owners, for different reasons: bulk cargo owners who have enough cargo to fill a ship, either for one voyage or for a period of time; shipping lines who do not wish to own their own ships or who are temporarily supplementing their fleet (**slot chartering**). Generally speaking, ships are **chartered (out)** by shipowners who do not wish to operate them commercially.

As far as cargo interests are concerned, shipping falls into two main categories: liner shipping and tramp shipping. **Liner shipping** involves regular services provided by shipping companies between scheduled, advertised ports of loading and discharging, with freight rates based on the company's tariff.

In general terms, **tramp shipping**, or **tramping**, concerns ships which will call at any port to carry whatever cargoes, most commonly bulk cargoes, are available. These ships are chartered by cargo interests from their owners in different ways and for different periods: a **voyage charter** is a contract of carriage in which the charterer pays for the use of a ship's cargo space for one, or sometimes more than one, voyage. This is as distinct from a **time charter** which is the hiring of a ship for a period of time. Occasionally, where a cargo owner has a requirement for a series of voyages to be undertaken between two specific ports or areas, he may hire ships from a shipowner under a contract of **affreightment**. This is a variation on the voyage charter.

A charterer may, in turn, charter the ship to another party. This is known as a **sub-charter**, or **sub-let**. This may happen when a time chartered ship is to be redelivered to its owner at a place other than the port where the (final) cargo is discharged. Rather than try to find another cargo, the charterer sub-lets the ship to another charterer, the **sub-charterer**. If the sub-charter is a voyage charter, the sub-charterer pays **sub-freight**; if time charter, **sub-hire**.

There is another category of charter, the **bareboat charter** or **charter by demise**. This is the hiring or leasing of a ship for a period of time during which the shipowner provides only the ship while the charterer provides the crew together with all stores and bunkers and pays all operating costs. This type of charter is favoured by persons or companies who wish to own a ship for investment purposes but who do not have the desire or expertise to operate the ship. For example, banking organisations may finance a newbuilding and charter it out to a ship operator.

The parties to these contracts are the shipowner and the charterer. In the case of a sub-charter, the parties are the disponent owner and the charterer. These are also described respectively as the charterer and sub-charterer. Normally, intermediaries act for both parties; these are the shipbrokers who may be charterer's agent or owner's broker (*see* **Shipbroker**).

The document containing the chartering contract is the **charter-party**, often referred to simply as the charter. This may be a **voyage charter-party**, a **time** charter-party or bareboat charter-party, depending on the type of contract. There are many standard forms of charter-party which are described and reproduced elsewhere in this book.

Associated abbreviations:
t/c time charter
v/c voyage charter

Associated definitions:
A charter The chartering or hiring of a ship. Also short form for charter-party
Charterable quantity Cargo sufficient to fill the size of ship likely to be found for a particular voyage
Part charter The chartering of a ship to carry a quantity of goods which represents only a part of the cargo. Very often, although the size of the cargo is not enough to fill a ship, it is sufficient to warrant the ship calling at a separate berth where loading or discharging is controlled by the charterer
To charter Said of a shipowner, to hire or charter his ship out to a charterer. Said of a charterer, to hire or charter a ship from its owner

Associated terms:
A slot charter
To slot charter
To sub-charter
Tramp ship

See also:
Bareboat charter
Contract of affreightment
Time charter
Voyage charter

Chartering—offer and counter-offer

Exchange of correspondence between a shipowner and a charterer, often by means of intermediaries acting for each, respectively owner's broker and chartering agent, leading to the chartering of a ship.

Offers (and **counter-offers**) can be firm or conditional. To conclude a contract is **to fix a ship**, the conclusion of a contract being known as a **fixture**.

A **firm offer** is one which is not conditional in any way and is binding on the party making it, provided that it is accepted in full and within any time limit specified in it.

Normally, offers have conditions attached, known as **subjects**, particularly in the early stages of negotiations, such that an acceptance will only result in a contract when the **subjects are lifted**, that is to say, when the conditions are met (*but see* **subject details** *below*). A counter-offer may commence with the words **accept except**; the message will then list the details or clauses not agreed to together with any amendments sought. A ship is said to be **fixed on subjects** when the terms and conditions of chartering her have been agreed except for a few, often minor, details.

Examples of subjects include: **subject free**, meaning that the acceptance of the offer will only result in a fixture if a contract has not been concluded in the meantime with a third party. This is also known as **subject open** or **subject unfixed**. **Subject stem** denotes that the offer is made subject to the availability of the cargo on the dates when the ship is being offered.

Subject details means that only minor details remain to be agreed. It is widely accepted that the conclusion of a contract is conditional on these details being agreed although an American court has ruled that the acceptance of such an offer or counter-offer is sufficient to create a contract, leaving the details to be agreed subsequently.

The correspondence can start with an offer either of a ship or of a cargo. The exact content will differ according to each set of circumstances and whether it concerns a time charter or voyage charter.

The initial offer for a voyage charter from a shipowner might specify the ship's name, deadweight, the date and place when she is open, possible voyage and an idea of the rate required. A charterer would state the size and type of cargo, readiness dates, voyage and also indicate the rate sought. These initial offers are sent out by telex, fax, e-mail, from Internet web sites and by circulars distributed by brokers acting for both sides.

Once a potential match is found between ship and cargo, the shipowner is able to estimate the costs of the proposed voyage and so the exchange of correspondence becomes more detailed in respect of, for example, the freight rate or hire being offered and indications or guarantees of how much the ship will lift. Particular details may be made **without guarantee**.

The exact cargo size may not be known at this stage and may be qualified with the word **about** (often abbreviated to abt). A shipowner may offer his ship to a prospective charterer with a large spread of dates, known as a **wide laycan**, in order to minimise the risk of the ship arriving after the cancelling date. The prospective charterer may want to **narrow the laycan**, that is, to reduce the number of days between the first of the laydays and the last, because of berth or labour availability or because of cargo readiness or delivery requirements.

During the negotiating stage, the shipowner may have more than one ship **coming free** (becoming available) and may not know which one will perform the voyage. He may therefore offer a named ship or (similar) substitute, or a **vessel TBN** (**to be nominated**) or a **vessel TBA** (**to be advised**), or simply a **TBN** or a **TBA**. He will be required to **nominate**, or designate, the exact ship by a certain time before commencement of the charter.

However, at the time when the contract for a voyage charter has been made, the shipowner may not know which of his ships will perform the voyage. It may then be described as a "named ship" or **similar substitute**.

A typical counter-offer for a voyage charter, made by a shipowner partway through negotiations, would contain:

—the ship's name, if it is known which ship is proposed
—year of build
—ship's deadweight
—cargo type
—cargo quantity and any qualifications, for example 5 per cent **more or less in owners' option**
—stowage factor
—laycan
—voyage, for example the names of the load and discharge ports
—rate of freight or lump sum
—terms of freight, for example fio
—excepted periods, for example Saturdays, Sundays and holidays excluded
—rate of demurrage/despatch
—commission amount
—amendments sought to any details or clauses
—time limit; generally, offers (and counter-offers) will specify a time limit after which the offer lapses.

An offer for a vessel on time charter would include her speed and consumption of fuel and diesel and possibly the place or area where she will be delivered and/or redelivered.

Finally, it should be noted that much of this correspondence is made up of abbreviations because, traditionally, negotiating had been by cable or telex with the need to save on the cost of communications.

Associated definitions:
Counter short for counter-offer
More or less in charterers' option option to the charterer to provide a specified percentage more or less than the quantity stipulated
To lift subjects to remove conditions
To offer firm to make a firm offer

Associated terms:
Substitution
To substitute

Associated abbreviations:
abt about
a/c account
charts charterers
fio free in and out
laycan laydays cancelling
l/c laycan

molchop more or less in charterers' option
moloo more or less in owners' option
shex Sundays and holidays excepted
shinc Sundays and holidays included
sim. sub. similar substitute
sshex Saturdays, Sundays and holidays excepted
sshinc Saturdays, Sundays and holidays included
sub. subject or substitute
sub. dets. subject details
tba to be advised
tbn to be nominated
wog without guarantee

See also:
Cancellation of a charter
Laytime—calculation
Laytime—commencement
Penalties

Charter-party

Document containing all the terms and conditions of the contract between a shipowner and a charterer. Charter-parties, or **charters** as they are often referred to, fall into two main categories: **voyage charter-parties** and **time charter-parties**. Time charters are contracts for the hire of a ship whereas voyage charters cover the space in a ship.

Most charter-parties are standard forms. Different standard forms have evolved for different trades. The Baltic and International Maritime Council (BIMCO) publishes voyage charter-parties for cement, coal, fertilisers, gas, grain, ore, stone, tankers and wood, as well as a number of general charters. It also publishes a number of time charters, for use in different situations. There are also a number of so-called private forms, that is, charter-parties developed and published by individual companies, both for voyage and time charters. The majority of these are produced by the major oil companies. Examples are BeePeeVoy, a BP voyage charter-party, and ExxonTime, a time charter published by Exxon.

Charter-parties contain various clauses setting out the rights and responsibilities of both parties in relation to such matters as payment of freight or hire, and contingencies for strikes, general average and war. They also contain details relating to the individual contract, such as the amount of freight, lay time, demurrage, the ship's construction, speed and consumption. The older forms leave spaces for this information, while the newer types, known as **box-layout charters**, have boxes into which the specific information is inserted. *For an example of a box-layout charter, see* **Gencon** *under* **Voyage charter**.

The standard clauses may be varied and/or added to by agreement of the two parties. When a significant number of clauses is added, these may be included in an **addendum to the charter**.

Charter-parties are signed by both the shipowner and the charterer or their agents. When signed by an agent, it is normal to add the words **as agent only**.

Abbreviations:
c/p Charter-party
t/c Time charter
v/c Voyage charter

Alternative spellings:
Charter party
Charterparty

See also:
Bareboat charter
BIMCO (Baltic and International Maritime Council)
Chartering
Sundry charter-party clauses (found in both voyage and time charters)
Sundry time charter-party clauses
Sundry voyage charter-party clauses
Time charter
Voyage charter

Charter-party bills of lading, waybills and cargo receipts

A variety of documents arise from the chartering of a ship, commencing with the document containing the contract itself, the **charter-party**. The type of charter-party and its content depend on whether it is a time charter or voyage charter and the type of commodity to be carried (*see* **Chartering** *and* **Charter-party**) .

A **charter-party bill of lading** is issued by the shipowner for a shipment of cargo on a chartered ship when it is intended that the bill of lading be passed to the receiver and that the receiver be bound by the terms and conditions of the charter-party. A clause to this effect incorporating the date and place of signature of the charter-party appears on the bill of lading.

Occasionally the charterer or his agent will want to issue a bill of lading, particularly when he acts as carrier. Such a document is called a **charterer's bill of lading**.

A variety of **waybills** and **cargo receipts** exist for situations where only one function of the bill of lading, that of receipt for the cargo on board the vessel, is required. Unlike a bill of lading, the waybill and cargo receipt are not documents of title—they contain a clause specifying that delivery will be made by the carrier to the party named in the document. Again, unlike a bill of lading, which is evidence of a contract of carriage, charter-party waybills and cargo receipts contain a clause or box identifying the charter-party governing the contract of carriage. The Baltic and International Maritime Council (BIMCO) publishes several waybills and receipts for different purposes:

—a Non-negotiable Tanker Waybill, codenamed **Tankwaybill 81**;
—a Non-negotiable Chemical Tanker Waybill, codenamed **Chemtankwaybill 85**;
—a Non-negotiable Gas Tank Waybill for use in the LPG Trade, codenamed **Gastankwaybill**;
—a Non-negotiable Cargo Receipt for heavy lifts, codenamed **Heavyconreceipt**;
—a Non-negotiable Cargo Receipt for food shipped by the World Food Programme in Rome, codenamed **Worldfoodreceipt**.

Associated abbreviations:
b/l bill of lading
c/p charter-party
w/b waybill

See also:
Bill of lading
Bill of lading as document of tide
Bill oflading as evidence of contract of carriage
Bill of lading as receipt
Waybill

Classification societies

Organisations whose main function is to carry out surveys of ships whilst being built and at regular intervals after construction, their purpose being to set and maintain standards of construction and upkeep for ships and their equipment. Each classification society has a set of rules governing the requirements for surveys and a number of classes; these are categories denoting the type of ship and the classification society with which she is **classed**. Probably the best known **class** is 100A1 used by Lloyd's Register of Shipping and other classification societies. The assigning of a class depends on a ship being constructed in accordance with the classification society's rules and, for a ship to **maintain her class**, she must continue to comply with these rules.

Each classification society has its own general conditions; those of Bureau Veritas, the French classification society, are reproduced below.

Expiry of class occurs when the term of classification expires and is not renewed. **Suspension of class** occurs when recommendations of the classification society have not been implemented or when surveys have not been carried out on time or when the ship is operated in conditions not allowed for in the classification certificate. Class may also be suspended when fees are unpaid. In order to be reinstated, the ship must undergo the necessary surveys.

If the shipowner does not comply with reinstatement surveys, the classification society may decide to **withdraw the class**. The ship is then removed from the classification register (*see below*).

Periodically, and after any collision, ships are surveyed by a classification society surveyor to ensure that they meet the minimum standards for continued trading set by the society. These are known as **classification surveys**.

In most countries, it is not obligatory for a shipowner to have his ship classed but there would be considerable difficulties in trading if the ship were not, since it is often a condition of the ship's insurance and a requirement of most charterers and shippers. Classification societies also inspect and approve the construction of shipping containers.

Charterers often stipulate a **first class ship**, that is, a ship to which the highest class has been given.

Some classification societies publish a **classification register**, listing all the ships classed by that society, and, in the case of the register published by Lloyd's Register of Shipping, all ships over a certain size. Against each ship is recorded such information as the place and date of build, the tonnages and capacities, dimensions, number of decks, holds and hatches and details of engines and boilers.

Classification societies exist in most of the principal maritime countries. Major ones include:

—**American Bureau of Shipping (ABS)**
—**Bureau Veritas (BV)** (France)
—**China Classification of Shipping (CCS)**
—**Croatian Register of Shipping (CRS)**
—**Det Norske Veritas (DNV)** (Norway)
—**Germanischer Lloyd (GL)** (Germany)
—**Hellenic Register of Shipping (HRS)** (Greece)
—**Indian Register of Shipping (IRS)**
—**Korean Register of Shipping (KRS)**
—**Lloyd's Register of Shipping (LR)** (United Kingdom)
—**Nippon Kaiji Kyokai (Class NK)** (Japan)
—**Polish Register of Shipping (PRS)**
—**Registro Italiano Navale (RINA)** (Italy)

Many of the major classification societies are represented internationally by the **International Association of Classification Societies (IACS)**.

One of the major classification societies, Uoyd's Register (LR), describes its services as follows:

Classification societies

MARINE DIVISION
GENERAL CONDITIONS

ARTICLE 1

1.1. - BUREAU VERITAS is a Society the purpose of whose Marine Division (the "Society") is the classification ("Classification") of any ship or vessel or structure of any type or part of it or system therein collectively hereinafter referred to as a "Unit" whether linked to shore, river bed or sea bed or not, whether operated or located at sea or in inland waters or partly on land, including submarines, hovercrafts, drilling rigs, offshore installations of any type and of any purpose, their related and ancillary equipment, subsea or not, such as well head and pipelines, mooring legs and mooring points or otherwise as decided by the Society.

The Society:
* prepares and publishes Rules for classification, Guidance Notes and other documents ("Rules");
* issues Certificates, Attestations and Reports following its interventions ("Certificates");
* publishes Registers.

1.2. - The Society also participates in the application of National and International Regulations or Standards, in particular by delegation from different Governments. Those activities are hereafter collectively referred to as "Certification".

1.3. - The Society can also provide services related to Classification and Certification such as ship and company safety management certification; ship and port security certification, training activities; all activities and duties incidental thereto such as documentation on any supporting means, software, instrumentation, measurements, tests and trials on board.

1.4. - The interventions mentioned in 1.1., 1.2. and 1.3. are referred to as "Services". The party and/or its representative requesting the services is hereinafter referred to as the "Client". **The Services are prepared and carried out on the assumption that the Clients are aware of the International Maritime and/or Offshore Industry (the "Industry") practices.**

1.5. - The Society is neither and may not be considered as an Underwriter, Broker in ship's sale or chartering, Expert in Unit's valuation, Consulting Engineer, Controller, Naval Architect, Manufacturer, Shipbuilder, Repair yard, Charterer or Shipowner who are not relieved of any of their expressed or implied obligations by the interventions of the Society.

ARTICLE 2

2.1. - Classification is the appraisement given by the Society for its Client, at a certain date, following surveys by its Surveyors along the lines specified in Articles 3 and 4 hereafter on the level of compliance of a Unit to its Rules or part of them. This appraisement is represented by a class entered on the Certificates and periodically transcribed in the Society's Register.

2.2. - Certification is carried out by the Society along the same lines as set out in Articles 3 and 4 hereafter and with reference to the applicable National and International Regulations or Standards.

2.3. - **It is incumbent upon the Client to maintain the condition of the Unit after surveys, to present the Unit for surveys and to inform the Society without delay of circumstances which may affect the given appraisement or cause to modify its scope.**

2.4. - The Client is to give to the Society all access and information necessary for the performance of the requested Services.

ARTICLE 3

3.1. - **The Rules, procedures and instructions of the Society take into account at the date of their preparation the state of currently available and proven technical knowledge of the Industry. They are not a code of construction neither a guide for maintenance or a safety handbook.**

Committees consisting of personalities from the Industry contribute to the development of those documents.

3.2. - The Society only is qualified to apply its Rules and to interpret them. Any reference to them has no effect unless it involves the Society's intervention.

3.3. - The Services of the Society are carried out by professional Surveyors according to the Code of Ethics of the Members of the International Association of Classification Societies (IACS).

3.4. - **The operations of the Society in providing its Services are exclusively conducted by way of random inspections and do not in any circumstances involve monitoring or exhaustive verification.**

ARTICLE 4

4.1. - The Society, acting by reference to its Rules:
* reviews the construction arrangements of the Units as shown on the documents presented by the Client;
* conducts surveys at the place of their construction;
* classes Units and enters their class in its Register;
* surveys periodically the Units in service to note that the requirements for the maintenance of class are met.

The Client is to inform the Society without delay of circumstances which may cause the date or the extent of the surveys to be changed.

ARTICLE 5

5.1. - **The Society acts as a provider of services. This cannot be construed as an obligation bearing on the Society to obtain a result or as a warranty.**

5.2. - The certificates issued by the Society pursuant to 5.1. here above are a statement on the level of compliance of the Unit to its Rules or to the documents of reference for the Services provided for.

In particular, the Society does not engage in any work relating to the design, building, production or repair checks, neither in the operation of the Units or in their trade, neither in any advisory services, and cannot be held liable on those accounts. Its certificates cannot be construed as an implied or express warranty of safety, fitness for the purpose, seaworthiness of the Unit or of its value for sale, insurance or chartering.

5.3. - The Society does not declare the acceptance or commissioning of a Unit, nor of its construction in conformity with its design, that being the exclusive responsibility of its owner or builder, respectively.

5.4. - The Services of the Society cannot create any obligation bearing on the Society or constitute any warranty of proper operation, beyond any representation set forth in the Rules, of any Unit, equipment or machinery, computer software of any sort or other comparable concepts that has been subject to any survey by the Society.

ARTICLE 6

6.1. - The Society accepts no responsibility for the use of information related to its Services which was not provided for the purpose by the Society or with its assistance.

6.2. - **If the Services of the Society cause to the Client a damage which is proved to be the direct and reasonably foreseeable consequence of an error or omission of the Society, its liability towards the Client is limited to ten times the amount of fee paid for the Service having caused the damage, provided however that this limit shall be subject to a minimum of eight thousand (8,000) Euro, and to a maximum which is the greater of eight hundred thousand (800,000) Euro and one and a half times the above mentioned fee.**

The Society bears no liability for indirect or consequential loss such as e.g. loss of revenue, loss of profit, loss of production, loss relative to other contracts and indemnities for termination of other agreements.

6.3. - All claims are to be presented to the Society in writing within three months of the date when the Services were supplied or (if later) the date when the events which are relied on of were first known to the Client, and any claim which is not so presented shall be deemed waived and absolutely barred.

ARTICLE 7

7.1. - Requests for Services are to be in writing.

7.2. - **Either the Client or the Society can terminate as of right the requested Services after giving the other party thirty days' written notice, for convenience, and without prejudice to the provisions in Article 8 hereunder.**

7.3. - The class granted to the concerned Units and the previously issued certificates remain valid until the date of effect of the notice issued according to 7.2. hereabove subject to compliance with 2.3. hereabove and Article 8 hereunder.

ARTICLE 8

8.1. - The Services of the Society, whether completed or not, involve the payment of fee upon receipt of the invoice and the reimbursement of the expenses incurred.

8.2. - **Overdue amounts are increased as of right by interest in accordance with the applicable legislation.**

8.3. - **The class of a Unit may be suspended in the event of non-payment of fee after a first unfruitful notification to pay.**

ARTICLE 9

9.1. - The documents and data provided to or prepared by the Society for its Services, and the information available to the Society, are treated as confidential. However:

* Clients have access to the data they have provided to the Society and, during the period of classification of the Unit for them, to the classification file consisting of survey reports and certificates which have been prepared at any time by the Society for the classification of the Unit;
* copy of the documents made available for the classification of the Unit and of available survey reports can be handed over to another Classification Society Member of the International Association of Classification Societies (IACS) in case of the Unit's transfer of class;
* the data relative to the evolution of the Register, to the class suspension and to the survey status of the Units are passed on to IACS according to the association working rules;
* the certificates, documents and information relative to the Units classed with the Society may be reviewed during IACS audits and are disclosed upon order of the concerned governmental or inter-governmental authorities or of a Court having jurisdiction.

The documents and data are subject to a file management plan.

ARTICLE 10

10.1. - Any delay or shortcoming in the performance of its Services by the Society arising from an event not reasonably foreseeable by or beyond the control of the Society shall be deemed not to be a breach of contract.

ARTICLE 11

11.1. - In case of diverging opinions during surveys between the Client and the Society's surveyor, the Society may designate another of its surveyors at the request of the Client.

11.2. - Disagreements of a technical nature between the Client and the Society can be submitted by the Society to the advice of its Marine Advisory Committee.

ARTICLE 12

12.1. - Disputes over the Services carried out by delegation of Governments are assessed within the framework of the applicable agreements with the States, international Conventions and national rules.

12.2. - Disputes arising out of the payment of the Society's invoices by the Client are submitted to the Court of Nanterre, France.

12.3. - Other disputes over the present General Conditions or over the Services of the Society are exclusively submitted to arbitration, by three arbitrators, in London according to the Arbitration Act 1996 or any statutory modification or re-enactment thereof. The contract between the Society and the Client shall be governed by English law.

ARTICLE 13

13.1. - These General Conditions constitute the sole contractual obligations binding together the Society and the Client, to the exclusion of all other representation, statements, terms, conditions whether express or implied. They may be varied in writing by mutual agreement.

13.2. - The invalidity of one or more stipulations of the present General Conditions does not affect the validity of the remaining provisions.

13.3. - The definitions herein take precedence over any definitions serving the same purpose which may appear in other documents issued by the Society.

BV Mod. Ad. ME 545 j – 16 February 2004

"LR provides classification, statutory and technical advisory services for all types of ships, craft and floating structures covering structural design and construction, and materials and equipment used.

Classification

LR classification sets and maintains standards of quality and reliability for all kinds of vessels by establishing requirements for the structural design and construction of ships and their machinery. These standards are maintained by periodic surveys.

Statutory Certification

LR is authorised by 135 national administrations to carry out surveys on their behalf and issue appropriate certification in accordance with various IMO Conventions.

Specialist advisory services

—New constructions and modifications
—Classification and statutory services for existing ships
—Marine quality services
—Technical planning and development
—Research and development projects
—Safety emergency response
—Marine specification

Plan appraisal services

—Control engineering
—Electrical engineering
—Lifting appliances and materials handling
—Machinery design and dynamics
—Piping systems
—Pressure plant design and advisory services
—Refrigeration

Specialist technical services

—Environmental engineering
—Fluid analytical consultancy
—Materials—selection and use
—Non-destructive examination
—System integrity and risk management
—Technical investigation
—Type approval."

LR also operates a container certification scheme which provides for a system of quality control during the manufacture of containers. LR is authorised to issue certification for containers in accordance with the following:

—International Convention for Safe Containers (CSC)
—International Customs Convention
—International Maritime Organization Dangerous Goods Code for Sea Transport (IMDG)
—International Regulations concerning the Carriage of Dangerous Goods by Rail (RID)
—European Agreement concerning the Carriage of Dangerous Goods by Road (ADR)

Classification societies

—US DOT Regulations CFR49 for the Transportation of Intermodal Portable Tanks (IM101 and IM102)

Associated abbreviation:
IACS International Association of Classification Societies

Associated definition:
Classification certificate Certificate issued by a classification society which states the class attributed to a ship

Associated term:
Withdrawal of class

See also:
International Association of Classification Societies (IACS)

CLECAT

CLECAT, the European association for forwarding, transport, logistic and customs services, was established in 1958 in Brussels, where it represents 24 national organisations of European multinational, medium and small freight forwarders and Customs agents, thus representing the largest and oldest institution of its kind.

CLECAT promotes the activity and defends the interests of its members in connection with a large number of institutional and non-institutional counterparts. It has a voice where a regulatory environment concerning transport formalities and transport modes is created, in the intent of securing a uniform and seamless environment, where cargo can move freely and securely for the benefit of the whole international trade, with due respect to issues such as security and environment.

CLECAT is a founding member and board member of the Alliance of European Industry Sectors involved in the Transport of Dangerous Goods (INDA) and the European Rail Freight Customers Platform (ERFCP), member of the EU Customs Trade High-Level Dialogue and the technical Customs Trade Contact Group *et al.*

CLECAT also represents FIATA, the World Federation of Freight Forwarders, on European issues, thus indirectly representing 38 European countries and 100 countries more worldwide.

See also:
Forwarding agent

Combined transport

Combined transport is often used synonymously with intermodal transport and multimodal transport, although these three expressions can be distinguished. Through transport can also be distinguished from the others. There are two main distinctions: first, the precise modes of transport used and, secondly, to what extent the provider of the service is deemed to be the carrier. This tends to identify the party responsible for the goods during the voyage.

These types of contract are provided by shipping lines and forwarding agents wishing to offer shippers an inclusive service. In some instances, the provider of the service is an ocean carrier who sub-contracts to other companies for the performance of the inland leg or legs. In other cases, the service is provided by forwarding agents.

Combined transport consists of a voyage involving more than one leg. Although very often made up of an ocean leg and one or more inland legs, it could simply be a voyage with two legs using the same mode, such as two ocean legs. The provider of this type of service, generally a shipping line, is deemed to be the carrier for the entire voyage. Responsibility for the goods rests with the carrier from the time they are received into his care until the time they are delivered at destination. The document evidencing the contract is the **combined transport document** or **combined transport bill of lading**. The Baltic and International Maritime Council (BIMCO) publishes a combined transport bill of lading, **Combiconbill**. BIMCO also publishes a **combined transport sea waybill**, codenamed **Combiconwaybill**.

The term **intermodal transport** is used when the voyage includes an inland as well as an ocean leg. This term tends to be used to refer purely to container traffic. Containership operators or liner conferences issue an **intermodal tariff** which sets out ocean freight rates, and rail and road rates for the inland parts of the voyage. This type of voyage may be covered by a combined transport contract.

Multimodal transport involves transport by more than one mode, normally, but not necessarily, including an ocean leg. Often forwarding agents act as carrier when offering a door to door service and are known as a **multimodal transport operator** or **MTO**. As with combined transport, the provider of a multimodal transport contract accepts responsibility for the goods from the time they are received into his care until the time they are delivered at destination. Both the Baltic and International Maritime Council (BIMCO) and the International Federation of Freight Forwarders Associations (FIATA) have published a multimodal transport bill of lading covering this situation. Additionally BIMCO has published a multimodal transport sea waybill.

Through transport is a term applied to any voyage involving an ocean leg and an element of **on-carriage**, that is the onward transport to an inland destination by another means, such as train, truck or barge. Freight for the move is covered by a **through rate** and a **through bill of lading** is issued, normally by the ocean carrier but occasionally by the **on-carrier**. The bill of lading will have

Combined transport

a box not only for the port of discharge but also for the final destination. The name of the on-carrier may be specified as well. Less commonly, there may be a leg of the voyage from a point of origin to the loading port; this is known as **pre-carriage** and is performed by a **pre-carrier**. It is less often arranged by the shipping line than on-carriage because shippers operating in the country of origin of the goods are often able to make the necessary arrangements themselves without difficulty.

Depending on the individual contract, the issuer may be responsible for the goods throughout the voyage or only for the ocean leg. Since often the on-carriage is not performed by the ocean carrier, it is important for the shipper or receiver to know the identities of all the parties involved and their contractual responsibilities in the event of loss or damage.

Associated abbreviations:
i/m intermodal
MTO multimodal transport operator

Associated definition:
Through bill through bill of lading

Associated term:
To on-carry

See also:
Bill of lading
BIMCO (Baltic and International Maritime Council)
Multimodal transport bill of lading

Combined transport bill of lading

Combined transport consists of a voyage involving more than one leg. Although very often made up of an ocean leg and one or more inland legs, it could simply be a voyage with two legs using the same mode, such as two ocean legs. The provider of this type of service, generally a shipping line, is deemed to be the carrier for the entire voyage. Responsibility for the goods rests with the carrier from the time they are received into his care until the time they are delivered at destination.

The document evidencing the contract is the **combined transport document** or **combined transport bill of lading**. The Baltic and International Maritime Council (BIMCO) publishes a combined transport bill of lading, codenamed **Combiconbill**. BIMCO also publishes a combined transport sea waybill, called **Combiconwaybill**.

The Combiconbill and Combiconwaybill resemble a liner bill of lading and sea waybill respectively except that, first, the goods are declared by the carrier as merely being received by him. This is because the place of receipt of the goods may well be somewhere other than the ocean vessel. Both the bill of lading and the waybill, as well as representing evidence of the contract of transport, therefore act as a receipt for the goods, when these are received into the care of the carrier. In this respect, they differ from standard liner bills of lading and sea waybills which cover goods received on board the ocean vessel (*although please also see* **Received for shipment bill of lading** *under* **Bill of lading as receipt**).

Secondly, there is a clause in both documents which provides that the carrier is responsible for the whole voyage but which allows him to sub-contract to other companies for the performance of any of the legs of the voyage.

The bill of lading is a document of title and can be negotiated and endorsed to a third party in the same way as an ocean bill of lading. The appearance of the waybill, as well as the terms and conditions, follow those of the bill of lading, except that the waybill is non-negotiable and cannot be endorsed to a third party. The waybill contains a clause to this effect.

See also:
Bill of lading
Combined transport
Waybill

Congestion

Congestion is the accumulation of ships at a port to the extent that ships arriving to load or discharge are obliged to wait some days, or, in extreme cases, weeks for a vacant berth so as to load or discharge their cargo. A port is also said to be **congested** when loading or discharging operations are unusually protracted, resulting in considerable delays. There are various reasons for congestion, such as strikes, severe weather or a seasonally high number of cargoes, for example after a harvest when a large number of vessels is required over a relatively short period of time. An example of seasonal weather is monsoon rain which may severely hamper port working and create a queue of ships. Congestion also arises from inefficiencies at the port, for example due to an inability to clear cargo from the quay as fast as ships can discharge.

Liner operators may try to absorb the extra costs arising from delays, notably extra daily running costs or time-charter hire, provided that these delays are short-lived. Indeed, the lines, or liner conferences on behalf of their members, will generally publish a **notice to the trade** warning their customers that congestion has built up in a particular port and that a surcharge will be necessary if the situation does not improve within a certain time. When the delays are prolonged, very often shippers are charged a surcharge, known as a **congestion surcharge**. There is no one method of calculating this surcharge but it is intended to cover the daily running costs of the ships involved, including any diesel oil needed to run the ships' generators for the period during which they

Congestion

are delayed waiting for a berth. This surcharge is expressed as an amount per freight ton or as a percentage of the freight or, in the case of containers, as an amount per twenty foot equivalent unit.

A shipowner who charters his ship out on voyage charter may build in a provision in the freight for delay in berthing; this is easier for a tramp owner to do than it would be for a shipping line since most frequently the charter will apply to a single voyage whereas the freight rates of a shipping line are set for a much longer period and are, in any event, not intended to provide for temporary changes in circumstances. A common alternative for the tramp owner is to include a provision for **demurrage**. This is a penalty which cargo interests have to pay for taking longer than the time allowed for loading and/or discharging. In many charter-parties, any delay in reaching the berth, including delay caused by congestion, will count in the calculation of demurrage.

In the same way as demurrage is often built in to contracts for movement by barge, a congestion surcharge may also be imposed on barge shippers when congestion, for example at a transhipment port, becomes a cause of serious delays to barges.

Since congestion incurs extra costs to cargo interests and ship operators, pressure is often put on port authorities by these port users to find solutions to the problem.

Associated abbreviations:
cs congestion surcharge
teu twenty-foot equivalent unit

See also:
Liner surcharges

Consignment

A **consignment** consists of goods which are placed in the care of a carrier for delivery to a person or company, termed the **consignee**. Normally the consignee is the importer of the goods or his agent. The person who places the goods in the care of the carrier is known as the **consignor**. This may be the exporter of the goods or his agent.

A **consignment note** is a document, prepared by the shipper, which contains details of the consignment to be carried by road or rail to its destination. It is signed by the carrier as proof of receipt into his care.

Two consignment notes are reproduced on pp. 107 and 108. These contain full details of the consignor and consignee, together with details of the cargo:

—the **CIM Rail Consignment Note**. This document is used for international rail freight movements. The CIM is not a standard UN aligned form (*see* **SITPRO (The Simpler Trade Procedures Board)**). It is not negotiable and is not a document title.

LETTRE DE VOITURE INTERNATIONALE **CMR** INTERNATIONAL CONSIGNMENT NOTE

Sender (name, address, country) Expéditeur (nom, adresse, pays) **1**	Sender's/agent's reference Référence de l'expéditeur/de l'agent **2/3**
Consignee (name, address, country) Destinataire (nom, adresse, pays) **4**	Carrier (name, address, country) Transporteur (nom, adresse, pays) **5**
Place & date of taking over the goods (place, country, date) Lieu et date de la prise en charge des marchandises (lieu, pays, date) **6**	Successive carriers Transporteurs successifs **7**
Place designated for delivery of goods (place, country) Lieu prévu pour la livraison des marchandises (lieu, pays) **8**	This carriage is subject, notwithstanding any clause to the contrary, to the Convention on the Contract for the International Carriage of Goods by Road (CMR) Ce transport est soumis nonobstant toute clause contraire à la Convention Relative au Contrat de Transport International de Marchandises par Route (CMR)

Shipping marks; no kind of packages; descriptions of goods* Marques et nos; no et nature des colis; désignation des marchandises* **9**	Gross weight (kg) **10** poids brut (kg)	Volume (m3) **11** Cubage (m3)

Carriage charges Prix de transport **12**	Senders instructions for customs, etc... Instructions de l'expéditeur (optional) **13**	
Reservations Réserves **14**	Documents attached Documents annexes (optional) **15**	
	Special agreements Conventions particulières (optional) **16**	
Goods received Marchandises reçues **17**	Signature of Carrier Signature du transporteur **18**	Company completing this note Société émettrice **19**
		Place and date: signature Lieu et date: signature **20**

CMR International Consignment Note

Consignment

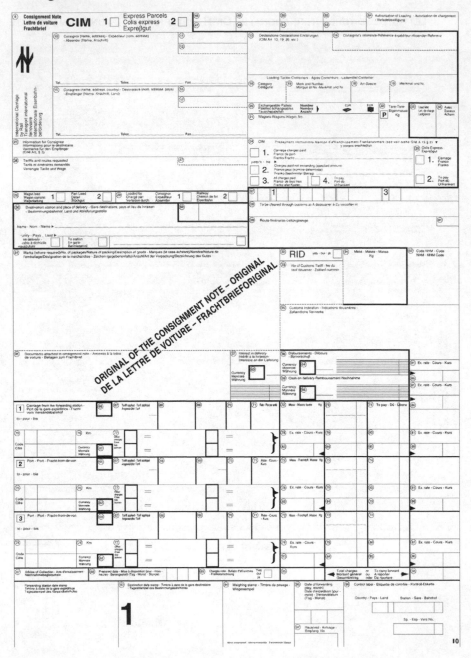

CIM Rail Consignment Note

—The **CMR International Consignment Note** or **CMR Road Consignment Note**. This fulfils the same function as the CIM Consignment Note except that the CMR Note is SITPRO aligned (*see* **SITPRO (The Simpler Trade Procedures Board)**) and is used for international road transport.

Associated definitions:
Consignment Act of placing goods in the care of a carrier for delivery to the consignee
To consign To address a consignment to (a person or company)

See also:
SITPRO (The Simpler Trade Procedures Board)

Container freight

Full container load (fcl)

As its name suggests, the full container load is a consignment which fills a container to capacity, either by weight or volume. It is from one shipper to one destination. The shipper is responsible for packing, or as it is known, **stuffing** the container and the consignee for unpacking (**destuffing** or **stripping**). Responsibility and costs are shared as follows:

- packing (stuffing) of the container—this is arranged and paid for by the shipper;
- haulage to the container terminal at the port of loading—may be arranged and paid for by the shipper. This is known as **merchant haulage**. In some trades, shippers who arrange their haulage pay a **handover charge** when delivering to the terminal. Alternatively, haulage may be arranged by the shipping line (known as **carrier haulage**). The shipper pays a rate for this element in accordance with the line's haulage tariff;
- **terminal handling charge** (at the port of loading)—the charge for moving the container around the port and loading onto the ocean vessel. This is paid separately to the freight by the shipper;
- ocean carriage—paid for by the shipper in the form of freight;
- terminal handling charge (at the discharging port)—the charge for off-loading and positioning of the container in readiness for the overland movement. This is paid as a separate charge by the merchant, often the consignee;
- haulage to destination—again paid by the merchant;
- unpacking (destuffing) of the container—arranged and paid for by the merchant.

When a shipping line quotes a full container load rate, it may specify that the rate applies only when the goods are shipped in the line's standard 20 foot general purpose containers. If so-called specialist equipment, such as open top

Container freight

or half height containers are required, the rate might be subject to an additional charge.

The movement is sometimes designated **fcl/fcl** to show that the merchant is responsible for both packing and unpacking.

Less than container load (lcl)

It is not necessary for a shipper to have sufficient cargo to fill a container before being able to make use of this method of shipment. This is the sequence of events when a small quantity of goods are shipped in this way:

- the shipper arranges and pays for the goods to be sent to an **inland container depot** or **container freight station**;
- the goods are then grouped together with other small consignments for the same destination and all packed into one container. This is known as **groupage** or **consolidation**. An **lcl service charge** is levied for the handling, and sometimes storage, of the cargo at the container freight station;
- haulage of the container to the port is charged at a separate rate depending on the location of the inland container depot;
- ocean carriage—as with full container load consignments, this is paid for by the shipper in the form of freight;
- at the country of destination, the goods are delivered by the carrier to a container freight station where the merchant pays a less than container load service charge for the handling and, if necessary, storage prior to arranging for the goods to be despatched to their final destination.

Variations

As with conventional cargoes, there are variations in the way container shipments can be effected. An **fcl/lcl** shipment requires the merchant to pack the container while leaving the shipping line to perform the unpacking. Conversely, an **lcl/fcl** shipment is packed into the container by the shipping line and unpacked by the merchant.

As well as variations in the responsibilities for packing and unpacking, there is a wide selection of options available to the shipper when it comes to the points where the carrier collects and delivers the cargo. These include:

- **quay to quay**—also described as port to port or terminal to terminal, this covers the ocean freight alone. If a comparison were to be drawn with conventional (breakbulk) shipments, the quay to quay rate is closer to the liner terms rate than to anyother;
- **door to door**—this is, as the name suggests, a service whereby the goods are collected from the shipper's or exporter's premises and delivered to the consignee's premises (also called **house to house**);
- **quay to door** and **door to quay** are further possibilities which may be used depending on the needs of cargo interests.

Freight all kinds

The amount of the freight rate usually varies according to the particular class in which a commodity is included. Sometimes, however, a carrier will quote a single rate irrespective of the commodity, hence the designation **freight all kinds**, almost always abbreviated to **fak**. Fak rates tend to be offered in trades where there is competition between lines and are usually pitched somewhere in the middle of the range of rates available from other carriers in the hope of attracting shippers of all types of commodities. Often, though, they succeed in attracting the higher value cargoes for which higher freight rates are charged by other lines.

Container shipments

Prior to containerisation, liner cargoes were normally freighted on a weight ton or measurement ton basis and this is largely how breakbulk (and lcl) shipments continue to be freighted. With full container loads, however, the tendency is for lines to charge a rate per container, known widely as a **box rate**, leaving it to the shipper to load as much as he wants or can within the container. The basic box rate applies to 20-foot general purpose containers. For 40-foot containers, lines either charge a different (higher) rate or apply a formula to the 20-foot rate according to the weight/measurement ratio of the cargo. In some cases, the rate for a 40-foot container is simply double that of the 20-foot container. There is sometimes an extra charge for special containers such as insulated containers or flatracks and this again is charged as amount per container. Box rates are generally base rates and as such are subject to any surcharges in force, such as the currency adjustment factor or bunker surcharge.

All in rate

There are occasions when freight rates are not subject to extra charges, when circumstances on a particular trade route dictate that rates should be all inclusive. Such rates are termed all in rates. Much less frequently, if at all, there may be no extra charges in force at a given moment.

Ad valorem freight

There are two instances where some or all of the freight is calculated according to the value of the goods, or, as it is referred to, **ad valorem**.

Some tariffs call for certain commodities to be rated according to their value rather than simply being put into tariff classes. This may be because a particular commodity may have variations of finish or content which result in a range of goods with widely varying values. In such cases, the tariff may contain a range of **ad valorem** rates for a commodity which increase as the fob value increases.

Sometimes, the maximum liability of a shipping line for loss or damage is insufficient for a shipper, particularly in the case of higher value goods. The shipper may be given an option of a higher limit of liability in exchange for his paying an extra sum or ad valorem charge on top of the freight. This charge

Container freight

varies from shipping line to shipping line but is generally between 1 and 3 per cent of the value of the goods. In both cases, the line will require some evidence of the value of the goods, such as consular invoice.

Associated abbreviations:
fak freight all kinds
fcl full container load
icd inland container depot
lcl less than container load
thc terminal handling charge

See also:
Containers and associated ancillary charges

Containers and associated ancillary charges

Containers are large boxes designed to enable goods to be sent from door to door without the contents. being handled. There are several standard sizes used worldwide such that the same container can be transferred from one mode of transport to other modes in the course of a single voyage. Indeed, specially designed road and rail vehicles and special ships and barges are frequently used to carry containers.

The most common sizes of containers are the **twenty-footer**, which measures about 20 feet (6.1 metres) long by 8 feet (2.4 metres) wide by 8 feet 6 inches (2.6 metres) high and the **forty-footer**, measuring about 40 feet (12.2 metres) long and having the same width and height as the twenty-footer.

Typically made of steel, there are containers of several types whose use depends principally on the nature of the cargo, for example dry bulk, liquid or perishable cargoes. The most common type is the **general purpose container**, also known as the **dry freight container**. This is used mainly for general merchandise. It is typically made from steel, is fully enclosed and is loaded and discharged through a set of full height rear doors. The floor is covered with timber planking or plywood sheeting and cargo is secured to lashing points normally along the sides at floor level.

Some shipping lines and liner conferences make an extra charge for providing containers which are not the usual 20-foot or 40-foot general purpose containers. This surcharge is variously known as a **special equipment surcharge**, **special equipment premium** or **special container additional**. The reason for the extra charge is the extra investment needed for non-standard equipment. The surcharge or premium is a lump sum per container and is normally subject to any surcharges, such as the currency adjustment factor, levied as a percentage of the freight. Shipping lines do not always levy a surcharge for special equipment but below is a list of the types of containers which can be subject to such a premium:

- **open top container**—this has an open top covered by a waterproof tarpaulin instead of the solid roof found on general purpose containers. This is to enable cargoes to be carried in containers, and hence on containerships, which cannot easily, or at all, be loaded through end doors and need to be loaded from the top. Cargoes which are too high for general purpose containers can also be shipped in open tops. These containers normally have end doors to give flexibility to loading and discharging operations.

- **half-height container**—known also as a **half-height**, this has standard dimensions except for the height. It is used for dense cargoes which take up little space in relation to their weight, such as scrap metal, steel bars or pipes and stone. Often these containers also have an open top so that the cargo can be loaded from the top. The half height is also suitable for loading and discharging in premises with insufficient height to take a full height container. Two half heights occupy one cell in a containership. As with the full height open top, the half height is covered by a waterproof tarpaulin.

- **flatrack** (also known as a **flat**)—an open flat bed onto which cargoes of awkward shape, such as large heavy pieces of machinery, can be placed.

- **dry bulk container**—specially designed for free-flowing bulk cargoes such as grain or sugar which is loaded through hatchways in the top and emptied through hatchways at one end by tipping the container.

- **insulated container**—this container is lined, normally with plywood, so as to minimise the effects of changes in temperature on the cargo and to reduce condensation. It is suitable for perishable goods and other cargoes which require protection from temperature changes without the necessity of refrigeration. The inside dimensions are less than those of a general purpose container because of the lining. In trades where there is an imbalance in one direction of cargo requiring insulated containers, these may be used on the return leg to carry clean general merchandise.

- **refrigerated container**—this is an insulated container used for the carriage of goods requiring refrigeration in transit, such as fruit, vegetables, dairy products and meat. It is fitted with a refrigeration unit which is connected to the carrying ship's electrical power supply. While the container is on the road, it can be fitted with a demountable generator. The refrigerated container is also known as a **reefer container**, **reefer box** or simply **reefer**.

- a variation on the refrigerated container is the **high cube reefer** which has a higher cubic capacity than the standard size reefer and can thus carry a greater volume of cargo. The extra capacity is achieved either by increasing the height of the container or by designing it so that the space taken by the clip-on diesel generator is over and above the standard dimensions of the container.

- **produce carrier**—this is a container with an open side to give unrestricted access for loading and discharging. The side of the container has removable steel grilles or gates and may have drop down doors covering the lower part. This type of container has two uses: for ventilation when carrying certain perishable goods and for loading and discharging at premises where side access is preferred, such as where cargo operations are carried out in a railway siding. The produce carrier is also known as an **open sided container** or **open side container**.

- **porthole container** or **porthole type container**—this type of insulated container has two apertures, known as portholes, through which air of the correct temperature for the cargo is delivered from (and returned to) a terminal's refrigeration unit or a clip-on unit.

The majority of containers in use are owned by the shipping lines or are leased from container leasing companies, with fees paid on the basis of a **per diem** (daily) rate. In some cases, shippers use their own containers, termed **shipper's own** containers or **shipper's owned** containers.

Every container has a **data plate** attached to it, specifying the tare and the gross weight.

Container capacity in ships or terminals is measured in **teu's** (twenty-foot equivalent units). Each container occupies a **cell** or **slot** in a containership.

Containerisation has brought with it problems for some shippers, particularly when a complete trade has become containerised, that is to say that there are no more of the traditional conventional ships. Containers have, without doubt, been of benefit to most commodities in terms of minimising handling and security from pilferage but there are commodities which cannot physically be accommodated in even the biggest container. These are the so-called **uncontainerable** (sometimes shortened to **uncon**) cargoes. An example might be a railway locomotive. At the carrier's discretion, such a cargo may be carried on a containership conventionally. Freighting is normally achieved by the line applying the LCL rate and charging the heavy lift charge and long length additional if these are applicable.

Out of gauge cargo is a cargo on a containership which exceeds the dimensions of the container. A long length cargo might overhang a flatrack, for example, and so occupy more space than was intended for the flatrack. Lines generally charge according to the overall measurement of the cargo, provided that the resulting figure is not less than any container rate which may be applicable. Alternatively, they may consider the number of slots lost by virtue of taking this cargo and charge accordingly. The line may also specify that any extra costs associated with handling out of gauge cargo will be charged to the merchant.

Terminal handling charges, also known as **terminals**, are the equivalent of the fob charges levied on breakbulk cargoes, for export cargoes in full container loads. This charge is levied by the shipping line who in turn remits it to the terminal operator. It covers:

- receiving the container into the terminal;
- movement to any stacking area;
- storage pending arrival of the ship;
- delivery from the stacking area to the ship.

Terminal handling charges are also payable at the terminal in the country of import. They cover:

- receiving the container from the ship to the terminal;
- movement within the terminal to any stacking area;
- storage pending haulage being arranged;
- delivery at the terminal to the haulier.

Terminal handling charges are normally quoted and payable in local currency as a lump sum per container. Less frequently, they are expressed as an amount per tonne, in which case there may be a minimum and a maximum lump sum. They do not attract any of the surcharges applicable to the freight.

It is not necessary to fill a container to capacity in order to be able to make use of this method of shipment. For those shippers who use consolidation or groupage services, a separate charge, the **lcl service charge**, is payable to the carrier. This is for:

- receiving and handling goods for export at the container freight station;
- storage pending delivery to the ship;
- loading into the container (along with goods from other shippers to the same destination).

As with the terminal handling charge, the lcl service charge applies to the reverse operation for import cargo:

- receiving and handling at the container freight station goods brought from the importing ship;
- storage pending delivery to the merchant.

For both imports and exports, the merchant is given a certain amount of free storage time at the container freight station before having to pay additional charges. The lcl service charge is normally quoted and payable in local currency and may be per metric ton or on a weight/measure basis, that is per metric ton or cubic metre whichever produces the greatest amount.

At the beginning of the era of containerisation, commodities were rated as they had always been, that is per freight ton. In this respect, all shippers were treated alike. Shipping lines were quick to see the operational advantages of a container being filled to capacity by just one shipper but shippers needed to be given an incentive. So they were offered an **fcl (full container load) allowance** of an amount per freight ton if they achieved a minimum quantity in the container. This amount was deducted from the freight rate. More recently, most conferences and container lines have switched to box rates (rates per container) so that the quantity actually shipped in the container does not affect the amount payable. Under this arrangement the fcl allowance does not apply.

Associated abbreviations:
cfs container freight station
fcl full container load

Containers and associated ancillary charges

feu forty-foot equivalent unit
fob free on board
gp (container) or **gp (box)** general purpose (container)
lcl less than container load
pd per day or per diem
teu twenty-foot equivalent unit

Associated definitions:
box widely used to denote container
to destuff to unload (a container)
to strip to unload (a container)
to stuff to load (a container)

See also:
Container freight

Contract of affreightment

In its general sense, a contract of affreightment is any contract for the hire of a ship. However, it has a specialised meaning, that is, a contract for a series of voyages involving bulk cargoes.

BIMCO, the Baltic and International Maritime Council, publishes two forms to cover this type of contract: a Standard Volume Contract of Affreightment for the Transportation of Bulk Dry Cargoes, codenamed **Volcoa**, and a Tanker Contract of Affreightment, codenamed **Intercoa 80**, this latter being issued by INTERTANKO, the International Association of Independent Tanker Owners.

In both cases, the object of the form is to identify all the elements applicable to a series of voyages. Principal ones are:

—period of the contract;
—total quantity of cargo;
—quantity per shipment, normally qualified by minimum and maximum quantities in the owner's option;
—a programme of shipments, if one has been calculated;
—a list of the performing vessels; and
—contingencies for charterers' failure to accept a vessel and owners' failure to nominate a vessel for a specific voyage.

Intercoa 80 requires details of:

—the maximum number of grades of cargo;
—the specific gravity;
—heating coils; and
—pumping capacity.

In both cases, the form is used in conjunction with a (separate) voyage charter-party which contains the terms relating to the total contract, rather than to individual shipments. In the case of Intercoa 80, the **Intertankvoy 76** charter-party is incorporated into the contract as a standard condition.

Associated abbreviation:
coa contract of affreightment

Convention on Facilitation of International Maritime Traffic

Few activities have been more subject to over-regulation than international maritime transport. This is partly because of the international nature of shipping: countries developed customs, immigration and other standards independently of each other and a ship visiting several countries during the course of a voyage could expect to be presented with numerous forms to fill in, often asking for exactly the same information but in a slightly different way.

As shipping and trade developed, so did the paperwork involved until by the 1950s it was being regarded not simply as an inconvenience but as a positive threat.

The actual number of separate documents required varied from port to port; yet the information sought was often identical. The number of copies required of some of these documents could often become excessive. To the variety of forms and the number of copies required could be added other burdens such as local language translations, consular visa requirements, variations in document size and paper stock used and the necessity for authentication by the shipmaster of the information submitted.

A report, *Merchant Shipping on a Sea of Red Tape*, compared the documentary requirements and procedures associated with international shipping with those related to the international airline industry and made it clear that merchant ships were foundering in self-inflicted bureaucracy. Analysis showed that whereas only three or four documents were required of aircraft, ports frequently required no fewer than 22, 32 or even 46 separate documents of a ship. The report concluded that:

—The need to simplify ships' documents was urgent and the demands of individual Governments had to be put into clear perspective with the overall welfare of merchant shipping.
—The cost savings which could be achieved from simplification and standard-isation were significant both to industry and to Governments and should be sufficient motivation to spur those concerned into immediate action.

The report recommended that all possible efforts should be directed towards inter-governmental action, preferably through IMO, which had met for the first time just a few weeks before the report was published. It revealed a great need to eliminate duplicative forms and to simplify, unify and standardise the remaining maritime documents. The report defined the various tasks as:

Convention on Facilitation of International Maritime Traffic

—Simplification—the process whereby superfluous data and unnecessary documents are eliminated or at least modified.

—Unification—the combining of several similar documents whenever possible.

—Standardisation—the development of definite size, format and language for documents designed for a specific purpose and use, and their general acceptance by and use throughout the industry.

The Facilitation Convention

The problems outlined in the 1959 report, if anything, grew worse over the next few years and by the early 1960s the maritime nations had decided that the situation could not be allowed to deteriorate further. International action was called for and to achieve it Governments turned to IMO.

In 1961 the 2nd IMO Assembly adopted resolution A.29(II) which recommended that IMO take up the matter. An Expert Group was convened which recommended that an international convention be adopted to assist the facilitation of international maritime traffic. In October 1963 the 3rd IMO Assembly adopted resolution A.63(III) which approved the report of Expert Group and in particular recommended that a convention be drafted which would be considered for adoption at a conference to be held under IMO auspices in the spring of 1965. The conference duly took place and the Convention on Facilitation of International Maritime Traffic (FAL), 1965, was adopted on 9 April.

Its purpose is summed up in the Foreword, which says:

"The Convention was originally developed to meet growing international concern about excessive documents required for merchant shipping. Traditionally, large numbers of documents are required by customs, immigration, health and other public authorities pertaining to the ship, its crew and passengers, baggage, cargo and mail. Unnecessary paperwork is a problem in most industries, but the potential for red tape is probably greater in shipping than in other industries, because of its international nature and the traditional acceptance of formalities and procedures.

The Convention emphasizes the importance of facilitating maritime traffic and demonstrates why authorities and operators concerned with documents should adopt the standardized documentation system developed by IMO and recommended by its Assembly for world-wide use."

The Convention is a "co-operative" treaty whereby Contracting Parties undertake to bring about uniformity and simplicity in the facilitation of international maritime traffic. It entered into force on 5 March 1967 and outlines general principles relating to international maritime facilitation.

The Conference concluded that formalities, documentary requirements and procedures on the arrival and departure of ships should be simplified and, in particular, that public authorities should not require for retention any declaration other than the eight referred to below under "The IMO Standardised Forms (FAL 1–6)".

The Conference agreed that, normally, public authorities should keep the number of individual items of information on a small number of standardised declarations to a minimum but that this would not preclude Governments from requiring further documents or information, as necessary in cases of suspected fraud or to deal with matters endangering public order, security or health, or to prevent the introduction or spread of diseases or pests.

It was accepted that Governments would continue to require for inspection, as opposed to retention, ships' certificates relating to registry, tonnage measurement, safe manning and similar matters and that the Convention should not be interpreted as preventing Governments from granting wider facilities to international shipping. The Convention's provisions apply to all ships, except ships of war and pleasure yachts.

The Conference invited Governments to adjust their national legislation when practicable and, to this effect, drafted international standards to facilitate their incorporation into national legislation.

Contracting Governments to the Convention agreed to adopt appropriate measures to:

1. facilitate international maritime traffic;
2. prevent unnecessary delays to ships, their crews, passengers and cargoes;
3. secure the highest practicable degree of uniformity in formalities, documentary requirements and procedures; and
4. keep to a minimum any alterations needed to meet special national requirements.

These measures should be practical and no less favourable than those applied to other means of international transport.

Standards and recommended practices

In its Annex, the Convention contains "Standards" and "Recommended Practices" on formalities, documentary requirements and procedures which should be applied on arrival, stay and departure to the ship itself, and to its crew, passengers, baggage and cargo. The Convention defines standards as internationally-agreed measures which are "necessary and practicable in order to facilitate international maritime traffic" and recommended practices as measures the application of which is "desirable".

The Convention provides that any Contracting Government which finds it impracticable to comply with any international standard, or deems it necessary to adopt differing regulations, must inform the Secretary-General of IMO of the "differences" between its own practices and the standards in question. The same procedure applies to new or amended standards.

In the case of recommended practices, Contracting Governments are urged to adjust their laws accordingly but are only required to notify the Secretary-General when they have brought their own formalities, documentary requirements and procedures into full accord.

This flexible concept of standards and recommended practices, coupled with the other provisions, allows continuing progress to be made towards the formulation and adoption of uniform measures in the facilitation of international maritime traffic.

Convention on Facilitation of International Maritime Traffic

IMO GENERAL DECLARATION

☐ Arrival ☐ Departure

1. Name and description of ship		2. Port of arrival/departure	3. Date - time of arrival/departure
4. Nationality of ship	5. Name of master	6. Port arrived from/Port of destination	
7. Certificate of registry (Port; date; number)		8. Name and address of ship's agent	
9. Gross tonnage	10. Net tonnage		
11. Position of the ship in the port (berth or station)			
12. Brief particulars of voyage (previous and subsequent ports of call; underline where remaining cargo will be discharged)			
13. Brief description of the cargo			
14. Number of crew (incl. master)	15. Number of passengers	16. Remarks	

Attached documents
(indicate number of copies)

17. Cargo Declaration	18. Ship's Stores Declaration	
19. Crew List	20. Passenger List	21. Date and signature by master, authorized agent or officer
22. Crew's Effects Declaration*	23. Maritime Declaration of Health*	

For official use

IMO Convention on Facilitation of International Maritime Traffic (vertical, left margin)

IMO General Declaration

120

Convention on Facilitation of International Maritime Traffic

IMO CARGO DECLARATION

☐ Arrival ☐ Departure

Page No.

1. Name of ship	2. Port where report is made

3. Nationality of ship	4. Name of master	5. Port of loading/Port of discharge

B/L No.*	6. Marks and Nos.	7. Number and kind of packages; description of goods	8. Gross weight	9. Measurement

10. Date and signature by master, authorized agent or officer

* Transport document No.

Also state original ports of shipment in respect of goods shipped on multimodal transport document or through bills of lading.

IMO Convention on Facilitation of International Maritime Traffic

IMO Cargo Declaration

Convention on Facilitation of International Maritime Traffic

IMO SHIP'S STORES DECLARATION

☐ Arrival ☐ Departure

Page No.

1. Name of ship	2. Port of arrival/departure	3. Date of arrival/departure
4. Nationality of ship	5. Port arrived from/Port of destination	
6. Number of persons on board	7. Period of stay	8. Place of storage

9. Name of article	10. Quantity	11. For official use

IMO FAL Form 3

12. Date and signature by master, authorized agent or officer

Convention on Facilitation of International Maritime Traffic

IMO CREW'S EFFECTS DECLARATION

| | | Page No. |

1. Name of ship	2. Effects which are dutiable or subject to prohibitions or restrictions*	
3. Nationality of ship		
4. No. 5. Family name, given names	6. Rank or rating					7. Signature
....	....					....
....	....					....
....	....					....
....	....					....
....	....					....
....	....					....
....	....					....
....	....					....
....	....					....
....	....					....
....	....					....
....	....					....
....	....					....
....	....					....
....	....					....
....	....					....
....	....					....
....	....					....
....	....					....
....	....					....
....	....					....

IMO FAL Form 4

8. Date and signature by master, authorized agent or officer

* e.g. wines, spirits, cigarettes, tobacco, etc..

IMO Crew's Effects Declaration

Convention on Facilitation of International Maritime Traffic

IMO CREW LIST

☐ Arrival ☐ Departure

Page No.

1. Name of ship	2. Port of arrival/departure	3. Date of arrival/departure

4. Nationality of ship	5. Port arrived from	6. Nature and No. of identity document (seaman's passport)

7. No. 8. Family name, given names	9. Rank or rating	10. Nationality	11. Date and place of birth	

IMO FAL Form 5

12. Date and signature by master, authorized agent or officer

IMO Crew List

Vertical text (left margin): IMO Convention on Facilitation of International Maritime Traffic

Convention on Facilitation of International Maritime Traffic

IMO PASSENGER LIST

				Page No.
	☐ Arrival ☐ Departure			

1. Name of ship		2. Port of arrival/departure	3. Date of arrival/departure	
4. Nationality of ship				

5. Family name, given names	6. Nationality	7. Date and place of birth	8. Port of embarkation	9. Port of dis-embarkation
....	....	....	....	....

IMO FAL Form 6

10. Date and signature by master, authorized agent or officer

IMO Passenger List

IMO Convention on Facilitation of International Maritime Traffic

Convention on Facilitation of International Maritime Traffic

The IMO Standardised Forms (FAL 1–6) *(reproduced on pp. 120–125)*

Standard 2.1 lists the eight documents which public authorities can demand of a ship and recommends the maximum information and number of copies which should be required. IMO has developed Standardised Forms for six of these documents. They are the:

— **IMO general declaration**
— **cargo declaration**
— **ship's stores declaration**
— **crew's effects declaration**
— **crew list**
— **passenger list.**

Another two documents are required under the Universal Postal Convention and the International Health Regulations.

The general declaration, cargo declaration, crew list and passenger list constitute the maximum information necessary. The ship's stores declaration and crew's effects declaration incorporate the agreed essential minimum information requirements.

Benefits of the Convention and the model forms

The adoption of the Convention was an important step, but the next step was to encourage as many Governments as possible to ratify it. IMO prepared a document which lists the various advantages to be gained from doing so. They are:

1 General

—A standardised rapid system of clearing ships inwards and outwards with easy completion of clearance documents in advance of the arrival of the ship eliminates delay and contributes to a quick turn-around.
—Minimisation of passenger clearance requirements reduces dock-side congestion and eliminates the need for correspondingly larger facilities.
—Easy reproduction on small inexpensive machines by shipboard or shore-based personnel of the simplified standardised documents reduces filing and storage space requirements.
—The uniform layout makes the use of Automatic Data Processing (ADP) techniques possible.

2 To Governments

—Reduction of the administrative burden and better utilisation of personnel in customs and other public authorities is achieved by eliminating non-essential documents and information.
—Formalities are no more onerous than those of competing ports.
—Governments have the benefit of forms designed by international experts. Simple, well-designed forms make for more efficient and less-expensive

administration and help increase port throughput by preventing unnecessary delay to ships, passengers and cargoes.

—National forms which follow an international model are more readily understood by ships' masters and, therefore, more likely to be correctly completed. Language difficulties are minimised.

—The uniform position of similar items of information on each form makes it easier to check the documents and extract the required information.

3 To shipowners

—General benefits derive from the acceptance of the principle that formalities and procedures in respect of maritime traffic should be no more onerous than those for other modes of transport.

—Fewer and simpler forms need to be completed. Less information is required and less work is therefore involved.

—If no changes are foreseen with regard to crews, ship stores or passengers during the voyage or any part of it, identical forms for several ports can be completed at the same time. In such circumstances the same forms can be submitted both on arrival and on departure.

—The ship's manifest and cargo declaration can be completed in one run, thus keeping down costs and reducing the possibility of errors.

—The uniform position of information makes typing easier and contributes to quicker familiarisation of new personnel with document processing. It also facilitates the use of ADP.

4 To shippers

—The enhanced efficiency of clearing ships and cargo saves time and expense.

—The use of standardised commercial documents, e.g. bills of lading, simplifies the production of documents.

—Cargoes awaiting shipment or collection are exposed for a shorter time to the risk of damage or pilfering within port facilities.

—The utilisation of containers and pallets is improved.

—It becomes possible to utilise documents produced by ADP techniques.

—Requirements for authentication of documents are simplified.

—Time savings reduce the charges for services rendered by public authorities outside regular working hours.

Although many countries have benefited from applying the principles of the Convention and using the Standardised Forms, IMO strongly emphasises that they would benefit still further, as would all others, if the Convention were ratified and the forms were adopted worldwide. Acceptance and use of the international standardised shipping documents is regarded as the basis of effective facilitation of maritime traffic. In view of these extensive benefits and to further encourage adoption of the Convention, IMO has recommended that:

—Governments which have not yet accepted the Convention should consider doing so as soon as practicable.

Convention on Facilitation of International Maritime Traffic

—Governments which cannot accept the Convention at present should nevertheless examine the possibilities of simplifying and reducing their legislative and documentary requirements respecting the arrival, stay and departure of ships and of using forms based on the IMO Model.

—Governments should encourage universal adoption of the Standardised Forms and the highest possible degree of uniformity in documentary requirements and procedures by keeping to a minimum any alterations needed to meet their national requirements.

—Governments should create national and, if necessary, regional facilitation committees consisting of representatives of governmental and commercial sectors for the purpose of developing facilitation measures.

IMO also recognises that the shipping industry's co-operation is essential if the benefits of these facilitation efforts are to be realised. It is hoped that operators and masters might be made aware of the advantages of facilitation and, with the assistance of their port agents, might press for the early replacement of national forms by internationally standardised forms.

The 1986 amendments

One of the main purposes of the amendments was to permit the use of automatic data processing (ADP) and other modern communications techniques, which had developed rapidly during the preceding years. They entered into force on 1 October 1986 and also made it possible for the shipping world to make use of another development known as electronic data interchange (EDI). This is basically a means of enabling computers to talk directly to each other. Because modern business transactions were increasingly being computerised this had a number of advantages.

The 1987 amendments

The amendments, which entered into force on 1 January 1989, include the upgrading of a number of recommended practices to standards. Standard 2.3.4 requires public authorities to accept a cargo manifest in place of the Cargo Declaration. Standard 2.6.1 simplifies the contents of the Crew List.

Other amendments are designed to facilitate the arrival and departure of ships engaged in disaster relief work, pollution combating operations and similar activities where speed is especially important.

Associated abbreviations:
ADP Automatic Data Processing
EDI Electronic Data Interchange
IMO International Maritime Organization

See also:
International Maritime Organization (IMO)

Conventional freight and the export contract

A contract of carriage between the shipper and the shipping line in which freight is levied on a liner terms basis dovetails neatly with two very popular types of export sales contract: **fob** (standing for free on board) and **cif** (cost, insurance and freight) (with **c&f**—cost and freight—a less frequent but very similar type of contract to cif).

There are two main variations on rates quoted by conventional shipping lines. In each of these, the word "in" represents the port of loading and "out" the discharging port. The word "free" means free of cost to the shipping line.

The most common type of freight rate is one on **full liner terms**, often simply called **liner terms**. This qualification signifies that it consists of the ocean carriage and the cost of cargo handling onto and off the ship at the loading and discharging ports, according to the custom of those ports. This varies widely from country to country and, within countries, from port to port: in some ports, the freight excludes all cargo handling costs while in others, the cost of handling between the hold and the ship's rail or quay is included in the freight.

Free in liner out, also known as **free in liner terms discharge**, stipulates that the loading and stowing are to be arranged and paid for by the shipper. This could apply only when the entire cargo to be loaded at a port belongs to one party who in all likelihood has his own loading facility. As the handling of cargo is not under the control of the shipping line, the shipper may be required to load at a certain rate or within a certain time. Alternatively he may be required to load **fast as can** (this means literally what it says) or **fast as can (according to the) custom of the port**. The contract of carriage might, under these circumstances, contain clauses more usually found in voyage charter-parties. One such clause might require the payment by the shipper of **demurrage** if he exceeds the time allowed to load or he might be paid **despatch**, also termed **despatch money**, if he loads the cargo in a quicker time. When freight is free in liner out, the discharging is on ordinary liner terms as previously explained.

In the case of **liner in free out**, the loading is on liner terms but the cost of discharging is excluded from the freight. It is likely that there is only one cargo receiver at the discharging port and that he has his own discharging facility. He may well be subject to the same constraints at the discharging port as the shipper was at the port of loading in the free in liner out example above.

Whatever the basis of assessing or calculating freight, most shipping lines and liner conferences have a provision for the minimum amount of freight payable by a shipper when he has a very small quantity of cargo to ship on one bill of lading. Called simply **minimum freight**, the amount varies from line to line but is normally a very modest sum below which it would not be economic to accept bookings.

There are two instances where some or all of the freight is calculated according to the value of the goods, or, as it is referred to, **ad valorem**.

Some tariffs call for certain commodities to be rated according to their value rather than simply being put into tariff classes. This may be because a particular commodity may have variations of finish or content which result in a range of goods with widely varying values. In such cases, the tariff may contain a range of ad valorem rates for a commodity which increase as the fob value increases.

Sometimes, the maximum liability of a shipping line for loss or damage is insufficient for a shipper, particularly in the case of higher value goods. The shipper may be given an option of a higher limit of liability in exchange for his paying an extra sum or ad valorem charge on top of the freight. This charge varies from shipping line to shipping line but is generally between 1 and 3 per cent of the value of the goods.

In both cases, the line will require some evidence of the value of the goods, such as consular invoice.

There are occasions when freight rates are not subject to extra charges, when circumstances on a particular trade route dictate that rates should be all inclusive. Such rates are termed **all in rates**. Much less frequently, if at all, there may be no extra charges in force at a given moment.

Because of the constraints of weight and measurement on stowage, commodities fall into three broad categories for freighting purposes, certainly when being shipped LCL or breakbulk:

- weight cargoes—those one tonne of which measures less than one cubic metre;
- measurement cargoes—those one tonne of which measures more than one cubic metre;
- cargoes which do not automatically fall into one of the above two categories, perhaps because they belong to a tariff class which includes variations of a commodity, some denser than others.

Weight cargoes are the denser cargoes as described above. For many years, these were freighted per long ton (2240 lbs). However, with the increasing use of the metric system, it is now more usual to find weight cargoes being charged per tonne (1000 kilogrammes). Liner tariffs often refer to the freight payable on weight cargoes as being **per weight ton**. If a liner conference wanted a particular class in the tariff to be payable on the weight, that is, per weight ton, it would normally put a W suffix to the class number, for example Class 15W. Such goods sometimes said to **stow deadweight**.

Measurement cargoes are the less dense cargoes. With the advance of the metric system, these cargoes are now usually freighted per cubic metre, often abbreviated to cbm or m^3. Jargon surrounds measurement cargoes as much as it does weight cargoes and one cubic metre of such a commodity is sometimes referred to as a **measurement ton**. This term is not as paradoxical as it may seem since the ton is said to have originally related to volume rather than weight and even now the gross and net register tonnages of ships represent cubic measures, not weights. Measurement cargoes are also said **to measure**, that is, they have a capacity in cubic metres greater than their weight in tonnes. Liner tariff classes for goods which measure and which are freighted solely on their cubic measurement often have the suffix M, i.e. Class 12M.

Summing up the previous two paragraphs, cargoes which are known to stow deadweight normally are rated per 1000 kilogrammes and their class number will have the suffix W. Those which are known to measure will be assessed per cubic metre and their class number will have the suffix M. There are many classes with no suffix in the average liner tariff; the tariff will, however, state somewhere that such cargoes will be rated either per tonne or per cubic metre, whichever produces the greatest revenue. Such a rate is called a **weight or measure rate** or a **weight or measurement rate**. This is normally abbreviated to **W/M** (when written) and **WM** (when spoken). Prior to the widespread use of the metric system, the comparison was between one long ton and 40 cubic feet.

The ratio of a commodity's measurement to its weight is known as its **stowage factor**. This is expressed in cubic feet to the ton or cubic metres to the tonne and may be referred to when assessing the way in which freight will be calculated. A measurement ton is 1 cubic metre and a weight ton is 1000 kilogrammes. There is a more general term, the **freight ton**, which could mean either a **measurement ton** or a **weight ton**, depending on the way the cargo to which it refers has been rated by the shipping line.

Whether per long ton, metric ton, cubic metre or whatever, there needs to be an agreement between the two parties to the contract of carriage about the quantity on which freight is payable. With (relatively) small consignments shipped on liner vessels, very often the weight or measurement declared by the shipper is accepted by the shipping line and appears on the bill of lading. It is thus the bill of lading quantity which determines the freight. Liner bills of lading usually contain a provision for the carrier to check the contents of containers, trailers, packages, etc., to determine their correct weight or measurement if there is any doubt about what was declared by the shipper.

Relationship between liner terms freight and fob contract

In a fob contract, the seller is required to deliver the cargo to the port of loading stipulated in the contract and to load it on to the vessel nominated by the buyer. In practice, the seller pays the **fob charges** and from there the liner terms freight takes over and is paid for by the buyer.

Relationship between liner terms freight and cif contract

Here the seller is required not only to load the goods onto the ocean vessel but to pay the freight as well. The difference between a cif contract and a c&f contract is that, in the former, the seller arranges marine insurance cover whereas in the latter, it is the responsibility of the buyer. There are variations on cif contracts which entail a qualification to the term, such as **cif landed** or **cif free out** but when the term is unqualified, it is assumed to mean liner terms.

Relationship between lifo freight and ciffo contract

Freight on **liner in free out** terms fits neatly with a **cif free out** contract, at least in concept. Caution is needed by the seller so as to agree terms with the shipping line or shipowner which match those agreed with the buyer. In this way any delay in discharging the ship will incur the same amount of demurrage in both the contract of carriage and the export sales contract. As a footnote, the expression cif free out is not always correctly interpreted as, although it may be readily accepted that "fo" stands for free out, it may not be self-evident from the term as to who is responsible for discharging. This may be because free out is a shipping term, not a sales term, and signifies free (of the cost of discharging) to the ship. The sales term **cif ship's hold** may perhaps be used with greater confidence.

Associated abbreviations:
c&f cost and freight
cif cost, insurance and freight
ciffo cost, insurance and freight free out
fac fast as can
faccop fast as can custom of the port
filo free in liner out
filtd free in liner terms discharge
flt full liner terms
fio free in and out
fo free out
fob free on board
lifo liner in free out
lt liner terms
pft per freight ton
w/m weight or measure(ment)

See also:
Liner and conference tariffs
Penalties

Currency adjustment factor

Shipping lines may be exposed to many currencies when involved in a given trade. These may be summarised as follows:

- tariff currency
- cost currencies
- revenue currencies
- currency of account.

The **tariff currency** is the currency in which the freight rates in the tariff are expressed. Coincidentally, the tariff currency may also be a cost currency (explained below).

Cost currencies are those required to pay all expenses such as operating and crew costs, port charges, fuel and cargo handling charges. A hypothetical line,

XYZ Line, trading between Belgium and India, might pay for crew, operating costs and fuel in US Dollars and port charges and cargo handling costs in Euros and Rupees.

Revenue currencies are the currencies in which freight is paid. Although the tariff currency may be, say, the US Dollar, the freight is normally converted to the currency of the country of shipment or possibly the country of residence of the shipper (particularly when freight is paid in the country of destination). Indeed, a shipper might well need the agreement of the shipping line to pay in the tariff currency.

It is important to note that each direction of a two-way trade is dealt with separately from the point of view of costs and revenues. Thus, in the case of XYZ Line, most if not all of the revenue from the eastbound leg from Belgium to India would be in Euros.

The **currency of account** is the currency in which the shipping line does its bookkeeping. Thus if XYZ Line were South African, it would gauge its profitability in terms of the Rand. The currency of account is often ignored when calculations are made concerning the effects of currency fluctuations. This is especially so in the case of liner conferences with many members, some of whom are based in third countries, that is to say, countries outside the range of the conference's service.

The currency adjustment factor, also known as the **currency adjustment charge,** originated when currencies started to fluctuate significantly in relation to the tariff currency and shipowners began to realise that currencies could have a significant effect on their bottom line. A shipping line would lose money if the tariff currency weakened in relation to the currencies in which costs were incurred or revenues derived. As the tariff currency weakened, so the freight received by the line reduced in value. It became necessary to introduce a surcharge, expressed as a percentage of the freight, to return the shipping line's revenue, or its ability to cover its costs to where it was before the fluctuation.

There are various methods in use for calculating the currency adjustment factor. Perhaps the most common and most widely accepted by shipowner and shipper alike is the one based on costs incurred. Other methods include basing it on revenues and even on the quantity of cargo carried.

The currencies used to calculate the currency adjustment factor make up what is known as the **basket of currencies**. To determine the currency adjustment factor, several elements are needed:

- base date rates of exchange—a list of all the rates of exchange on a given starting date. At this point, the currency adjustment factor stands at zero (or has been reduced following a partial incorporation into tariff rates—see "rolling in" below);
- current rates of exchange—rates prevailing at the date when the currency adjustment factor is to be introduced or changed;
- percentage increase or decrease of all cost currencies in relation to the tariff currency;

Currency adjustment factor

- weighting factors—the percentage of the total of all costs expended in each of the cost currencies. These add up to 100 per cent;
- weighted percentage change—the effect of the fluctuation of each individual currency against the tariff currency. This figure is determined by multiplying the percentage increase or decrease in the value of the currency by the weighting factor.

The total of all the weighted percentage changes becomes the currency adjustment factor. One important effect of fluctuations is that the calculation of the currency adjustment factor can bring a negative result; the currency adjustment factor becomes a minus percentage applied to the freight.

Surcharges can be brought in (and withdrawn) at relatively short notice but shipping lines and liner conferences often review fluctuations on a monthly basis and/or delay changes to the currency adjustment factor until **trigger points** are reached. These trigger points represent a movement in the weighted change of the currency adjustment factor of a certain minimum percentage. The smaller the trigger point, the more frequently the currency adjustment factor would need to be amended. Indeed, the idea of a trigger point is precisely to avoid constant alterations to the level of the currency adjustment factor as currencies fluctuate.

Many liner conferences tend to incorporate or roll in some or all of the currency adjustment factor at the time of a general rate increase. This has the effect of keeping the level of the surcharge relatively small.

Some liner conferences combine the currency adjustment factor and the bunker surcharge into one surcharge. In their internal calculations, the lines calculate the two elements separately then add them together and express as a single percentage of the freight. This combined surcharge is known as a **currency and bunker adjustment factor**. Since the two constituent elements of this surcharge can be negative, or their combined result negative, the surcharge itself can therefore be negative. Trigger points exist for this surcharge in the same way as they do for the surcharges when quoted and used separately. The difference is that the currency and bunker adjustment factor will only change when the combined effect of the movements in the two reaches the minimum level required to trigger an increase.

Although mention of the currency adjustment factor has so far revolved around shipping lines and liner conferences, tramp owners may negotiate a currency adjustment factor into voyage charters, although usually this is confined to charters for several consecutive voyages or so-called contracts of affreightment which are performed over a relatively long period of time.

Associated abbreviations:
cabaf currency and bunker adjustment factor
cac currency adjustment charge
caf currency adjustment factor

See also:
Bunker surcharge
Liner surcharges

Dangerous goods

Dangerous goods are goods which are potentially hazardous, such as inflammable or toxic goods. Dedicated terminals exist in ports for receiving, storing and loading dangerous goods. Safety is paramount and such terminals are equipped with fire-resistant walls, sprinkler systems and good ventilation. Terminals have separate compartments for different products and may have bottling plants.

In recognition of the special needs of such cargoes for segregated stowage and additional documentation, shipping lines sometimes levy a **hazardous cargo surcharge** or **hazardous cargo additional**. This may take the form of a monetary amount, particularly in the case of container shipments for which a lump sum is charged, or a percentage of the basic freight, particularly for breakbulk shipments. In both cases, the surcharge is subject to any currency adjustment factor.

In some trades, in the case of breakbulk and LCL goods, the surcharge is levied by the shipping line pending clearance of the cargo by the merchant in the country of import. If this is done within the specified period, the surcharge is refunded in full. If, on the other hand, clearance is not effected in time, some of the money may be used to cover the line's extra costs such as special storage and the balance returned to the merchant. Delays to full container loads caused by the merchant are more likely to be the subject of demurrage than a hazardous cargo surcharge. It should be noted that there are trades where there is no hazardous cargo surcharge at all, any extra costs being incorporated into the tariff rates.

When dangerous goods are being consigned by sea, the consignment must be accompanied by a document which contains information indicating the nature of the hazards of the goods. The 1995 SITPRO **Dangerous Goods Note** (DGN), reproduced overleaf, reflects the requirements of the Merchant Shipping (Dangerous Goods and Marine Pollutants) Regulations 1990 and the 1994 consolidated edition of the **International Maritime Dangerous Goods (IMDG) Code** (incorporating Amendment 27–94).

Only goods for one shipment to one port of discharge or one sailing (and sometimes one bill of lading) may be grouped on one DGN.

If a consignment containing compatible dangerous and non-dangerous substances is documented on a DGN, the dangerous goods should be listed first, or otherwise emphasised. Wherever possible, non-dangerous material should be documented separately on a SITPRO Standard Shipping Note.

Ideally, the DGN should be completed by mechanical means, e.g. aligned documentation system or computer, as hand-written documents are often illegible and prone to inaccuracies.

Dangerous goods

DANGEROUS GOODS NOTE

© SITPRO 1999

Exporter	1	Customs reference/status	2

Booking number	3	Exporter's reference	4
		Forwarder's reference	5

Consignee — 6

DSHA Notification (in accordance with DSHA Regulations (as amended)) given by: — 6A

Shipper	Cargo agent	Transport operator	Shipping line

Freight forwarder — 7

International carrier — 8

For use of receiving authority only

Other UK transport details (e.g. ICD, terminal, vehicle bkg. ref., receiving dates) — 9

10A I hereby declare that the contents of this consignment are fully and accurately described below by the proper shipping name, and are classified, packaged, marked and labelled/placarded and are in all respects in proper condition for transport according to the applicable international and national governmental regulations and in accordance with the provisions shown overleaf. The shipper must complete and sign box 17.

Vessel	Port of loading	10

Port of discharge	Destination	11

TO THE RECEIVING AUTHORITY
Please receive for shipment the goods described below subject to your published regulations and conditions (including those as to liability).

Shipping marks	Number and kind of packages; description of goods;	12	Net weight (kg) of goods	13	Gross weight (kg) of goods	13A	Cube (m³) of goods	14

SPECIFY: Proper Shipping Name*, Hazard Class, UN No. Additional information (if applicable) see overleaf
For RID/ADR/CDG Road requirements see notes overleaf

* Proper Shipping Name - Trade names alone are unacceptable

CONTAINER/VEHICLE PACKING CERTIFICATE
I hereby declare that the goods described above have been packed/loaded into the container/vehicle identified below in accordance with the provisions shown overleaf.
THIS DECLARATION MUST BE COMPLETED AND SIGNED FOR ALL CONTAINER/VEHICLE LOADS BY THE PERSON RESPONSIBLE FOR PACKING/LOADING

Name of company

Name/Status of declarant

Place and date

Signature of declarant

	15	Total gross weight of goods	Total cube of goods

Container identification number/ vehicle registration number	16	Seal number(s)	16A	Container/vehicle size and type	16B	Tare (kg)	16C	Total gross weight (including tare) (kg)	16D

DOCK/TERMINAL RECEIPT

Name and telephone number of shipper preparing this note — 17

HAULIER DETAILS	RECEIVING AUTHORITY REMARKS	
Haulier's name	Received the above number of packages/containers/trailers in apparent good order and condition unless stated hereon.	Name/status of declarant
Vehicle reg. no.		Place and date
Driver's signature	Receiving authority signature and date	Signature of declarant

630 Non-completion of any boxes is a subject for resolution by the contracting parties

Dangerous goods note

For short sea roll-on/roll-off consignments less information is required. Important elements are:

Box 6A (**DSHA Notification**); under the Dangerous Substance in Harbour Regulations 1987, ports must be given prior notice of arrival of dangerous substances.

Box 12 calls for the Proper Shipping Name of the goods as specified in IMDG Section 7.1. For most Not Otherwise Specified (N.O.S.) and certain other descriptions, the chemical name(s) must be included in parentheses, e.g. Flammable Liquid N.O.S. (contains Isopropanol). Trade names alone are not acceptable. "Dangerous Goods in limited quantities of Class/Classes ..." is acceptable.

Also in Box 12 it is necessary to provide additional information in certain circumstances. These are detailed in Section 9 of the IMDG Code. Particular attention should be paid to the following:

—**Flashpoint** (if 61 degrees Celsius or below): the flashpoint in degrees Celsius must be shown for a liquid which gives off a flammable vapour at or below 61 degrees Celsius (141 degrees Fahrenheit) even if this is not the main hazard.

—**Marine Pollutants**: the words "MARINE POLLUTANT" must be shown for substances which are identified as "Marine Pollutants" in the IMDG Code, or preparations of mixtures containing 1 per cent or more of a substance identified as being a severe marine pollutant or 10 per cent or more of a substance identified as a marine pollutant.

Box 15 is the **Container/vehicle packaging certificate and declaration**. For container/vehicle loads, this section requires the name of the company, the name and status of the declarant, the place and date (where and when signed) and the signature of the person responsible for the packing/loading of the dangerous goods into the container/vehicle. The container/vehicle packing certificate and declaration serves a separate function to the **dangerous goods declaration**, and the two are very often signed by different people. However, for the sake of convenience the two declarations are included in the same document. The consignor (exporter) of the goods is responsible for signing the dangerous goods declaration (Box 17), but the declaration under the container/vehicle packing certificate (Box 15) must be signed by whoever is responsible for packing/loading the dangerous goods into the container/vehicle. It is clearly inappropriate for the consignor to sign the packing certificate if the packing/loading of the container/vehicle is undertaken elsewhere—for example at a groupage depot, or at an outside warehouse.

Where dangerous goods are being carried by sea as part of an international road transport journey to/from Europe, under the terms of the European Agreement concerning the International Carriage of Dangerous Goods by Road (ADR) the documentation of ADR must be met. Provided that it is correctly completed, the 1995 SITPRO DGN may be used as a combined road/sea transport document for journeys between the UK and Europe.

The SITPRO 1995 DGN may also be used as a combined rail/sea transport document for journeys between the UK and Europe provided that the docu-

Dangerous goods

mentation requirements of the Regulations concerning the International Carriage of Dangerous Goods by Rail (RID) are met.

FIATA has a special form for freight forwarders for the shipper's declaration relating to the transport of dangerous goods: the **Shipper's Declaration for the Transport of Dangerous Goods (FIATA SDT)**. If a freight forwarder deals with the transport of dangerous goods, the FIATA SDT allows him to identify the goods and to clarify the question of responsibility in case of accident or damage. Therefore it is important that the FIATA SDT is not filled in by the freight forwarder. In each case the FIATA SDT must be completed and signed by the shipper and then handed over to the freight forwarder. The FIATA SDT is reproduced on page 139.

BIMCO (The Baltic and International Maritime Council) also produces two documents: a **Dangerous Goods Declaration** and a **Dangerous Goods Container/Trailer Packing Certificate**.

IMO also publishes a Dangerous Goods Declaration which incorporates a Container packing certificate/vehicle declaration.

It should be noted that the ADR/RID and the IMDG (referred to above) classifications are not identical. They are listed here:

ADR/AID classification

Class 1 Explosive substances and articles with explosive substances
Class 2 Gases: compressed, liquefied or dissolved under pressure
Class 3 Inflammable liquids Class 4.1 Inflammable solids
Class 4.2 Substances liable to spontaneous combustion
Class 4.3 Substances which give off inflammable gases on contact with water
Class 5.1 Oxidising substances
Class 5.2 Organic peroxides
Class 6.1 Toxic substances
Class 6.2 Substances liable to cause infection
Class 7 Radioactive substances
Class 8 Corrosive substances
Class 9 Miscellaneous dangerous substances and articles

IMDG classification

Class 1 Explosives
    1.1 Substances and articles which have a mass explosion hazard
    1.2 Substances and articles which have a projection hazard but not a mass explosion hazard
    1.3 Substances and articles which have a fire hazard and either a minor blast hazard or a minor projection hazard or both, but not a mass explosion hazard
    1.4 Substances and articles which present no significant hazard
    1.5 Very insensitive substances which have a mass explosion hazard
    1.6 Extremely insensitive articles which do not have a mass explosion hazard

FIATA SDT

Shipper (Name & Address) / Chargeur (Nom & Adresse)

Emblem of National Association

No.		Country Code

SHIPPERS DECLARATION FOR THE TRANSPORT OF DANGEROUS GOODS
(approved by FIATA)

Consignee (Name & Address) / Destinataire (Nom & Adresse)

Forwarder / Transitaire

Ref. nr.

In accordance with the European Agreement concerning the international carriage of Dangerous Goods by Road (ADR) with Annexes A+B of 30. 9. 1957, or the International Regulations concerning the Carriage of Dangerous Goods by Rail (RID) as Annex I of the International Convention concerning the Carriage of Goods by Rail (CIM) of 1.7.1977, or in accordance with Chapter VII – Carriage of Dangerous Goods – of the International Convention for the Safety of Life at Sea, 1960 (or 1974) supplemented by the provision of the IMCO International Maritime Dangerous Goods (IMDG) Code, 1965 as amended, or national official regulations when applicable giving the precise listing of relevant ADR/RID Class, and/or IMDG IMCO Class, and/or Marginal Reference No., the undersigned, as principal of the forwarder remits to him together with the order of shipment of Dangerous Goods the following informations:

Conformément à l'Accord européen relatif au transport international des marchandises dangereuses par route (ADR) et ses Annexes A+B du 30.0.1957 ou au Règlement international concernant le transport des marchandises dangereuses par chemin de fer (RID) et à l'Annexe 1 de la Convention internationale concernant le transport des marchandises par chemin de fer (CIM) du 1.7.1977, ou conformément au Chapitre VII – Transport de marchandises dangereuses – de la Convention internationale pour la sécurité des vies en mer, 1960 (ou 1974) complété par les dispositions du Code maritime international des marchandises dangereuses (IMDG) 1965, amendé, de l'OMI ou aux réglementations nationales officielles d'application donnant la liste précise des classifications ADR/RID et/ou IMDG/OMI applicables, et/ou le No. de référence marginal, le soussigné, commettant du transitaire, lui remet en même temps que l'ordre d'expédition de marchandises dangereuses les renseignements suivants:

Marks & Numbers, Number & Kind of Packages; Correct Technical Name of Substances. Indicate ADR/RID Class, IMDG/IMCO Class, UN-No., Flashpoint (in °C). Marques et Numéros, Nombre et Nature des colis; dénomination technique appropriée des substances Indiquer la Classe ADR/RID, Class IMDG/IMCO, n° d'ordre UN, Point Eclair (en° C).

Gross Weight (kg)	Poids brut (kg)
Net quantity	Quantité nette
(when required)	(s'il y a lieu)

specimen

Characteristics:

Caractéristiques:

Special information is required for (a) dangerous goods in limited quantities. and (b) radioactive substances (class 7). In certain circumstances, (c) a wheathering certificate, or (d) a Container/Trailer packing certificate is required.

Des renseignements supplémentaires sont nécessaires pour (a) des marchandises dangereuses en quantités limitées et (b) les substances radioactives (classe 7). Dans certains cas, (c) un certificat d'intempéries, ou (d) un certificat d'emballage pour conteneur/remorque est requis.

ADR/RID and/or IMDG/IMCO Declaration
The undersigned declares that goods to be shipped are authorized for transport by road according to ADR or by rail according to RID and/or transport by sea and that their nature conditions, packing and labelling are in accordance with ADR/RID and/or IMDG/IMCO prescriptions.
If several dangerous substances are packed together in a collective package or in a single container it is furthermore declared that the mixed packing is not prohibited (ADR/RID).

Déclaration ADR/RID et/ou IMDG/OMI
Le soussigné déclare que les marchandises à expédier sont admises au transport par route suivant l'ADR ou par fer suivant la RID et/ou par mer et que les conditions de leur nature, l'emballage et l'étiquetage sont en concordance avec les prévisions de l'ADR/RID et/ou IMDG/OMI.
Si plusieurs marchandises dangereuses sont emballées ensemble dans un colis collectif, ou dans un même conteneur, il est déclaré également que cela n'est pas prohibé (ADR/RID).

Instructions in case of accidents ☐ are joined ☐ will be given

Des consignes en prévision d'accidents ☐ sont jointes ☐ seront avisées

The packages ☐ have been labelled ☐ are not labelled

Les colis ☐ ont été étiquetés ☐ n'ont pas été étiquetés

Special remarks
Remarques particulières

Place and date of issue
Lieu et date d'émission

26

Shippers signature and stamp
Sceau et signature du chargeur

Shipper's Declaration for the Transport of Dangerous Goods (FIATA SDT)

Dangerous goods

Class 2   Gases: compresses, liquefied or dissolved under pressure
Class 3   Inflammable liquids
   3.1   Low flashpoint group of liquids
   3.2   Intermediate flashpoint group of liquids
   3.3   High flashpoint group of liquids
Class 4.1 Inflammable solids
   4.2   Inflammable solids, or substances, liable to spontaneous combustion
   4.3   Inflammable solids, or substances, which in contact with water emit flammable gases
Class 5.1 Oxidising substances
   5.2   Organic peroxides
Class 6.1 Poisonous (toxic) substances
Class 6.2 Infectious substances
Class 7   Radioactive substances Class 8 Corrosives
Class 9   Miscellaneous dangerous substances and articles

Associated abbreviations:
BIMCO Baltic and International Maritime Council
DG Dangerous Goods
DGN Dangerous Goods Note
DSHA Dangerous Substance in Harbour Area (Regulations)
FCL full container load
FIATA International Federation of Freight Forwarders Associations
IMDG Code International Maritime Dangerous Goods Code
LCL Less than container load
N.O.S. Not Otherwise Specified
SITPRO Simpler Trades Procedures Board

See also:
BIMCO (Baltic and International Maritime Council)
SITPRO (Simpler Trades Procedures Board)
Standard Shipping Note

Delivery and re-delivery (time-charter)

Delivery of a time-chartered ship by the shipowner is the placing of the ship by the shipowner at the disposal of the charterer at the beginning of the period of the charter, at the time and place agreed. The place of delivery is often a location, such as a pilot station, where it is relatively easy to verify the time of arrival and hence the time when the charter commences. A typical charter-party might specify delivery as being on **arrival pilot station any time day or night Sundays and holidays included**.

It is often a requirement of time charter-parties that the holds of a ship be clean or clean-swept by the shipowner on delivery.

Normally, an **on hire survey**, or **on hire condition survey**, is carried out as soon as practicable. This is done in order to determine the condition of the ship which may subsequently be compared with her condition at the end of the charter. The charter-party specifies a quantity of fuel and diesel estimated to be on board at time of delivery and agreed prices payable by the time charterer to the owner; the quantity of bunkers actually on board is ascertained during the on hire survey and the two sets of figures compared. By agreement, the ship is inspected by one surveyor only or one surveyor for each of the two parties. Which party pays for the survey and whether the time taken counts for the purpose of calculating hire money are matters agreed in the charter-party.

A **delivery certificate** is issued to the time charterer by the shipowner and signed by him or on his behalf. It certifies the time, date and place of delivery of the ship. It also states the quantity of bunkers on board at the time of delivery and any notations by the charterer concerning the failure of the ship to comply in any respect with the terms of the charter-party.

At the end of the period of the charter, the ship is given back to the shipowner. This is termed **re-delivery**. The main consequence of re-delivery is that hire money ceases to be paid for any period beyond this time. The place of re-delivery is anywhere the two parties agree and might be a particular port, any port within a range of ports or simply within an agreed area. The time charterer must give the shipowner **notice of re-delivery**, that is, a written notice of the date when the ship is to be returned to the shipowner and the place of re-delivery. Charter-parties often stipulate that several such notices be given at agreed intervals as the date of re-delivery approaches. A typical re-delivery might be at the point the ship finishes discharging her (last) cargo or on leaving the (last) port of discharge at the point where the pilot disembarks. These are known, respectively, as **when where ready on completion of discharge** and **dropping outward pilot**.

Time charter-parties often require that the holds of a ship be clean or clean-swept by the charterer on re-delivery.

In a similar way to delivery, an **off hire survey**, or **off hire condition survey**, is carried out at the time the ship is re-delivered. This is done in order to determine whether the ship is in the same condition, wear and tear excepted, as on delivery. The quantity of bunkers is ascertained for comparison with the amounts specified in the charter-party. By agreement, the ship is inspected by one surveyor only or one surveyor for each of the parties. As with the on-hire survey, the question of who pays for the survey and whether the time taken counts for the purpose of calculating hire money are dealt with in the charter-party .

A **re-delivery certificate**, signed by or on behalf of the shipowner and charterer, certifies the time, date and place of re-delivery of the ship. It states the quantities of bunkers remaining on board at the time of re-delivery.

Delivery and re-delivery (time charter)

Associated abbreviations:
aps arrival pilot station
atdn any time day or night
dly delivery
dop dropping outward pilot
redly re-delivery
redly cert re-delivery certificate
shinc Sundays and holidays included
wwr when where ready
wwrcd when where ready on completion of discharge

Associated terms:
to deliver
to re-deliver

Alternative spelling:
Redelivery

Disbursements

Sums paid out by a ship's agent on behalf of a shipowner at a port and recovered from the shipowner by means of a **disbursements account**. The Baltic and International Maritime Council (BIMCO) publishes a standard disbursements account which divides the charges into three categories: port charges, cargo charges and ship charges. Port charges include harbour dues, light dues, pilotage, towage, mooring and unmooring, shifting, Customs charges, launch hire and car hire, agency remuneration and communications. Cargo charges are stevedoring expenses, charges for winchmen and cranes, tally charges and overtime. Ship charges are cash to master, water, stores and provisions, crew expenses and repairs. Space is left for other unspecified charges.

It is common for the agent to send the shipowner a **pro forma disbursements account** in advance of the ship's call at the port in order to put the agent in funds before he is required to pay the accounts. It is also used in a different way, to help the shipowner estimate the viability of a voyage before fixing his ship.

See also:
BIMCO (Baltic and International Maritime Council)
Ship operating costs
Ship's agent

Draught

Depth to which a ship is immersed in the water; this depth varies according to the design of the ship and will be greater or lesser depending not only on the weight of the ship and everything on board, such as cargo, ballast, fuel and spares, but also on the density of the water in which the ship is lying (*see* **water density** *below*). A ship's draught is determined by reading her **draught marks**, a scale marked on the ship's stem and stern. A ship's draught is important in working out how much cargo she is allowed to lift (calculated before and during loading), in determining what ports or places are accessible to her at different times of year, and in contributing to her safe navigation.

The **draught limitation** is the maximum depth of water to which the hull of a ship may be immersed at a certain port or place. Normally expressed in metres or feet, this figure is used in conjunction with the ship's deadweight scale to determine the quantity in tonnes of cargo, known as the **lift**, which the ship can carry. This limitation is determined either by the ship's load line (see below) or by virtue of the depth of water at the port or place in question or by some limitation on the way to or from the port or place.

The word draught is itself widely used to designate **depth of water**. In the context of the depth of water available at a port or place, it is a factor at a port or place which helps to determine the type of ship, or maximum size of ship, capable of reaching there and the maximum cargo which can be carried to or from it.

The depth of water to which a ship is immersed when fully loaded is her **laden draught**.

The average of the draughts forward and aft of a ship is the **mean draught**.

Water density is the ratio of the weight of water to its volume. This ranges from 1,000 kilogrammes per cubic metre for **fresh water** to 1,206 kilogrammes for **sea water**, with **brackish water** in between. Sea water provides greater buoyancy than fresh water so a ship loaded in fresh water to her fresh water load line will rise to her summer load line by the time she reaches the open sea. A **fresh water allowance** is the extra draught allowed by the load line regulations for loading in fresh water.

A **load line** is one of a number of lines painted on the sides of a ship which show the maximum depths to which the ship may be immersed when arriving at, sailing through or putting to sea in the different **load line zones**. Draughts corresponding to these zones are as follows:

summer draught   summer zone at all times and seasonal zone at certain times
tropical draught   tropical zone
winter draught   winter zone at certain times

A ship whose hull is immersed to the appropriate load line and which cannot therefore load any more cargo is said to be **down to her marks**.

A ship whose cargo holds are full and whose hull is immersed as far as the permitted load line is said to be **full and down**. Such a condition is the ideal one for a ship operator since it maximises the use of a ship's cubic capacity and her permitted draught.

For any given quantity carried of cargo, fuel, fresh water and stores, expressed as a ship's deadweight, she will have a **corresponding draught** and vice versa.

Draught

A **bar draught** is a sand-bank which forms at the mouths of rivers and very often limits the type of ship able to reach up-river destinations. In many cases, ships have to **lighten**, that is, to discharge some of their cargo to barges or small ships, before being able to navigate over a bar and complete the voyage. Equally, ships loading at an up-river port may only be able to load part of the cargo, the balance being taken on board after the ship has cleared the bar.

The **trim of a ship** is the relationship between her draughts forward and aft. Consideration is given to the trim when loading cargo since it is desirable to sail with a reasonably even keel. Failing this, a ship is safer **trimmed by the stern** or **down by the stern**, that is, with the draught aft slightly deeper than the draught forward. Adjustments can be made to the trim by the way in which the cargo is distributed in the hold or holds and by means of water ballast, for example in the peak tanks. A ship is said to be **down by the head** or **trimmed by the head** if her draught forward is slightly deeper than her draught aft. This often makes the handling of a ship difficult at sea.

A ship's **air draught** is one of three possible measurements:

(1) the maximum height from the water-line to the topmost point of a ship, that is, the superstructure or the highest mast. This information is required for ships having to navigate bridges;
(2) the clearance between the topmost point of a ship and a bridge over a river;
(3) the maximum height from the water-line to the top of the hatch coamings. This figure is necessary in some bulk trades where loading is effected by conveyor belt which projects over the hatchway. The ship must be low enough in the water, if necessary by retaining sufficient ballast on board, to allow the conveyor to clear the hatch coamings.

Associated abbreviations:
bw brackish water
fw fresh water
fwa fresh water allowance
sw salt water

Associated definitions:
draft widely used alternative spelling of draught.
to draw to have a draught of (a certain number of metres or feet). For example, it may be said that a particular ship draws four metres when immersed to her summer load line.
to trim a ship to adjust the draughts forward and aft of a ship so as to enable her to sail on a reasonably even keel. *See* **trim of a ship** *above.*

See also:
Freeboards and load lines

Dry cargo ships

In addition to the ship types mentioned in **Multipurpose ships** and **Vehicle carriers**, these are the major dry cargo specialised ships:

Banana carrier: any ship dedicated to the banana trade. Such a ship is required to have considerable ventilation capability combined with the ability to cool the cargo and she must be fast because of the way bananas mature on passage. Most of these ships are designed to carry palletised goods although cartons are still used. More recently, bananas are being carried in specially designed refrigerated containers.

Barge-carrying ship: ocean ship which carries barges. These barges are loaded with cargo, often at a variety of locations, towed to the ocean ship, sometimes referred to as the **mother ship**, and lifted or, in some cases, floated on board. After the ocean crossing, the barges are off-loaded and towed to their various destinations. The ocean ship then receives a further set of barges which have been assembled in readiness. This concept was designed to eliminate the need for specialised port equipment and to avoid transhipment with its consequent extra cost. One example of barge-carrying ships are the **LASH ships** (lighter aboard ship).

Cable ship: ship designed to lay and repair power cables or communications cables on the sea bed. Cable for laying is held in tanks or holds, of which there may be several, and played out over the bows.

Cassette carrier: ship designed for the carriage of cassettes. Cassettes are a type of flat bed resembling a flatrack used to convey cargoes such as rolls of paper or steel coils. They are lifted onto a trailer, known as a cassette trailer, and towed by a tractor unit which is part of the port terminal's facilities. The cassettes are placed on decks, similar to the car decks of ro-ro ships, which have bulkheads positioned at intervals to prevent their shifting while in transit.

Cattle carrier: ship used for the carriage of live cattle. Many are converted from oil tankers and dry cargo ships of various types, although a few have been purpose-built. The cattle are loaded and unloaded along ramps and carried in pens on several decks, all of which are weather-protected. The pens have troughs for feed and water. Some deck space is set aside for the carriage of hay, for which the ship may be equipped with a dedicated crane.

Dredger: vessel designed to remove mud or sand from the sea bed or from a river bed. This is often done at or near a port to increase the depth of water or to restore it to its previous depth. The methods of dredging are by suction, buckets and grabs. The suction method uses a pipe and a submersible pump to suck sand. The bucket method uses a continuous supply of buckets which reach to the sea bed and scrape up the sand or aggregate. A grab may also be employed on the end of a crane. All three operations transfer the sand or aggregate into the hold or into hoppers and thence to barges for removal. In some cases, the ship's hold may have a bottom opening through which the sand is dropped out at sea. Dredgers are sometimes referred to as **sand dredgers** or **sand carriers**.

Fruit carrier: ship equipped with a refrigerating system for carrying perishable goods, such as fruit, vegetables, meat and fish. Basic constructional features are similar to those of a general cargo ship. Refrigeration of cargo spaces is effected by circulating cool air at temperatures appropriate to the particular cargo. The cargo spaces are insulated, normally with aluminium or galvanised steel, to assist in maintaining the desired temperature. She is called a fruit carrier when dedicated to the fruit trade, otherwise she is termed a **refrigerated ship** or **reefer ship**.

Heavy lift ship: ship designed to lift and carry exceptionally heavy loads such as railway locomotives or offshore drilling rigs. There are three basic methods of loading and discharging such cargoes: **lift-on lift-off** by means of a heavy lift derrick fixed to the deck of the ship; **float-in float-out** whereby the ship is partially submerged during loading and discharging; **roll-on roll-off** whereby the cargo is wheeled on and off the ship.

Ice-breaker: ship whose hull is specially strengthened to enable her to crush ice using her own weight in order to make a passage sufficient for other ships to navigate.

Livestock carrier or **sheep carrier**: ship used for the carriage of livestock, mainly sheep. Many are converted from oil tankers and dry cargo ships, although a few have been purpose-built. Ships which have been converted have essentially only had livestock decks added; these consist of weather-protected pens in which the livestock are carried.

Pallet carrier: ship designed to carry palletised goods and shipping containers. Although the ship is capable of carrying general cargo, the interior generally carries paper products on pallets. These are loaded through a side door, taken by **pallet lift** (alternatively called **pallet elevator**) to the appropriate level and thence by fork-lift truck to the desired positions. The containers are carried on deck.

Refrigerated trailer ship: vessel with decks on which refrigerated trailers are carried. Essentially she is a roll-on/roll-off ship with a large number of electrical socket connections to enable the trailers' refrigeration units to be operated. When carrying shiploads of bacon, these ships are referred to as **refrigerated meat carriers**.

Supply ship: ship used in the offshore drilling industry. As well as carrying out the normal duties of delivering supplies, her duties include towing (when she is sometimes termed a **tug/supply ship**), anchor handling, survey work and rescue work.

Support ship: vessel used in the offshore industry for testing and servicing undersea construction work. Typically she has her own cranes, diving bell, a helicopter deck, and possibly photographic and research laboratories. If engaged in diving support, she might have compression chambers.

Associated abbreviations:
LASH lighter aboard ship
ro-ro roll-on/roll-off

See also:
Ship types
Multipurpose ships
Vehicle carriers

European Sea Ports Organisation (ESPO)

The European Sea Ports Organisation represents over 98 per cent of the seaports of the European Union and has direct contacts in some 500 ports across Europe.

The Organisation was set up in 1993 in response to a growing perception among seaports that a body should represent their interests within the European Community. The ESPO General Assembly, the decision making body, comprises three national delegates of ports from each of the 13 maritime Member States of the EU together with observers from four further states which may ultimately seek membership of the European Union.

The seaports represented within ESPO reflect a complete spectrum of size, development, ownership and management philosophy, but are united in their determination to secure an effective voice for ports in the development of the policies of the European Union. To achieve this objective, ESPO first set up a permanent office in Brussels, the Secretariat, which acts as a clearinghouse and ensures the communication of information between the European institutions and the ports throughout Europe.

ESPO asserts that:

- Seaports are vital to the enlarged European Community.
- Ports need a flexible response to market forces.
- Ports serve their customers best by the efficient handling of goods and people.
- The desire for clean seas which it supports must be based on the polluter pays principle.
- The Environmental Code of Practice which it prepared and published, with financial support from the European Commission and which ESPO is actively encouraging ports across Europe to implement fully, indicates the commitment of seaports to the environment and self regulation.

ESPO also has set up organizational structures to develop responses that include an Executive Committee and three standing Technical Committees.

European Sea Ports Organisation (ESPO)

General Assembly and Executive Committee

The General Assembly of ESPO is the policy making body comprising three delegates from each Member State. It meets at least twice a year to determine the general policy of the Organisation, based on the work undertaken by ESPO's Technical Committees.

The Executive Committee comprises the Chairman, two vice-chairmen and two other members, drawn from the General Assembly. The Committee is empowered by the General Assembly to deal with urgent matters of policy and response to the Commission and other European institutions.

The Executive Committee meets regularly once a month and works in close liaison with the Secretary General and the Chairmen of the Technical Committees. The Technical Committees include: the Environment, the Marine and the Transport Committees that, between them, deal with all the different subjects that may impact on port life and operations. Where appropriate, the Technical Committees have sub-committees attached to them, which are set up to deal in depth with a specific subject, requiring specialist input. The fruits of all this work are then submitted to the General Assembly for decision and the resulting policies and positions are communicated to the appropriate European institutions.

Transport Committee

The Transport Committee looks at ports from the point of view of the ports' role as a link within the transport chain. Thus the Trans-European Transport Network has, for example, been high on its agenda for a number of years, as are indeed various other issues that were the object of Commission Communications and papers, such as maritime strategy, short sea shipping, and last but not least a major part of the Green Paper on Sea Ports and Maritime Infrastructure.

The Committee also deals with those subjects relating to port efficiency and port performance. These cover issues such as free and fair competition within and between ports, as well as the thorny subject of state aids.

Because of its heavy workload it also seconds work to several specialist sub-groups that examine specific and sometimes specialist subjects on which they produce a report. This can then be fed back into the main Committee and ultimately it may be adopted as a policy position for ESPO.

The main subjects being dealt with by the current sub-committees deal with port statistics, added value and vocational training.

Customs procedures, notably within the context of the Customs 2000 Programme are a further subject dealt with by this Committee, as indeed are public procurement and transparency of accounts.

All these subjects are debated within the Committee, sometimes together with Commission staff who take this opportunity to discuss them with industry. In the light of such discussions and debates draft policy positions can be developed for ESPO and put forward, through the Executive Committee, for debate and final decision by the General Assembly.

Perhaps because of this, but maybe also because of the Committee's concerns with developing policies, many public relations initiatives have stemmed from ideas developed by the Transport Committee, not least of which is this present handbook.

Marine Committee

As the name implies the Marine Committee has mainly been concerned with the interface between the port and the seaward side.

A task which has taken up much of the Committee's time during 1997–1998 has been reception of ships' waste in port as required under the MARPOL Convention. Although the Commission's directive is not yet finalised, the Committee and the specialists in their MARPOL Sub-group can claim some success in shaping the draft directive to meet the principles set out in ESPO's own MARPOL policy statement. The Marine Committee and the MARPOL Sub-group have worked very closely.

Much of the Committee's work has been linked to the International Maritime Organization (IMO) whether it is dealing with safety at sea or environmental protection. In general, the Committee are on their guard against the transposition into EU directives or regulations of some of the IMO's more tentative resolutions. The Committee has studied for example the discussions on safety of bulk carriers, the handling of disabled ships and the implications of compulsory insurance.

Environment Committee

ESPO attaches the highest priority to the environment. This commitment entails not only the tasks of monitoring and responding to new legislation and policy but also making recommendations on the action ESPO members might take to improve their environmental situation.

Associated abbreviation:
ESPO European Sea Ports Organisation

European Shippers' Council

The European Shippers' Council (ESC) represents

- the interests of companies trading in Europe as users of freight transport services;
- companies who ship the vast majority of goods distributed by sea, road, rail, air and inland waterways;
- the 12 national transport user organisations/shippers' councils from 12 countries;
- a number of key European commodity trade associations, such as CEFIC— The European Chemical Industry Council;

European Shippers' Council

- European industry interests as users of freight transport services on a variety of international governmental and non-governmental organisations including: OECD, the Consultative Shipping Group, International Maritime Organisation, the United Nations, WTO and The International Chamber of Commerce.

ESC maintains an on-going dialogue, and is regularly consulted by, the European Commission and other Community institutions on transport policy and logistics issues. The ESC also has reciprocal representative arrangements with UNICE (the European Employers Organisation). Another unique aspect of the European Shippers' Council is that it is the only multi-modal shippers organisation in Europe.

ESC is the leading platform for discussions with transport providers. ESC maintains contact with, and holds regular liaisons with, the key transport industry representative organisations and their members. These include ECSA, CENSA, ICS, Intertanko, and Intercargo (shipowners), CLECAT, FFE and FIATA (freight forwarders), CER (railways), IRU (road transport), ESPO and FEPORT (ports), UIRR (combined transport) and TEEO (European Express carriers).

Through the Shippers' Tripartite, ESC meets annually with the US National Transportation League, the Canadian Shippers' Council and the shippers' organisations in Asia to develop common strategies to the benefit of shippers in Europe, the Americas and Asia.

- To promote efficient and competitive freight transport services to enhance the competitiveness of companies conducting business in Europe and overseas transport markets.
- To encourage and persuade transport policy makers to develop open and competitive markets which enhance industrial competitiveness and efficiency.
- To promote industry best practice and key performance indicators to improve the efficiency of industry's transport and logistics supply chains.

Key activities and achievements

ESC is the pre-eminent body responsible for efforts to liberalise/de-regulate liner shipping markets. It has achieved this through curtailment of the power of liner conference cartels to impose cartel/monopoly prices on shippers and unfair contracts/contract terms through the pursuit of various complaints with the European Commission.

ESC is largely responsible for the development of individual and confidential service contract/agreements which have diminished the power of cartel conferences.

Its activities in the maritime sector have extended to the development of a policy framework for European ports. This has been in response to the European Commission Green Paper on Sea Ports and Maritime Infrastructure.

Development of best practices

Today shippers are paying far greater attention to the performance of their transport and logistics supply chains. For many manufacturers supply chain costs, including inventory and investment costs, can represent 20/30 per cent of total company or product costs. Transport and logistics costs are estimated to represent about 30 per cent of total supply chain costs. Because of this magnitude of costs tied up in the supply chain, shippers now require greater reliability and better performance in their transport and logistics supply chain to give them enhanced competitive edge.

In light of this, the European Shippers' Council has taken the lead in assisting shippers to improve the performance of their transport and logistics supply chains by working with transport providers to encourage them to benchmark their services. To date some progress has been made in the air cargo market with the launch in 1998 of the ESC Air Council's key performance indicators and the publication of the ESC code of best practice in the dry bulk shipping sector. Similar exercises are planned with regard to the rail, road and short sea shipping sectors.

It should be stressed that we are only at the very beginning of implementing key performance indicators and best practice in the transport sector. The first task has been to raise the awareness of the need for continuous improvement in the transport sector through best practice techniques, largely through promotion and dissemination of the ESC. The main task is assisting in the implementation of the KPIs and the use of benchmarking in order to measure the competitiveness and performance of one mode of transport over another. ESC stands ready to play its full part in these developments.

The development of best practices and key performance indicators so far have focused on the air freight industry, the bulk shipping industry and the European rail freight industry.

Bulk shipping voluntary code of best practice

ESC was mindful of the responsibility shippers had towards the safety of ships and their crews moving their bulk products. ESC, with the full support of the European Commission developed a voluntary code of best practice which European shippers should follow in order to avoid contracting sub-standard and unsafe ships.

Associated abbreviations:
CENSA Council of European and Japanese National Shipowners' Associations
ECSA European Community Shipowners' Associations
ESC European Shippers' Council
FIATA International Federation of Freight Forwarders Associations
ESPO European Sea Ports Organisation
FEPORT Federation of European Port Operators
ICS International Chamber of Shipping
OECD Organisation for Economic Co-operation and Development

UIRR International Union of combined Road-Rail transport companies
WTO World Trade Organization

Federal Maritime Commission (FMC)

The Federal Maritime Commission was established in 1961 as an independent United States Government agency, responsible for the regulation of shipping in the foreign trades of the USA. The Commission's five members are appointed by the President with the advice and consent of the Senate. The FMC is headquartered in Washington, DC, with four Area Representatives around the nation.

The Federal Maritime Commission:

—protects shippers, carriers and others engaged in the foreign commerce of the USA from restrictive rules and regulations of foreign Governments and from the practices of foreign-flag carriers that have an adverse effect on shipping in US trades;

—investigates, upon its own motion or upon filing of a complaint, discriminatory, unfair, or unreasonable rates, charges, classifications, and practices of ocean common carriers, terminal operators, and freight forwarders operating in the foreign commerce of the USA;

—receives agreements among ocean common carriers or marine terminal operators and monitors them to assure that they are not substantially anti-competitive or otherwise violate the US Shipping Act of 1984;

—receives, reviews, and maintains electronic tariff filings which contain the rates, charges and rules established by water carriers operating between the United States and another country;

—regulates rates, charges, classifications, rules, and regulations contained in tariffs of carriers controlled by foreign Governments and operating in US trades to ensure that such matters are just and reasonable;

—licenses US-based international ocean freight forwarders;

—requires bonds of non-vessel operating common carriers (NVOCCs); and

—issues passenger vessel certificates showing evidence of financial responsibility of vessel owners or charterers to pay judgments for personal injury or death or to repay fares for the nonperformance of a voyage or cruise.

The FMC's jurisdiction encompasses many facets of the maritime industry. However, it has no jurisdiction over the bulk trades, vessel operations, navigation, vessel construction, vessel documentation, vessel inspection, licensing of seafaring personnel, maintenance of navigational aids or dredging. These activities are handled by other federal, state and local agencies.

The principal shipping statutes administered by the FMC are the Shipping Act 1984 (46 USC app. 1710 *et seq.*), the Foreign Shipping Practices Act 1988 (46 USC app. 1701 *et seq.*), and section 19 of the Merchant Marine Act 1920 (46 USC app. 876). The FMC's regulations are published in 46 CFR 500 *et seq.*

Tariff publishing services

The FMC provides complete new tariff creation, filing and maintenance for companies operating as common carriers in the domestic and foreign commerce of the United States that are required to file public tariffs with the Federal Maritime Commission as per the Shipping Act of 1984 in accordance with Title 46 of the Code of Federal Regulations, Part 514. Tariff requests are prepared and transmitted to the FMC's ATFI System the same day the request is received and made available in either hard copy or data via their Apex for Windows retrieval service.

Associated abbreviation:
FMC Federal Maritime Commission

Federation of European Maritime Associations of Surveyors and Consultants (FEMAS)

In 1988 the then Vice-President of VESW, the Society of Marine Surveyors and Consulting Engineers in the Netherlands, with their Secretary, conceived the idea that it would be prudent for the various national societies to form a federation in order that their voice could be heard in international forums in maritime affairs. These matters were aired at a meeting which was attended by one UK and two German representatives.

After this meeting it was proposed by the VESW that the captioned Federation be set up. The first meeting was called in Amsterdam in 1989 since which time meetings have been held in the centres in which member-societies are in operation, namely, Belgium, France, Germany, Greece, Italy and the United Kingdom.

The Constitution of the Federation, Memorandum and Articles of Association were presented for ratification at the General Assembly in the Netherlands in September 1993.

Whilst some countries within the European Union are not yet members of the Federation, it has been found that in the main they sometimes do not have societies of consultants or surveyors in the maritime field.

The Federation's membership is exclusively for societies or associations working with a membership in the maritime field, thus individuals are not members.

The day-to-day business of the Federation is looked after by a professional secretary.

Within the European Union there is a wide difference in the combined education and experience requirements for professional engineers, but after protracted consideration a compromise acceptable to the member countries has been drawn up. The differences highlight the difficulty of establishing free movement of professionals in that particular field and it will probably be equally difficult in the various professions involved in maritime consultancy.

Fed. of European Maritime Assocs of Surveyors & Consultants (FEMAS)

If the naming of persons as professionals under the titles of maritime technical consultants or surveyors, be they engineers, naval architects or cargo surveyors, is to be protected within the EU, it will require that there is some suitable basis for their acceptability as to qualifications, experience and ethics.

If the interest of member organizations were to be confined to those involved in ship and machinery aspects of maritime transportation, there is already in the UK established recognition of marine engineers and naval architects within the "professions" recognised in a provisional list of regulated professions provided to the EU Commissioners concerning their Directive 89/48/EEC. The recognition is either on the basis of being regulated by statute, common law or professional associations and similar arrangements will apply to other member countries.

The objectives of FEMAS are:

a. To provide an organization which is available to EU Commissioners, Government departments, international bodies and others for consultation concerning matters affecting maritime safety and operations.

b. To provide a central organization within the EU capable of presenting a unified approach to, or being approached by, national or EU governmental bodies upon any matters affecting its member organizations or their members.

c. To disseminate and update professional knowledge and information amongst the member organizations.

d. To foster the exercise of the highest quality of professional service in the field of maritime surveying.

e. To protect the professional title **Marine Surveyor** and/or **Maritime Consultant** or the national equivalent so that within the ED they can only be used by persons duly registered within their professions as being suitably qualified and experienced.

f. To keep member organizations informed of proposed legislation affecting maritime affairs coming before the European Union Commissioners or any other governmental body.

g. To consider and endeavour to obtain improvements or amendments to laws or rules which may be desirable to improve the status and customer confidence placed upon the membership of the member organizations.

h. To promote dialogue amongst the member organizations ensuring unified standards and working practices within the EU.

i. To represent and defend the interests of the profession at the highest possible level.

Associated abbreviation:
FEMAS Federation of European Maritime Associations of Surveyors and Consultants

See also:
Maritime engineering
Royal Institution of Naval Architects (RINA)

FIATA Warehouse Receipt (FIATA FWR)

The following definition and sample document (reproduced on p. 156) has been provided by the International Federation of Freight Forwarders Associations (FIATA).

The freight forwarder often provides warehousing services. When doing so he has to issue a receipt for the merchandise.

The **FIATA Warehouse Receipt** (**FWR**) is a warehouse receipt for use in freight forwarders' warehousing operations. It is a standard document mainly used at national level. It is published by FIATA, the International Federation of Freight Forwarders Associations, and distributed by the national organizations affiliated to FIATA to their member firms in accordance with official instructions and explanatory notes on its use.

The FWR is not a "récépissé-warrant", which means a formal document recognised as a warrant according to the applicable law. When a warehouse keeper is requested to issue a "récépissé-warrant", the FWR cannot be used. If the issue of a legally recognised document of this kind is not required, the FWR can be issued in almost all cases. Its commercial character is practically the same as that of a "récépissé-warrant". The FWR incorporates detailed provisions regarding the rights of the holders-by-endorsement of the document, the transfer of ownership, and the agreement that presentation of the warehouse receipt amounts to good delivery of the merchandise. For all practical purposes, such legal functions intended by the use of the FWR are recognised in most jurisdictions.

The FWR is not negotiable, unless it is marked "negotiable".

It must be decided individually in each country which standard trading conditions are to be applied to the FIATA Warehouse Receipt. In countries where forwarders use standard trading conditions which include also provisions regarding the activity of warehouse keepers, such standard conditions are to be applied.

Associated abbreviation:
FWR FIATA Warehouse Receipt

FIATA Warehouse Receipt (FIATA FWR)

FIATA Warehouse Receipt (FIATA FWR)

Supplier	Emblem of National Association	**FWR** **FIATA WAREHOUSE RECEIPT**
		No.
		ORIGINAL

Depositor	Warehouse Keeper
	Warehouse

Identification of means of transport	Insurance
	☐ Covered
	☐ Against fire
	☐ Against burglary / pilferage ☐ not covered
	☐ Other risks covered (specify)
	Insurance amount

Marks and numbers;	Number and kind of packages;	Description of goods	Gross weight

specimen

Received in apparent good order and condition		Gross weight	
Description of merchandise (contents):	☐ Stated by Depositor	☐ Stated by Depositor	
	☐ Controlled by warehouse keeper	☐ Controlled by warehouse keeper	

Warehousing is subject to standard business conditions; vide reverse
As warehouse keepers we are liable to deliver the stored merchandise against presentation of this document only, and in case of cession of rights exclusively to the holder of this document being legitimated by an uninterrupted chain of transfers as outlined overleaf.
We acknowledge that we can only lodge a complaint with the legitimated holder of this document if and when this refers to the validity of issue of said document and / or results therefrom.
Our legal lien or right of retention will not be affected by this clause.
In case of partial deliveries warehouse receipt must be submitted for entering outgoing stock.

	Place and date of issue
	Stamp and signature

Text authorized by FIATA. COPYRIGHT FIATA / Zurich – Switzerland 2.82

FIATA Warehouse Receipt (FIATA FWR)

Flag

Nationality of a ship, the country in which the ship is registered. Hence, a British flag vessel is a vessel registered in the United Kingdom.

A **flag of convenience** is the registration of a ship in a country whose tax on the profits of trading ships is low or whose requirements concerning manning or maintenance are not stringent. This is sometimes referred to as a **flag of necessity**. This latter conveys the idea that trading from the shipowner's country of nationality is too costly and that flagging out is the only way for a shipowner to continue trading the ship.

To **flag out** is to change the registration of a ship from the nationality of the shipowning company to that of another country. Normally flagging out is to a flag of convenience.

Flag discrimination is the action taken by the Government of a country to restrict all, or some proportion, of shipments, both imports and exports, to ships of that country's fleet. The main purpose is to build up or protect the fleet by providing it with employment. In some countries, this practice is designed to avoid or restrict the spending of foreign currencies. Very often, priority is given to cargo in a national flag ship or to the ship herself in the form of lower import duty, lower port charges or priority berthing. Some countries reserve coastal trade to their own ships. This is known as **cabotage**.

A **flag waiver** is a dispensation given by a country which reserves the carriage of goods by sea to ships of its own national fleet, to ship goods in a ship of another nationality. This dispensation is given when the national fleet does not have a ship available or one which is suitable to carry the goods.

A flag is also the emblem or logo of the shipowner or shipping line. This may be made of material and flown from a standard or painted on the funnel of a ship. Some time charter-parties allow the charterer to fly his **house flag**, that is to say, his company emblem, on the ship during the period of the charter. This is particularly appropriate when the charterer is a shipping line who is supplementing his fleet by chartering in and who wishes to maintain his corporate identity.

Associated abbreviation:
foc flag of convenience

See also:
International Transport Workers' Federation (ITF)

Forwarder's Certificate of Receipt (FIATA FCR)

(Definition and sample document (reproduced on p. 158) provided by FIATA.)

The Forwarder's Certificate of Receipt (FCR) was introduced by FIATA for the use by international forwarders who come within the ambit of FIATA. The

Forwarder's Certificate of Receipt (FIATA FCR)

Suppliers or Forwarders Principals

Emblem of National Association

FIATA FCR

Forwarders Certificate of Receipt

No.

Country Code

ORIGINAL

Forw. Ref.

Consignee

Marks and numbers	Number and kind of packages	Description of goods	Gross weight	Measurement

according to the declaration of the consignor

The goods and instructions are accepted and dealt with subject to the General Conditions printed overleaf

We certify having assumed control of the above mentioned consignment in external apparent good order and condition

☐ at the disposal of the consignee

with irrevocable instructions*

☐ to be forwarded to the consignee

Remarks

Instructions as to freight and charges

* Forwarding instructions can only be cancelled or altered if the original Certificate is surrendered to us, and then only provided we are still in a position to comply with such cancellation or alteration.

Instructions authorizing disposal by a third party can only be cancelled or altered if the original Certificate of Receipt is surrendered to us, and then only provided we have not yet received instructions under the original authority.

Place and date of issue

Stamp an signature

Forwarder's Certificate of Receipt (FIATA FCR)

FIATA FCR document enables the freight forwarder to provide the consignor with a special document as an official acknowledgement that he has assumed responsibility of the goods.

The FIATA FCR can be handed to the consignor immediately after the consignment has been received by the freight forwarder.

By completing the FIATA FCR the freight forwarder certifies that he is in possession of a specific consignment with irrevocable instructions for despatch to the consignee shown in the document or to keep it at his disposal. These instructions may only be cancelled if the original FIATA FCR document is handed over to the issuing freight forwarder and only if he is in a position to comply with such cancellation or alteration.

The FIATA FCR will primarily be used when the supplier sells the goods **ex works** and needs to prove that he has complied with his obligations to the buyer by presenting a FIATA FCR. In the case of a Letter of Credit the seller will under such conditions be able to present a FIATA FCR issued by a forwarder in order to obtain payment of the sales price placed at his disposal by the buyer under the terms of the Letter of Credit. The seller can no longer dispose of the goods handed over to the forwarder once the FIATA FCR document has been handed over to the buyer.

The FIATA FCR is not negotiable. As the delivery of the consignment to the consignee does not depend on the handing over of this document, only one original is issued. Should further copies be required, forms specially over-printed with the words "Copy not negotiable" should be used.

When issuing a FIATA FCR, the freight forwarder should ensure:

(1) that he or his agent (branch, intermediate freight forwarder) has taken over the consignment specified therein and that the right of disposal of the goods is vested in him;
(2) that the goods appear to be in apparent good order and condition;
(3) that the details on the document clearly correspond with the instructions he has received;
(4) that the conditions of freight documents (B/L etc.) are not contrary to the obligations he has assumed according to the FIATA FCR document.

The FIATA FCR bears the general national freight forwarding conditions of the issuing country on the reverse (see **British International Freight Association (BIFA)**). The document may only be used by freight forwarders who adhere to these general conditions in their forwarding activities.

It is recommended that the freight forwarder covers his liability in accordance with the FIATA FCR requirements.

The FCR is published by FIATA and distributed by the national organizations affiliated to FIATA to their member firms in accordance with official instructions and explanatory notes on its use.

Associated abbreviation:
FCR Forwarder's Certificate of Receipt

Forwarder's Certificate of Transport (FIATA FCT)

(Definition and sample document (reproduced on p. 161) provided by FIATA.)

The **Forwarder's Certificate of Transport (FCT)** was introduced by FIATA for the use by international freight forwarders within the FIATA organizations.

By issuing a FIATA FCT document to the consignor, the freight forwarder assumes the responsibility to deliver the goods at destination through the medium of an agent appointed by him. The FIATA FCT can be handed over to the consignor immediately after the consignment has been handed over to the freight forwarder for shipment.

By issuing the FIATA FCT the freight forwarder certifies that he has assumed responsibility for dispatch and delivery of a specific consignment according to instructions he has received from the consignor as indicated in the document.

The freight forwarder is responsible for the delivery of the consignment at destination through a delivery agent appointed by him to the holder of the document in accordance with the conditions stipulated on the reverse of the FIATA FCT.

The FIATA FCT has a "block" function. The freight forwarder is only responsible for the forwarding and delivery of the goods. The FIATA FCT, as distinguished from the FBL, is not a document subjecting the freight forwarder to a liability as carrier but his liability is governed by the applicable freight forwarding conditions.

The FIATA FCT will therefore be of importance in all cases where the transport has to be arranged for delivery to the consignee. The seller will be able to obtain payment of the selling price from his bank against the FIATA FCT "cash against Documents".

The FIATA FCT is negotiable, as the delivery of the consignment may only be effected against presentation of the original document, duly endorsed. The FIATA FCT is also negotiable when made out "to Order" (see also ICC Doc. 470/251 Art. 24).

When issuing the FIATA FCT document the freight forwarder should ensure:

(1) that he or his agent (branch, intermediate freight forwarder) has taken over the consignment specified therein and that the right of disposal of the goods is vested solely in him;
(2) that the goods appear to be in apparent good order and condition;
(3) that the details on the document clearly correspond with the instructions he has received;
(4) that conditions of freight documents (B/L etc.) are not contrary to the obligations he has assumed according to the FIATA FCT document;
(5) that responsibility for the insurance of the consignment has been agreed;
(6) that it is clearly specified whether one or more originals have been issued.

It is recommended to dispatch the FIATA FCT documents by registered post only.

Forwarder's Certificate of Transport (FIATA FCT)

Suppliers or Forwarders Principals		Emblem of National Association	**FIATA FCT**	
			No.	Country Code
Consigned to order of			**Forwarders Certificate of Transport**	
			ORIGINAL	Forw. Ref.

Notify address

Conveyance	from / via

Destination

Marks and numbers	Number and kind of packages	Description of goods	Gross weight	Measurement

according to the declaration of the consignor

The goods and instructions are accepted and dealt with subject to the General Conditions printed overleaf.

Acceptance of this document or the invocation of rights arising therefrom acknowledges the validity of the following conditions, regulations and exceptions also of the trading conditions printed overleaf, except where the latter conflict with conditions 1–6 below.

1. The undersigned are authorized to enter into contracts with carriers and others involved in the execution of the transport subject to the latter's usual terms and conditions.
2. The undersigned do not act as Carriers but as Forwarders. In consequence they are only responsible for the careful selection of third parties, instructed by them, subject to the conditions of Clause 3 hereunder.
3. The undersigned are responsible for delivery of the goods to the holder of this document through the intermediary of a delivery agent of their choice. They are not responsible for acts or omissions of Carriers involved in the execution of the transport or of other third parties. The undersigned Forwarders will, on request, assign their rights and claims against Carriers and other parties.
4. Insurance of the goods will only be effected upon express instructions in writing.
5. Unforeseen and/or unforeseeable circumstances entitle the undersigned to arrange for deviation from the envisaged route and/or method of transport.
6. Unforeseen and/or unforeseeable disbursements and charges are for the account of the goods.

Insurance through the intermediary or the undersigned Forwarders

☐ Not covered

☐ Covered according to the attached Insurance Policy / Certificate

All disputes shall be governed by the law and within the exclusive jurisdiction of the courts at the place of issue.

For delivery of the goods please apply to:

Freight and charges prepaid to:

thence for account of goods, lost or not lost.

We, the Undersigned Forwarders in accordance with the instructions of our Principals, have taken charge of the abovementioned goods in good external condition at: ....

for despatch and delivery as stated above or order against surrender of this document properly endorsed.

In witness thereof the Undersigned Forwarders have signed originals of this FCT document, all of this tenor and date. When one of these has been accomplished, the other(s) will lose their validity. ....

Place and date of issue

Stamp and signature

Forwarder's Certificate of Transport (FIATA FCT)

Forwarder's Certificate of Transport (FIATA FCT)

The FIATA FCT bears the national forwarding conditions of the issuing country on the reverse. The document may only be used by freight forwarders who adhere to these general conditions in their forwarding activities.

Greatest possible care must be taken in the preparation of these documents as the particulars contained therein must reflect accurately the full details of the consignment, such that a fee covering the preparation of the document by the issuing freight forwarder is therefore agreed and justified.

The FCT is published by FIATA and distributed by the national organizations affiliated to FIATA to their member firms in accordance with official instructions and explanatory notes on its use.

Associated abbreviations:
B/L bill of lading
FCT Forwarder's Certificate of Transport
ICC International Chamber of Commerce

Forwarding agent

Person or company who arranges the carriage of goods and the associated formalities on behalf of an exporter or importer. The duties of a forwarding agent include booking space on a ship, providing all the necessary transport documentation and arranging Customs clearance. Also referred to as a **forwarder** or **freight forwarder** or **freight service professional** or **freight intermediary**. Revenue comes from charges made to the shipper and, especially on the Continent of Europe, from a **forwarding agent's commission**, which is payable by the ocean carrier.

Depending on the individual circumstances, the forwarder may act as agent or as principal. For example, a forwarder issuing a FIATA multimodal transport bill of lading does so as carrier.

Some forwarders act as **consolidators** or **groupage operators**, grouping together several compatible consignments into a full container load. This grouping is known as **consolidation** or **groupage**. The consolidator issues a **house bill of lading** to a shipper covering that shipper's consignment which the forwarding agent has grouped with consignments from other shippers to the same destination. The forwarding agent receives one **groupage bill of lading** from the carrier which covers all the consignments.

The house bill of lading reproduced on p. 163 is published by the British International Freight Association (BIFA) and only available for use by BIFA members. It has BIFA's Standard Trading Conditions on the reverse (*these are reproduced under the entry for BIFA—see pp. 68–69*).

Forwarders often form agreements with other forwarders in countries to which they may be arranging transport. It may be advantageous, especially when problems arise, to have signed an agreement, termed an **agency agreement**, with the other forwarder.

162

HOUSE BILL OF LADING

(c) SITPRO 1992

B/Lading number	Customs reference/status
	Shipper's reference
	Forwarders reference

U N I C

Shipper · VAT no.

Consignee · VAT no.

Notify party and address

Other UK transport details

Conveyance	Point of loading
Point of discharge	Destination

Shipping marks; container number	No. and kind of packages; description of goods	Gross weight (kg)	Cube (m3)

SHIPPED by or RECEIVED for shipment from in apparent good order and condition, except as noted in the Particulars. Contents, weight, value and measurement according to sender's declaration.
This house BILL of Lading shall have effect subject to our Trading Conditions.

IN WITNESS whereof the Undersigned have signed the number of Bills of Lading shown all of this tenor and date. One Bill of Lading, duly endorsed, is to be given up in exchange for the goods or for a delivery order for same upon which the other Bills of Lading contained in the set shall be void

Freight payable at	
Number of original Bills of lading	

Format approved by BIFA

For particulars of delivery apply with this Bill of lading to	Place and date of issue
	Signature

SITPRO Licensee No. 000.

House bill of lading

Forwarding agent

Associated abbreviation:
fac forwarding agent's commission

See also:
British International Freight Association (BIFA)
Multimodal transport bill of lading

Forwarding Instructions (FIATA FFI)

Document, prepared by the shipper, which provides the freight forwarder with full instructions regarding the consignment. It includes a description of the cargo, its place of origin and final destination together with any special handling or other instructions.

The following definition and sample document (reproduced on p. 165) has been provided by the International Federation of Freight Forwarders Associations (FIATA).

FFI—FIATA Forwarding Instructions
Freight forwarders mostly design and print their own forwarding instructions forms which have to be filled in by their clients. However, the instruction forms of the various freight forwarders are non-uniform.

FIATA, the International Federation of Freight Forwarders Associations, therefore thought that it would be advantageous for Freight Forwarders to agree on a common layout and drafted the FIATA Model for Uniform Forwarding Instructions. The form is aligned to the UN layout key for trade documents (*see* **SITPRO (The Simpler Trade Procedures Board)**), which aims at providing an international basis for the standardisation of documents used in international trade.

The form is designed to be used in the aligned series and to combine functions in sets of forms, of which integral parts serve various purposes in the procedures for cargo handling.

The member organizations of FIATA may adapt this instruction form to their national requirements, however, it is fundamental that such changes are made within the margin of the UN layout key.

FIATA recommends its national member organizations to adopt and to introduce this instruction form, as it is an important tool to improve professional standards and will serve to foster the corporate identity of our trade.

The FFI is published by FIATA and distributed by the national organizations affiliated to FIATA to their member firms in accordance with official instructions and explanatory notes on its use.

Associated abbreviation:
FFI FIATA Forwarding Instructions

Associated definition:
shipping instructions forwarding instructions

FIATA FORWARDING INSTRUCTIONS FFI

3336 Consignor 1	Emblem of National Association	(approved by FIATA) 1492 Consignor's reference No. 2
3132 Consignee 3		3170 Freight Forwarder 4

3180 Notify party 5	3238 Country of origin 6	Documentary credit 7

Goods ready for shipment Place _____ Date _____ 8	4490 Conditions of sale 9	

8066 Mode of transport 10		Transport insurance 11	4112 Insurance conditions
Air	Road	Covered by us	
Rail	Sea	Covered by consignee	6345 Currency and 5011 value insured
3258 Place of destination		To be covered by you	

7102 Marks & numbers 12	7224 Number & 7064 type of pkgs.	7002 Description of goods 13	7357 Commodity code	6292 Gross weight 15	6322 Cube 16
				6048 Net net weight	Value

specimen

The goods and instructions are accepted and dealt with subject to the Trading Conditions printed overleaf.

4078 Handling instructions (dangerous goods etc.) 17	
Dimensions / Measurement and weight of each package	4052 Terms of delivery 19

1346 Document enclosed:	1160 Document required:	Orig. Copy 18	3410 Place and 2006 date of issue 20
			4426 Authentication 21

Text authorized by FIATA, COPYRIGHT FIATA/Zurich-Switzerland 4.84

Forwarding Instructions (FIATA FFI)

165

Freeboards and load lines

A ship's freeboard is the distance between the **deck line**, that is, the line representing the uppermost continuous deck, and the relevant load line, painted on the side of a ship. Freeboards are assigned by a Government department or, if authorised by that department, by a classification society.

A **load line** is one of a number of lines painted on the sides of a ship which show the maximum depths to which the ship may be immersed when arriving at, sailing through or putting to sea in the different **load line zones**. The positioning of these lines is determined by the rules agreed at the **International Conference on Load Lines** which has been ratified by many maritime countries. The zones are geographical areas, defined by the International Conference on Load Lines. There are five types of zone: **tropical zone, summer zone, winter zone, seasonal tropical zone** and **seasonal winter zone**. The first three types of zone are permanent, that is, the one appropriate load line applies all year round. The last two zones are seasonal and the corresponding load lines apply at certain periods only, depending on the particular zone; for the rest of the year in these seasonal zones, the summer load line applies.

Load lines are marked with corresponding letters (shown below in parentheses) and have free boards associated with them as follows:

The distance between the deck line and the	is the
fresh water load line (F)	**fresh water freeboard**
fresh water timber load line (LF)	**fresh water timber freeboard**
tropical load line (T)	**tropical freeboard**
tropical fresh water load line (TF)	**tropical fresh water freeboard**
tropical timber load line (L T)	**tropical timber freeboard**
tropical fresh water timber load line (LTF)	**tropical fresh water timber freeboard**
summer load line (S)	**summer freeboard**
summer timber load line (LS)	**summer timber freeboard**
winter load line (W)	**winter freeboard**
winter North Atlantic load line (WNA)	**winter North Atlantic freeboard**
winter North Atlantic timber load line (LWNA)	**winter North Atlantic timber freeboard**
winter timber load line (LW)	**winter timber freeboard**

A ship's summer load line is also known as her **summer marks** or **Plimsoll Line**. A **load line mark** is a ring painted on the sides of a ship bisected by a horizontal line which is level with the ship's summer load line. Her winter load line is known as her **winter marks**.

A **fresh water allowance** is the extra draught allowed by the load line regulations for loading in fresh water. This is because a ship's draught will be reduced when reaching the open sea where the density of water is greater.

Load lines are also marked on the walls of shipping containers and warehouses to show the maximum height to which goods may be stacked.

Alternative spellings:
loadline or **load-line**

Associated abbreviation:
fwa fresh water allowance

Associated definition:
lumber load line alternative to timber load line

See also:
Draught
International Conference on Load Lines

Freight

Freight is the amount of money paid to a shipowner or shipping line for the carriage of cargo. The freight may include the cost of loading and/or discharging the cargo or may simply cover the ocean carriage. This will depend on the type of contract and the particular terms, particularly whether it is a liner or charter shipment and, in some cases, on the custom of the port involved.

When freight is payable

Freight is either prepaid or payable at destination. **Freight prepaid** is freight payable before the contract of carriage has been performed. Very often, the bills of lading are signed and exchanged with the shipper for his payment of freight. By agreement, freight may be payable by the shipper within a certain number of days of signing bills of lading. **Freight payable at destination**, also known as **freight collect** or **freight forward**, applies to freight normally paid by the consignee, often in cases of bulk cargoes whose weight is established on discharge from the ship.

Through transport and combined transport

As far as freight is concerned, there is no difference between through transport and combined transport; in both cases the ocean carrier arranges at least one extra leg of the voyage (in addition to the sea or ocean crossing). Normally, there are overland legs in the country of export and the country of import and these can be a combination of road, rail and barge transport. The difference between

Freight

the two types of service lies in the responsibility borne by the ocean carrier for the cargo:

- through transport—the ocean carrier is responsible as principal for the sea transit but as agent only on the other modes of transport. On occasion, one document, a through bill of lading, is issued but very often the through movement is covered by several documents issued by the different carriers;
- combined transport—here the ocean carrier assumes responsibility throughout the combined voyage as principal. One document is issued, a combined transport document or combined transport bill of lading. Any shipment of a container involving more than one mode of transport is said to be intermodal. Examples of intermodal movements are door to door, quay to door and door to quay.

Associated abbreviation:
frt freight

Associated definitions:
to freight (1) to determine or calculate the freight for a particular consignment
to freight (2) to show the freight (amount) on a document such as a ship's manifest or bill of lading

See also:
Breakbulk liner ancillary charges
Charter freight terms
Container freight
Containers and associated ancillary charges
Conventional freight and the export contract
Liner and conference tariffs
Liner surcharges

ICC International Maritime Bureau (IMB)

The ICC International Maritime Bureau (IMB) is a specialised division of the International Chamber Of Commerce (ICC). The IMB is a non-profit making organisation, established in 1981 to act as a focal point in the fight against all types of maritime crime and malpractice. The International Maritime Organization (IMO) in its resolution A 504 (XII) (5) and (9) adopted on 20 November 1981 has, *inter alia*, urged governments, all interests and organizations to cooperate and exchange information with each other and the IMB with a view to maintaining and developing a co-ordinated action in combating maritime fraud. The IMB has an MOU with the World Customs Organization (WCO) and has an observer status with Interpol (ICPO).

IMB's main task is to protect the integrity of international trade by seeking out fraud and malpractice. For over 20 years, it has used industry knowledge, experience and access to a large number of well-placed contacts around the world to do this: identifying and investigating frauds, spotting new criminal methods and trends, and highlighting other threats to trade.

The information gathered from sources and during investigations is provided to members in the form of timely advice via a number of different communication routes. It lists the threats and explains how members can reduce their vulnerability to them. Over the years, this approach has thwarted many attempted frauds and saved the shipping and trading industry many millions of dollars.

The IMB provides an authentication service for trade finance documentation. It also investigates and reports on a number of other topics, notably documentary credit fraud, charter party fraud, cargo theft, ship deviation and ship finance fraud.

As well as helping to prevent crime, the IMB also has a duty to educate both the shipping community and a wider audience that comprises just about every entity engaged in trade. To this end, the IMB runs a regular series of courses and training programmes that have a wide-ranging syllabus and many proven benefits. It also offers bespoke consultancy services in areas such as ship and port security.

One of the IMB's principal areas of expertise is in the suppression of piracy. Concerned at the alarming growth in the phenomenon, this led to the creation of the IMB Piracy Reporting Centre in 1992. The Centre is based in Kuala Lumpur, Malaysia. It maintains a round-the-clock watch on the world's shipping lanes, reporting pirate attacks to local law enforcement and issuing warnings about piracy hotspots to shipping.

With its multi-lingual and multi-disciplined staff, experience, unique structure, industry support and well-placed contacts, the IMB can rightly claim to be the world's premier independent crime-fighting watchdog for international trade.

Associated abbreviation:
ICC International Chamber Of Commerce
IMB International Maritime Bureau

Ice clause

Clause in a bill oflading or charter-party which sets out the options available to the parties to the contract of carriage in the event that navigation is prevented or temporarily delayed by severe ice conditions. The wording of the clause and the options vary according to the individual contract: a master may have the right to divert the ship to the nearest safe port to discharge cargo destined for an ice-bound port. Equally, a charterer may have the option of keeping a ship waiting for ice conditions to clear on payment of demurrage.

Gencon, BIMCO's general purpose voyage charter-party, contains a **General Ice Clause** which caters for the different possibilities arising separately at both loading and discharge ports, both before and after arrival. It reads as follows:

Ice clause

"Port of loading

(a) In the event of the loading port being inaccessible by reason of ice when the vessel is ready to proceed from her last port or at any time during the voyage or on the vessel's arrival or in case frost sets in after vessel's arrival, the Captain for fear of being frozen in is at liberty to leave without cargo, and this Charter shall be null and void.

(b) If during loading the Captain, for fear of vessel being frozen in, deems it advisable to leave, he has liberty to do so with what cargo he has on board and to proceed to any other port or ports with option of completing cargo for Owners' benefit for any port or ports including port of discharge. Any part cargo thus loaded under this Charter to be forwarded to destination at vessel's expense but against payment of freight, provided that no extra expenses be thereby caused to the Receivers, freight being paid on quantity delivered (in proportion if lumpsum), all other conditions as per Charter.

(c) In case of more than one loading port, and if one or more of the ports are closed by ice, the Captain or Owners to be at liberty either to load the part cargo at the open port and fill up elsewhere for their own account as under section (b) or to declare the Charter null and void unless Charterers agree to load full cargo at the open port.

(d) This Ice Clause not to apply in the Spring.

Port of discharge

(a) Should ice (except in the Spring) prevent vessel from reaching port of discharge Receivers shall have the option of keeping vessel waiting until the re-opening of navigation and paying demurrage, or of ordering the vessel to a safe and immediately accessible port where she can safely discharge without risk of detention by ice. Such orders to be given within 48 hours after Captain or Owners have given notice to Charterers of the impossibility of reaching port of destination.

(b) If during discharging the Captain for fear of vessel being frozen in deems it advisable to leave, he has liberty to do so with what cargo he has on board and to proceed to the nearest accessible port where she can safely discharge.

(c) On delivery of the cargo at such port, all conditions of the Bill of Lading shall apply and vessel shall receive the same freight as if she had discharged at the original port of destination, except that if the distance of the substituted port exceeds 100 nautical miles, the freight on the cargo delivered at the substituted port to be increased in proportion."

Associated abbreviation:
BIMCO Baltic and International Maritime Council

Incoterms

Rules governing the interpretation of terms used in international trade, published by the International Chamber of Commerce (ICC). Against each of the terms are defined the duties of buyer and seller. These rules are incorporated into a contract of sale by agreement of the two parties. This is done by means of a clause in the contract.

CFR—Cost and freight (. . . named port of destination)
"Cost and Freight" means that the seller must pay the costs and freight necessary to bring the goods to the named port of destination but the risk of loss of or damage to the goods, as well as any additional costs due to events occurring after the time the goods have been delivered on board the vessel, is transferred from the seller to the buyer when the goods pass the ship's rail in the port of shipment.

The CFR term requires the seller to clear the goods for export.

This term can only be used for sea and inland waterway transport. When the ship's rail serves no practical purpose, such as in the case of roll-on/roll-off or container traffic, the CPT term is more appropriate to use.

CIF—Cost, insurance and freight (. . . named port of destination)
"Cost, Insurance and Freight" means that the seller has the same obligations as under CFR but with the addition that he has to procure marine insurance against the buyer's risk of loss of or damage to the goods during the carriage. The seller contracts for insurance and pays the insurance premium.

The buyer should note that under the CIF term the seller is only required to obtain insurance on minimum coverage. The CIF term requires the seller to clear the goods for export. This term can only be used for sea and inland waterway transport. When the ship's rail serves no practical purposes such as in the case of roll-on/roll-off or container traffic, the CIP term is more appropriate to use.

CPT—Carriage paid to (. . . named place of destination)
"Carriage paid to . . ." means that the seller pays the freight for the carriage of the goods to the named destination. The risk of loss of or damage to the goods, as well as any additional costs due to events occurring after the time the goods have been delivered to the carrier, is transferred from the seller to the buyer when the goods have been delivered into the custody of the carrier.

"Carrier" means any person who, in a contract of carriage, undertakes to perform or to procure the performance of, carriage, by rail, road, sea, air, inland waterway or by a combination of such modes.

If subsequent carriers are used for the carriage to the agreed destination, the risk passes when the goods have been delivered to the first carrier.

The CPT term requires the seller to clear the goods for export.

This term may be used for any mode of transport including multimodal transport.

CIP—Carriage and insurance paid to (. . . named place of destination)
"Carriage and insurance paid to . . ." means that the seller has the same obligations as under CPT but with the addition that the seller has to procure cargo insurance against the buyer's risk of loss of or damage to the goods during the carriage. The seller contracts for insurance and pays the insurance premium.

The buyer should note that under the CIP term the seller is only required to obtain insurance on minimum coverage. The CIP term requires the seller to clear the goods for export. This term may be used for any mode of transport including multimodal transport.

DAF—Delivered at frontier (. . . named place)
"Delivered at Frontier" means that the seller fulfils his obligation to deliver when the goods have been made available, cleared for export, at the named point and place at the frontier, but before the Customs border of the adjoining

country. The term "frontier" may be used for any frontier including that of the country of export. Therefore, it is of vital importance that the frontier in question be defined precisely by always naming the point and place in the term. The term is primarily intended to be used when goods are to be carried by rail or road, but it may be used for any mode of transport.

DES—Delivered ex ship (. . . named port of destination)

"Ex Ship" means that the seller fulfils his obligation to deliver when the goods have been made available to the buyer on board the ship uncleared for import at the named port of destination. The seller has to bear all the costs and risks involved in bringing the goods to the named port of destination. This term can only be used for sea or inland waterway transport.

DEQ—Delivered ex quay (duty paid) (. . . named port of destination)

"Delivered Ex Quay (duty paid)" means that the seller fulfils his obligation to deliver when he has made the goods available to the buyer on the quay (wharf) at the named port of destination, cleared for importation. The seller has to bear all risks and costs including duties, taxes and other charges of delivering the goods thereto.

This term should not be used if the seller is unable directly or indirectly to obtain the import licence.

If the parties wish the buyer to clear the goods for importation and pay the duty the words "duty unpaid" should be used instead of "duty paid".

If the parties wish to exclude from the seller's obligations some of the costs payable upon importation of the goods (such as value added tax (VAT)), this should be made clear by adding words to this effect: "Delivered ex quay, VAT unpaid (. . . named port of destination)".

This term can only be used for sea or inland waterway transport.

DDU—Delivered duty unpaid (. . . named place of destination)

"Delivered duty unpaid" means that the seller fulfils his obligation to deliver when the goods have been made available at the named place in the country of importation. The seller has to bear the costs and risks involved in bringing the goods thereto (excluding duties, taxes and other official charges payable upon importation) as well as the costs and risks of carrying out Customs formalities. The buyer has to pay any additional costs and to bear any risks caused by his failure to clear the goods for import in time.

If the parties wish the seller to carry out Customs formalities and bear the costs and risks resulting therefrom, this has to be made clear by adding words to this effect.

If the parties wish to include in the seller's obligations some of the costs payable upon importation of the goods (such as value added tax (VAT)), this should be made clear by adding words to this effect: "Delivered duty unpaid, VAT paid (. . . named place of destination)".

This term may be used irrespective of the mode of transport.

DDP—Delivered duty paid (. . . named place of destination)

"Delivered duty paid" means that the seller fulfils his obligation to deliver when the goods have been made available at the named place in the country of importation. The seller has to bear the risks and costs, including duties, taxes and other charges of delivering the goods thereto, cleared for importation.

If the parties wish to exclude from the seller's obligations some of the costs payable upon importation of the goods (such as value added tax (VAT)), this should be made clear by adding words to this effect: "Delivered duty paid, VAT unpaid (. . . named place of destination)".

This term may be used irrespective of the mode of transport.

EXW—Ex works (. . . named place)

"Ex works" means that the seller fulfils his obligation to deliver when he has made the goods available at his premises (i.e. works, factory, warehouse, etc.) to the buyer. In particular, he is not responsible for loading the goods on the vehicle provided by the buyer or for clearing the goods for export, unless otherwise agreed. The buyer bears all costs and risks involved in taking the goods from the seller's premises to the desired destination. This term thus represents the minimum obligation for the seller. This term should not be used when the buyer cannot carry out directly or indirectly the export formalities. In such circumstances, the FCA term should be used.

FCA—Free carrier (. . . named place)

"Free Carrier" means that the seller fulfils his obligation to deliver when he has handed over the goods, cleared for export, into the charge of the carrier named by the buyer at the named place or point. If no precise point is indicated by the buyer, the seller may choose within the place or range stipulated where the carrier shall take the goods into his charge. When, according to commercial practice, the seller's assistance is required in making the contract with the carrier (such as in rail or air transport) the seller may act at the buyer's risk and expense.

This term may be used for any mode of transport, including multimodal transport.

"Carrier" means any person who, in a contract of carriage, undertakes to perform or to procure the performance of carriage by rail, road, sea, air, inland waterway or by a combination of such modes. If the buyer instructs the seller to deliver the cargo to a person, e.g. a freight forwarder who is not a "carrier", the seller is deemed to have fulfilled his obligation to deliver the goods when they are in the custody of that person.

"Transport terminal", means a railway terminal, a freight station, a container terminal or yard, a multi-purpose cargo terminal or any similar receiving point.

"Container" includes any equipment used to unitise cargo, e.g. all types of containers and/or flats, whether ISO accepted or not, trailers, swap bodies, ro-ro equipment, and applies to all modes of transport.

Incoterms

FAS—Free alongside ship (. . . named port of shipment)
"Free Alongside Ship" means that the seller fulfils his obligation to deliver when the goods have been placed alongside the vessel on the quay or in lighters at the named port of shipment.

This means that the buyer has to bear all costs and risks of loss of or damage to the goods from that moment. The FAS term requires the buyer to clear the goods for export. It should not be used when the buyer cannot carry out directly or indirectly the export formalities.

This term can only be used for sea or inland waterway transport.

FOB—Free on board (. . . named port of shipment)
"Free on Board" means that the seller fulfils his obligation to deliver when the goods have passed over the ship's rail at the named port of shipment. This means that the buyer has to bear all costs and risks of loss of or damage to the goods from that point.

The FOB term requires the seller to clear the goods for export.

This term can only be used for sea or inland waterway transport. When the ship's rail serves no practical purpose, such as in the case of roll-on/roll-off or container traffic, the FCA term is more appropriate to use.

The different terms are suitable for different types of transport as follows:

Applicable for sea and inland waterway transport:
FAS, FOB, CFR, CIF, DES, DEQ

Any mode of transport including multimodal:
EXW, FCA, CPT, CIP, DAF, DDU, DDP

Rail transport:
FCA

Air transport:
FCA

Associated abbreviations:
CFR cost and freight
CIF cost, insurance and freight
CIP carriage and insurance paid to
CPT carriage paid to
DAF delivered at frontier
DDP delivered duty paid
DDU delivered duty unpaid
DES delivered ex ship
DEQ delivered ex quay
EXW exworks
FAS free alongside
FCA free carrier
FOB free on board

174

See also:
International Chamber of Commerce (ICC)

Inland haulage

One important feature of containerisation is the ease with which goods are transferred from road vehicle, rail wagon and barge to ocean vessel and back again. Taking advantage of this facility of handling, container shipping lines in many trades will carry goods overland in the country of export and the country of import. This element in the through movement of containers is called **carrier haulage**. Carriers do not have to own the vehicles that they use but can use private haulage companies with whom they negotiate haulage charges. This applies equally to the way in which rail and barge are used. It is not, however, at these rates that the merchant is debited: the line or conference will have a set of rates for this purpose known as **zone haulage rates** or **grid haulage rates**. In the country of export, the rates cover the portion of the journey from the place of acceptance of the goods in the contract of carriage to the terminal. The place of acceptance could be the supplier's premises or a container yard, wherever the container is loaded. The terminal is usually at the port but could be a delivering-in point elsewhere, sometimes at a port formerly served by the line but which, for reasons of rationalisation, is no longer called at. In the country of import, the haulage rate covers from the terminal to the place of delivery which could be a container yard or the consignee's premises, wherever the container is unpacked. The rates are known as zone rates or grid rates because each country is divided up by the line or conference by means of a grid or into zones with individual rates applicable from any zone to the terminal or terminals in the country of export and vice-versa in the country of import. When the container is placed by the merchant in the care of the carrier, the latter decides on the best way of delivering it to the terminal and it is not unknown for the inland leg of the voyage to be effected using more than one means of transport. **Carrier haulage rates** are normally expressed in local currency as a lump sum. They are usually not subject to surcharges.

Some merchants prefer to undertake the inland haulage themselves, and this can be done both in the country of export and in the country of import. Not unexpectedly, this is known as **merchant haulage**. The container is made available to the merchant at a specified container yard either for the exporter to take away for loading or for the importer to take to his premises for unloading. Generally, the place where the container is made available is the place where the merchant is required to return it. Wherever merchant haulage is used, lines tend to impose a charge called a **handover charge** or sometimes **transfer charge** to cover the cost of transferring the container to and from the merchant's vehicle. Some users of merchant haulage have argued that the handover charge is a disincentive on the part of shipping lines who prefer merchants to use carrier haulage. When using their own haulier, merchants are also able to make use of the carrier's trailers and for this lines charge a hire charge which is specified in the tariff. When the carrier's equipment (container or container and trailer) is used in conjunction with merchant haulage, the merchant is allowed a period of free time while the equipment is under his control. If at the expiry of free time he has not returned the equipment he will be subject to penalties.

Institute of Chartered Shipbrokers (ICS)

The Institute of Chartered Shipbrokers, based in London, England, is the professional body for those engaged in all aspects of the shipping business.

When the Institute was founded in 1911 shipbrokers had, for generations, been the intermediaries for finding ships for cargoes or cargoes for ships or attending ships in port.

In 1920, it was realised that attaining real professionalism required education and discipline: the Institute set standards which were able to satisfy His Majesty's Privy Council and a Royal Charter was granted.

At that time membership was limited to the United Kingdom, Ireland and the British Commonwealth. Also at that time a big ship was 7,000 tons, tankers were almost unheard of and liners were the monopoly of a few Western nations. Since then many changes both evolutionary and revolutionary have taken place in the shipping industry.

In 1984, a supplementary Royal Charter was granted and now membership of the Institute is open to citizens of any country of the world, company membership is possible and qualifying examinations cover the full spectrum of shipping commerce.

Membership is now enjoyed by over 3,500 men and women throughout the world with Institute branches established in Canada, Cyprus, Germany, Hong Kong, India, Ireland, Pakistan, Singapore, South Africa, Sri Lanka and the United Arab Emirates as well as 10 branches in the United Kingdom.

The qualifying examinations are held annually to test candidates in certain general subjects relating to shipping plus a choice of specialist papers in dry cargo chartering, ship management, ship sale and purchase, tanker chartering, liner trades and port agency.

Membership of the Institute (MICS) is achieved by candidates passing the examinations and satisfying the Controlling Council of their suitability.

Promotion to Fellowship status (FICS) which permits the person to be described as a Chartered Shipbroker, is granted to those members who reach positions of seniority and influence in the shipping world.

Membership of the Institute is internationally recognised as a mark of professionalism in shipping business.

The Institute is a member of the **Federation of National Associations of Shipbrokers and Agents (FONASBA)**.

Associated abbreviations:
FICS Fellow of the Institute of Chartered Shipbrokers

FONASBA Federation of National Associations of Shipbrokers and Agents
ICS Institute of Chartered Shipbrokers
MICS Member of the Institute of Chartered Shipbrokers

Alternative spelling:
ship broker

Associated definition:
broking shipbroking

See also:
Shipbroker

InterManager—International Ship Managers' Association (ISMA)

The International Ship Managers' Association – InterManager – is a trade association representing the views of the practitioners in ship management, both third party managers and in-house managers, at the IMO, with governments and industry. InterManager seeks to encourage the highest standards in ship management through innovation, creativity and knowledge sharing. Experience shows that a compliance culture doesn't lead to the highest standards: quality comes from self regulation with verification.

Membership is open the ship managers, ship owners, crew managers. Associate membership is open to other maritime enterprises supporting the aims of the association.

The origins of InterManager can be traced back to the late 1980s. At that time, ship management was emerging as an important sector of the shipping industry in its own right, but it lacked any real forum for debate as an homogeneous group. The idea of forming an association of ship managers was first floated at that time, partly to serve this need but also in response to what was perceived as unfair criticism of a growing industry sector.

A perceived deterioration in shipping standards over the preceding two decades was blamed by many industry commentators on the ship management sector. The argument ran that, with the replacement of the traditional ship owner structures by new types of owner such as K/S investors, third party managers had become the instrument of cost-cutting and substandard operations.

InterManager president and Eurasia Group president and group managing director, Rajaish Bajpaee says, "In the late 1980s the worldwide consciousness of the need for quality practices in the day-to-day management of ships had yet to emerge as a pressing pan-industry issue. This was a difficult period for shipping in general, and the industry faced a depression of historic proportions. The situation was only worsened by a spate of serious accidents, which were blamed on human error and management failures.

InterManager—International Ship Managers' Association (ISMA)

The mood at the time has been succinctly captured by Lord Justice Sheen in his inquiry into the loss of the *Herald of Free Enterprise* where he described the management failures as 'the disease of sloppiness', which pervaded every level of the vessel operator's hierarchy."

During the late 1980s the ship management sector was still in its infancy, and lacked a common voice. Mr Bajpaee believes this made the sector vulnerable to the witch hunts, which inevitably followed the shipping casualties of the day. It soon became clear that the maritime industry had found a convenient scapegoat to blame.

Acknowledging the pressure on standards, the ship management sector reacted and embarked on a quality assurance system by which negative trends could be brought under control. The result of this initiative was the creation of the International Ship Managers' Association (then known as ISMA) in the spring of 1991. The association is Company Limited by Guarantee registered in Limassol, Cyprus.

"Recognising the possibility that the very existence of the sector was at stake, the leading quality ship managers of the day resolved to present a united front to the pressures being faced by the industry", explains Mr Bajpaee. "The ship management sector achieved this by way of self-regulation, and by voluntarily binding themselves to a Code of Conduct and Management Practice. It was only a matter of time thereafter that this united front was incorporated in 1991 into an independent association of ship management companies."

The Association was incorporated to act as the visible and united face of a movement within the ship management community towards quality assurance and accountability. According to Mr Bajpaee, "The most substantial achievement of the Association was in providing the ship management sector with a homogenous voice, and in the formulation of the 'ISMA Code' ... an exceedingly rigorous code of conduct, which had to be compulsorily followed by the Association's membership, and verified independently by way of an external audit mechanism."

The ISMA Code of Ship Management Standards was unique and revolutionary because it was proactive in nature and advocated voluntary self regulation. There were several codes of conduct, which emerged as reactions to the rash of highly publicised casualties and incidents, but these codes were just that – reactionary. These codes did not subscribe to the higher ideal of excellence in ship management, and eventually lost their relevance when the ISM Code made basic safety practices in shipping mandatory under Chapter IX of the SOLAS Convention.

Mr Bajpaee believes the ISMA Code has continued to retain its relevance even in the present day when shipping is highly regulated since the Code subscribes to the rigorous pursuit of excellence in many more dimensions as opposed to focusing upon the basic standards of quality and safety which are achievable in day-to-day ship management.

More recently the Association has come to recognise that excellence within the ship management sector alone cannot guarantee quality in shipping. The maritime value chain is only as strong as its weakest link, and accordingly each link within the chain needs to be strengthened. The Association has therefore embraced a broader and more inclusive philosophy of inviting the participation of each link within the value chain, in the pursuit of excellence.

Supporting this objective the Association in 2005 introduced a category of associate members, that is, industry players who are not engaged in ship management as their core business but who contribute to the sector through their involvement as partners within the maritime value chain. These Associate Members are admitted on the basis of the commitment they demonstrate towards the Association's pursuit of excellence.

Mr Bajpaee said the re-branding of the "erstwhile ISMA occurred in the context of this expansion of the membership, and nearly simultaneously with this significant paradigm shift in the Association's approach to quality".

This broadening of the Association's approach to excellence has occurred under the umbrella of what is known as the "KPI Initiative". The KPI Initiative is a movement for the establishment of pan-industry objective Key Performance Indicators (KPIs) against which the performance of ships and their operators would be judged.

The movement aims at harnessing the expertise of each link within the maritime value chain, and developing a set of universal KPIs through the participation of all sectors in ocean transport within the Initiative. Hence the need for an active constituency of Associate Members that will be called upon to contribute their unique expertise in the formulation of the pan-industry KPIs. These Associate Members are today very actively involved in InterManager's work, and the success of the KPI Initiative rests on their continued involvement and engagement.

InterManager has grown considerably over the years and, to spread the quality ideal, in 1994 membership was extended to crew managers. InterManager is widely acknowledged as the voice of quality conscious players within the ship management industry and allied industries. The Association is evolving into an increasingly visible and proactive trade association, which will act in synergy with other similar associations, governmental and non-governmental organisations for promoting and enhancing sustainable and objective quality in shipping.

Today, InterManager represents shipmanagers worldwide controlling a fleet of over 1,000 ships. Today the entry ticket to InterManager membership for ship and crew managers is a commitment to work towards ISO 9001:2000 compliance.

InterManager chronology

1988: The formation of a professional, homogeneous organisation to represent the ship management sector was first aired in Hong Kong partly as a response to perceived unfair criticism and partly in recognising the possibility that the very existence of the sector was at stake.

1989: Five of the major ship management companies Columbia Shipmanagement Ltd, Cyprus; Denholm Ship Management, UK; Hanseatic Shipping Co

Ltd, Cyprus; V Ships, Monaco and Wallem Group Ltd, Hong Kong form a group, later to be replaced by ISMA, to prepare the foundations for an Association and to compile a Code of Ship Management Standards for members, which was the forerunner of the ISM Code.

1990: By the end of 1990, the Code and articles of association for the proposed new Association are completed and circulated to about 50 ship management companies and interested parties.

1991: In April 1991, ISMA officially comes into being at a meeting in London. Marisec becomes the secretariat for the Association's 35 initial members. Denholm managing director David Underwood is elected founder president.

1994: ISMA president Joachim Meyer of Hanseatic welcomes the ISM Code but states it is not as comprehensive as the ISMA Code, which covers all aspects of ship operations and ship management. Membership is extended to include crew managers.

1995: The first full-scale revision of the ISMA Code takes place. All the requirements of the final ISM Code are included and new provisions are made to allow for crew management members.

1996: The revised Code is issued in February. Rules for associate membership are eased to accept companies deemed to have equivalent quality standards, but this brings in only a few new recruits. The executive committee, as a result, decides against becoming a full trade association to return ISMA to an Association of quality ship managers.

1998: Increased business is anticipated by ship managers as a result of the implementation of the first phase of ISM and the fallout from the Asian financial crisis. Members are warned to assess carefully any potential new clients seeking ship management services to solve their ISM requirements.

1999: Speculation about consolidation within the ship management sector mirrors developments in the wider shipping market. This leads to talk of a two-tier market with the big ship managers set to grow in size to achieve economies of scale, while the smaller operations are forced to offer restricted services.

2000: The ISMA Code is totally reviewed and a new version issued.

2005: InterManager is launched in Hong Kong. The new trade association is armed with new articles of association and a broad mandate to galvanise the contribution of the global ship management sector to the industry-wide drive for improving the image and performance of shipping.

For more information see *www.intermanager.org*
Contact the General Secretary: *secretary@intermanager.org* Tel: +44 1403 733070.

Associated abbreviation:
ISMA International Ship Managers' Association

International Association of Classification Societies (IACS)

Leading the way: dedicated to safe ships and clean seas, IACS members make a unique contribution to maritime safety and regulation through technical support, compliance verification and research and development. More than 90% of the world's cargo carrying tonnage is covered by the classification design, construction and through-life compliance rules and standards set by the 10 Member Societies and one Associate of IACS.

Classification societies are organizations that establish and apply technical standards in relation to the design, construction and survey of marine related facilities including ships and offshore structures. The vast majority of ships are built and surveyed to the standards laid down by classification societies. These standards are issued by the classification society as published rules. A vessel that has been designed and built to the appropriate rules of a society may apply for a certificate of classification from that society. The society issues this certificate upon completion of relevant classification surveys. Such a certificate does not imply, and should not be construed as an express warranty of safety, fitness for purpose or seaworthiness of the ship. It is an attestation only that the vessel is in compliance with the standards that have been developed and published by the society issuing the classification certificate.

More than 50 organizations worldwide define their activities as providing marine classification. Ten of those organizations form the International Association of Classification Societies (IACS). It is estimated that these 10 societies, together with the additional society that has been accorded associate status by IACS, collectively class about 94% of all commercial tonnage involved in international trade worldwide.

Classification is one element within a network of maritime safety partners. Other elements are parties such as the shipowner, the shipbuilder, the flag State, port States, underwriters, shipping financiers, and charterers among others.

The role of classification and classification societies has been recognized in the International Convention for the Safety of Life at Sea, (SOLAS) and in the 1988 Protocol to the International Convention on Load Lines. This statutory role is addressed later in this note.

As an independent, self-regulating, externally audited, body, a classification society has no commercial interests related to ship design, ship building, ship ownership, ship operation, ship management, ship maintenance or repairs, insurance, or chartering. In establishing its rules, each classification society may draw upon the advice and review of members of the industry who are considered expert in their field.

International Association of Classification Societies (IACS)

Classification rules are developed to assess the structural strength and integrity of essential parts of the ship's hull and its appendages, and the reliability and the function of the propulsion and steering systems, power generation and those other features and auxiliary systems which have been built into the ship in order to maintain essential services on board. Classification rules are not intended as a design code and in fact cannot be used as such. A ship built in accordance with an IACS Member's rules will be assigned a class designation by the society on satisfactory completion of the relevant surveys. For ships in service, the society carries out surveys to ascertain that the ship remains in compliance with those rules. Should any defects that may affect class become apparent, or damages be sustained between the relevant surveys, the ship owner and operator are required to inform the society concerned without delay.

Compliance with the IACS Quality System Certification Scheme (QSCS) and observance of the IACS Code of Ethics is mandatory for both IACS Member and Associate status.

IACS is governed by a Council, with each Member represented by a high management figure. Under the Council is the General Policy Group (GPG), made up of a senior management figure from each Member, which develops and implements actions giving effect to the policies, directions and long term plans of Council. The chair of GPG is taken by the Member holding the Council chair.

The Code of Ethics is the bedrock of the IACS members' work. It states, *inter alia*:

"Classification Societies live on their reputation. Acceptance of their technical work can only be maintained by continuously proving integrity and competence."

and

"Competition between Societies shall be on the basis of services (technical and field) rendered to the marine industry but must not lead to compromises on safety of life and property at sea or to the lowering of technical standards."

Associated abbreviation:
IACS International Associations of Classification Societies

See also:
Classification Societies

International Association of Dry Cargo Shipowners (Intercargo)

Since 1980, Intercargo has represented the interests of owners, operators and managers of dry cargo shipping and works closely with the other international associations to promote a safe, high quality, efficient and profitable industry.

182

Membership benefits include the provision of information on technical, commercial and operational issues relating to the dry cargo industry, an active Committee structure, and participation in the work of the International Maritime Organisation (IMO) where it enjoys observer status.

Intercargo believes that a new approach is needed to maintain a safe, efficient, environmentally friendly and profitable dry cargo shipping industry.

Dry bulk trades comprise iron ore, coal, grain, timber, steel and other similar cargoes which are shipped in bulk as opposed to carried in containers or other unit loads. Delivering approximately 5 million tons of these commodities every day requires an efficient dry cargo shipping industry—without which, world trade as we know it would cease.

Concern for the lives of seafarers and the safety of ships means that safety is very much at the forefront of the activities of Intercargo. Indeed, Intercargo runs a Technical Committee, known as CASTEC, which meets twice a year alternating between venues in Asia and Europe, to discuss technical matters. It also runs technical seminars on a wide range of subject matters.

Intercargo also continues to work closely with IACS to develop safe, efficient, environmentally friendly and operationally streamlined bulk carriers. Intercargo and IACS hold regular technical and policy meetings, concentrating on important issues such as the Joint Bulker Project Common Rules. The ultimate aim of the JBP project is to reduce the interpretive differences between individual classification societies—the importance of which cannot be understated.

Intercargo also continues to monitor bulk carrier losses. It has been compiling statistics since 1990, and produces an annual Bulk Carrier Casualty Report that lists the losses each year and analyses the previous 10-year period. The trends indicate that the number of ships, lives and amount of deadweight tonnage lost continues to fall, while the average age of the bulk carriers that sink is rising.

The international conventions like SOLAS, STCW and MARPOL form the framework of the safety, security, training and pollution prevention regulations with which ships should comply. The primary task of enforcing compliance and the issuing of certificates falls on the flag State. Under control provisions that date back to the 1929 SOLAS convention, port States also have certain rights to exercise authority over foreign ships that enter its ports. Checking that a ship complies with convention standards, is one of those rights. A ship found to have deficiencies and considered unsafe to proceed to sea is likely to be detained.

Port State control (PSC) activity has developed along regional lines. In 1982 the Paris Memorandum of Understanding on Port State Control, now simply referred to as the Paris MOU, was signed between north European States, Canada and the Russian Federation. Agreements in South America and Asia quickly followed. The United States, however, chose to remain outside of any regional grouping and operate its own programme.

Intercargo actively supports the PSC inspection regime as an effective method of eliminating substandard shipping. It has written a guide for ships involved in the dry bulk trades and it encourages members and non-members alike to complete an Inspection Reporting Form to comment on inspection experiences that have caused concern. That guide has also been reproduced and published jointly with the North of England P&I Association and it features in its series of loss prevention guides. One other aspect which now falls under the remit of the PSC regime is security with Inspectors charged with ensuring that vessels are compliant with the International Ship and Port Facility Security Code (ISPS). Intercargo monitors PSC data and encourages members to lodge appeals to the small minority of inspections/detentions which are deemed grossly unfair.

Intercargo continues to monitor the detentions of bulk carriers reported by the Paris and Tokyo MOU's and the US Coast Guard. Preliminary evidence shows that the ships entered with Intercargo accounted for around 8% of these detentions.

Intercargo releases to the EQUASIS database, the names of the ships it has entered for membership. Checking this publicly accessible database enables interested parties to see the PSC deficiency and detention record of all internationally trading ships, and not just those entered with Intercargo.

Intercargo has devoted a considerable amount of time attempting to galvanise support against what it perceives as erosion of free market principles on the Mississippi River. Intercargo believes that the differential charges levied between the tug company and the Marine Terminal Operator (MTO), and the MTO and the ship operator, raise costs and limit the right of shipowners to select a tug company of its choice.

Associated abbreviations:
ISPS International Ship and Port Facility Security Code
JBP Joint Bulker Project
IACS International Association of Classification Societies
MOU Memorandum of Association
mto marine terminal operator
PSC Port State Control

International Association of Independent Tanker Owners (INTERTANKO)

INTERTANKO has been the voice of independent tanker owners since 1970, ensuring that the oil that keeps the world turning is shipped safely, responsibly and competitively.

Membership is open to independent tanker owners and operators of oil and chemical tankers, i.e. non-oil companies and non-state controlled tanker owners, who fulfil the Association's membership criteria. Independent owners operate some 80% of the world's tanker fleet and the vast majority are INTERTANKO members. As of January 2005, the organisation has 235 members, whose combined fleet comprises more than 2,230 tankers totalling 170 million dwt, which is 70% of the world's independent tanker fleet. INTERTANKO's associate membership stands at 285 companies with an interest in shipping of oil and chemicals.

INTERTANKO is a forum where the industry meets, policies are discussed and statements are created. It is a valuable source of first-hand information, opinions and guidance. INTERTANKO has a vision of a professional, efficient and respected industry, that is dedicated to achieving Safe transport, cleaner seas and free competition.

The strong support that INTERTANKO enjoys allows it to speak authoritatively and proactively on behalf of tanker operators at international, regional, national and local level. It is also able to maintain a 25-strong secretariat and a network of 14 committees and four regional panels that coordinate an extensive work programme that comprises more than 50 agenda items. Governments and shipping regulators have taken a closer interest in tanker shipping in recent years. INTERTANKO has responded by establishing, strengthening and maintaining relationships with legislators on all levels, working with them to ensure a fair and equitable distribution of the responsibilities and liabilities involved in carrying oil and chemicals by sea.

Underlining its commitment to representing its members where key decisions are made, INTERTANKO opened offices in Singapore and Washington DC in 1999, in addition to its principal offices in Oslo and London. Within the shipping industry itself, INTERTANKO participates in discussions within the International Maritime Organisation (IMO) where it has NGO status and the International Oil Spill Compensation Fund. In addition, it has consultative status at the United Nations Conference on Trade and Development.

Oil and its derivatives will remain the world's most critical commodity in the foreseeable future and tankers will be needed to distribute it to where it is needed. As long as tankers are vital to this distribution INTERTANKO will provide leadership in the development and implementation of industry standards and practices, and international regulations for maritime safety and environmental protection.

INTERTANKO is actively involved in a wide range of topics, which include commercial, technical, legal and operational matters. INTERTANKO's direct contact with the members and original sources enables it to select and promulgate the information which is essential to the tanker industry.

INTERTANKO's information and advisory services include the Weekly NEWS, courses, seminars and free access to a range of web based services. INTERTANKO produces publications, specialising in technical, operational, environmental, documentary and market issues. Members and associate members are also entitled to direct expert opinions from resourceful and experienced lawyers, mariners, naval architects, marine engineers, economists and other specialists within INTERTANKO. Their wide network of contacts routinely benefit directly members and associate members.

International Association of Ports and Harbors (IAPH)

On 7 November 1955, the International Association of Ports and Harbors (IAPH) was founded in Los Angeles, USA, where delegates from 38 ports and maritime organisations in 14 countries gathered to celebrate the birth of this worldwide body of ports and harbours. The past five decades have seen IAPH steadily grow and develop as a truly leading organisation of the global port community representing, if not all, a majority of ports and harbours in the world. In 2005, IAPH will be celebrating the 50th Anniversary of its founding world wide. It is a non-profit-making and non-governmental organisation (NGO) headquartered in Tokyo, Japan.

Since its inception, IAPH has served the global port industry and formed a global alliance of ports and harbours over the past decades. Being the World Ports Association, IAPH comprises now some 230 Regular Members—leading ports in 90 countries and economies, who are public port authorities, private port operators and government agencies. In 2002, a total of 7.1 billion tons—accounting for some 60% of the world sea-borne trade—was handled by IAPH member ports, and over 80% of world container traffic in 2001 was handled by them. In addition, more than 100 shipping, stevedoring and warehousing businesses, national and regional port associations, port and maritime research institutes, and manufacturers of port-related products are represented as Associate members.

Though "unity" characterises IAPH, its membership is in reality diverse. In terms of port operation, it has landlord ports, operating ports, and a mixture of both. As to ownership, it has public port authorities—national, state, municipal—and private port/terminal operating companies, and a joint venture of public and private sectors. IAPH seeks ways and means to harmonise such diversity, but at the same time diversity is often our strength and assets!

IAPH is often referred to as the "United Ports of the World", in which active players in the global port community, namely Port CEOs, Port Directors and Port Managers are represented to promote and advance their common cause and interests. To accomplish its goals, IAPH strives to achieve the following mission:

- to promote the development of the international port and maritime industry by fostering cooperation among members in order to build a more cohesive partnership among the world's ports and harbours, thereby promoting peace in the world and the welfare of mankind;
- to ensure that the industry's interests and views are represented before international organizations involved in the regulation of international trade and transportation and that they are incorporated in the regulatory initiatives of these organizations; and
- to collect, analyse, exchange and distribute information on developing trends in international trade, transportation, ports and the regulations of these industries.

186

IAPH's motto is "World Peace Through World Trade—World Trade Through World Ports". As clearly stated in its constitution, IAPH is committed to "promoting peace in the world and the welfare of mankind" as its ultimate goal.

Associated abbreviation:
IACS International Association of Ports and Harbours

International Bunker Industry Association Ltd (IBIA)

The International Bunker Industry Association Ltd (IBIA) was conceived in October 1992 by eight members of the industry. Since then it has expanded steadily with a world wide membership comprising Ship Owners, Charterers, Bunker Suppliers, Traders, Brokers, Barging Companies, Storage Companies, Surveyors, Port Authorities, Credit reporting companies, Lawyers, P&I Clubs, Equipment Manufacturers, Shipping Journalists and Marine consultants.

The aims of IBIA are:

- To provide an international forum to address the concerns of all sectors of the international bunker industry.
- To improve and clarify industry practices and documentation.
- To represent the industry in discussions with relevant governmental and non-governmental bodies and to make the concerns of the industry known to such bodies.
- To assist members in the event of disputes by identifying the options and exploring the alternatives open to them and eventually to provide a panel of suitably experienced mediators and arbitrators.
- To increase the professional understanding and competence of those working in the industry.

Associated abbreviation:
IBIA International Bunker Industry Association

See also:
Bunkers

ICHCA International Limited (IIL)

ICHCA International Limited (IIL) is a membership organisation established in 2003 dedicated to the promotion of safety and efficiency in the handling and movement of goods by all modes and during all phases of both national and international transport chains.

It has 900 members in over 80 countries and members consist of ports, terminals, port authorities, container depots, academics and cargo specialists.

ICHCA International Limited (IIL)

It is an independent, non political, non-governmental and non profit distributing organisation. It has an influential and international membership in many countries, spanning all five continents, with National Sections in Japan and the USA.

Its membership represents a substantial cross-section of senior corporate executives, leading consultants, academics and authorities in the world of cargo handling and transport. It can provide management information and exchange of technical data relating to methods and techniques in the industry whilst being conscious of future trends and training needs.

It arranges opportunities for its membership to meet at international, national and regional levels at conferences, symposia, meetings, workshops and other social occasions for the interchange of information. It can assist with both formal and informal contacts in the industry.

It produces publications for members, including bi-monthly electronic newsletters with the latest cargo handling news, an annual review incorporating topical trends and developments, plus individual "best practice" publications gained from the research and study activities of its Panels. The latter cover a wide variety of issues and technical matters.

It participates in and monitors the activities of the regulatory bodies of government, non-governmental and inter-governmental organisations to ensure that practical difficulties encountered by its membership are voiced at the earliest discussion stage in the formulation of agreements, rules, regulations and laws. Following a recently new appointment to the Board, IIL will liaise more closely with the international agencies and also develop training initiatives for business management levels.

It promotes policies and projects that will improve the safety and efficiency of physical handling of cargo in all transport modes.

It enjoys non governmental (NGO) consultative status with a number of inter-governmental agencies whose programme of work impacts on the activities of the international cargo handling and transportation industry. Perhaps the chief amongst these are the International Maritime Organization (IMO), United Nations Conference on Trade and Development (UNCTAD), United Nations Economic and Social Councils (ECOSOC) particularly for Europe (UNECE), Asia Pacific (ESCAP), European Council of Ministers of Transport (ECMT), European Commission (EC), and the Organisation for Economic Co-operation and Development (OECD). It also maintains observer and liaison status with a number of international industry bodies and takes an active role in several international industry fora.

These organisations include the International Standards Organisation (ISO), European Standards Organisation (CEN), International Chamber of Shipping (ICS), International Air Transport Association (IATA) and the International Association of Ports and Harbours (IAPH). Following a recent new appointment to the Board, IIL will liaise more closely with the international agencies and also develop training initiatives for business management levels.

It makes important contributions to the debate on a wide range of industry issues around the world and, in many cases, has a direct effect on the formation of international regulations and legislation. Its representative function is carried out by staff of the Registered Office, as well as International Safety Panel members and others.

One of the ways in which it fulfils its objective of promoting efficiency in the movement of goods by all modes of transport and at all phases of the transport chain is through the work of its Panels of industry experts.

The International Safety Panel is made up of some 40 acknowledged experts in the ports and related industries who specialise in all aspects of cargo as well as personnel. Their remit includes: legal issues, safe working practices, equipment and training. Meeting three times a year at various global venues, they debate issues and attend IMO, ISO, BSI, etc. sessions, representing the views of IIL's membership. They have also an on-going task in preparing a series of publications such as Briefing Pamphlets, Study Reports and Research Papers. Their expertise is drawn from over 15 countries and a number liaise on a correspondence basis only.

The Bulk Panel represents a sector of the industry for which representation is fragmented and, in some cases, missing altogether. Springing from a prototype working group in Australia, it has widened the activities into a truly international forum.

Associated abbreviation:
IIL ICHCA International Limited

International Chamber of Commerce (ICC)

The International Chamber of Commerce:

—promotes international trade, investment and the market economy system worldwide;
—makes rules that govern the conduct of business across borders;
—provides essential services, foremost among them the ICC International Court of Arbitration, the world's leading institution of its kind.

Members from 63 national committees and over 7,000 member companies and associations from over 130 countries throughout the world present ICC views to their Governments and co-ordinate with their membership to address the concerns of the business community.

The ICC has top-level consultative status with the United Nations where it puts forward the views of business in industrialised and developing countries.

It also maintains close relations with the World Trade Organization (WTO), the Organization for Economic Co-operation and Development (OECD), the European Union and other inter-governmental and non-governmental bodies.

ICC permanent representatives at the UN in New York and Geneva monitor developments affecting business within the UN and its specialised agencies.

International Chamber of Commerce (ICC)

The ICC ensures that business concerns are brought to the attention of Governments, both through its international secretariat in Paris, and the representations of national committees throughout the world.

Activities of the ICC Commissions

Most of the 500 commission members are senior executives of major companies who

—make critical assessments of legislative proposals and other developments affecting their fields, and communicate these views to Governments and international organisations;

—meet regularly to review issues affecting business, covering a wide range of sectors, such as banking, competition, the environment, financial services, insurance, intellectual property, marketing, air, maritime and surface transport, taxation, and trade and investment policy;

—harmonise trade practices;

—draw up voluntary codes for business which set ethical standards.

ICC services

Foremost amongst the ICC's practical services to business is the International Court of Arbitration, the world's leading body for the resolution of international disputes by arbitration.

The International Bureau of Chambers of Commerce (IBCC) strengthens co-operation between chambers in every part of the world, linking those in the industrialised world with their counterparts in the developing countries and transition economies of east and central Europe. IBCC also manages the ATA Carnet system for temporary duty-free imports.

ICC Conferences was created in 1996 to disseminate ICC expertise in international arbitration, trade, banking and commercial practice, through a worldwide programme of conferences and seminars. The ICC international business law and practice conducts research and training, and facilitates information exchange between the legal academic community and practitioners.

ICC Commercial Crime Services

This specialised division is the umbrella organisation of three ICC units dealing with different aspects of crime affecting business:

—Commercial Crime Bureau, set up to combat the increase in commercial frauds worldwide;

—International Maritime Bureau, which deals with all types of maritime crime, including fraud, cargo theft, and piracy;

—Counterfeiting Intelligence Bureau which helps companies to prevent the faking of their products;

—ICC Publishing SA offers business people practical reference works for the conduct of international trade. Topics include banking practice, international arbitration, commercial fraud, international contracts and joint ventures.

Associated abbreviations:
ICC International Chamber of Commerce
IMB International Maritime Bureau

See also:
ICC International Maritime Bureau (IMB)

International Convention on Load Lines

Recognising that the establishment by international agreement of minimum freeboards for ships engaged on international voyages constitutes a most important contribution for the safety of life and property at sea, the International Conference on Load Lines was held in London from 3 March to 5 April 1966, upon the invitation of the Inter-Governmental Maritime Consultative Organization (IMCO), subsequently renamed International Maritime Organization (IMO), for the purpose of drawing up an International Convention on Load Lines.

The Convention, which has been adopted by a large number of countries, contains the following main provisions:

—Application and exceptions and exemptions: the Convention applies essentially to ships registered in contracting countries which are engaged on international voyages. Smaller vessels and all fishing vessels are excepted. There are also various exemptions, such as vessels not normally engaged on international voyages but required to undertake one such voyage only.
—Surveys: there are requirements for periodical surveys and inspections, including what these cover and who is authorised to carry them out.
—Certificates: representatives of the government of a country who has ratified the Convention, or persons authorised by them, may issue certificates.

The Convention has a number of Regulations relating mainly to:

—Application: the Convention makes provision for ships carrying timber deck cargoes, sail-assisted ships and ships constructed of wood or of composite construction.
—**Deck Line**: the line representing the uppermost continuous deck; this is a horizontal line 300 millimetres in length and 25 millimetres in breadth, marked amidships.
—**Load Line Mark**: a ring 300 millimetres in outside diameter and 25 millimetres wide which is intersected by a horizontal line 450 millimetres in length and 25 millimetres in breadth, the upper edge of which passes through the centre of the ring. The mark is placed amidships.
—Lines to be used with the Load Line Mark: the various **load lines**—summer, winter, winter North Atlantic, tropical, fresh water and tropical fresh water.

Conditions of assignment of freeboard are defined: the Convention specifies a number of requirements relating mainly to the construction of the ship, for example, doors, hatchways, machinery space openings, ventilators and freeing ports.

There is a section on the computation of freeboards, including special requirements for ships assigned timber freeboards, in particular methods of stowage and securing of deck cargoes.

The zones, areas and seasonal periods are defined, together with any applicable dates or relevant ship size. These are:

—Northern Winter Seasonal Zones and Area.
—North Atlantic Winter Seasonal Area.
—North Pacific Winter Seasonal Zone.
—Southern Winter Seasonal Zone.
—Tropical Zone.
—Seasonal Tropical Areas.
—Summer Zones.

See also:
International Maritime Organization (IMO)
Freeboards and load lines

International Harbour Masters' Association (IHMA)

The International Harbour Masters' Association was formed in June 1996 with more than 250 members in 52 countries worldwide. Its headquarters are in Bristol, United Kingdom. The objects of the association are:

—to promote safe and efficient marine operations in port waters;
—to develop and foster collaboration and good relations among **harbour masters** worldwide;
—to represent the views of harbour masters internationally, regionally and nationally;
—to promote the professional standing and interests of harbour masters generally;
—to collect, collate and supply information of professional interest to the membership and to provide any other service that may be deemed appropriate.

IHMA provides harbour masters with opportunities to consult about technical and professional matters with colleagues in their region or around the world—to learn about their experiences, their problems and their solutions. Deputies and assistants also gain important strengths from the opportunities to broaden their knowledge of port maritime affairs.

IHMA was founded as the result of an earlier study by the European Harbour Masters' Association (EHMA) and detailed consultation by its IHMA Founding Group Committee comprised of harbour masters from around the world.

The founding of IHMA has been based upon major amendments to EHMA's Constitution so as to create a democratic and well focused worldwide organisation. EHMA is now an integrated part of IHMA.

EHMA began in the 1950s as an informal meeting of harbour masters of some of the major ports of north-west Europe. It became "officially" established with a Constitution in 1985 and a funded organisation in 1994.

Membership grew from fewer than 100 in 1994 (when the IHMA Founding Group was established) to more than 250 in June 1996.

A "harbour master" is defined in the IHMA Constitution as:

"that person who, whatever may be his local title of office, is the principal person who normally exercises jurisdiction at a place in ways that meet the following criteria:

(a) the jurisdiction is exercised over a water area of a port or port approach.
(b) in the exercise of this jurisdiction he should possess an authority conferred on him by national law, regulation or rules.
(c) the duties should encompass a legal and/or operational responsibility for the movement of shipping and
(d) the duties should involve him significantly in ensuring that shipping movements within the area of his jurisdiction are carried out safely."

Associated abbreviation:
IHMA International Harbour Masters' Association

International Maritime Organization (IMO)

Shipping is perhaps the most international of all the world's great industries— and one of the most dangerous. It has always been recognised that the best way of improving safety at sea is by developing international regulations that are followed by all shipping nations and from the mid-nineteenth century onwards a number of such treaties were adopted.

Several countries proposed that a permanent international body should be established to promote maritime safety more effectively, but it was not until the establishment of the United Nations itself that these hopes were realised. In 1948 an international conference in Geneva adopted a convention formally establishing IMO1. It entered into force in 1958 and the new Organization met for the first time the following year.

Its first task was to adopt a new version of the International Convention for the Safety of Life at Sea (SOLAS), the most important of all treaties dealing with maritime safety. This was achieved in 1960 and IMO then turned its attention to such matters as the facilitation of international maritime traffic, load lines and the carriage of dangerous goods.

But although safety was and remains IMO's most important responsibility, a new problem was emerging—pollution. The growth in the amount of oil being transported by sea and in the size of oil tankers was a particular concern.

International Maritime Organization (IMO)

Pollution prevention was part of IMO's original mandate but in the late 1960s a number of major tanker accidents resulted in further action being taken.

During the next few years IMO introduced a series of measures designed to prevent accidents and to minimise their consequences. It also tackled the environmental threat caused by routine operations such as the cleaning of oil cargo tanks and the disposal of engine room wastes—in tonnage terms a bigger menace than accidents.

The most important of all these measures was a treaty usually known as MARPOL 73/78—it was adopted in two stages, in 1973 and 1978. It covers not only accidental and operational oil pollution but also pollution by chemicals, goods in packaged form, sewage and garbage.

Recent changes to the Convention will make it necessary for all new tankers to be fitted with double-hulls or a design that provides equivalent cargo protection in the event of a collision or grounding. Since 1 July 1995 these changes have also been applied to existing tankers when they reach 25 years of age. An enhanced programme of surveys for tankers and bulk carriers aged five years and more came into operation on the same day. It is expected that these and other changes will result in many existing ships being scrapped or upgraded in the next few years.

IMO was also given the task of establishing a system for providing compensation to those who had suffered financially as a result of pollution. Two treaties were adopted, in 1969 and 1971, which enabled victims of oil pollution to obtain compensation much more simply and quickly than had been possible before. IMO followed up this success by developing a number of other legal conventions, most of which concerned liability and compensation issues.

Shipping, like all of modern life, has seen many technological innovations and changes. Some of these have presented challenges for the Organization and others, opportunities. The enormous strides made in communications technology, for example, have made it possible for IMO to introduce major improvements into the maritime distress system.

In the 1970s a global search and rescue system was initiated. The 1970s also saw the establishment of the International Mobile Satellite Organization (INMARSAT) which has greatly improved the provision of radio and other messages to ship.

In 1992 a further advance was made when the Global Maritime Distress and Safety System became operative. When it is fully in force in 1999, it will mean that a ship that is in distress anywhere in the world can be virtually guaranteed assistance, even if its crew does not have time to radio for help, as the message will be transmitted automatically.

Other measures introduced by IMO have concerned the safety of containers, bulk cargoes, liquefied gas tankers and other ship types. Special attention has been paid to crew standards, including the adoption of a special Convention on Standards of Training, Certification and Watchkeeping.

The adoption of maritime legislation is still IMO's best known responsibility. Around 40 conventions and protocols have been adopted by the Organization and most of them have been amended on several occasions to ensure that they are kept up to date with changes taking place in world shipping.

But adopting treaties is not enough—they have to be put into effect. This is the responsibility of Governments and there is no doubt that the way in which this is done varies considerably from country to country.

IMO has therefore developed a technical co-operation programme which is designed to assist Governments which lack the technical knowledge and resources that are needed to operate a shipping industry successfully. The emphasis of this programme is very much on training and perhaps the best example is the World Maritime University in Malmo, Sweden, which was established in 1983 and provides advanced training for the men and women involved in maritime administration, education and management.

With a staff of 300 people IMO is one of the smallest of all United Nations agencies. But it has had considerable success in achieving its aim of "safer shipping and cleaner oceans". The rate of serious casualties at sea fell appreciably during the 1980s and estimates indicate that oil pollution from ships was cut by around 60 per cent during the same period.

The challenge now facing IMO and its 156 Member States is how to maintain this success at a time when shipping is changing more rapidly than ever before.

There follows a list of the IMO Conventions accepted by many maritime nations:

Maritime Safety

International Convention for the Safety of Life at Sea (SOLAS), 1960 and 1974
International Convention on Load Lines (LL), 1966
Special Trade Passenger Ships Agreement (STP), 1971
International Regulations for Preventing Collisions at Sea (COLREG), 1972
International Convention for Safe Containers (CSC), 1972
Convention on the International Maritime Satellite Organization (INMARSAT), 1976
International Convention on Standards of Training, Certification and Watch-keeping for Seafarers (STCW), 1978
The Torremolinos Convention on Maritime Search and Rescue (SAR), 1979
International Convention on Standards of Training, Certification and Watch-keeping for Fishing Vessel Personnel (STCW-F), 1995

Marine Pollution

International Convention for the Prevention of Pollution of the Sea by Oil (OILPOL), 1954
Convention on the Prevention of Marine Pollution by Dumping of Wastes and Other Matter (LDC), 1972
International Convention for the Prevention of Pollution from Ships, 1973, as modified by the Protocol of 1978 relating thereto (MARPOL 73/78)
International Convention Relating to Intervention on the High Seas in Cases of Oil Pollution Casualties (INTERVENTION), 1969

International Maritime Organization (IMO)

International Convention on Oil Pollution Preparedness, Response and Co-operation (OPRC), 1990

Liability and Compensation

International Convention on Civil Liability for Oil Pollution Damage (CLC), 1969

International Convention on the Establishment of an International Fund for Compensation for Oil Pollution Damage (FUND), 1971

Convention Relating to Civil Liberty in the Field of Maritime Carriage of Nuclear Materials (NUCLEAR), 1971

Athens Convention Relating to the Carriage of Passengers and their Luggage by Sea (PAL), 1974

Convention on Limitation of Liability for Maritime Claims (LLMC), 1976

International Convention on Liability and Compensation for Damage in Connection with the Carriage of Hazardous and Noxious Substances by Sea (HNS), 1996

Other subjects

Convention on Facilitation of International Maritime Traffic (FAL), 1965

International Convention on Tonnage Measurement of Ships (TONNAGE), 1969

Convention for the Suppression of Unlawful Acts Against the Safety of Maritime Navigation (SUA), 1988

Protocol for the Suppression of Unlawful Acts Against the Safety of Fixed Platforms Located on the Continental Shelf (SUAPROT), 1988

International Convention on Salvage (SALVAGE), 1989

Associated abbreviations:
IMCO Inter-Governmental Maritime Consultative Organization (IMO's previous name)
IMO International Maritime Organization

See also:
International Convention on Load Lines
Convention on Facilitation of International Maritime Traffic

International Safety Management (ISM) Code

The Code's origins can be traced back to the late 1980s, when concern was growing about poor management standards in the shipping industry. In 1989, IMO adopted Guidelines on management for the safe operation of ships and for pollution prevention "to provide those responsible for the operation of ships with a framework for the proper development, implementation and assessment of safety and pollution prevention management in accordance with good practice".

These Guidelines were revised in November 1991 and the ISM Code itself was adopted as a recommendation in 1993. However, after several years of practical experience, it was felt that the Code was so important that it should be mandatory.

It was decided that the best way of achieving this would be through the International Convention for the Safety of Life at Sea, 1974 (SOLAS). This was done by means of amendments adopted on 24 May 1994, which added a new Chapter IX to the Convention entitled "Management for the Safe Operation of Ships". The Code itself is not actually included in the Convention, but is made mandatory by means of a reference in Chapter IX. By adding the ISM Code to SOLAS it is intended to provide an international standard for the safe management of ships and for pollution prevention.

The safety management objectives established by the ISM Code are:

—to provide for safe practices in ship operation and a safe working environment;
—to establish safeguards against all identified risks;
—to continuously improve safety management skills of personnel, including preparing for emergencies.

The Code requires a **safety management system** (SMS) to be established by "the Company", which is defined as the shipowner or any person, such as the manager or bareboat charterer, who has assumed responsibility for operating the ship. This system should be designed to ensure compliance with all mandatory regulations and that codes, guidelines and standards recommended by IMO and others are taken into account.

The SMS in turn should include a number of functional requirements:

—a safety and environmental protection policy;
—instructions and procedures to ensure safety and environmental protection;
—defined levels of authority and lines of communication between and amongst shore and shipboard personnel;
  procedures for reporting accidents, etc.;
—procedures for responding to emergencies;
  procedures for internal audits and management review.

The company is then required to establish and implement a policy for achieving these objectives. This includes providing the necessary resources and shore-based support. Every company is expected "to designate a person or persons ashore having direct access to the highest level of management".

The Code then goes on to outline the responsibility and authority of the master of the ship. It states that the SMS should make it clear that "the master has the overriding authority and the responsibility to make decisions ...". The Code then deals with other seagoing personnel and emphasises the importance of training.

Companies are required to prepare plans and instructions for key shipboard operations and to make preparations for dealing with any emergencies which might arise. The importance of maintenance is stressed and companies are required to ensure that regular inspections are held and corrective measures taken where necessary.

The procedures required by the Code should be documented and compiled in a Safety Management Manual, a copy of which should be kept on board. Regular checks and audits should be held by the company to ensure that the SMS is being complied with and the system itself should be reviewed periodically to evaluate its efficiency.

After outlining the responsibilities of the company, the Code then stresses that the responsibility for ensuring that the Code is complied with rests with the Government. Companies which comply with the Code should be issued with a document of compliance, a copy of which should be kept on board. Administrations should also issue a Safety Management Certificate to indicate that the company operates in accordance with the SMS and periodic checks should be carried out to verify that the ship's SMS is functioning properly.

The new Chapter IX of SOLAS entered into force under the tacit acceptance procedure on 1 July 1998. It will apply to passenger ships, oil and chemical tankers, bulk carriers, gas carriers and cargo high speed craft of 500 gross tonnage and above not later than that date and to other cargo ships and mobile offshore drilling units of 500 gross tonnage and above not later than 1 July 2002.

Associated abbreviations:
doc document of compliance
SMS safety management system

See also:
International Maritime Organization (IMO)

International Ship Suppliers Association (ISSA)

ISSA is the international association representing nearly 2,000 ship suppliers throughout the world. It has 36 national associations of ship suppliers as full ISSA members and associate members in 52 other countries where no national association exists. Over 500 locations are served by ISSA members.

ISSA members have to undergo a rigorous vetting procedure before gaining admittance. Members and the goods and services they offer can be found in every major port in the world.

The Association was formed in 1955 and has over half a century of service to the maritime industry.

Ship supply is recognised as very much a "relationship" business. To ensure fair trading and best practice ISSA has developed a set of Conditions, which form the basis of any supply contract.

To strengthen the relationship between ship supplier and buyer still further, ISSA drew up a Code of Ethics, which Members abide by to ensure the highest standards are applied in day-to-day operations.

ISSA publishes a magazine called *The Ship Supplier* at regular intervals containing news, views and relevant articles to the vibrant world of ship supply.

The ISSA Ship Stores Catalogue is ISSA's premier publication.

One of ISSA's declared aims is to provide a better understanding between buyers and suppliers through consultation and communication.

ISSA enjoys Non-Governmental Organisation (NGO) status with both the International Maritime Organisation (IMO) and UNCTAD and takes part in promoting e-commerce through membership of MeCA (Maritime e-Commerce Association) and the Baltic Exchange.

Associated abbreviation:
ISSA International Ship Suppliers Association

International Transport Workers' Federation (ITF)

The International Transport Workers' Federation is an international trade union federation of transport workers' unions. Any independent trade union with members in the transport industry is eligible for membership of the ITF.

624 unions representing 4,400,000 transport workers in 142 countries are members of the ITF. It is one of several Global Federation Unions allied with the International Confederation of Free Trade Unions (ICFTU).

The ITF's headquarters is located in London and it has offices in Nairobi, Ouagadougou, Tokyo, New Delhi, Rio de Janeiro, Georgetown, Moscow and Brussels.

Objectives

The aims of the ITF are set out in its Constitution (see below). They are:

- to promote respect for trade union and human rights worldwide;
- to work for peace based on social justice and economic progress;
- to help its affiliated unions defend the interests of their members;
- to provide research and information services to its affiliates;
- to provide general assistance to transport workers in difficulty.

Although the range of ITF activities is very wide, they can be best summed up under three key headings:

- representation;
- information;
- practical solidarity.

International Transport Workers' Federation (ITF)

The ITF represents the interests of transport workers' unions in bodies which take decisions affecting jobs, employment conditions or safety in the transport industry, such as the International Labour Organisation (ILO), the International Maritime Organisation (IMO) and the International Civil Aviation Organisation (ICAO).

A major function of the ITF is informing and advising unions about developments in the transport industry in other countries or regions of the world. The ITF also maintains a specialist education department, dedicated to the development of strong and democratic transport unions.

The ITF organises international solidarity when transport unions in one country are in conflict with employers or government and need direct help from unions in other countries.

The kind of solidarity needed can range from protest messages, demonstrations and political pressure, to direct industrial action in the form of strikes, boycotts etc. The ITF's worldwide campaign in the maritime industry against the use by ship owners of Flags of Convenience (FOCs) to escape from national laws and national unions is a good example of solidarity.

The ITF is unique amongst international trade union organisations in having a powerful influence on wages and conditions of one particular group of workers, seafarers working on ships flying Flags of Convenience (FOCs). FOCs provide a means of avoiding labour regulation in the country of ownership, and become a vehicle for paying low wages and forcing long hours of work and unsafe working conditions. Since FOC ships have no real nationality, they are beyond the reach of any single national seafarers' trade union.

The ITF has therefore been obliged to take on internationally the role traditionally exercised by national trade unions—to organise and negotiate on behalf of FOC crews. For 50 years the ITF, through its affiliated seafarers' and dockers' unions, has been waging a vigorous campaign against shipowners who abandon the flag of their own country in search of the cheapest possible crews and the lowest possible training and safety standards for their ships.

Over the past 50 years the ITF's maritime affiliates have developed a set of policies which seek to establish minimum acceptable standards applicable to seafarers serving on FOC vessels. The policies form the basis of an ITF Standard Collective Agreement which sets the wages and working conditions for all crew on Flag of Convenience vessels irrespective of nationality. It is the only agreement normally available to shipowners who run into industrial action. All FOC vessels covered by an ITF-acceptable agreement are issued an ITF Blue Certificate by the ITF Secretariat, which signifies the ITF's acceptance of the wages and working conditions on board. About a quarter of all FOC vessels are currently covered by ITF agreements, thus giving direct protection to over 90,000 seafarers.

Compliance with ITF-recognised agreements is monitored by a network of over 100 ITF inspectors in ports throughout the world. ITF Inspectors are union officials who are either full time or part time working directly with the ITF. By inspecting FOC ships they monitor the payment of wages and other social and employment conditions and if necessary take action to enforce ITF policy. In recent years the number of inspectors has doubled and they are now to be found in ports in every region of the world.

The FOC Campaign is the joint responsibility of the Seafarers' and Dockers' Sections and it is the Fair Practices Committee (FPC) which has, since 1952, provided the key forum by which both sections' representatives have come together to review the day to day running and effectiveness of the Campaign. The involvement of the dockers' unions, whether through direct action or through co-operation with seafarers' unions, has continued to be vital to the success of the Campaign.

The FPC is elected at each Congress by a joint Conference of the Seafarers' and Dockers' Sections. It usually meets once a year (around May–June). Between meetings, urgent matters may be referred to the Fair Practices Committee Steering Group which deals with matters connected with the approval of collective agreements and non-compliance with ITF policy by ITF maritime affiliates, monitors and develops the strategy and direction of the FOC Campaign, and considers new initiatives and means for expanding and developing the FOC Campaign. The role of the FPC steering group is to monitor the activities of the ITF Inspectors and to make recommendations to the appropriate ITF bodies on the practical implementation of FOC policies and on any other matter relating to the effectiveness of the campaign.

While the political campaign has not so far succeeded in preventing a constant growth in ships using FOC registers, the industrial campaign has succeeded in enforcing decent minimum wages and conditions on board nearly 5,000 FOC ships. In addition, the ITF has become the standard-bearer for exploited and mistreated seafarers, irrespective of nationality or trade union membership, throughout the world. Every year millions of dollars are recovered by the ITF and its affiliated unions in backpay and in compensation for death or injury on behalf of seafarers who have nowhere else to turn.

Associated abbreviations:
foc flag of convenience
IMO International Maritime Organization
ITF International Transport Workers' Federation

ISMA Code

ISMA (the International Ship Managers' Association) was established in the spring of 1991 in response to the need to achieve and maintain high standard **ship management** practices. An integral part of the establishment of ISMA was the adoption of the Code of Shipmanagement Standards.

The ISMA Code is based upon the experience of people directly involved in ship management, deriving from intensive discussions and a co-operative effort, assisted by representatives of Lloyd's Register of Shipping, Germanischer Lloyd and Det Norske Veritas classification societies.

In order to introduce the standards for quality management required by the ISMA Code of Shipmanagement Standards to an even wider field of companies involved in the management of ships, ISMA revised and extended the Code of Shipmanagement Standards to enable those companies solely involved in the management of ships' crews to implement quality management systems.

The revised ISMA Code is issued as being suitable for use by:

—Shipmanagers.
—Crewmanagers.
—Ship and crew management divisions of shipowners.

An independent body is responsible for assessing the quality assured management of ISMA members. The body will audit the company's operations and will conduct shipboard audits annually. The exact number will depend upon the size and composition of the company's fleet.

The ISMA Code is updated and revised according to the following procedures:

(i) The ISMA Code Committee together with the representatives of the independent auditing body meet at least once a year to discuss the need for updating and/or revising of the ISMA Code.
(ii) The ISMA Secretariat will co-ordinate and circulate information regarding the ISMA Code.
(iii) Revisions or amendments to the ISMA Code are authorised by the ISMA Executive Committee.

It is hoped that the ISMA Code will continue to be welcomed by the industry and further strengthen its confidence in the efficiency, reliability and standards of those companies involved in the providing of management services to the industry who have introduced QA systems and by their having been certified by an independent auditing body.

Scope and field of application

The Code of Shipmanagement Standards is issued in three parts as follows:

Part 1 General Services
Part 2 Crewmanagement Services
Part 3 Shipmanagement Services

A crewmanager will be required to comply with Parts 1 and 2 only. A shipmanager will be required to comply with Parts 1,2 and 3.

The Code of Shipmanagement Standards (ISMA Code) specifies requirements for quality assured ship and crewmanagement services.

Compliance with the applicable Parts (1 + 2 or 1 + 2 + 3) of the ISMA Code by a company will ensure that a company operates with quality assured systems for crewmanagement or shipmanagement.

The ISMA Code specifies those areas where systems and controls are essential to meet the objectives. The requirements of the ISMA Code apply to both shorebased and shipboard management.

Verification of compliance with the ISMA Code will be carried out by an independent body.

The requirements of the ISMA Code apply to all ships under management; where a Management Agreement does not require the company to provide all of the services detailed in the ISMA Code, the company shall, having received certification, apply the relevant requirements of the ISMA Code to the services it provides.

By the ISMA Code, the International Ship Managers Association establishes quality assured systems within its scope and field of application. The ISMA Code is not intended to be read or construed as a product guarantee/warranty.

Objectives

To provide quality assured crewmanagement services, through the expedience of arranging employment of seafarers for the purpose of manning each ship (in accordance with the conditions of limitation imposed by the individual management agreement):

- with qualified, medically fit and suitably experienced seafarers;
- with adequate numbers of seafarers for the trade in which it is engaged;
- in accordance with the requirements for training, certification and watch-keeping standards of the particular flag state;

so as to provide, but not be limited to, the human element of:

- operating the ship safely and efficiently;
- avoiding injuries to personnel and loss of life;
- conserving and protecting the environment;
- complying with all applicable national and international rules and requirements;
- applying recognised industry standards when appropriate;
- providing the client with sufficient, accurate and timely information about the status of the crew;
- continuous development of skills and systems in the business;
- preparing for emergencies.

To provide quality assured shipmanagement services, which entails, but is not limited to:

- operating the ship and transporting cargo safely and efficiently;
- avoiding injuries to personnel and loss of life;
- conserving and protecting the environment;
- protecting the owners' assets that are entrusted to the company;
- complying with statutory and classification rules and requirements;
- applying recognised industry standards when appropriate;

ISMA Code

- providing the client with sufficient, accurate and timely information about the operation and status of the ship;
- continuous development of skills, systems and understanding of the business;
- preparing for emergencies.

Reference

Requirements of the following documents are incorporated in the ISMA Code:

- ISO-9002 Quality Systems—Model for Quality Assurance in Production and Installation;
- IMO—Resolution A-741(18). International Management Code for the Safe Operation of Ships and for Pollution Prevention (International Safety Management (ISM) Code).
- Note: The requirements of the ISM Code will not be applied to a company that only provides crewmanagement services.

The requirements of the following documents are to be complied with in meeting the requirements of the ISMA Code:

- appropriate national and international rules and regulations for the relevant ship;
- appropriate classification society rules and regulations for the relevant ship;
- appropriate industry guidelines including codes, guidelines and standards recommended by IMO, flag administrations, classification societies and other maritime industry organisations as pertinent and relevant.

The ISMA Code covers the following:

Part 1 (for Crewmanagers and Shipmanagers)
Business Ethics
Management Agreement
Organisation
Shorebased Personnel
Accounting
Management System
Corrective and Preventative Actions
Document Control
Records
Internal Audits
External Audits

Part 2 (for Crewmanagers and Shipmanagers)
Personnel
Safety
Environmental Protection
Contingency Planning
Cost Efficiency, Purchasing and Contracting

204

Support
Insurance
Compliance with Rules and Regulations
Communication Procedures

Part 3 (for Shipmanagers)
Personnel
Safety
Environmental Protection
Contingency Planning
Operational Capability
Cost Efficiency, Purchasing and Contracting
Maintenance and Maintenance Standard
Technical Support
Insurance
Certification and Compliance with Rules and Regulations
Cargo Handling and Cargo Care
Communication Procedure

Associated abbreviation:
ISMA International Ship Managers' Association

See also:
Classification societies
International Ship Managers' Association (ISMA)
International Safety Management (ISM) Code

Laytime—Calculation

It is the responsibility of the ship's agent at the loading and discharging ports to prepare a **statement of facts**, detailing the dates and times of arrival of the ship and the commencement and completion of loading and discharging. This statement also details:

—the quantity of cargo loaded or discharged each day;
—normal working hours at the port;
—the hours worked and the hours stopped with the reasons for the stoppages, such as bad weather, a strike or breakdown of equipment;
—the number of gangs;
—any relevant remarks.

This document, sometimes referred to as a **port log**, forms the basis for the **time sheet**, also completed by the agent. This is a similar document to the statement of facts, but its purpose is to correlate the time used with the laytime allowed. It has a section in which laytime is computed and this provides the parties with the necessary information to compute demurrage or despatch.

Laytime—Calculation

The Baltic and International Maritime Council (BIMCO) publishes two standard statements of facts, one all-purpose, the other for oil and chemical tank vessels. This latter type has provision for commencement of ballasting and deballasting, connection and disconnection of hoses and other operations in which these vessels are involved. Both types of statements are in two formats: short form and long form, the long form being for long and complex cargo operations. BIMCO also publishes a standard time sheet (short form and long form formats). Both the statement of facts and the time sheet are recommended both by BIMCO and by the Federation of National Associations of Ship Brokers and Agents (FONASBA).

Laytime can be expressed as a number of **tonnes per day** or a number of **workable hatches per day**. In the latter case, it is necessary to divide the quantity of cargo in the largest hatch by the quantity per workable hatch per day as stipulated in the charter-party. Difficulties of interpretation may arise in the calculation of laytime when expressed in this way, particularly if the ship has hatches capable of being worked by two gangs simultaneously. A workable hatch is also known as a **working hatch**.

What constitutes a day needs to be made clear in order to avoid disputes. A **working day** is a day when normal working is carried out in a port. A **working day of 24 hours** is a period of time which contains 24 normal working hours. If it is the custom of a port that eight hours represents the normal working time per day, then a working day of 24 hours would be considered as three laydays. A **working day of 24 consecutive hours** equates to one layday. The word consecutive was introduced after it was ruled in court that a working day of 24 hours might be considered as more than one layday according to the length of normal working time each day in a port. **Running days** are consecutive calendar days of 24 hours including weekends and holidays.

Laytime may be reversible, non-reversible, averaged or all purposes, as the case may be, for the purpose of calculating demurrage or despatch. If **reversible**, the charterer may, if he so wishes, add the time for loading to the time for discharging. If **non-reversible**, these times must be treated separately.

When laytime may be **averaged**, the charterer is allowed to offset the time used in loading cargo against that used in discharging. If, for example, a charterer earns five days' despatch at the loading port but there is a period of three days' demurrage at the discharging port, the charterer has a net claim for two days' despatch money.

If despatch money is to be calculated on **working time saved**, the charterer can deduct laytime used from lay time allowed. If, for example, a charter-party provides for six laydays for loading and the charterer uses $2\frac{1}{2}$ days, he is entitled to $3\frac{1}{2}$ days' despatch money. This is also known as **laytime saved**. If, on the other hand, despatch is to be calculated on **all time saved**, time used for loading and/or discharging, as the case may be, is deducted from a theoretical time up to the expiry of laytime which includes excepted periods. For example, a charterer may be allowed 10 days for loading. He calculates the expiry of lay-time taking account of excepted periods, such as weekends, and arrives at a theoretical number of calendar days, say 15. Should he use only four days to load, he is entitled to 11 days' despatch money.

If laytime is **all purposes**, or simply **purposes**, it is expressed as one figure, for example 72 hours all purposes, representing a combined time for loading and discharging.

Charter-parties normally contain provisions, varying from one contract to the next, for periods during which any time used for loading or discharging does not count for the purpose of calculating demurrage or despatch, other than by prior agreement. Such periods are known as **excepted periods**. These periods must be expressly stated in the charter-party and may include weekends, public holidays, bad weather and time used shifting from anchorage to berth. It should be noted that, once laytime has expired, time counts during excepted periods in the calculation of demurrage. Time during excepted periods is sometimes termed **suspension of laytime**.

Whether, and to what extent, time counts during weekends and public holidays depends on the specific provision. Variations are:

—Saturdays, Sundays and holidays excepted (or excluded)
—Saturdays, Sundays and holidays included
— Sundays and holidays included
—Sundays and holidays excepted (or excluded)
—Fridays and holidays excepted (or excluded). This applies to those countries where Friday is the Sabbath, notably in the Middle East.

Bad weather may also be an excepted period. A **weather working day** is a day on which work is normally carried out at a port and which counts as laytime unless loading or discharging ceases because of bad weather or would have ceased had work been in progress. The difference between this and **weather permitting** is that, in the latter case, laytime stops only when work stops as a result of bad weather.

Excepted periods, when specified in the charter-party, may be accompanied by the term **unless used**. In this case, time will count if used to the extent specified in the charter-party, sometimes all time, sometimes half. Alternatively, the charter-party will specify that time will not count during an excepted period **even if used**.

Associated term:
Average (laytime) (to)

Associated abbreviations:
fhex Fridays and holidays excepted (or excluded)
shex Sundays and holidays excepted (or excluded)
sshex Saturdays, Sundays and holidays excepted (or excluded)
shinc Sundays and holidays included
wwd weather working day
wp weather permitting

See also:
Laytime—commencement
Penalties

Laytime—Commencement

Time allowed by the shipowner to the voyage charterer or bill of lading holder in which to load and/or discharge the cargo. It is expressed as a number of days or hours or as a number of tonnes per day (*see further below*). These days are known as laydays. Laytime itself is often abbreviated to **time**, especially in the expressions **time to count** or **time does not count**, both of which are used to describe periods during which time accumulates or not, as the case may be, in the calculation of demurrage or despatch.

The charter-party normally contains provisions for:

—the period during which the shipowner must present the ship;
—when laytime commences;
—periods when laytime does not count, for instance during bad weather, weekends or holidays;
—when laytime is exceeded, when demurrage or damages for detention become payable;
—how laytime is to be calculated, such that demurrage or despatch may be computed; and
—when laytime has not been fully used, when despatch may be payable.

All of these are further explained below and in **Laytime—calculation** *and* **Demurrage**.

The shipowner (or master on his behalf) must **tender notice of readiness** to the charterer that the ship has arrived at the port of loading and is ready to load. There is normally a provision in the charter-party for the **commencement of laytime**, which is often at a certain hour after notice of readiness has been tendered by the master. The period during which the owner must tender this notice is called **laydays cancelling**. This period is expressed as two dates, for example, laydays 25 March cancelling 2 April, or, when abbreviated to **laycan**, laycan 25 March/2 April. The charterer is not obliged to commence loading until the first of these dates if the ship arrives earlier and may have the option of cancelling the charter if the ship arrives after the second of the dates, known as the **cancelling date**.

If the ship is likely to be delayed in reaching the loading port, the shipowner may ask the charterer **to extend the cancelling date**. If the charterer agrees, the contract is amended accordingly. If not, the charterer may have the option to cancel the charter either before the cancelling date by mutual consent or after the cancelling date within a time specified in the charter-party. Alternatively, the shipowner may be obliged to present his ship at the loading port, however late.

Different charter-parties have different provisions for the commencement of laytime when the ship has arrived at the port and has tendered notice of readiness: **whether in berth or not** means that laytime will start to count whether or not the ship has reached the berth; in the case of a provision **whether in port or not**, the ship does not need to be within the port limits—she need only arrive at the anchorage; **whether in free pratique or not** will mean that laytime will start to count whether pratique has been granted by the authorities or not.

Free time is the period between the time a ship is ready to load or discharge, having given notice of readiness, and the time laytime commences in accordance with the charter-party. During this time, the charterer is not obliged to load or discharge. It is important to make a provision in the charter-party for the effect on laytime should the charterer or receiver elect to load or discharge during this period.

Associated abbreviations:
l/c laycan
wibon whether in berth or not
wifpon whether in free pratique or not
wipon whether in port or not

Associated term:
Extension of the cancelling date

See also:
Laytime—calculation

Liner and conference tariffs

The **liner tariff** or **freight tariff**, or **conference tariff** in the case of a liner conference, is a schedule published by a shipping line (or conference as the case may be) containing freight rates for a variety of commodities likely to be carried by the line. Tariffs are produced by shipping lines and by conference **secretariats** on behalf of the member lines of a conference. Some tariffs contain the lines' rules, but sometimes these are published in a separate document. The rules contain the general terms and conditions of the shipping line or conference.

The liner tariff is the bible of shipping lines and liner conferences and is very much the framework within which shippers and shipping lines carry on business together. The essentials contained in the tariff are:

- a list of the member lines;
- the geographical area covered;
- an index to the tariff classes;
- the range of freight rates;
- measurement rules;

Liner and conference tariffs

- pallet rules;
- heavy lift charges;
- long length cargo additional charges;
- tariff currency.

One of the pages of the conference tariff will list all the shipping lines who are members of that conference. It is important for a shipper tied by a contract or agreement of one sort or another to know, when booking his cargo, which are **member lines** and which are **non-conference lines**. This may not be as straightforward as it seems if a conference has, say, over 30 member lines.

Shipping is an international business in which vessels of many nationalities compete to carry cargo. Shipping lines incur costs and derive revenue in different currencies according to the trades in which they are involved. It is for convenience therefore that the lines elect to quote freight rates in a single currency, the **tariff currency**. By far the most common tariff currency worldwide is the US Dollar, a traditionally stable currency and one in which some costs such as fuel and charter rates are normally expressed. Tariffs can be expressed in any currency and even artificial currencies such as the ECU (European Currency Unit) have been used.

Mainly because the tariff is expressed in, for instance, Dollars does not mean that freight is paid in that currency. Very often, freight is converted to, and paid in, the local currency. Various elements of the contract with the shipping line are normally both quoted and paid in the local currency; examples are inland haulage and Terminal Handling Charges or FOB charges.

Every commodity likely to be carried is listed in alphabetical order and each is placed in a category known as a **class** corresponding to a rate of freight. Most tariffs contain listings of hundreds of different commodities, the exact number and precise description of which vary from one tariff to another according to past experience of each line or conference. It is normally both impractical and unnecessary for every one of the many commodities to have a different freight rate and so frequently they are grouped together into a relatively small number of classes. The reason for having classes and different freight rates is that these reflect the cost of handling and the varying risks which the shipping lines take on when carrying goods with wide-ranging values, shapes, sizes and susceptibilities to damage.

The class numbers are set out on separate pages in the tariff together with their associated freight rates. This method is preferable to putting a freight rate against every commodity in the tariff since every page would need to be reprinted each time the rates changed. Freight on less than container load and breakbulk shipments is generally payable per tonne (1000 kilogrammes) or per cubic metre, whichever produces the greater revenue for the shipping line. Full container load rates are normally per 20-foot general purpose container. The method of calculating rates for 40-foot containers will either be found on the same tariff page as the rates for 20-foot containers or, if not, then on a nearby page. Very often, rates for 40-foot boxes are double those of 20-footers (note the colloquialisms). If the goods require shipment in a special container, such as a refrigerated or open top container, then an additional charge may apply. A list of these special containers, together with the associated charge, appears elsewhere in the tariff.

Liner tariffs should contain every commodity likely to be carried but it will be appreciated that, with the large number of products, a particular commodity, or variation, may not appear in the tariff. Alternatively, the definition provided by the shipper may not coincide with any tariff entry. To provide for this eventuality, tariffs have additional categories, variously known as **unenumerated**, **not otherwise specified** and **not otherwise enumerated**. A good example of the way in which this works is with machinery: the tariff may have any number of entries for specific items of machinery, such as pile drivers or welding machines, but if the piece of machinery which you happen to be shipping is not listed, the solution is for the shipping line to class it as Machinery and Machines NOS (or NOE or equivalent, according to the particular tariff).

Because of the imprecision of this category and the need for there to be no upward limit on the value of goods so shipped (in order to ensure that all unforeseen goods can be included), the rate is generally higher than the rates for specified commodities. For this reason, it is important for the shipper to discuss the description of the goods with the shipping line to see whether they are, in fact, NOS or whether they fit into one of the enumerated categories.

Tariffs often have a number of classes or categories each of which consists of a single freight rate and a group of commodities to which that rate applies. The classes are numbered for ease of use and may include the suffix W or M denoting that the freight is payable on the weight or measurement respectively. Some tariffs have only one freight rate, known as **freight all kinds**, which as its name suggests, is charged irrespective of the commodity.

Shipping lines must be prepared to carry cargoes of different shapes and sizes and this creates difficulties of stowage particularly for the breakbulk lines but the question here is how unusually shaped cargoes are freighted. Shipping lines have devised rules, known as **measurement rules**, for determining the measurement of goods. Knowing the cubic measurement is necessary either when the freight rate is payable on this basis, that is per cubic metre, or when it is payable on the basis of weight or measurement (per tonne or cubic metre, whichever produces the greatest revenue). In this case, it is necessary to have an agreed method of calculating the measurement.

Possibly the easiest formula is:

$$\text{extreme length} \times \text{extreme width} \times \text{extreme height}$$

Most tariffs apply this formula to each piece or package supplied by each shipper. This presents no difficulties when the cargo has no projections of any sort. Thus a crate 3 metres long by 1.5 metres wide by 1.5 metres high measures 6.75 cubic metres. However, different tariffs have different approaches to projections and, in some cases, the calculation depends on the nature of the projection. Essentially, many tariffs do not count projections which assist in the handling of the goods. These include:

- hooks;
- eyes;
- lugs;
- handles;
- rings;
- skids and runners.

Disagreements do occur sometimes when cargoes have projections which do not fall into the category of lifting or handling aids. For example, a shipper supplies a number of metal bars strapped together into a bundle with all the bars measuring 30 feet long except for one at 40 feet. Some shipping lines take the view that the whole bundle should be measured on the basis that the overall length is 40 feet. This might be justified if the shipping line were unable to make use of the resulting space, known as broken stowage.

From time to time, a shipper will require a freight rate lower than the tariff rate because of particular market circumstances. He then requests a **special rate quotation**. Shipping lines and liner conferences are generally prepared to consider requests for concessions if a shipper has difficulties in this respect. It is up to the shipper to make a good case and he would normally put it in writing as succinctly as possible but including the following important details:

- port(s) or place(s) of shipment;
- port(s) or place(s) of discharge or delivery;
- full details of the commodity requiring a special rate—this may be only one of several commodities from the one shipper;
- dimensions of the pieces to be shipped and details of the packaging;
- period of shipment;
- type of equipment needed, e.g. 20-foot or 40-foot or special container;
- the reason why a special rate is required and the rate level required;
- the anticipated quantity to be shipped.

If a special rate is granted, it may take the form of an amount (per freight ton or per container) or it may be by means of a special rebate on the tariff rate. In some cases, the rate may be all in, that is, inclusive of all extras and surcharges.

One occasion when a shipper or exporter seeks a special rate is when he exports a product for the first time. If the product is unfamiliar to the lines, it may attract an unexpectedly high freight rate (high as far as the shipper is concerned, that is). This is so because the lines are unsure as to the costs and risks associated with it. If the exporter adds the freight rate to his FOB price and finds that his price is too high to enable him to sell, he may decide to approach the lines with a view to obtaining a **promotional rate**. This is a reduced rate which shipping lines sometimes agree to grant to enable exporters to break into a market.

Export orders are often awarded for entire projects, such as the construction of a building complex or factory with delivery spread over a period of time. The shipper may seek a reduced rate from a line or conference in exchange for shipping all the cargo for the one project on ships of that line or conference. Such a rate is called, not surprisingly perhaps, a **project rate**. In the rate application, the shipper specifies the name of the project and mentions it in his shipping instructions for each lot to ensure that the line can identify it an apply the special rate.

Open rates are rates which are not set out in the tariff of a liner conference but are negotiated with any of the member lines, independently of the others, by a shipper. For the most part, this situation arises when a commodity is susceptible to competition from non-conference lines and enables member lines to react quickly to market conditions when assessing the rate level. Cargoes which are not usually carried in liner ships may be **open rated**, that is, subject to open rates. This applies in particular to commodities which may be carried in liner ships in small quantities but not normally in large quantities. For these, tariff rates may apply for small quantities, but for lots over a certain amount specified in the tariff, rates are negotiated by the shipper with the member line of his choice. Often, this rating arrangement will be confined to shipments of a minimum quantity shipped form one port of loading to one port of discharge on one bill of lading. In some trades, member lines have the right of independent action on all cargoes for which no special rates exist. This is a form of open rating.

Every so often, a line or conference decides to increase all the rates in its tariff. This is known as a **general rate increase**. How frequently this happens is a function of the stability of market conditions, movements in costs and the forces of competition. While in some trades the rates may not have increased for several years, in others there may be more than one increase in the space of one year. Both these examples are perhaps the exceptions as, in many trades, increases are on an annual basis.

According to the custom of each trade, notice of a general rate increase is given to shippers. It is the extent of the notice and the way in which it is announced which may vary; commonly, a minimum of 30 days' notice is given of rate increases. In most cases, notice of an increase is published in the shipping press, advising the amount and effective date. General rate increases can take the form of a monetary increase per freight ton or per container or a percentage to be applied to all tariff rates. In some instances, it is a combination of the two types.

Base freight rates in the tariff may be raised by means of a general rate increase. There are periods when rates may remain unchanged, or even fall, as a result of conditions in a particular trade. When the opportunity arises, the conference may impose a **rate restoration** with a view to bringing rates back to previous levels.

Associated abbreviations:
ECU European Currency Unit
fak freight all kinds

fcl full container load
gri general rate increase
lcl less than container load
noe not otherwise enumerated
nos not otherwise specified

See also:
Containers and associated ancillary charges
Freight
Liner
Liner surcharges
Shipping—how it is structured

Liner contracts

Loyalty is a method which conferences use to attract cargoes and to keep shippers, to a greater or lesser degree, from using the services of competitors.

The **deferred rebate** system is the oldest of the methods used by conferences to encourage loyalty from shippers. It is an agreement whereby the shipper is entitled to a rebate from the freight for shipping all of his goods destined for places served by a conference on the ships of the lines who are members of that conference. The rebate applies to shipments made over a specific period of time and is deferred for a further period of time before it is paid, normally several months after the date of shipment. The level of the rebate can vary from conference to conference but typically it is 10%, calculated on the basic freight rate, that is to say the rate before the application of surcharges and any extras.

The shipper is effectively tied to the conference for the combined period of shipment and deferment, for if he ships any goods to one of the places served by the conference on a non-conference ship at any time before receiving his accumulated rebate, he stands to forfeit the entire amount. The only exception to this is when the shipper obtains a **dispensation** from the conference to use an independent line. This situation tends to arise only infrequently, for instance when none of the member lines is able to carry a particular cargo because of its shape or size.

A **loyalty contract** is a more formal arrangement than the deferred rebate system in that a shipper signs a document stating that he will confine shipment of all the goods in question to vessels of member lines in return for a level of service and a discount, known as a **contractor's rebate**, or a special freight rate. This is also known as an **immediate rebate** since it is deducted from the freight at the time the freight is payable. Non-contractors might be entitled to a deferred rebate which is payable at some agreed time, provided that the shipper does not ship any cargoes during this period with a non-conference line to any destination served by the conference. Like the deferred rebate, the immediate rebate is calculated on the base rate of freight. The level is often 9.5% although it too can vary from conference to conference.

Shipment by a **contractor** (the name given to a shipper who signs a loyalty contract) on a non-conference vessel without the dispensation referred to above is considered a breach of contract. The penalty for such a breach is set out in the written contract, often damages for loss of expected business payable to member lines.

One area of contention arises when goods supplied by a contractor are sold on an ex-works, free alongside or free on board basis and shipped by the buyer on a non-conference vessel. Some conferences have viewed this as a breach of the loyalty contract on the part of the supplier.

Traditionally conferences have insisted on 100% loyalty. There is a school of thought that this so inhibits competition from independent lines that something less than 100% should prevail, allowing a measure of flexibility to shippers to use non-conference operators for a relatively small proportion of their shipments. In recent years, different percentages of loyalty have emerged for discussion, the most popular being 70% although it is widely felt that such an arrangement would be at best difficult to police. In different countries, antitrust legislation deals differently with the notion of 100% loyalty. In Canada, for example, conferences may not insist on it, whereas in the USA, it is possible although such contracts do not enjoy the protection of antitrust legislation.

A **dual rate contract** is a system whereby a liner terms and conditions to all shipments but whose tariff contains two sets of rates: one level for shippers who undertake to ship all, or an agreed amount, of their cargo on conference line ships, and a higher rate for all other shippers.

Other types of contract include the **service agreement** or **service contract**. This is an agreement in which the shipper undertakes to ship all of his cargo, or some agreed amount or percentage, as the case may be, on conference line ships for a specific period in return for an agreed level of freight and level of service. Some contracts require the shipper to achieve a minimum quantity of cargo over the agreed period.

The service contract is a more recent development in the history of shipper/shipping line arrangements. It is worth making a comparison between this arrangement and traditional loyalty.

- cargo—in a service contract the shipper is required to commit a certain quantity which could be in tonnes or could be a certain number of containers. Assuming the shipper is able to make reasonably accurate forecasts, he can contract for the carriage of a certain percentage of his anticipated shipments, opting to keep some of his cargo for shipment by other lines;
- area—since the service contract is specific in respect of the cargoes involved, the shipper can restrict his involvement with the line or conference to certain destinations only;
- period—traditional rating has seen freight rates capable of being increased simply after a notice period, often after 30 days. This has in some cases meant

more than one increase in the space of a year and, perhaps more importantly, an element of uncertainty as to the duration of the rates. The service contract, on the other hand, is designed to be valid for a specific period;

- service—by virtue of a quantity being specified, the line or conference is more aware of the level of service necessary to satisfy the shipper. In particular, the shipper will expect the lines to have sufficient space to accommodate the anticipated flow of cargo. Additionally, factors such as transit times and port rotation may be agreed.

In return, the lines may be entitled to damages if the shipper fails to meet the minimum quantity set out in the contract. These may be liquidated damages, that is agreed in advance, as it may be difficult to quantify actual damages.

A discount, known as a **volume-related discount**, is often granted where a shipper achieves certain target figures for cargo shipped. This arrangement is different to the service contract which calls for a minimum quantity. In the volume-related arrangement, the shipper is given several rates, reducing as the quantity shipped increases. Thus on the one hand the shipper has flexibility in not being committed to the one line or conference but on the other hand he has the real incentive of a lower freight rate the more he ships with that line or conference.

Associated abbreviations:
fas free alongside
fob free on board

See also:
Liner shipping—how it is regulated
Liner shipping—how it is structured

Liner ship positions

Shipping lines advertise primarily by means of a **sailing schedule**. This is a printed list of current and future sailings and contains, typically, the names of the ships, receiving dates (*see below*) and sailing dates against each of the load ports, and estimated arrival dates at the discharge ports. It also contains the names and telephone numbers of the line's agents for enquiries, bookings and documentation. Each departure often has a **voyage number** and this is shown on the schedule: many shipping lines employ the same ships again and again between the same ports, and distinguish one voyage from another by means of a sequential number, for example one and up. This voyage number is used on correspondence as a virtual extension to the ship's name.

The ship's **itinerary** is, effectively, that portion of the sailing schedule which contains a list of all the ports which she calls at on a particular voyage to load and discharge cargo, together with her ETAs and ETSs. The rotation is the sequence in which the ship calls at these ports.

The sailing schedule might take the form of an advertisement in the trade press; alternatively, it may be a **sailing card**, literally a card with the schedule printed on, which may be a looseleaf insert in a newspaper or may be sent to the shipping line's customers. More recently, schedules are made available electronically, for example on the Internet.

At the time when the sailing schedule is published, the shipping line may not know which ships will perform all the voyages specified, especially the ones in the schedule which are furthest into the future. Against the vessel name they may show a **vessel TBN (to be nominated)** or a **vessel TBA (to be advised)**, or simply a **TBN** or a **TBA**. In the case of a parcel service, the line may advertise a TBN and charter in a (suitable) ship only once the quantity of cargo is known.

The date when the vessel is expected at a port or place, for example the load port or the discharge port, is the **ETA (estimated time of arrival)**. She may **come forward**, have an estimated date of arrival which is earlier than previously given, or **go back** (alternatively **drop back**) with an estimated date later than previously given.

Once the ship is in the load port and on the loading berth, her **receiving dates** are two inclusive dates between which she can receive cargo for loading. These dates are advertised by the shipping line or its agent. The final date for delivering cargo is the **closing date,** when the ship is said **to close**. Cargo booked but arriving after the ship closes is ordinarily not loaded and is said to be shut out or short shipped (*see also* **Tally (to)**).

Shippers may well be interested in the ship's **ETD, estimated time of departure** and **ETS, estimated time of sailing** as well as her ETA at the discharge port, so that they can keep their customers advised.

Associated abbreviations:
v or **voy** voyage

Associated term:
nomination designation of a specific ship for a particular voyage by the shipowner

Liner shipping—how it is regulated

There are different types of co-operation between shipping lines. The first of these chronologically are **liner conferences**, otherwise known as **shipping conferences**, or simply **conferences**, which came into existence during the late 19th century. There have been many and far-reaching developments to the liner conference system since the 1990s, many of which have focused on their anti-competitive nature, but in many trades they exist in much the same form which is described in the section **Liner shipping—conferences**. Conferences were recognised by the **United Nations Conference on Trade and Development** which established the Convention on a Code of Conduct for Liner Conferences, known widely as the **UNCTAD Liner Code**, in 1974. This had the following objectives and basic principles:

(a) the objective to facilitate the orderly expansion of world sea-borne trade;
(b) the objective to stimulate the development of regular and efficient liner services adequate to the requirements of the trade concerned;
(c) the objective to ensure a balance of interests between suppliers and users of liner shipping services;
(d) the principle that conference practices should not involve any discrimination against the shipowners, shippers or the foreign trade of any country;
(e) the principle that conferences hold meaningful consultations with shippers' organizations, shippers' representatives and shippers on matters of common interest, with, upon request, the participation of appropriate authorities;
(f) the principle that conferences should make available to interested parties pertinent information about their activities which are relevant to those parties and should publish meaningful information on their activities.

National shipping lines were given the right to become members of any conference whose members served that particular country, and be given loading rights. The so-called 40/40/20 rule was devised, whereby shipping lines at both ends of a given trade were entitled to 40% each of the traffic, and other lines 20%. Conference agreements were required to be made available to the authorities of the countries served. The Code allowed for loyalty contracts to be instituted, and for loyalty rebates to be given to shippers. It also provided for consultation with shippers' organisations in respect of, for example, rates, surcharges and changes in tariff conditions. A minimum of 150 days' notice was required for any general rate increase.

Block exemption

In the European Community, Article 81 (1) of the Treaty of Rome of 1986 prohibited organisations from creating agreements or acting in concert in such a way that trade might be affected, such as fixing prices. The Commission granted conferences serving European Community countries a block exemption with a view to retaining stability of service and prices in the liner trades. Elsewhere in the world, various countries followed suit. In Canada, for example, the Shipping Conferences Exemption Act, 1987 (SCEA), exempted certain shipping conference practices, such as collective rate setting, from the provisions of the Competition Act.

In 1995, the European Commission extended block exemption to consortia by introducing the Consortia Regulation. These are groups of shipping lines, often but not necessarily members of a conference, who pool their ships and other resources, such as terminals, to benefit from the economies of scale and provide a combined service in a particular trade. The Regulation prohibits consortia from price fixing but it allows lines to establish groups to gain economies of scale and share equipment. It gives automatic exemptions for lines in consortia but outside conferences where the market share threshold is equal to or below 30% if the consortium operates within a conference and below 35% if it operates outside a conference, and below 50% in those cases approved by the EC.

In the United States of America, the ability of conferences legally to enter set common rates and to share resources, goes back to the Shipping Act of 1916. This was rewritten in 1984 with a new Shipping Act.

In 1998, the Ocean Shipping Reform Act modified the Shipping Act of 1984 by guaranteeing that conference members can take independent action, meaning that shippers were now permitted to deal with individual carriers within a conference and to be able to conclude confidential service contracts with individual carriers within the conference. The Act also prohibited conferences from requiring its members to make individually negotiated rates available to all similarly situated shippers; it eliminated the need for carriers to file tariffs with the FMC although it required lines to publish their tariffs electronically.

In 2002 the Organisation for Economic Co-operation and Development produced a report recommending that anti-trust immunity was inappropriate for conferences as it conferred no benefits on shippers. However, one of its main proposals was that shippers and shipping lines be allowed to agree confidential contracts. The report, while not recommending the scrapping of agreements between shipping lines, did say that these should be subject to scrutiny in case they distorted the market.

Associated abbreviations:
OECD Organisation for Economic Co-operation and Development
OSRA Ocean Shipping Reform Act
SCEA Shipping Conferences Exemption Act
UNCTAD United Nations Conference on Trade and Development

See also:
Liner shipping—how it is structured

Liner shipping—how it is structured

Liner conferences, also referred to as **freight conferences** or **shipping conferences** or simply **conferences**, consist of two or more shipping lines operating a service in common between designated geographical areas, such as Europe to the Far East, generally in one direction only, for example eastbound. The lines, known as **member lines**, agree a set of freight rates and any special rates for shippers, and each line charges the same as the others. The ships used are of types suitable for the trade. Unlike tramp shipping where freight rates are a function of daily supply and demand, conference rates are relatively stable.

Liner shipping—how it is structured

Lines in a conference are governed by the rules of membership which may include loading rights and discharging rights and pooling of cargo. **Loading rights** and **discharging rights** are authorisations granted by all the member lines to a particular member line to load or discharge cargo, as the case may be, on a regular basis at a certain port, coastline or country. **Pooling** is the sharing of cargo or the profit or loss from freight by member lines.

Conferences can be open or closed. A **closed conference** is one in which the member lines vote on the admission of a new line. The purpose of this is to restrict the number of ships in a particular trade. An **open conference** is one which does not require such a vote.

One of the principal functions of the conference is to consult with shippers on all matters of mutual interest, including levels of freight rates and surcharges.

Conferences are administered by **secretariats** who co-ordinate activities on behalf of the member lines. Functions include publishing a common tariff, called a freight tariff or liner tariff, and periodic amendments to it, keeping shippers informed of proposed changes to the level of surcharges and receiving requests from shippers for special freight rates and conveying the responses and offers of the lines.

Conference lines do not necessarily have the monopoly on their particular trade routes: other shipping lines may also operate on the same route but choose not to become a member of the conference, generally in order to have the freedom to set different, often lower, freight rates. Such a line is termed an **independent line**, a **non-conference line** or an **outsider**. In the past, outsiders have had agreements with conferences covering the level of service provided, particularly in respect of the freight rates which it offers to shippers. These operators were known as **tolerated outsiders**. Shippers were allowed by the conference to ship cargo in ships operated by tolerated outsiders without infringing their loyalty contract.

Consortia

These are modern-day groups of shipping lines, often but not necessarily members of a conference, who pool investment including their ships and other resources, such as terminals, to benefit from the economies of scale and provide a combined service in a particular trade. In Europe, they are provided with block exemption to the competition provisions of the Treaty of Rome in respect of their sharing arrangements, but not in respect of price fixing which is not allowed.

Alliances, sometimes termed **strategic alliances**, are the most recent form of grouping. They are similar to consortia in that they share resources, facilities and equipment, but whereas consortia relate to a particular trade, alliances are multi-trade or global. They are not covered by the block exemption given to conferences or consortia.

Discussion agreements, sometimes described as **stabilisation agreements**, are non-binding groupings of lines who collaborate for the purpose of discussing trade factors and recommending freight rate levels, in particular the stabilisation of rates and recommendations on surcharges, although they do not actually set rates.

Recent **mergers and acquisitions** of shipping companies have produced large groupings of lines. On the one hand, they produce economies of scale but, on the other hand, they tend to reduce competition.

See also:
Liner contracts
Liner shipping—how it is regulated
Liner shipping—trades

Liner shipping—trades

Traditionally, liner services operate between ports in an individual **trade**, that is, between ports of loading in a particular country or a particular coastline or ports within a range, and similarly defined ports of discharging. This is sometimes called a **pendulum service**. A route used by a pendulum service is a **pendulum route**. In cases where the ships load or discharge at more than one port, the distance is generally not great between the first and last port of loading (and between the first and last port of discharging) in relation to the ocean crossing. More and more, especially in container trades, ports are divided into main ports, outports and feeder ports. **Main ports** are ports called at regularly; these have a wide range of facilities and can often accommodate a large number of ships. Often they become main ports because of their geographical position combined with a good inland transport infrastructure which makes them suitable for cargoes coming from, or going to, a number of inland points. The increase in size of ships in recent years has also limited the number of ports which can be served, often a question of draught. **Outports** are ports served infrequently or by transhipment. These ports tend not to have sufficient cargo to warrant a regular call. **Feeder ports** are ports which have regular cargoes but these may be insufficient to warrant a call by an expensive deep sea vessel because of an insufficient depth of water or length of berth or inadequate cranage. These are now generally known as **hub and spoke services**, where the main port is the hub and the feeder ports are the spokes. In this case, the shipping line will provide a **feeder ship**, often simply called a **feeder**, normally a smaller ship which takes cargo to and from the nearest main port. Where a ship is only prepared to call at a port when there is a minimum amount of cargo to load or discharge, the shipping line will designate it an **inducement port**.

More recently, some shipping lines have introduced **round the world services**; instead of limiting themselves to one trade, for example Europe to and from South America, these services involve ships sailing in one direction only, for example Europe to the US Gulf, then on to the US Pacific Coast, then the Far East and back to Europe. This reduces the possibility of having to take low-paying cargoes, particularly when there is an imbalance of traffic.

Liner shipping—trades

A variation on this concept of combining several trades into one service involves several consecutive routes, with outward and return voyages, for example from the Pacific Coast of North America to Asia and Europe and back. This is often also called a pendulum service as it features an outward and return voyage which distinguishes it from the round the world service which is in one direction only.

Associated charges

The extra charge which an outport attracts is called an **outport additional**. This in turn is qualified depending on whether the ship has to make a special call at a port or whether the cargo has to be brought to the port of loading, for example in a smaller ship. The outport additional takes two forms depending on whether shipment is direct or not:

- The **direct additional** is an extra charge made by a shipping line for calling at an outport to load or discharge cargo. Very often, such a call will depend on there being a certain minimum quantity of cargo available, sufficient to justify what is known as an inducement call. The charge is per tonne or per cubic metre or per container according to the way that the cargo has been freighted.
- A shipping line may decide that it is not viable to call at a port because the amount of cargo and the revenue derived from it are small in relation to the cost of putting a large ocean vessel in. In this case, a smaller vessel, called a **feeder vessel**, may be used to carry the cargo between the outport and the main port and the cargo transhipped. The charge for this is known as a **feeder additional** or **transhipment additional**. In some trades, the word feeder is used solely for container shipments and transhipment for conventional cargoes while in other trades the two terms are used synonymously. Again the basis of this charge is the same as the basic freight rate, that is, per tonne, per cubic metre or per container.

When a shipper has a large enough cargo to induce (attract) a ship to a (smaller) port not normally called at, the shipping line may charge a direct additional. Such a cargo is termed **inducement cargo**.

If the cargo has to be taken to the port of loading by another ship, known as a feeder ship, a **feeder additional** or **transhipment additional** is usually charged.

Associated abbreviation:
rtw round the world

See also:
Cargo types
Containers
Dry cargo ships
Liner shipping—how it is structured

Liner surcharges

Shipping lines impose surcharges when situations occur which cause them to bear extra costs. This can happen in three ways: events of a temporary nature, fluctuating costs and differences in costs between areas served. Generally, shipping lines will put a **notice to the trade** in suitable newspapers to warn shippers about impending surcharges. Indeed, it is in the rules of some conferences, as agreed with shippers, that such notices be published.

Of events of a temporary nature, the most common reason for unforeseen costs is congestion. Congestion is the accumulation of ships at a port to the extent that ships arriving to load or discharge are obliged to wait for a vacant berth. There are various reasons for congestion, such as strikes, severe weather or a seasonally high number of cargoes. When liner ships suffer prolonged delays as a result of congestion, their operators very often charge shippers a **congestion surcharge**.

In the case of war breaking out in the area of the load or discharge port, shipping lines are obliged to pay additional insurance premiums and may seek to recover this from shippers by means of a **war risk surcharge**, which may be a percentage on the freight.

Certain costs are continually fluctuating, which may cause shipping lines to have difficulty in estimating the total cost of their operation with any accuracy. Most lines reserve the right to impose surcharges in these situations, at least when the costs concerned exceed a certain amount or percentage. The currency adjustment factor is the most common of these surcharges. The bunker surcharge is a charge which reflects fluctuations in the price of bunkers. Some conferences have combined both of these into one surcharge, the currency and bunker adjustment factor.

When the country of shipment is affected by inflation, shipping lines may impose an **inflation adjustment factor** to cover extra costs incurred.

When a shipping line or liner conference has a tariff common to all countries of shipment, but where one of these countries has inordinately higher costs, the line or conference may impose an **area differential**, which is an extra charge on shippers of that country.

Associated abbreviations:
ad area differential
b/s bunker surcharge
cabaf currency and bunker adjustment factor
caf currency adjustment factor
iaf inflation adjustment factor

See also:
Bunker surcharge
Congestion
Currency adjustment factor

Lloyd's Agents

Lloyd's Agents are agents of the Corporation of Lloyd's rather than the Underwriters. The global network comprises over 400 main Lloyd's Agents and over 500 Lloyd's Sub-Agents. The first Lloyd's Agency appointments were made in 1811, primarily for the reporting of shipping movements and although most Agents still carry out this function their main role today is one of conducting or arranging surveys on ships and cargoes. About 250 Agents have also been granted authority to adjust and settle claims arising under Lloyd's certificates of insurance.

Primary role of the Agent

Other than providing shipping information, the main function of Lloyd's Agents is to provide a surveying service and evidence of this is usually reflected in the wording of cargo insurance certificates which often use the clausing: "In the event of loss or damage which may result in a claim under this insurance immediate notice should be given to the Lloyd's Agents at the port or place where the loss or damage is discovered, in order that he may examine the goods and issue a survey report." It should be noted however that in carrying out surveys or other tasks, whether for insurers or other principals, the company would be employed directly by these parties, and would not be acting as an Agent of Lloyd's underwriters unless specifically instructed by them.

Additional roles

Most Lloyd's Agents are traditionally known for conducting a variety of marine surveys. With the increased scope and complexities of insurance some Lloyd's Agents have widened their activities into other fields including aviation and non-marine surveys and investigations. Although much of the routine work of Lloyd's Agents relates to cargo loss or damage, there is a whole range of other cargo and/or hull related survey activity carried out by Lloyd's Agents worldwide. These include: **draft surveys**, **bunker surveys**, ship damage and collision surveys, **on-and-off-hire condition surveys**, **pre-shipments surveys** and **cargo out-turn surveys**.

Surveyors

Many Lloyd's Agents employ their own staff surveyors to carry out day-to-day surveying activities on damaged cargoes and on occasions when specialist knowledge is required they will find and appoint the appropriate person to conduct the survey on behalf of the applicant.

Claims settlement

In 1866 certain selected Lloyd's Agents were authorised by Lloyd's to adjust, settle and purchase from underwriters claims on Lloyd's policies and certificates which made special provisions for the settlement of claims abroad. Around 250 Lloyd's Agents currently have authority to act as claims settling agents.

Agency Department, Lloyd's

Lloyd's Agency Department provides central office support for the agency system. The department, headed by the Controller of Agencies, also conducts inspection of Agents where common business issues and ways of improving still further the standard of professional surveying skills required of Lloyd's Agents are discussed and explored. The Agency Department may be contacted for any Agency user questions and problems, for advice on which Agent to instruct and their capabilities, Agency contact detail changes and for orders of the Directory of Lloyd's Agents.

Alternative spelling:
outturn

London Shipping Law Centre

The overriding aim of the London Shipping Law Centre is to assist the shipping industry to manage commercial risks and legal tasks as effectively as possible. It aims to do this by bringing all sectors of the shipping community together, not just fractions of it.

This provides opportunities to exchange ideas and experiences and to communicate perceptions and expectations in a neutral place without inhibitions.

The opportunity to improve communications is facilitated by formal lectures, role-playing seminars, question and answer sessions, workshops and informal lobbying or gathering for a specific purpose. Paramount considerations for these activities are high quality as well as cost and time efficiency. Most of the events are hosted by members.

A broad range of topics which are of interest to the industry are covered. They explore—by an interactive method—the different commercial and legal pressures that underpin typical recurring problems or the feasibility of new initiatives.

By improving knowledge and expanding meaningful contacts the industry will find it easier to manage their affairs, to make preparation for new legislation and to appreciate the consequences of changes in dispute resolution processes. The Centre is, in a sense, a mutual learning club of quality, for the advancement of its members' interests.

The ultimate aim of the Centre is to promote London, and those who serve the industry, as the world's leading shipping capital.

The London Shipping Law Centre seeks to improve management of risks in all branches of the maritime industry. The definition of "risks" in this context includes primarily legal risks and liabilities that might arise. Legal risks are interwoven with commercial, technical, scientific and financial risks, and to the extent that they are "risks", include those as well.

London Tanker Brokers' Panel

The London Tanker Brokers' Panel was formed in 1953 at the instigation of Shell, who wished to have available an independent and impartial body to act as adjudicators in connection with various contracts they proposed to conclude with both independent owners and affiliated companies.

Early in 1954 Shell decided to introduce a sophisticated indicator of freighting values for use between affiliated companies and drew up the first terms of reference for AFRA (Average Freight Rate Assessment), the calculation of which was entrusted to the Panel. The first results were issued on 1 April 1954.

In 1964, Shell and BP agreed to sponsor AFRA jointly and did so until early 1983 when they decided to relinquish their sponsorship; whereupon the Panel undertook to provide AFRA results on a subscription basis and became a limited company in February 1983.

AFRA results have been acknowledged by taxation authorities of various countries to be an acceptable method of charging freight between affiliated companies of multi-national groups.

Recently the results have been used by oil traders and government agencies as the basis for the freight element in various types of oil sale agreements.

The Panel meets regularly twice each month to ratify the AFRA results and to deal with requests for a variety of rate assessments and will convene additional meetings as client needs arise.

For many years regular clients for rate assessments (apart from AFRA) have included most of the major oil companies and companies such as Kuwait Petroleum, and many other well known companies, some of them oil companies, some oil traders, some shipowners.

Occasionally rate assessments are made for solicitors in connection with arbitration or court proceedings but the Panel does not provide expert witnesses.

Although the Panel will consider any request for assistance in the determination of a tanker charter rate (some have to be refused), most of the assessments it makes fall into the following categories:

(1) Single voyage rate.
(2) Time charter rate.
(3) Consecutive voyage rate.
(4) Contract of affreightment rate.
(5) Assessments of average single voyage rates in specified trades over a specified period for a stipulated size range.

Although the Panel is able to provide current and historical rate assessments, it makes a strong point of always refusing to deal with any forecasting. In other words, it is quite prepared to give its opinion of what the rate for a particular piece of business might have been in the recent or distant past or is today, but it is not prepared to give an opinion as to what the rate might be tomorrow, next week or next month.

Every month the Managing Director of the Panel prepares an agenda for the regular meeting detailing the various assessments (with notes of the relevant terms of reference) which the Panel is required to make.

The agenda is distributed at least one week in advance of the meeting and the directors are therefore able to ensure that they attend the meeting well briefed with details of relevant fixtures and the market situation relating to each assessment.

All the Panel members are active shipbroking companies in the international shipping markets and, individually, participate in negotiations of tanker charters, gathering of market information and providing market reports for their business clients. The participating companies produce statistical and research data for the industry. They have market information based upon those transactions in which their companies are involved and, also, information gathered from the international market which is a major part of their function as shipbrokers.

Where a rate award is requested, the Directors seek to find market fixtures that compare as closely as possible to the terms of reference given for the award being requested. When a close comparison is not available then the Directors will use their judgement as brokers based on whatever information is available which will provide some basis for such judgement and/or their day to day activities involving market intelligence, negotiations in which they may be involved and from their continuous dialogue with owners and charterers and other brokers. Then, in a discussion, a consensus is reached and a decision taken as to the result to be provided to the client.

At its formation, the Panel realised that in order to maintain a reputation for independence and impartiality it was important never to provide details or explanations or enter into discussions as to why or how it arrived at a particular rate assessment and this policy has always been followed. This policy is always made clear to solicitors that seek the Panel's assistance. In most cases, companies using its services will have agreed in advance with the other contractual party that the Panel's assessment will be accepted.

The results of AFRA are available on the first business day of each month. Results are provided for five different deadweight groups as follows:

Medium Range	— 25,000/44,999	(long) tons dw.
Large Range 1	— 45,000/79,999	(long) tons dw.
Large Range 2	— 80,000/159,999	(long) tons dw.
VLCC	— 160,000/319,999	(long) tons dw.
ULCC	— 320,000/549,999	(long) tons dw.

The calculations are made over a monthly period running from the 16th of one month to the 15th of the following month and the assessments represent the weighted average cost of tonnage that has been commercially chartered and is in service for the carriage in bulk of crude oil and/or its dirty products during the calculation period. Certain categories of vessels are excluded from the assessments, e.g. vessels owned by oil companies and Governments (except when operating on commercial charter), vessels employed in specialised trades, such as the carriage of petro-chemicals, luboils and bitumen etc. and vessels engaged in protected trades. Vessels known to be engaged in the carriage of clean products are also excluded; as are vessels used for storage and vessels in lay up.

In each size group tonnage is divided into the following three categories:

  (i) vessels engaged on long term charters;
 (ii) vessels engaged on short term charters;
(iii) vessels engaged on single voyage charters.

Long term is defined as charters originally fixed for a period of 12 months or more or for a number of consecutive voyages that extend over 12 months or more; while short term is defined as charters originally fixed for a period of less than 12 months or for a number of consecutive voyages that do not extend over 12 months or more.

The carrying capacity of each vessel operating during the calculation period in each of these charter categories is calculated on the basis of a standard voyage taking into account the various characteristics of each vessel, e.g. size, type of propulsion, speed and bunker consumption. Then the weighted average rate in US dollars per (metric) tonne for carrying a (metric) tonne of oil on the basis of that standard voyage is obtained for each of these three categories; time charters being converted to a voyage cost per (metric) tonne. The result for each size group is the overall weighted average obtained by multiplying the carrying capacity for each of the charter categories by the weighted average rate for that charter category. The answer thus arrived at in US dollars per (metric) tonne is converted to a Worldscale equivalent on the basis of the standard voyage and this is the published result.

The results are expressed in terms of the Worldscale rates effective on the first day of the calendar month following the last day of the calculating period.

It should be noted that AFRA represents the cost of all chartered tonnage actually operating during the calculation period, irrespective of fixture date. Fixtures concluded during the period under review will not affect the result unless the vessel concerned is actually performing under that fixture during the period. On the other hand, a charter made some years ago will still be reflected in the result, provided the vessel is actually trading under it during the calculation period.

Associated abbreviation:
AFRA Average Freight Rate Assessment

See also:
Worldscale

Manifest

Document containing a full list of the ship's cargo, extracted from information shown on the bills of lading. Each bill of lading consists normally of one sheet of paper and relates to one consignment; the information is generally laid out in boxes covering one side of the sheet and the conditions of carriage are printed on the reverse. The manifest does not follow this format: essentially it is a statement of the bills of lading and has headings taken from the bills which are normally displayed side by side across the page. A page of a manifest could contain one bill of lading or, more often, many, depending on the amount of information relating to each bill of lading. The headings normally include: shipper, consignee, marks and numbers, description of the cargo including its packaging, its dimensions, weight and any remarks as to its condition.

A copy, known as the **outward manifest**, or **Customs manifest**, is lodged by the ship's agent with the Customs authorities at the port of loading. A further copy, known as the **inward manifest**, is similarly lodged at the discharge port, with one copy going to the ship's agent so that the unloading of the ship may be planned in advance.

Manifests do not usually show the freight charged by the shipping line, but some countries require this to be shown so a **freighted manifest** is drawn up, detailing the freight charges bill of lading by bill of lading.

See also:
Bill of lading

Maritime and Coastguard Agency (MCA)

The Maritime and Coastguard Agency was established on 1 April 1998 as an executive agency of the Department of the Environment, Transport and the Regions (DETR). The Agency was created by the merger of The Coastguard Agency (TCA) and the Marine Safety Agency (MSA) and is responsible for carrying out the functions of both organisations.

The MCA is responsible for:

—responding to maritime emergencies, 24 hours a day;
—developing, promoting and enforcing high standards of marine safety;
—minimising the risk of pollution of the marine environment from ships and where pollution occurs.

The MCA carries out inspections and surveys to ensure that high standards are maintained. It educates the maritime community and the public, about how to prevent accidents. However, should an incident occur, it has teams of experts ready to respond at a moment's notice. If the cause of the incident is found to be attributable to negligent behaviour, it has a Prosecution Unit ready to ensure seafarers are held accountable for illegal actions.

Maritime and Coastguard Agency (MCA)

A unique role of MCA is that of Receiver of Wreck, responsible for any finds recovered from UK waters, whatever the archaeological significance.

The MCA is responsible for implementation of the Government's strategy for marine safety and prevention of pollution from ships. The Agency's overall aim is to develop, promote and enforce high standards of marine safety and to minimise the risk of pollution of the marine environment from ships.

The MCA promotes the safety of shipping and safe navigation in UK coastal, estuarial and inland waters in consultation with other Government departments and marine organisations. It develops and promotes the highest reasonable safety standards for various types of vessel by active participation in IMO and EU maritime activities.

The MCA manages the provision of statutory survey and classification services to meet the needs of the UK shipping industry on all types and classes of vessels from passenger ships to small commercial motor and sailing vessels.

The MCA carries out inspections on UK and foreign registered ships using UK ports to ensure they comply with international safety, pollution prevention and operational standards.

The Government is advised by the MCA, in close consultation with industry, on the need for new legislation. It provides the input required for the drafting of this legislation and prepares advice and instructions to the maritime community.

Safety, pollution prevention and operational standards are enforced by the MCA and it applies relevant sanctions.

The MCA provides advice in the event of an accident or on the recommendations of the Marine Accident Investigation Branch or other accident reports and implements relevant recommendations.

The MCA sets standards, monitors training, examination and certification of seafarers and establishes the safe manning levels of UK ships. Counter services are provided at District Marine Offices for the issuing of documents such as boatmaster's licences, discharge books and British Seaman's Cards and for conducting sight tests.

As part of the MCA, the Register of Shipping and Seamen (RSS) provides a central register of UK merchant ships, fishing vessels and other classes of ships. It issues and revalidates various seafarers certificates and documents. RSS also maintains a record of the Merchant Navy Reserve and registers all births and deaths at sea.

Maritime engineering

Great Britain owes much of its long and proud tradition as a seafaring nation to the skills of marine engineers who built and operated the machinery used in the great merchant ships and naval vessels of the past. Nowadays, the tradition continues, with engineers playing an important role in the Royal Navy and the Merchant Navy, in shipbuilding and ship repair, and in industries supplying marine equipment.

The marine engineering role has become so broad that the term **maritime engineering** is now usually preferred, because it reflects a wide range of roles and responsibilities. **Marine engineering** is now generally used in a narrower sense, to describe the design, construction and operation of a vessel's propulsion machinery and associated systems.

There are three main branches of maritime engineering:

1. Ocean engineering

Ocean engineering involves all aspects of the exploration and production of oil, gas and minerals found under the seabed. It includes offshore engineering, platforms and other structures and deep water technology, which makes use of equipment such as remotely operated vehicles to carry out operations on the seabed.

The range of activities includes oil and gas extraction, mining the seabed for minerals, and development of renewable energy resources. Engineers are also actively involved in looking for cost effective, environmentally-friendly ways of disposing of redundant facilities taking into account all considerations.

2. Marine engineering

Seagoing marine engineers are responsible for the safe and efficient operation of a vessel's main propulsion machinery, associated equipment and systems. They work on passenger liners and ferries, ships carrying cargo, offshore oil and gas supply and pipelaying vessels, warships and submarines, and a variety of specialised craft.

The traditional career path in marine engineering is to train with the Merchant Navy or the Royal Navy, gain qualifications and experience at sea and then, after a number of years, to move into a shore-based job.

Engineers employed by merchant shipping companies work on a wide variety of vessels, varying from tankers and container ships to cruise liners and ferries. At sea, their main task is to operate and maintain the ship's main propulsion machinery. They are also responsible for the electrical systems and for the high-tech electronic equipment used on board.

There may be additional responsibilities on specific types of vessel. Many cargo ships have an engineer who specialises in refrigeration, which is essential for the carriage of cargoes such as fruit or meat.

3. Shore-based industries

Many types of shore-based work are open to maritime engineers. Some enter onshore employment after a career at sea; others, particularly graduates, go straight into posts in which they can use their technical education. Shore-based work includes:

—**superintendent engineer**: based in the head office of a shipping company, responsible for the running, maintenance and operation of a fleet of ships;
—classification societies employ **marine surveyors** who ensure that ships and

offshore structures are well designed, well built, and properly maintained;
—engineers with experience at sea or in shore-based industries are recruited as
surveyors by the UK Government's Marine Safety Agency. Their responsibilities include all aspects of marine safety, including the setting, monitoring
and enforcing of safety and pollution prevention on all UK vessels, enforcing
international standards on foreign ships visiting UK ports, and working for
the improvement of international standards.

Other areas include shipbuilding and ship repair, the manufacture of marine
plant and equipment, education and consultancy, the latter especially in survey
work and advice on the insurance of cargo.

There are three main levels of qualification within the engineering profession:
Chartered Engineer (CEng), **Incorporated Engineer** (Eng) and **Engineering
Technician** (EngTech).

The **Institute of Marine Engineers** is a long-established professional
engineering institution based in the City of London. Membership of the
Institute is multi-disciplinary, spanning the whole range of maritime engineering disciplines including marine engineering, ocean (offshore and sub-sea)
engineering, shore-based industries and the marine applications of chemical,
electrical, electronic, mechanical and structural engineering.

The Institute has a strong international dimension. Forty per cent of its
17,000 members are based overseas, and their interests are represented by a
network of 30 overseas branches. There are also 13 branches in the UK. All
branches—both in the UK and overseas—provide local technical and social
facilities.

The Institute gives guidance to and works closely with a wide range of organizations such as the International Maritime Organization (IMO), the Engineering Council, The Maritime Safety Agency, to name a few.

There is a strong interest from abroad in British maritime engineering courses,
and the Institute can advise people overseas considering applying for courses in
the UK. Equally, as the Institute accredits certain overseas qualifications, advice
can also be sought about these.

Associated abbreviations:
MCA Maritime and Coastguard Agency
MSA Marine Safety Agency
RSS Register of Shipping and Seamen

Multimodal transport bill of lading

Multimodal transport involves transport by more than one mode, normally, but
not necessarily, including an ocean leg. Often forwarding agents act as carrier
when offering a door-to-door service and are known as a **multimodal transport
operator** or **MTO**. As with combined transport, the provider of a multimodal

Multimodal transport bill of lading

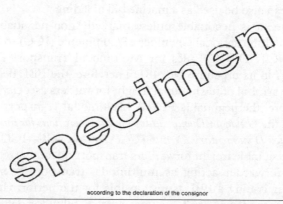

Consignor		
Consigned to order of		
Notify address		
	Place of receipt	
Ocean vessel	Port of loading	
Port of discharge	Place of delivery	

Marks and numbers	Number and kind of packages	Description of goods	Gross weight	Measurement

FBL

NEGOTIABLE FIATA
MULTIMODAL TRANSPORT
BILL OF LADING
issued subject to UNCTAD/ICC Rules for
Multimodal Transport Documents (ICC Publication 481).

Emblem of National Association

ICC

specimen

according to the declaration of the consignor

Declaration of interest of the consignor in timely delivery (Clause 6.2.)		Declared value for ad valorem rate according to the declaration of the consignor (Clauses 7 and 8.)

The goods and instructions are accepted and dealt with subject to the Standard Conditions printed overleaf.

Taken in charge in apparent good order and condition, unless otherwise noted herein, at the place of receipt for transport and delivery as mentioned above.

One of these Multimodal Transport Bills of Lading must be surrendered duly endorsed in exchange for the goods. In Witness whereof the original Multimodal Transport Bills of Lading all of this tenor and date have been signed in the number stated below, one of which being accomplished the other(s) to be void.

Freight amount	Freight payable at	Place and date of issue
Cargo Insurance through the undersigned ☐ not covered ☐ Covered according to attached Policy	Number of Original FBL's	Stamp and signature
For delivery of goods please apply to:		

Multimodal transport bill of lading (FIATA FBL)

transport contract accepts responsibility for the goods from the time they are received into his care until the time they are delivered at destination.

The two types of document evidencing a contract for multimodal transport are the **multimodal transport bill of lading** and the **multimodal transport sea waybill**. Both the Baltic and International Maritime Council (BIMCO) and the International Federation of Freight Forwarders Associations (FIATA) have published multimodal transport bills of lading covering this situation. Additionally BIMCO have published a multimodal transport sea waybill. The terms and conditions of the waybill follow those of the bill of lading, except that the waybill is non-negotiable and cannot be endorsed to a third party. The waybill contains a clause to this effect.

(The following definition, notes and sample document are provided by FIATA.)

The FIATA Multimodal Transport Bill of Lading (FBL) is a carrier-type transport document set up by FIATA for the use by freight forwarders acting as multimodal transport operators (MTO).

The FBL can also be used as a marine bill of lading.

The document is negotiable unless marked "non-negotiable". It has been deemed by the International Chamber of Commerce (ICC) to be in conformity with the UNCTAD/ICC Rules for Multimodal Transport Documents published by ICC in its brochure No. 481. Therefore, the FBL bears the ICC logo alongside the symbol of the national freight forwarders association.

Furthermore, the negotiable FIATA Multimodal Transport Bill of Lading is referred to in the *Guide for Documentary Credit Operations for the Uniform Customs and Practice for Documentary Credits (UCP 500)* of ICC (ICC publication No. 515) as an acceptable freight forwarders transport document.

A freight forwarder acting as multimodal transport operator (MTO) as marine carrier issuing a FBL is responsible for the performance of transport. The freight forwarder not only assumes responsibility for delivery of the goods at destination, but also for all carriers and third parties engaged by him for the performance of the whole transport.

By issuing a FBL, the freight forwarder accepts a basic liability limit of 666.67 SDR per package or unit, or 2 SDR per kilogramme of gross weight of the goods lost or damaged, whichever is the higher (Art. 8.3 of the FBL conditions) or, if a multimodal transport does not include carriage of goods by sea or inland waterways, a basic liability limit of 8.33 SDR per gross weight (Art. 8.5 of the FBL conditions). When loss or damage to the goods can be attributed to a particular stage of transport in a multimodal transport operation, the freight forwarder's liability is limited according to mandatory national or international law applicable to this stage of transport (Art. 8.6a of the FBL conditions).

When issuing a FBL, the freight forwarder should ensure:

(1) that he has taken over the goods specified therein and that the right of disposal of the goods is solely vested in him;

(2) that the goods appear to be in apparent good order and condition;

(3) that details on the document correspond with the instructions he has received;

(4) that responsibility for cargo insurance cover has been agreed upon with the consignor; and

(5) that it is clearly specified how many original FBLs are issued.

Freight forwarders issuing FBLs have to insure their liability in accordance with the FBL conditions.

Associated abbreviations:
FIATA International Federation of Freight Forwarders Associations
mt multimodal
MTO multimodal transport operator
SDR Special Drawing Rights
UNCTAD United Nations Conference on Trade and Development

See also:
Bill of lading
Combined transport
Waybill

Multipurpose ships

Ships capable of carrying several types of cargo, either in combination with each other or as full cargoes. This flexibility reduces the number of voyages in ballast and makes such ships adaptable to changing trade patterns. There are a number of different types of multipurpose ship, and the principal ones are mentioned here.

Bulk newsprint carrier: ship designed to carry rolls of newsprint, having gantry cranes to lift the cargo on and off. Such ships may also be suitable for the carriage of timber cargoes and containers, thus reducing the number of voyages in ballast.

Bulk/container carrier or container/bulk carrier: ship designed to carry a full cargo of containers or dry bulk, such as grain, coal and ore.

Con-ro ship *or* **ro-ro/containership**: ship designed to carry both shipping containers and ro-ro cargo. She has cell guides within which to accommodate the containers and also has decks to take roll-on/roll-off cargo.

Container/barge carrier: ship designed to carry barges and shipping containers at the same time. The barges are floated into the ship through large bow doors. The containers are stowed on deck.

Container/pallet carrier: ship designed to carry shipping containers and palletised goods. Although the ship is capable of carrying general cargo, the interior of the ship generally carries paper products on pallets. These are loaded through a side door, taken by pallet lift (pallet elevator) to the appropriate level and thence by fork-lift to the desired positions. The containers are carried on deck. This type of vessel is sometimes called a pallet carrier.

Ore/bulk/oil carrier *or* **bulk-oil carrier** *or* **oil/bulk/ore carrier**: large ship designed to carry cargoes either of ore or other bulk commodities, or of oil. The cargo is loaded into central holds and, if oil, into side tanks as well.

Ore/oil carrier: ore is carried only in the central holds whereas oil is carried in wing tanks and in the central holds as well, if required.

Paper/container carrier: ship designed to carry shipping containers and paper, the latter normally in the form of rolls. She has box-shaped holds suitable for the stowage of containers, a dehumidifying system to remove moisture from the holds, since dry conditions are necessary when carrying paper. The rolls are loaded through doors in the side of the ship.

Passenger/train/vehicle carrier: vessel having, typically, three decks onto which vehicles, both cars and trucks, are carried and having rails on several decks allowing wagons to be transported. The vessel has overnight accommodation for passengers and may well have entertainment and shopping facilities on board. The vehicle decks are inter-connected by internal ramps.

Passenger/vehicle ferry: vessel designed to carry passengers (with or without cars) and commercial vehicles with their drivers, usually on short sea crossings. Vehicles are driven on and off the ship on ramps and spend the voyage on special decks, with private cars normally kept separate from commercial vehicles.

Associated abbreviations:
obo ore/bulk/oil carrier
o/o ore/oil carrier
ro-ro roll-on/roll-off

See also:
Ship types

Nautical Institute

The Nautical Institute is an international professional body for qualified seafarers and others with an interest in nautical matters. It provides a wide range of services to enhance the professional standing and knowledge of members who are drawn from all sectors of the maritime world.

Its work is available to the whole industry to help improve the safety and efficiency of shipping. Its monthly journal *Seaways*, books, web services and projects help to provide real solution to problems facing the industry and provide mariners input to decision makers internationally and nationally.

The Nautical Institute is a thriving international professional body for qualified mariners—with over 40 branches worldwide, and over 6,500 members in over 110 countries.

Its objectives are to promote and co-ordinate in the public interest the development of nautical studies in all its branches by:

- Encouraging and promoting a high standard of qualification, competence and knowledge among those in control of seagoing craft including non-displacement craft.
- Facilitating the exchange and publication of information and ideas on nautical science, encourage research and publish its results.
- Establishing and maintaining appropriate educational and professional standards of membership.
- Co-operating with Government Departments and other bodies concerned with statutory and other qualifications, and with universities and other educational institutes and authorities in the furtherance of education and training in nautical science and practice.
- Encouraging the formation of Branches and professional groups in different areas worldwide.

The Marine Accident Reporting Scheme is a confidential reporting system run by The Nautical Institute to allow full reporting of Accidents (and Near Misses) without fear of litigation.

Organisation for Economic Co-operation and Development (OECD)

The aim of the OECD, pursuant to Article 1 of the Convention signed in Paris on 14 December 1960, and which came into force on 30 September 1961, is to promote policies designed:

—to achieve the highest sustainable economic growth and employment and a rising standard of living in Member countries, while maintaining financial stability, and thus to contribute to the development of the world economy;

—to contribute to sound economic expansion in member as well as non-member countries in the process of economic development; and

—to contribute to the expansion of world trade on a multilateral, non-discriminatory basis in accordance with international obligations.

The original member countries of the OECD are Austria, Belgium, Canada, Denmark, France, Germany, Greece, Iceland, Ireland, Italy, Luxembourg, the Netherlands, Norway, Portugal, Spain, Sweden, Switzerland, Turkey, the United Kingdom and the United States. The following countries became members subsequently through accession at the dates indicated hereafter: Japan (28 April 1964), Finland (28 January 1969), Australia (7 June 1971), New Zealand (29 May 1973), Mexico (18 May 1994), the Czech Republic (21 December 1995), Hungary (7 May 1996), Poland (22 November 1996) and the Republic of Korea (12 December 1996). The Commission of the European Communities takes part in the work of the OECD (Article 13 of the OECD Convention).

Organisation for Economic Co-operation and Development (OECD)

OECD has a Maritime Transport Committee, one important function of which is to report annually on "developments of interest within the framework of longer-term trends in international shipping and trade". The Committee has also involved itself in matters such as competition in international liner shipping, specifically the impact which diverging competition rules are having on the development on world trade in goods. The Committee has also been concerned with assessing the competitive advantages obtained by shipowners operating substandard ships.

Associated abbreviation:
OECD Organisation for Economic Co-operation and Development

Penalties

In most voyage charters, the charterer is allowed by the shipowner a certain amount of time within which to load and/or discharge the cargo. This time is known as **laytime**. It can be expressed as a number of tonnes per day, a number of tonnes per (workable) hatch per day or simply a number of hours or days. There are periods when laytime does not count; these may be weekends, public holidays or bad weather depending on the particular charter-party. Once laytime has been used up, the charterer is very often liable for **demurrage**, an agreed sum of money paid for every extra day taken to load or discharge the cargo.

There are many variations in the way that laytime and demurrage can be described which will affect the final calculation. The **rate of demurrage**, normally an amount of money per day, or part of a day on a pro rata basis, is agreed in the charter-party (or liner bill of lading).

One point is worthy of note: if the charterer has used all the laytime allowed in the charter-party before completing loading, demurrage is calculated continuously until completion; no allowances are made for so-called excepted periods such as holidays or weekends. This is a general rule which applies to loading and discharging and gives rise to the expression **once on demurrage, always on demurrage**.

Laytime is calculated on a **time sheet** and this is used as the basis of the calculation of demurrage.

Despatch, or **despatch money**, is the amount paid by the shipowner to the charterer, shipper or receiver, as the case may be, for loading and/or discharging in less than the time allowed in the charter-party. It is not found in every case, but in those cases where it is offered by a shipowner, it is an incentive to cargo interests to load or discharge as quickly as possible. Very often, the rate of despatch is half the rate of demurrage. When no despatch is agreed, the offer will show the amount of demurrage followed by the term **free despatch**. When set at half the rate of demurrage, it is termed half despatch and often appears in an abbreviated form in an offer or counter-offer as, for example, $5,000 **d 1/2 d** ($5,000 per day demurrage, $2,500 per day despatch).

Damages for detention are very similar to demurrage in that their purpose is to recompense a shipowner for an undue delay to his ship when loading or discharging if these operations are the responsibility of the charterer, shipper or receiver. These damages occur in two situations: firstly, in those charter-parties where demurrage is set for a certain number of days, damages for detention become payable at the expiry of that period and continue until completion of loading or discharging, as the case may be. An example of this is the universally accepted general purpose voyage charter, the Gencon, which specifies 10 running days on demurrage. Although there is no express provision for this period being exceeded, damages for detention are implied in the contract. The second situation is when no provision is made at all in the charter-party for damages should laytime be exceeded. Here too, damages for detention are implied but this time they take effect as soon as laytime expires, there being no provision for demurrage.

Where a charter-party does contain a provision for demurrage, the rate is agreed in advance. This is known in legal parlance as liquidated damages. Damages for detention, by contrast, are unliquidated, that is to say they are not agreed in advance but are determined after the event and generally are a reflection of the daily operating expenses of the shipowner.

Chartered ships are not alone in being delayed by their users. The advent of containerisation has meant that an enormous amount of equipment, in the form of shipping containers of many different types, is spread around in the countries at each end of the many shipping routes served by containership lines. While some containers are in transit, overland or on the high seas, others are in yards, depots, terminals and ports waiting for a shipper to load his cargo or a receiver to unload. In an FCL shipment, it is up to the merchant to load and discharge the container. Containers cannot earn money for the shipping line if they are sitting idle waiting for something to happen and hence penalties exist for merchants who fail to conclude their cargo operations and release the equipment back to the shipping line within a certain time.

Demurrage on equipment is a charge on the merchant for keeping equipment at the container yard or container terminal or berth beyond the free time specified in the liner tariff. It is essentially referred to in connection with FCL shipments, in other words, where the merchant controls the entire box. Most frequently, it arises at the terminal or yard in the country of destination when the merchant fails to strip (unload) the container soon enough. Less often, it can arise in the country of shipment when the merchant does not permit the shipping line to ship the container on the first available vessel.

There are three elements in the analysis of demurrage:

* amount of free time—taking the terminal in the country of destination as the commonest example, free time is the period within which the merchant can unload the container and make it available to the carrier without incurring demurrage charges. This period varies from line to line and country to country but is typically between two and five working days;

Penalties

- commencement of free time—free time may be two to five days. The starting point varies widely but could be the date of arrival of the container at the container yard or, if delivery is at the port, free time could commence immediately after discharge from the ship or one or two days after completion of discharge. All of this depends on the terms of the particular tariff;
- amount of demurrage—every line or conference has its own way of calculating demurrage. In all cases, it is a lump sum per container per day; but the period of demurrage varies: some lines exclude the first weekend; some charge an amount for an initial period followed by an increased amount. Others have steadily increasing charges the longer the container remains to be unpacked. Often, there will be an additional charge for refrigerated containers where generators must be kept working.

Demurrage can also be a daily charge payable by the user of a railway wagon (railcar) for detaining it beyond the time allowed. This is known as **wagon demurrage** or, in North America, **car demurrage**.

While demurrage charges on equipment relate to FCL shipments, LCL shipments can incur **storage charges**. These charges are payable by the merchant for failing to take delivery of the goods at the container freight station within the specified period (the container freight station is the place where goods for export are grouped together into containers and where imported goods shipped in this way are unpacked from the container for collection by the consignees). As with demurrage, there are three key elements:

- amount of free time—typically five to seven days or it could be the custom of the port;
- commencement of free time—this again varies from trade to trade. In some cases, it commences when the container arrives at the container freight station. In others, it runs from the day the container is unpacked or from the following day;
- amount of charges—the tariff will specify the amount per freight ton per day for storage at the container freight station. The carrier may have an option to transfer goods overdue for collection to a warehouse and may charge the merchant for this operation.

Demurrage and storage charges relate to delays occurring at the port or terminal or container yard or container freight station. Delays do also occur to containers and trailers at the supplier's or receiver's premises or at private yards where the merchant effects loading or unloading. If a merchant detains equipment in this way beyond the free time specified, he is liable to pay the carrier **detention charges**. These arise in the same way as demurrage and storage: the merchant is given free time, usually a (small) number of hours in which to load or unload, as the case may be. If this time is exceeded, he is liable to pay an amount per day to the carrier, as set out in the tariff. The tariff may specify a larger amount per day after a certain number of days.

While a high percentage of shipments proceed without a hitch, there are times when all does not go according to plan. The types of problem which can arise are:

- the consignee refuses to take delivery of the cargo;
- the consignee refuses to take delivery of the cargo within a reasonable time or fails to give appropriate instructions for delivery;
- a local prohibition of a particular commodity means that it cannot be landed;
- a shipowner or shipping line is unable to deliver the cargo by virtue of an excepted peril.

If it looks as if the cargo is going to be collected eventually, the master may arrange for it to be put into a warehouse at the expense of the consignee. In the other examples mentioned above, the cargo may be re-loaded (if, of course, it was initially landed) and shipped to another, convenient, port or indeed returned to the original port of loading. All the costs associated with this constitute **backfreight** and will be for the account of the merchant.

Some liner bills of lading contain a clause stipulating that if the discharge port is inaccessible or if to discharge there would result in an unreasonable delay to the ship, the shipping line reserves the right to proceed instead to another port, normally described as the nearest convenient and safe port, to discharge the cargo. Any additional costs incurred in discharging the cargo at this other port come under the heading of **additional freight** and are generally payable by the merchant to the shipping line.

Associated abbreviation:
d 1/2 d despatch half demurrage

Port types

A **main port** is a port which handles a significant proportion of a country's seaborne trade. It can normally accommodate a large number of ships of all types and has a variety of facilities and good inland transport connections. Often it provides loading, discharging, handling and storage facilities for a wide range of commodities.

For shipping lines, or member lines of a liner conference, a main port is a port called at regularly, as distinct from an **outport** which is served infrequently or by transhipment. Freight to outports sometimes attracts a surcharge known as an **outport additional**. Infrequent service of an outport by deep sea vessels occurs due to an insufficiency of cargo. Historically, this stems from the ever-increasing sizes of these ships and the tendency to reduce the number of ports called at directly.

A vessel may call at an outport **by inducement**, that is to say, only when there is sufficient cargo, either for loading or discharging, to warrant it. Such a port is then called an **inducement port** and the cargo termed **inducement cargo**. The quantity of cargo required to justify a port call depends on the profitability of the freight, taking into account the time and cost of the deviation from the normal schedule and the cost of calling at an extra port.

Transhipment arises when an outport does not have sufficient depth of water or facilities to accommodate deep sea vessels or when the cost of deviating, including extra port charges, makes such a call uneconomical. The outport may then be served by a smaller vessel known as a **feeder ship**. This plies between the outport, which is then termed a **feeder port**, and the port served directly by the ocean vessel, known as the **transhipment port**. This latter type of port is often one which is on a number of trade routes. It specialises in, and has facilities for, cargoes which arrive on one ship and are transferred, or transhipped, into or onto another. It may also have facilities for intermediate storage.

A **specialised port** is a port most of whose facilities are designed to handle one particular commodity, often a bulk cargo, such as oil, grain or iron ore. These facilities consist of loading or discharging equipment, as the case may be, vehicles and equipment for handling as well as storage.

A **bunkering port** is a port at which a ship calls to take on bunkers (fuel). It is not a port where cargo is normally loaded or discharged, particularly if the bunkers are taken on at an anchorage rather than on the berth. Sometimes, however, in the case of liner ships, an inducement cargo (*see above*) may be loaded or discharged, if necessary to or from barges.

A **free port**, **free trade zone** or **free zone** is a separate area within a port set aside for goods which are imported temporarily before being re-exported, sometimes after having been processed in some way. Facilities vary widely from one zone to another and the advantages of using such zones also vary from one to another and from country to country. Often, raw materials may be imported without payment of Customs duties provided they are used for manufacture within the zone. Temporary imports through a free trade zone may fall outside quota systems.

An **autonomous port** is a type of port in France which is self-funded and managed by a council made up of representatives of the municipality, dock workers and others.

Alternative spellings:
transship
transshipment
trans-ship
trans-shipment

Post fixture work

Work done after a ship has been **fixed**, that is, after the contract for the charter of a ship has been agreed. This work may be done by specialists working for the shipowner, charterer or shipbroker. Different functions need to be done according to whether the ship has been voyage chartered or time chartered. Many of the functions are as a result of requirements in the charter-party, for example, the notices of arrival which have to be given by the parties at various stages before and during the period of the charter.

In the case of a voyage charter:

—the **freight** needs to be calculated (if it is not a lump sum), collected from the charterer and passed on to the shipowner;
—**disbursements**, a vessel's expenses when in port, are checked and paid;
—a **time sheet** is completed and despatch and demurrage calculated. This is done by means of information provided by the port agents on the statement of facts; the calculation depends on the terms agreed in the charter-party.

In the case of time charters:

—**hire money** needs to be paid on time. Failure to do this might result in the ship being withdrawn from the service of the charterer;
—**orders to the master** need to be prepared and sent to the ship, instructing him regarding the intended ports of call, details of agents and cargoes and fuel and bunkering calculations;
—**bunkering**; prices and delivery need to be determined by the charterer;
—**on hire and off hire (condition) surveys** need to be arranged, normally done in conjunction with both the shipowner and the charterer.

In all types of charter:

—any disputes may need to be referred to arbitrators but each side needs to collate all the necessary documentation. It may also be necessary for representatives from each side to attend arbitration hearings;
—calculations are carried out by one side and verified by the other.

See also:
Penalties

Protection and Indemnity Club (P&I club)

Also known as **Protection and Indemnity associations**, these are associations of shipowners who, by means of contributions known as **calls**, provide mutual protection against liabilities not covered by insurance, such as claims for injury to crew and loss or damage to cargo. The protection or insurance of a ship is called an **entry**—the ship is said to be **entered** with the club. Shipowners, demise charterers and ship managers who contribute to a P&I club are **members** of that club. Charterers of ships, other than demise charterers, may also enter ships with P&I clubs in order to cover their liability as charterers.

An **advance call** is normally paid once a year in advance by shipowners. This is the basic fee for the service provided by the association and is based on the ship's gross tonnage, known as the **entered tonnage**. The total of members' calls represents the anticipated amount of claims against the association's funds. When the association's total exposure to claims has been calculated after the end of each year, and the anticipated amount has been exceeded, the P&I club may request a **supplementary call**.

More recently, some P&I clubs have introduced **fixed rate calls**, otherwise called **fixed rate premiums**, whereby no supplementary calls are made.

Associated abbreviations:
P&I or **pandi** Protection and Indemnity
F d & d freight, demurrage and defence

Associated definitions:
Call rate Amount of contribution payable to the P&I club per ton of the ship's tonnage.
Freight, demurrage and defence Class of insurance provided by a P&I club which covers legal costs incurred by a shipowner in conjunction with claims arising from the operation of his ship.
Interclub Agreement Agreement between a number of major P&I clubs on the method of apportioning liability for loss and damage to cargo carried in ships chartered under a New York Produce Exchange charter-party.
Certificate of Entry A document and any endorsement thereto issued by the Association in accordance with the Rules and the Articles of Association which records the names of Members interested in, and evidences the contract of insurance in respect of, an Entered Ship.

Royal Institution of Naval Architects (RINA)

Founded in 1860, and incorporated by Royal Charter in 1910, The Royal Institution of Naval Architects is an internationally renowned professional institution whose members are involved at all levels in the design, construction, repair and management of shipping. Based in London, England, the Institution has over 5,000 members in more than 80 countries, and is widely represented in the marine industry, universities and maritime organisations.

Membership is open to those qualified in naval architecture, or who are involved or interested in the marine industry. Membership demonstrates the achievement of internationally recognised standards of competence. The Institution publishes a range of technical journals, books and papers, and organises an extensive programme of conferences, seminars and training courses covering all aspects of naval architecture and marine technology.

Associated abbreviation:
RINA Royal Institution of Naval Architects

Sale and purchase (s&p)

Sale and purchase is a separate area of shipping and shipbroking. Buyers and sellers of ships are normally represented by specialist sale and purchase brokers. The standard contract containing the terms for the sale and purchase of ships is the Norwegian Shipbrokers' Association Memorandum of Agreement, code named the **Saleform 1993**. This was adopted by the Baltic and International Maritime Council (BIMCO) in 1956 and the form was subsequently revised in 1966, 1983 and 1986/87. It contains:

—details of the ship, such as its year of build, flag, call sign and capacities;
—the purchase price;
—deposit (10% being standard);
—payment terms;
—inspections of records and of the ship herself and when and where this is to take place;
—notices, time and place of delivery;
—drydocking, if agreed;
—what spares and other items, and what quantity of bunkers, are to be on board;
—the documentation to accompany the sale;
—any encumbrances such as liens;
—which party to pay which fees and taxes;
—condition and class on delivery;
—an arbitration clause;
—other formalities.

A **bill of sale** is issued to record the transaction. This contains the main elements of the sale, such as the names of the parties, the price, the description of the vessel and any encumbrances. BIMCO publishes a standard bill of sale code named **Bimcosale**.

BIMCO also publishes a standard contract, code named **Salescrap 87**, for the sale of vessels for demolition, or breaking up. This contract is similar to the Saleform but contains boxes and clauses specifically geared to the fact that the ship is being sold for demolition, notably the inclusion of the ship's light displacement tonnage, or lightweight. This is the weight of the ship's hull, machinery, equipment and spares and is normally the basis on which such ships are paid for.

Associated abbreviation:
s&p sale and purchase

Security

A raft of new security measures were initiated in the aftermath of the terrorist attacks on New York of September 2001. These apply to ships and shipping companies, to cargoes, to port authorities and port facilities, and to governments.

Security

International Code for the Security of Ships and Port Facilities

The International Maritime Organization introduced the **International Code for the Security of Ships and Port Facilities**, containing measures to enhance maritime security and safety. Effective July 2004 in contracting states, the ISPS Code applies to passenger ships, cargo ships of 500 gross tonnage and over, mobile offshore drilling units, and port facilities. It aims "to reduce the vulnerability of the industry to attack, thus countering the threat and reducing the risk". It does this by providing "a standardised, consistent framework for managing risk and permitting the meaningful exchange and evaluation of information between Contracting Governments, companies, port facilities, and ships".

The Code is actually made up of a number of amendments to the Safety of Life at Sea (SOLAS) Convention of 1974, and is mandatory for all the states who have signed up to SOLAS (currently 148). The Code is in two parts: there is a mandatory section with requirements for governments, port authorities and shipping companies, and a second part consisting of a set of guidelines as to how these requirements are to be carried out.

The Code covers ships and shipping companies, port authorities and port facilities, and the role of governments.

Ships and shipping companies

The Code requires shipping companies to have a **ship security plan** for each of its ships.

This is a plan developed to ensure the application of measures on board the ship designed to protect persons on board, cargo, cargo transport units, ship's stores or the ship from the risks of a security incident. The plan is based on a ship security assessment.

The ship security plan addresses issues such as:
—weapons and dangerous substances;
—restricted areas;
—unauthorised access to the ship;
—responding to security threats;
—evacuation in case of security threats;
—duties of shipboard personnel;
—auditing security activities;
—security training, drills and exercises;
—interfacing with port facility security activities;
—the periodic review of the plan;
—reporting security incidents;
—identification of the ship security officer;
—issues surrounding ship security equipment;
—ship security alert system.

The plan, which may be prepared by a **recognized security organization**, must make it clear that the Master has overriding authority in respect of the safety of the ship.

Ships which conform to the ISPS Code are issued with an **International Ship Security Certificate**. Conversely, those which do not are not issued with the certificate and are not permitted to trade. Such a ship may be detained in port, or refused access, until such time as she is issued with a certificate. The certificate is valid for a period not exceeding five years, depending on the Administration which issued it.

For every ship the company must designate a **ship security officer** who is answerable to the Master. This person is responsible for the security of the ship, including implementation and maintenance of the ship security plan and for liaison with the company security officer and port facility security officers.

Shipping companies are also required to designate a **company security officer** who is responsible for ensuring that a ship security assessment is carried out; that a ship security plan is developed, submitted for approval, and thereafter implemented and maintained and for liaison with port facility security officers and the ship security officer.

Port authorities and port facilities

Port facility security officers are to be designated, and certain security equipment must be put in place. A port facility security officer is the person designated as responsible for the development, implementation, revision and maintenance of the port facility security plan and for liaison with the ship security officers and company security. The **port facility security plan**, based on a **port facility security assessment**, is developed to ensure the application of measures designed to protect the port facility and ships, persons, cargo, cargo transport units and ship's stores within the port facility from the risks of a security incident.

The port facility security plan addresses issues such as:

—weapons and dangerous substances;
—unauthorised access to the ship;
—responding to security threats;
—evacuation in case of security threats;
—duties of shipboard personnel;
—interfacing with ship security;
—reporting security incidents;
—security of cargo and cargo-handling equipment;
—auditing security activities;
—the periodic review of the plan;
—reporting security incidents;
—identification of the port facility security officer.

The role of governments

Contracting Governments are responsible for setting security and providing guidance for protection from security incidents.

There are three levels of security provided for by the Code, numbered 1 to 3. One is the normal level of security provided by the ship or port facility, two is a

Security

heightened state of security, and three represents a situation where there is a credible threat to security.

A contracting government may appoint a recognized security organisation to act on its behalf for certain functions.

Each contracting nation lists its contact details in IMO's Global Integrated Shipping Information System for:

—ship security;
—port facility security;
—Ship Security Alert System alerts;
—maritime security related communications from other Contracting Governments;
—assistance with security incidents; and
—recognized security organizations approved by Contracting Governments.

Cargoes

The US has introduced security requirements for ocean carriers and NVOCCs with vessels scheduled to call at a US port, to file certain manifest information 24 hours before the ship's departure from the overseas port of loading, including details of cargo not to be discharged, known as freight remaining on board (frob). Known as the **24-Hour Advance Cargo Manifest Rule**, if the carrier or NVOCC puts inadequate information, such as "FAK" (freight all kinds) or "STC" (said to contain), in relation to the cargo on the advance manifest, a "do not load" order will be given by the US port, obliging the carrier or NVOCC to short ship the cargo.

A joint initiative, known as **Customs-Trade Partnership Against Terrorism**, has been established between the US Government and business aimed at protecting cargo destined for the USA against the threat of terrorism, while speeding up the flow of goods. The principle is that if business takes steps to secure its cargo against terrorism, it will be afforded a quick passage through US Customs. Businesses have to apply to participate in the scheme by completing questionnaires, carrying out a self-assessment of supply chain security, and notifying other parties to the supply chain about the measures required. C-TPAT membership is available to importers, carriers, brokers, warehouse operators and manufacturers.

Container Security Initiative—initiative by US Customs to protect the country from dangers of terrorism posed by the entry of shipping containers. It consists of four elements: (1) establishing security criteria to identify high-risk containers; (2) pre-screening containers in overseas ports, in other words before they arrive at US ports; (3) using technology to pre-screen high-risk containers; and (4) developing and using smart and secure containers with electronic seals capable of being monitored via a global network.

Other countries' security systems include Canada's **Partners in Protection**, Sweden's **StairSec Programme**, and New Zealand's **SEP Programme**.

248

The **World Customs Organisation**, whose official name is the **Customs Co-operation Council**, has developed its Framework of Standards to Secure and Facilitate Global Trade, which over 100 countries have undertaken to implement. The Framework, which takes account of the above US initiatives, aims to establish customs control standards that provide supply chain security while facilitating goods being traded internationally. Another of its key objectives is to strengthen co-operation between Customs administrations to improve their capability to detect high-risk consignments. It covers breakbulk as well as containerised cargoes.

The WCO Framework consists of four core elements. First, the Framework harmonises the advance electronic cargo information requirements on inbound, outbound and transit shipments. Second, each country that joins the Framework commits to employing a consistent risk management approach to address security threats. Third, the Framework requires that at the reasonable request of the receiving nation, based upon a comparable risk targeting methodology, the sending nation's Customs administration will perform an outbound inspection of high-risk containers and cargo, preferably using non-intrusive detection equipment such as large-scale X-ray machines and radiation detectors (termed non-intrusive inspection). Fourth, the Framework defines benefits that Customs will provide to businesses that meet minimal supply chain security standards and best practices.

The US Department of Energy has also established a programme called the **Megaport Initiative** which is aimed at providing ports around the world with radiation screening equipment capable of detecting nuclear materials which might be used in a terrorist attack.

Associated abbreviations:
CSI Container Security Initiative
cso company security officer
C-TPAT Customs-Trade Partnership Against Terrorism
frob freight remaining on board
GISIS IMO's Global Integrated Shipping Information System
IMO International Maritime Organization
ISPS International Code for the Security of Ships and Port Facilities
ISSC International Ship Security Certificate
nii non-intrusive inspection
nvocc non vessel owning (or operating) common carrier
pfsa port facility security assessment
pfso port facility security officer
pfsp port facility security plan
rso recognized security organizations
SOLAS Safety of Life at Sea Convention
ssa ship security assessment
sso ship security officer
ssp ship security plan

Security

stc said to contain
WCO World Customs Organisation

See also:
International Maritime Organization

Ship operating costs

There are two principal aspects of operating a ship: technical and commercial.

Technical operation includes crewing and supplying the ship, keeping her machinery and equipment in working order, which in turn means arranging the necessary surveys and keeping her certificates up to date, and stowing cargoes safely and efficiently.

Commercial operation is concerned more with finding cargoes, negotiating freight rates and bunker prices and appointing ship's agents at the ports of call.

Different people are involved in the different functions, principally the shipowner, time charterer and ship management company. The involvement of each depends on individual contracts.

Commercial operation

Ships may be operated in two basic ways:

—as tramps, that is, they call at any port to carry whatever cargoes are available, normally chartered out on the basis of a voyage charter (full charter or part charter) or time charter. When voyage chartered, the ship continues to be operated commercially by the owner, the charterer merely responsible for cargo handling. When time chartered, however, the ship is operated by its time charterer, often bulk cargo interests;

—as liners, plying between regular, advertised ports of loading and discharge on a regular basis, carrying a relatively large number of small consignments. In cases where a shipping line owns its ships, these are operated by their owner. Occasionally, a shipping line will charter in a ship when there is a surplus of cargoes or when one of the fleet is in drydock. In such cases, shipping lines may time charter and operate the ship as if it were one of their fleet of owned vessels.

Commercial operation includes:

—port charges;
—pilotage;
—towage;
—daily running cost (shipowner) or time charter hire (charterer);
—stevedoring charges (cargo handling);
—buying fuel;
—appointment of port agents;
—finding cargoes; and
—freight charges.

Technical operation

In all cases, technical operation is carried out by the shipowner or a nominated ship management company (ship managers).

Some of the technical responsibilities (with associated costs) are:

—quality of fuel (bunkers);
—crew wages;
—victuals;
—spares;
—surveys;
—annual drydocking;
—repairs;
—ship management;
—P&I club;
—certification; and
—(third party) insurance.

Alternative spelling:
shipmanager

Associated abbreviations:
drc daily running cost
P&I Protection and Indemnity

Ship types

There is a large diversity of ship types, varying in their equipment, their size and the configuration of their cargo spaces, which in turn has a bearing on their capacity to carry cargo. All of these factors combine to meet a need, that is to say, to be able to carry efficiently a particular product or combination of products, in a particular quantity, or over a certain distance.

When deciding on a ship to carry a specific cargo, it is important to know what the various ship types are, what they are called, their principal characteristics and what equipment they have which is likely to be required for the cargo, for example, heating coils, cranes of a minimum lifting capacity, or ice-breaking ability.

General cargo ship: the traditional ship designed to carry a wide variety of products unpacked and packed, in cartons, crates, bags or bales, or on pallets. Such ships have several decks to enable them to carry many consignments to and from a number of ports. These ships may also be termed **breakbulk ships** or **conventional ships** as they carry conventional cargoes, that is, dry cargoes which are lifted on and off one piece or bundle at a time by means of cranes or derricks.

Ship types

Box hold ship or **box holder**: vessel with a hold or holds whose sides are at right angles, or almost at right angles, to the floor. Such ships normally have wide hatchways to enable cargo to be lowered directly into the desired position in the hold.

Coaster: ship which carries cargoes between ports on the same coast or ports of the same country. This term is also used occasionally to refer to **short sea traders**, that is, ships which perform short international voyages. There is no real distinction in terms of construction between the two—ships in either trade are of varied types: they may have one deck or more than one, they may be geared or gearless, they may have one hatch or several and may be fitted to carry containers. As a rule, they are small in relation to ocean-going vessels (**deep sea vessels**), for example, typically 2,000 to 3,000 tonnes deadweight in Northern Europe and from 3,000 up to 8,000 tonnes deadweight on the Pacific coast of North America.

Geared ship: ship which is equipped with her own crane(s) or derrick(s). Such a ship is required for a voyage where the loading or discharging port does not have shore cranes or, if available, where shore cranes are of insufficient lifting capacity or inefficient. This is the opposite of a **gearless ship**, that is, a ship not so equipped. When chartering or scheduling a ship for a particular voyage, it is necessary to ensure that each of the ports of call has a crane capable of lifting up to the heaviest piece of cargo to be loaded or discharged or, failing this, that the ship should be suitably equipped.

Ships may have one deck or more than one. A deck is a horizontal division within the hold, used for stowing cargo. A ship with one deck is called a **single deck ship** or **single decker**. Single deckers are suitable for homogeneous cargoes of all types but are not suitable for general cargo. Bulk carriers are single deckers. Ships with two decks are called **tween deckers**. Some general cargo ships are constructed in this way as it allows for a range of products to be stowed safely. Where a voyage is likely to include a large number of ports, it is likely that a vessel with several decks, a **multideck ship**, would be required.

Containerships, also called **cellular containerships**, have cells into which the containers are lowered and where they are held in place by uprights called **cell guides**. Containers are frequently carried on deck where they require to be lashed and secured. Generally, containerships are not geared but some are **self-sustaining**, that is, they have their own crane, normally a gantry crane, for loading and discharging the containers. This enables them to serve ports which do not have suitable, or indeed any, lifting equipment.

Certain types of ship are classified according to their size:

Capesize ships are bulk carriers so called because they are too large to negotiate the Suez and Panama Canals. Vessels of over 150,000 tonnes deadweight fall into this category. **Panamax ships**, or **Panamaxes**, are bulk carriers whose dimensions enable them to transit the Panama Canal where lock width is the limiting factor. Vessels of 60,000 to 70,000 tonnes deadweight fall into this category although ships of even larger capacity have been built which are small enough in size for the Canal transit.

Paragraph ships are cargo-carrying ships so called because the regulations of various countries concerning the construction, equipment and manning of ships contain separate sections, or paragraphs, for ships of different gross tonnages. A paragraph ship is a ship whose gross tonnage is just below a certain figure which, if it had been exceeded, would have entailed more stringent requirements and a higher running cost.

Associated abbreviations:
osd open shelter decker
sd single decker

See also:
Bulk carriers
Multipurpose ships
Tankers
Vehicle carriers

Shipbroker

Person who negotiates the terms for the charter of a ship on behalf of a charterer or shipowner; when on behalf of a charterer, he or she is called a **chartering agent** or **charterer's broker**; when representing a shipowner, he or she is termed an **owner's broker**. Brokers tend to specialise in dry cargoes (**dry cargo brokers**) and wet cargoes (**tanker brokers**). Brokers may work exclusively for one principal, when they are termed **exclusive brokers**, or for several (**competitive brokers**). **Coasting brokers** specialise in the negotiation of charters for coastwise or short sea voyages. There is also a category which negotiates on behalf of a buyer or seller of a ship, known as a **sale and purchase broker**.

In many countries, these are the only categories of shipping business to comprise shipbroking. In the UK, the profession of shipbroker encompasses several other occupations: **ship's agent**, attending to the requirements of a ship, her master and crew when in port on behalf of the shipowner; **loading broker**, whose business is to attract cargoes to the ships of his principal; **bunker broker**, an intermediary in the negotiations between an oil company and a shipowner or ship operator for the purchase of bunkers. In certain ports in France, there exists a category of ship broker, known as a **sworn shipbroker**, who has a monopoly in the port in which he carries on business, in chartering negotiations and a monopoly in the translation of official and other documents, such as charterparties, bills of lading, and the formalities associated with the inward and outward clearance of ships. Shipbrokers are represented in the United Kingdom by the Institute of Chartered Shipbrokers.

Shipbroker

Shipbroking is done by telephone, telex, fax and e-mail. Additionally, brokers meet on the floor of the Baltic Exchange, the shipping market, located in London, England, whose main function is to provide facilities for the chartering of ships by its members. The Baltic, as it is widely referred to, has published a code for shipbrokers which contains guidance for brokers who operate within the self-regulated market of the Exchange. The **Baltic Code** was first produced in 1983 and revised in 1988. Basic Principles and Unacceptable Practices are reproduced below.

Basic Principles

The motto of the Exchange—"Our Word Our Bond"—symbolises the importance of ethics in trading. Members need to rely on each other and, in turn, on their principals for many contracts verbally expressed and only subsequently confirmed in writing. The foundation for ethical trading has long been regarded by the Baltic Exchange community as the principle of treating others as you would wish to be treated yourself.

Over the years the following basic tenets have been developed:

1. In the conduct of his profession a broker shall exercise great care to avoid misrepresentation and shall be guided by the principles of honesty and fair dealing.

2. Under no circumstances may a broker avail himself of, or make use of an authority if he does not actually hold it. Neither can he alter the terms of an authority without the approval of the principal concerned.

3. An owner's broker should offer his vessel fully "firm" only for one cargo at a time. A charterer's broker should similarly offer his cargo "firm" to one vessel only.

4. A broker can receive more than one firm offer for his vessel or cargo but must make it quite clear to others who wish to make him an offer that he has already received one or several firm offers for the particular order or vessel concerned.

5. No broker has authority to quote a vessel or a cargo unless duly authorised by a principal or by brokers acting on the instructions of principals.

6. An unsolicited offer or proposal does not in any way bind a broker who receives it unless the broker accepts such an unsolicited offer or proposal.

7. Before a broker quotes business on the Exchange from a source whose *bona fides* is unknown, it is expected that he makes reasonable investigations and communicates the result of those investigations to anyone entering into negotiations. If such checks have not been made or completed this fact should be conveyed clearly to the other principal or his broker.

8. A broker should respect the channel or channels through which a vessel or a cargo has been quoted to him but it is for the principal to direct which of those channels to use should he enter into firm negotiations.

254

Unacceptable Practices

1. Organisations operating as freight contractors/freight speculators offering named tonnage against tenders without the authority of owners/disponent owners.

2. Agents/brokers implying by telex messages or otherwise that they hold a ship/cargo firm when they do not, in order to secure a counter-offer from a principal.

3. Off-setting against hire sums representing unspecified or vague claims.

4. Withholding payment of commissions when due in respect of hire/freight/deadfreight/demurrage earned and paid.

5. Using information obtained through Exchange members for business transacted directly with non-Baltic members or their local brokers. This practice implies the use of market-sensitive information given to another member, who would conform to this Code, being used outside the market, thus avoiding the risk of entering a binding commitment with someone who will not necessarily operate to Baltic standards.

6. Passing market-sensitive information gained in the Exchange to non-Baltic brokers or agents so that they can deal directly with Baltic members' principals or their brokers. This has the effect of diluting the value of the market and runs the risk of an agreement being concluded with someone who may not be fully familiar with the practices of the market and may not observe the same standards of business ethics.

7. Offers made "subject to charterer's reconfirmation" when the offer is in fact made by the actual charterer.

8. Owners offering their vessel firm when they hold a firm offer from a charterer. The charterer's offer should be declined before the owner makes the offer. If a member of the Exchange fails to comply with any of the above items or practices he may be disciplined by the Directors under the Rules. The Directors have power to suspend or expel a member from the Exchange in these circumstances.

Associated definitions:
broker alternative for shipbroker
shipbroking The work or profession of a shipbroker
to broke To negotiate the terms for the charter of a ship

Alternative spellings:
ship broker
ship broking

See also:
Baltic Exchange
Chartering
Chartering—offer and counter-offer
Institute of Chartered Shipbrokers (ICS)

Shipping

The business of moving goods internationally involves many different types of activity. It starts with the sales contract between the exporter and the importer. This may be concluded with or without the intervention of intermediaries or agents. Terms of sale may be as agreed between the two parties or may be standard, such as Incoterms, produced by the International Chamber of Commerce. The parties agree between themselves as to the responsibilities of each. The exporter is required to make the goods available to his customer at a specific place, depending on the agreement he has with that customer. This might be, for example, the factory of manufacture (ex works), the port of loading (FOB), the port of discharge (C&F or CIF), or the customer's premises (delivered). There are a number of variations of these.

When the goods are ready for shipment, a number of functions need to be carried out to get them to their destination. The exporter or importer may have their own shipping department or they may employ the services of a **freight forwarder**, sometimes called a **forwarding agent**, to make the arrangements. The person who takes responsibility for arranging the shipping of the goods is called the **shipper** (sometimes **consignor**). In practice, this is normally the exporter, the freight forwarder or the importer.

Goods may need to be transported by one means of transport or more than one, depending on where the parties are situated. Often, the journey starts with a leg by road, involving a **road haulier** (**trucking company** in North America). Alternatively, the manufacturer's premises may have their own rail siding for direct loading to **rail**, or river berth for loading to a **barge**.

Many international moves involve a leg by sea. Depending mainly on the quantity of cargo to be shipped at anyone time, the shipper will require either a **shipping line** (**steamship line**) for smaller consignments, or a **tramp ship operator** for larger ones. A shipping line is one which operates a ship or ships between advertised ports on a regular basis and offers space for goods in return for freight based on a tariff of rates. A tramp (ship) operator is someone who operates a ship which will call at any port to carry whatever cargoes are available, normally on the basis of a charter or part charter. In between these, and a sort of mixture of the two, are the so-called **parcel carriers**, who advertise a service between named ports but on the basis of a suitably-sized cargo.

Shipping lines employ a **liner agent** or **loading broker** at the port of loading. Their principal duties are to advertise the line's sailings, obtain cargoes, co-ordinate their delivery to the ship and sign bills of lading on behalf of the master.

Tramp ship operators and their charterers normally use intermediaries called **shipbrokers**, often simply called **brokers**, to negotiate the terms of the charter on their behalf. There are various types of shipbroker—owner's brokers, charterers' agents, dry cargo brokers and tanker brokers (*see* **Shipbroker**).

In each of the ports, ship operators, whether liner or tramp, appoint a **port agent**, sometimes called **ship's agent**, to look after the interests of the ship while she is in port. The agent arranges pilotage, towage, a berth for the ship, he signs bills of lading and collects the freight. Charterers may also appoint a ship's agent at each of the ports. In this case, the shipowner may appoint another agent, known as a **protecting agent** or **protective agent** to protect his interests and supervise the work.

The shipper will require the services of a **Customs broker** to clear the goods through Customs, both outwards in the country of export and inwards at the port of entry or in the country of destination.

The person or company who enters into a contract of carriage with the shipper is the **carrier**. Normally, this includes road hauliers, barge and rail operators and shipowners or operators. However, some movements arranged by freight forwarders make them the carrier, in particular when they act as **nvocc** (**non vessel owning** or **operating common carrier**) or **MTO** (**multimodal transport operator**). In these cases, the forwarder enters into contracts himself with shipowners and others, normally in order to offer exporters and importers a door-to-door service.

The person or company to whom the goods are delivered is called the **receiver**. This is often used synonymously with **consignee**, but this latter person is strictly the person referred to in the "consign to" box on the bill of lading. In practice, this is generally either the receiver or a forwarding agent.

Other functions include those of **warehousekeepers** and **terminal operators**, who provide facilities, often highly specialised, for different commodities. These facilities might involve storage, loading and discharging ships, sorting, palletisation or bagging, and loading of vehicles.

Port authorities provide the land and infrastructure for private terminal operators; in some cases, the port authority operates the port itself.

Many contracts involve payment by letter of credit and this requires the involvement of a **bank** which advances the money to pay for the goods against production of a suitable **letter of credit**.

Disputes arising from contracts of carriage are subject to resolution by arbitration or litigation, depending on the individual contract. In the case of arbitration, a number of **arbitrators** may hear the case and issue an award. Arbitrators are often commercial people, rather than lawyers. **Maritime lawyers** may be brought in, especially in complex cases, to represent the parties even in disputes which are referred to arbitration.

A number of **trade associations** exist in the shipping industry, representing companies and individuals nationally and internationally. Many of them offer educational courses and act as the voice of their members in discussions with other trade organisations and Governments.

Associated abbreviations:
MTO multimodal transport operator
nvoc or **nvo** non vessel owning or operating carrier
nvocc non vessel owning or operating common carrier

See also:
Carrier
Forwarding agent

Shipping

International Chamber of Commerce (ICC)
Shipbroker
Ship's agent

Shipping documents

Shipping documents are prepared by the exporter and/or his freight forwarder. Their main purpose is to arrange for the movement of goods and associated activities. They also give instructions for the allocation of charges and can provide special instructions for the handling of the goods, e.g. the Dangerous Goods Note.

SITPRO publishes a number of shipping documents, many of which are in the aligned system of export documentation (*see* **SITPRO**). These are:

—**CIM Rail Consignment Note** (*see* **Consignment**)
—**CMR Road Consignment Note** (*see* **Consignment**)
—The **Certificate of Shipment** is a document for freight forwarders who need to send confirmation to the exporter and/or consignee that the goods have been shipped as per the information contained in the certificate. SITPRO's Certificate of Shipment is reproduced on p. 259.
—**Common Short Form Bill of Lading** (*see* **Bill of Lading** *for general definition*)
—**Dangerous Goods Note** (DGN) (see separate entry)
—**Export Cargo Shipping Instructions** (**ECSI**) (*see separate entry*)
—**FIATA Bill of Lading** (*see* **Bill of Lading** *for general definition*)
—**FIATA Forwarder's Certificate of Receipt** (**FCR**) (*see separate entry*)
—**House Bill of Lading** (*see* **Bill of Lading** *for general definition*)
—**Non-negotiable Sea Waybill** (*see* **Waybill** *for general definition*)
—**P&O Bill of Lading for Combined Transport** (*see* **Combined Transport Bill of Lading** *for definition*)
—**P&O Non-negotiable Waybill for Combined Transport** (*see* **Combined Transport Bill of Lading** *for definition*)
—**Shipping Specification**; this is a continuation document which contains details of Customs items which will not fit on a front sheet. It is used where these details are required by any party to a trade transaction.
—**Standard Shipping Note** (*see separate entry*)

Associated abbreviations:
b/l bill of lading
DGN Dangerous Goods Note
ECSI Export Cargo Shipping Instructions
FIATA International Federation of Freight Forwarders Associations
SITPRO Simpler Trades Procedures Board
w/b waybill

See also:
SITPRO

CERTIFICATE OF SHIPMENT

© SITPRO 1992

TO ▶

Exporter	VAT no.

Consignee	VAT no.

Customs reference/status	U
Exporter's reference	N
	I
Forwarder's reference	C

Other UK transport details

Vessel/flight no. and date	Port/airport of loading
Port/airport of discharge	Place of delivery

Shipping marks; container number	Number and kind of packages; description of goods	Gross weight (kg)	Cube (m³)

Dear Sirs,
We hereby certify that this consignment has been shipped in accordance with the above mentioned details.

Yours faithfully,

Certificate of Shipment (SITPRO)

Shipping documents

(c) SITPRO 2000

EXPORT CARGO SHIPPING INSTRUCTIONS v2.10

Approved by BIFA

To

* DANGEROUS GOODS:
Refer to IMDG, ADR, IATA CIM and UK regulations
as appropriate and specify:
proper shipping name, hazard class, Un no, flashpoint, dec C

A Exporter/shipper VAT no	Customs reference/status
	Booking number
	Exporter's reference
	Forwarder's reference

B Consignee VAT no

D Other address VAT no

C Freight forwarder VAT no

If required, this space may be used for other addresses, e.g. buyer, place of acceptance/delivery, additional notify party.

Country of origin of goods | Country of final destination

Other UK transport details

E If required this space may be used for extra addresses or other information

Vessel/flight no. and date | Port/airport of loading

Port/airport of discharge | Place of delivery

Please insure for

Unless otherwise instructed cover will be for ILU clauses "A" and will be charged to A

Shipping marks: container number and type	No. and kind of packages: description of goods *	Item No.	Commodity code		
			Quantity 2	Gross weight (Kg)	Cube (m3)
			Procedure	Net weight (kg)	Value(£)
			Summary declaration/previous document		
			Commodity code		
			Quantity 2	Gross weight (Kg)	Cube (m3)
			Procedure	Net weight (kg)	Value(£)
			Summary declaration/previous document		
			Commodity code		
			Quantity 2	Gross weight (Kg)	Cube (m3)
			Procedure	Net weight (kg)	Value(£)
			Summary declaration/previous document		

Identification of warehouse

FREIGHT ▷

Inland carriage to | Groupage depot/ICD

UK port/airport

Trade Term | Invoice price

◁ **DOCUMENTATION**

Certificate of shipment
Air, sea or other waybill
Bill of lading
Consular formalities/certs. of origin
Other documentation charges
Customs formalities Export
Transit
Import

Indicate services required, and to whom charges should be debited, by entering

A,B,C,D or **E**

in check box

Depot/ICD or port charges including unloading

No of freight containers | Total gross wt (kg) | Total cube (m3)

Freight to

Special instructions

Depot/ICD or port charges at destination

Oncarriage at destination to | Depot/ICD

Place of delivery

STATUS
Enter T1/T2/MiX or T2L
(as applicable)

Indicate who post enters if SCP

Make out documents as indicated and dispose of as follows:

Ocean Freight Payable at

Name of contact and telephone number

No. of bills of lading required
Original Copy

I/We hereby declare that the above particulars are correct and agree to your published Regulations and Conditions, including those as to liability.

Date

Signature

Export Cargo Shipping Instructions (ECSI) (SITPRO)

Shipping instructions

Document, prepared by the exporter, the purpose of which is to provide the freight forwarder with full instructions for an export shipment. It includes a description of the cargo, its place of origin and final destination, documentary requirements, the name of the carrying ship, the place and date of loading and any special requirements.

SITPRO publishes a UN aligned document (*see* **SITPRO**) for this purpose, called the **ECSI** (**Export Cargo Shipping Instructions**), reproduced on p. 260. Forwarders may have their own pre-printed equivalent of the ECSI, but these can be of non-standard formats. The SITPRO ECSI is, however, in general use. Two copies are normally required. The ECSI is an important document as it tells the forwarder or carrier exactly how to handle an export shipment, including which services are required, and who is to be charged for each. The five address boxes on the ECSI are coded A–E. These codes are used at the foot of the form to show who is responsible for each charge.

The ECSI can be used for all modes of transport.

It is important to enter in the centre of the form the Customs details required for the SAD (C88) document if the freight forwarder or carrier is completing the SAD on behalf of the exporter. The responsibility for the accuracy of the information, such as commodity code and procedure code, rests with the exporter. The VAT number must be quoted in the top left-hand box. Any extra information required by the carrier for certain destinations—such as quarantine or fumigation details—must be provided.

Associated abbreviation:
ECSI Export Cargo Shipping Instructions

See also:
SITPRO

Ship's agent

Person or company, acting on behalf of the shipowner, who looks after the interests of a ship, whether liner or tramp, while she is in port. His duties include the arranging of pilotage, towage and a berth for the ship, entering the ship in at Customs, signing bills of lading and the collection of freight. The agent is paid an **agency fee**, agreed in advance with the shipowner or ship operator. A ship's agent is widely known as **agent** or **port agent** or **ship agent**.

It is usual for the shipowner or ship operator to nominate the agent at each port. Indeed, this is case provided for in Gencon, BIMCO's general purpose voyage charter-party, which reads: "In every case, the Owner shall appoint his own Broker or Agent both at the port of loading and the port of discharge."

Ship's agent

However, it is open to negotiation as to whether owners' agents or charterers' agents are nominated. If the agent is nominated and paid for by the shipowner, he is known as an **owner's agent** or **owners' agents**; if by the charterer, **charterer's agent**, **charterers' agents** or **charts agents**. When the agent is nominated by charterers, the owner may appoint a person or company to protect his interests and to supervise the work carried out by charterers' agents. Such a person or company is known as a **protecting agent** or **protective agent** or **supervisory agent**. A protecting agent may also be appointed and brought in from elsewhere when the ship's agent is the only company at the port or the only one authorised to act as ship's agent.

When signing bills of lading, the ship's agent will usually add the words **as agent only**, signifying that he does so as agent and not as principal and has no rights or liabilities under the contract of carriage.

Associated definition:
Ship's agency business of looking after the interests of a ship while she is in port

See also:
Disbursements

Ship's dimensions and capacities

Various ship's dimensions are important for three main reasons as far as trading is concerned: the capacity of the ship to take cargo, the ability of the ship to enter a port and be accommodated at a loading or discharging berth and, lastly, the basis on which dues are assessed.

Capacities

The ship's **deadweight** or **deadweight all told** is the total weight of cargo, fuel, fresh water, stores and crew which the ship can carry when immersed to a particular load line, normally her summer load line. The deadweight is expressed in tons or tonnes. It is also referred to as the **total deadweight**. The combined weight of a ship's stores and spares is called her **constants**. The **deadweight cargo capacity** or **deadweight carrying capacity** is simply the weight of cargo which the ship can carry when immersed to the same load line.

Whereas deadweight reflects the weight of cargo able to be carried, a ship carrying conventional cargo also has a cubic capacity for cargo. In fact, ships have two such capacities, corresponding to the two basic types of cargo: the **bale capacity**, or **bale** for short, is the total capacity of a ship's holds available for the carriage of solid cargo, such as steel coils, which is not capable of filling the spaces between the ship's frames. It is expressed in cubic metres or cubic feet; the **grain capacity**, or **grain** for short, is the number of cubic metres or cubic feet of space for free-flowing cargoes, such as grain—it includes the spaces between the ship's frames and is therefore greater than the bale.

A **full and complete cargo** is a quantity of cargo sufficient to fill a ship to capacity either by weight or cubic measurement, depending on the **stowage factor** of the cargo, that is, the ratio of the cargo's weight to its cubic measurement, expressed either as cubic metres to the tonne (1,000 kg) or cubic feet to the ton (of 2,240 lb). When a ship's cargo holds are full and her hull is immersed as far as the permitted load line, she is said to be **full and down**. This condition is ideal for a ship operator since it maximises the use of the ship's cubic capacity and her permitted draught.

A conventional ship's ability to accept cargo depends on her hatch and hold sizes.

The capacity of a containership is normally expressed in **twenty foot-equivalent units** (**teu's**). That of a roll-on/roll-off ship is expressed in **lane metres**, with the total comprising the **lane length** of the ship.

Dimensions

Ports, and within ports, berths, have different lengths, widths and depths of water. As well, there are restrictions at locks, sand bars and river bridges. It is vital to know what these are and how they relate to the ship's dimensions before scheduling or fixing a ship.

The **length overall** is the maximum length between the extreme ends, forward and aft, of a ship. This measurement is often required to determine, for example, whether a ship can negotiate a particular lock or whether she can be accommodated at a specific berth. It is also known as the **overall length**.

The **beam** is the maximum breadth of a ship. This is sometimes a factor in determining whether a ship is able to be accommodated in a lock or whether the cranes at a port have a sufficient **outreach** to reach cargo on the seaward side.

The **draught** is the depth to which a ship is immersed in the water; this depth varies according to the design of the ship and will be greater or lesser depending not only on the weight of the ship and everything on board, such as cargo, ballast, fuel and spares, but also on the density of the water in which the ship is lying. A ship's draught is determined by reading her **draught marks**, a scale marked on the ship's stem and stern. Every ship has a **deadweight scale**, a table which shows in columns a set of draughts with the ship's corresponding deadweight tonnages when she is lying in salt water and fresh water. The quantity varies not only ship by ship but also according to the quantity already on board. The quantity of cargo needed to immerse a ship one further centimetre is expressed in **tonnes per centimetre**. The corresponding Imperial measurement is **tons per inch**.

Ships have a **capacity plan**, a document detailing the capacities of all the cargo spaces and all the tanks used for oil fuel, diesel oil, lubricating oil, fresh water and water ballast. The capacities are expressed in cubic metres or cubic feet and, in the case of tanks, the quantity in tonnes or tons which they can hold.

The **air draught** is one of three possible distances:

Ship's dimensions and capacities

(1) the maximum height from the water-line to the topmost point of a ship, that is, the superstructure or the highest mast. This information is required for ships having to navigate bridges;

(2) the clearance between the topmost point of a ship and a bridge over a river;

(3) the maximum height from the water-line to the top of the hatch coamings. This figure is necessary in some bulk trades where loading is effected by conveyor belt which projects over the hatchway. The ship must be low enough in the water, if necessary by retaining sufficient ballast on board, to allow the conveyor to clear the hatch coamings.

Register tonnages

All ships have **register tonnages** on which the various dues, such as port dues and pilotage, are charged. The **gross tonnage** is a figure representing the total of all the enclosed spaces, arrived at by means of a formula which has as its basis the volume measured in cubic metres. This has replaced the **gross register tonnage** or **gross registered tonnage**. The **net tonnage** is similarly calculated but on the basis solely of the enclosed spaces within a ship that are available for cargo. The net tonnage has replaced the **net register tonnage** or **net registered tonnage**. Ships are measured by a surveyor for this purpose and a **Tonnage Certificate** issued, showing the various tonnages. The Panama and Suez Canals have their own regulations concerning measurement of ships for the purpose of determining the tonnages which are used to calculate canal dues.

Alternative spelling:
draft

Associated abbreviations:
dwat deadweight all told
dwcc deadweight cargo capacity or deadweight carrying capacity
dwt deadweight
f&cc full and complete cargo
grt gross register tonnage or gross registered tonnage
gt gross tonnage
lbp length between perpendiculars
lm lane metre(s)
loa length overall
nrt net register tonnage or net registered tonnage
nt net tonnage
tdw tonnes deadweight
teu twenty-foot equivalent unit
tpc tonnes per centimetre
tpi tons per inch

Ship's documents

Certificate of Fitness: A certificate issued by or on behalf of the flag administration confirming that the structure, equipment, fittings, arrangements and materials used in the construction of a gas carrier are in compliance with the relevant IMO Gas Codes. Such certification may be issued on behalf of the administration by approved classification societies. (*Definition from the Society of International Gas Tanker & Terminal Operators.*)

Certificate of Seaworthiness: Document issued by a surveyor after repairs have been effected, certifying that the ship is seaworthy.

Classification Certificate: Certificate issued by a classification society which states the class attributed to a ship.

Dangerous Cargo Endorsement: Endorsement issued by a flag state administration to a certificate of competency of a ship's officer allowing service on dangerous cargo carriers such as oil tankers, chemical carriers or gas carriers. (*Definition from the Society of International Gas Tanker & Terminal Operators.*)

Deratting Certificate: Document issued by the health authorities in a port which certifies that any rats on board a ship have been exterminated.

Deratting Exemption Certificate: Document issued by the health authorities in a port which certifies that their inspector has found a ship to be free of rats.

Gas-Free Certificate: A gas-free certificate is most often issued by an independent chemist to show that a tank atmosphere has been tested, and is certified to contain adequate oxygen and is sufficiently free from toxic, chemical and hydrocarbon gases for a specified purpose such as tank entry and hot work. (In particular circumstances, such a certificate may be issued when a tank has been suitably inerted and is considered safe for surrounding hot work.) The certificate is valid only for a clearly defined length of time. (*Definition from the Society of International Gas Tanker & Terminal Operators.*)

International Load Line Certificate: Certificate required by ships undertaking international voyages. It gives the positions of a ship's freeboards relative to her deck line and the positions of her various load lines above and below her summer load line. The certificate states that the ship has been surveyed and the appropriate load lines marked on her sides. It is issued either by a Government department or, if authorised by that department, a classification society. As required by the International Convention on Load Lines, the ship is surveyed periodically and the certificate renewed.

International Load Line Exemption Certificate: Certificate exempting a ship from the requirements of the International Convention on Load Lines. An exemption may be given to a ship not normally involved in international voyages but which is to undertake a single such voyage.

Ship's documents

International Tonnage Certificate: Certificate issued to a shipowner by a Government department in the case of a ship whose gross and net tonnages have been determined in accordance with the International Convention of Tonnage Measurement of Ships. The certificate states the gross and net tonnages together with details of the spaces attributed to each.

ISM Code documents: Companies which comply with the ISM Code should be issued with a **Document of Compliance**, a copy of which should be kept on board. Administrations should also issue a **Safety Management Certificate** to indicate that the company operates in accordance with the safety management system (SMS) and periodic checks should be carried out to verify that the ship's SMS is functioning properly.

Safety Radio-telegraphy Certificate: Document, issued by the authorities of a country, which certifies that a ship is equipped with suitable radio equipment taking into consideration her size, number of crewmen and the types of voyage which she is likely to undertake.

Suez Tonnage Certificate: Certificate whose main function is to record the ship's tonnage calculated in accordance with the Suez Canal regulations. It is on this tonnage that Suez Canal dues are assessed each time the ship passes through the Canal. A similar certificate, the **Panama Tonnage Certificate**, exists for the Panama Canal. In each case, the tonnage measurement may be different from the ship's normal tonnage.

Associated abbreviations:
doc Document of Compliance
ISM Code International Safety Management Code
SMC Safety Management Certificate
SMS safety management system

SITPRO

SITPRO Limited, formerly The Simpler Trade Procedures Board, was set up in 1970 as the UK's trade facilitation agency. Reconstituted as a company limited by guarantee in April 2001, SITPRO is one of the Non-Departmental Public Bodies for which the Department of Trade and Industry has responsibility. It receives a grant-in-aid from the Department. SITPRO is dedicated to encouraging and helping business trade more effectively and to simplify the international trading process. Its focus is the procedures and documentation associated with international trade.

SITPRO's mission is to Make International Trade Easier.

The following strategic objectives underpin this mission:

- influencing the simplification of international trade procedures;
- promoting best trading practices;

- developing and promoting international standards for trade documentation;
- working towards better border regulations and the removal of international trade barriers; and
- remaining the world's premier trade facilitation agency.

SITPRO's work is guided by its Board and its Policy Groups. At any time there are about 100 executives and specialists taking part in this work. Its ability to obtain this voluntary support and guidance is essential for both its research and development and promotional roles.

SITPRO offers a wide range of services, including advice, briefings, publications and checklists covering various international trading practices. It manages the UK aligned system of export documents and licenses the printers and software suppliers who sell the forms and export document software.

Associated abbreviation:
SITPRO Simpler Trade Procedures Board

See also:
Consignment
Shipping Documents
Standard Shipping Note (SSN)

Standard Shipping Note (SSN)

The Standard Shipping Note, reproduced on p. 268 and published by SITPRO, the Simpler Trade Procedures Board, enables the shipper to complete one standard document for all consignments irrespective of port or inland depot. By doing so, it provides the receiving authority with complete, accurate and timely information as well as providing all those with an interest in the consignment with adequate information at each movement stage, until final loading on board the vessel (or aircraft).

The SSN has been widely and successfully used throughout the UK and has now been updated to take account of changing transport techniques and cargo handling practices.

The SSN should accompany all non-hazardous deliveries (containerised, unit loads, general cargo) from factories or warehouses to inland clearance depots, groupage depots, ports, airports and other cargo terminals.

However, the SSN must not be used if the delivery includes items classified as dangerous in UK, IMO, ADR, RID regulations. In this case, the SITPRO Dangerous Goods Note (DGN) 1995 version should be used. This incorporates the dangerous goods declaration, stowage order and container/packing certificate and is for use by all transport modes except air. However, the DGN can be used in support of the IATA Shipper's Declaration for Dangerous Goods (air transport).

267

Standard Shipping note (SSN)

© SITPRO 1999

STANDARD SHIPPING NOTE - FOR NON - DANGEROUS GOODS ONLY

IMPORTANT USE THE DANGEROUS GOODS NOTE IF THE GOODS ARE CLASSIFIED AS DANGEROUS ACCORDING TO APPLICABLE REGULATIONS SEE BOX 10A

Exporter	1	Customs reference/status	2
		Booking number	3	Exporters reference	4
		Forwarder's reference	5

Consignee	6

Freight forwarder	7	International carrier	8
		For use of receiving authority only	

Other UK transport details (e.g. ICD, terminal, vehicle bkg. ref. receiving dates)	9

The Company preparing this note declares that, to the best of their belief, the goods have been accurately described, their quantities, weights and measurements are correct and at the time of despatch they were in good order and condition; that the goods are not classified as being hazardous by reference to relevant national and international regulations applicable to the intended modes of transport. **10A**

Vessel/flight no. and date	Port/airport of loading	10

Port/airport of discharge	Destination	11

TO THE RECEIVING AUTHORITY - Please receive for shipment the goods described below subject to your published regulations and conditions (including those as to liability)

Shipping marks	Number and kind of packages; description of goods; non-hazardous special stowage requirements	12	Gross weight (kg) of goods	13A	Cube (m³) of goods	14

For use of Shipping company only		Total gross weight of goods	Total cube of goods

Container identification number/ vehicle registration number	16	Seal number(s)	16A	Container/vehicle size and type	16B	Tare (kg)	16C	Total gross weight (including tare) (kg)	16D

HAULIER DETAILS	**DOCK/TERMINAL RECEIPT**	Name and telephone number of company preparing this note	17
	RECEIVING AUTHORITY REMARKS		
Hauliers name	Received the above number of packages/containers/trailers in apparent good order and condition unless stated hereon.	Name/status of declarant	
Vehicle reg. no.		Place and date	
Drivers signature	Receiving authority signature and date	Signature of declarant	

Standard Shipping Note (SSN) (SITPRO)

268

The greatest benefit of using the SSN and DGN is that receiving authorities receive clear accurate and precise information on how the goods should be handled, and the Customs procedure applicable.

The SSN is a SITPRO aligned document (*see* **SITPRO**).

See also:
SITPRO (Simpler Trade Procedures Board)

Associated abbreviations:
DGN Dangerous Goods Note
SITPRO Simpler Trade Procedures Board
SSN Standard Shipping Note

Stowage

The placing of goods in a ship in such a way as to ensure, first, the safety and stability of the ship not only on a sea or ocean passage but also in between ports when a part of the cargo has been loaded or discharged, as the case may be; secondly, the safety of the individual consignments which should not be damaged or contaminated by being in proximity to goods with which they are not compatible; thirdly, the ability to unload goods at their port of discharge without having to move goods destined for other ports. Stowage is determined by the ship's cargo superintendent although responsibility rests with the master of the ship.

On conventional ships calling at a number of load ports and discharge ports, this can be a complicated exercise, and a knowledge of the characteristics of different products is called for. In particular, it is important for a cargo superintendent to know whether a particular product may be overstowed by another, or whether it can be overstowed at all, taking all the above factors into consideration (**to overstow** is to stow one item of cargo on top of another in a ship): some commodities have a **tier limit**, or **tier limitation**, which is the maximum number of levels of that commodity which may be stowed on top of each other without suffering **compression damage**; this type of damage may also arise when certain cargoes are overstowed by others. Alternatively, some sensitive cargoes can be contaminated and unfit for their original purpose if stowed close to other, possibly strong-smelling, cargoes.

Before loading commences a **cargo plan** is drawn up. This working document is a plan in the form of a longitudinal cross-section of the ship. It shows suggested locations in the ship of all the consignments, taking into consideration all the above factors. A cargo plan is often taken to be synonymous with a **stowage plan** which has the same format but is drawn up to show the actual locations of all the consignments once they have been stowed in the ship. The stowage plan is frequently colour-coded to highlight the various ports of discharge. It is very often sent to the stevedore at each of the discharge ports to assist them in planning the discharge of the ship.

Stowage

Occasionally, it is not known at the time of loading at which port a particular cargo is to be discharged. This cargo, termed **optional cargo**, must therefore be stowed in such a position that it can be removed at any of a number of selected ports, known as **optional ports**, without disturbing other cargo. The position in the ship is called an **optional stow**.

To help identification of consignments, goods or their packaging should have displayed distinctively on them a **shipping mark** which should include the port or place of destination, known as the **port mark**, and a package number, if there is more than one. These markings are also known as **marks and numbers**. To further assist in identifying separate consignments, and to make sure that they are not mixed or discharged at the wrong port, **separations** are employed which might consist of painting different colour marks on the cargo or putting tarpaulins or other materials between them.

Associated definitions:
mixing of cargo placing of goods in a ship in such a way that they require sorting before being delivered.
to pre-stow to decide in advance the stowage of a cargo on a ship.

Strike clause

Clause in a bill of lading or charter-party which sets out the options available to the parties to the contract of carriage in the event that a strike or lock-out (and in certain contracts, a riot or civil commotion) prevents or interrupts the loading or discharging of the cargo. The wording of the clause and the options vary according to the individual contract. Various standard strike clauses have evolved over the years, and these range from a few lines to many paragraphs which seek to cover every possible eventuality.

Charter-parties

A number of different charter-party strike clauses start by exonerating both owner and charterer from responsibility for the consequences of any strike preventing or delaying the carrying out of any obligations under the charter-party .

There are key stages of the voyage which many charter-parties make separate provision for when a strike commences. These are listed below together with commonly found options which vary according to the individual contract:

(a) before the ship has arrived at the load port or before loading has commenced:
    —owners and charterers may agree to cancel the charter;
    —owners may ask charterers to treat laytime as if there is no strike, failing which owners may have the right to cancel the charter;
(b) when a part of the cargo has been loaded:

—charterers may require the vessel to wait, paying the owners full demurrage;

—owners may have the option to sail and possibly complete with cargo from another port on the route;

(c) when the ship is on the way to the discharge port;

—charterers may require the vessel to proceed to the discharge port and wait on payment of half demurrage (after expiry of any time allowed) or possibly order the vessel to another port;

(d) when only a part of the cargo has been discharged:

—the vessel may be ordered by the charterers to another port to discharge.

Amwelsh, the Americanized Welsh Coal Charter, treats loading and discharging in the same way: provided the strike had not started when the charter was agreed, half the laytime counts during periods of strike. There is also a provision that demurrage is payable at half the rate agreed if the vessel goes on demurrage during the strike.

Some charter-parties extend the scope of the strike clause to include the place of manufacture or mine, and the inland transport required to bring the cargo to the load port, since such a stoppage or lock-out will affect the charterer's ability to provide cargo for the ship.

Charter-party bills of lading incorporate the provisions of the relevant charter-party and so the same strike clause will apply to both documents.

Liner bills of lading

Whereas in most charters, cargo interests are responsible for loading and discharging, where shipments are booked on liner terms, the shipping line is responsible. Generally, the liner bill of lading, which contains the carrier's standard terms and conditions, will exclude liability on the part of the carrier for loss or damage arising from strikes (as well as other situations outside of the carrier's control).

If either the loading or discharging is prevented or delayed by a strike, normally the carrier will be entitled to discharge the cargo at the loading port or at any other safe and convenient port.

Associated definitions:

Strike-bound (1) Said of a port where no loading or discharging is taking place because of a strike of dockers or where ships are unable to enter or leave because of a strike of pilots, tugmen or lock-gatemen.

Strike-bound (2) Said of a ship which is unable to leave a port because of a strike of pilots, tugmen or lock-gatemen.

See also:
Bill of lading
Charter-party

Sub-charter

Tramp owners and owners of bulk carriers may not operate the ships themselves but may charter them out to others (the charterers). Often, these charterers may employ the ships for the duration of the charter. However, there are occasions when a ship becomes surplus to requirements, possibly temporarily, or when the main purpose of the charter was to perform a trip in one direction but the charter stipulated a round voyage. In these cases a charterer may, in turn, charter the ship out to a third party. There may thus be several "layers" of companies, giving rise to a hierarchy of people, actions and documentation. When there are only two parties involved, the shipowner and the charterer, there is no confusion as to role. When there are more levels, all of the parties and their actions and contract types may need to be distinguished one from another, something which becomes crucial in the event of a dispute.

At the highest level, the party to whom the shipowner charters his ship is the head charterer. The charter-party is called the **head charter** or **head charter-party,** irrespective of what type of charter it is, for example, whether it is a Baltime charter-party or a New York Produce Exchange charter-party, or whatever type of voyage charter it may be. In the case of a voyage charter, payment to the owner is the freight or voyage freight. This is summarised as follows:

Owner: **Shipowner**
Charterer: **Head charterer**
Contract: **Head charter** or **head charter-party**
Payment: **Freight** or **voyage freight**

Should the charterer at some stage let the ship to a third party, that third party is known as the sub-charterer. The action is termed a sub-charter or a sub-let. The charter-party is called the sub-charter or sub charter-party. The freight is known as the sub-freight.

Effective owner: Head charterer becomes **disponent owner**
Charterer: **Sub-charterer**
Contract: **Sub-charter**
Payment: **Sub-freight**

This process may be repeated with the following relationships:

Effective owner: Sub-charterer who becomes disponent owner
Charterer: Sub-sub-charterer
Contract: Sub-sub-charter
Payment: Sub-sub-freight

Often, the parties at each level of sub-charter will agree terms and conditions, known as **back to back conditions,** which are identical to the level above and thereby to the head charter. The purpose of this is avoid having different rights and responsibilities between the various parties which could complicate the resolution of disputes.

Associated definitions:

to recharter said of a charterer of a ship, to charter or hire the ship out to another party. Also referred to as **to sub-let** or **to sub-charter**.

Sundry charter-party clauses (found in both voyage and time charters)

A number of types of clause are found in both voyage and time charter-parties and are equally applicable to both types of contract; in many cases the clause is identical, if produced by the same body. Below are the most commonly found clauses.

Address commission clause: **Address commission** is a commission payable by the shipowner to the charterer, expressed as a percentage of the freight or hire (depending on whether the charter is on a voyage or time basis). It is often 2½%; in a voyage charter, it normally applies to freight and any deadfreight or demurrage. In the case of a time charter, it is based on the hire (money). Although this commission is sought by charterers as a means of reducing the freight or hire, these are capable of being adjusted by the shipowner to compensate for it.

Arbitration clause: Clause which stipulates that any dispute arising from the contract be resolved by arbitration, as opposed to litigation. The clause also specifies the place where the arbitration is to be held, the number of arbitrators and their qualifications, and may also set out the procedure should one party fail to nominate an arbitrator, or should the arbitrators fail to agree.

Brokerage clause: Clause in a charter-party which stipulates the elements on which commission is payable to the shipbroker and the amount payable in the event of non-execution of the charter. Also called **brokerage commission clause**.

Clause paramount: Clause in a charter-party, and in a bill of lading, which stipulates that the contract of carriage is governed by the Hague Rules or Hague-Visby Rules or the enactment of these rules of the country having jurisdiction over the contract. Also referred to as the **paramount clause**.

Deviation clause: Clause in bill of lading or charter-party allowing the shipping line or shipowner to deviate from the agreed route or normal trade route. This clause varies from contract to contract and may permit the ship to call at unscheduled ports for whatever reason, or to deviate to save life or property. Also termed **liberties clause** (for example in the NYPE time charter) or **liberty clause** (the Worldfood and Bimchemtime charter-parties). It sometimes includes a provision for bunkering—*see* **p&i bunker deviation** *under* **Sundry voyage charter-party clauses**.

Exceptions clause: Clause in a charter-party or bill of lading which exonerates the carrying ship from responsibility for damage to cargo from certain named causes such as an Act of God or negligence of the master.

Sundry charter-party clauses (found in both voyage and time charters)

Ice clause: Clause which sets out the options available to the parties to the contract in the event that navigation is prevented or temporarily delayed by severe ice conditions. The wording of the clause and the options vary according to the individual contract: a master may have the right to divert the ship to the nearest safe port to discharge cargo destined for an ice-bound port. Equally, a charterer may have the option of keeping a ship waiting for ice conditions to clear on payment of demurrage.

Lien clause: Clause in a voyage charter-party which entitles the shipowner to exercise a lien on the cargo, that is, to retain control of the cargo until any freight, deadfreight or demurrage which is owing is paid. This provision is often incorporated into the cesser clause (*see* **Sundry voyage charter-party clauses**) which seeks to relieve the charterer of all responsibility under the charter-party once the cargo has been shipped.

Litigation clause: Clause which stipulates that any dispute arising from the contract be determined in a court of law, as opposed to arbitration. This is often accompanied by a stipulation as to which country's courts must hear any dispute and which country's laws must apply. These latter two stipulations sometimes appear in a clause on their own, termed a **jurisdiction clause**, or **law and jurisdiction clause**. Occasionally, a charter-party will contain a clause stipulating only which country's laws will apply; such a clause is called a **governing law clause**, or simply **law clause**.

Preamble: First few lines of the charter-party which serve to show that the parties agree to the contract contained in the document. In it, traditionally, the parties to the contract and the ship were identified. With box layout charter-parties becoming more prevalent, each of these elements has its own box to be filled in and so the preamble no longer contains these details but merely makes reference to the relevant box numbers. Indeed, in many cases, the preamble is not referred to as such.

Sub-let clause: To sub-let (or to sub-charter, or to assign), said of a charterer, is to charter or hire the ship out to another party, known as the sub-charterer. The sub-let clause gives the charterer permission to sub-let the vessel. Normally the clause holds the charterer responsible for the fulfilment of the contract even if he sub-lets the ship. *See* **Chartering**.

War clause: Clause which sets out the course of action open to the master of a ship in the event that the ship or her cargo or crew would be put at risk because of war should the voyage proceed. This clause often provides options not only for war, but also for blockade and civil commotion. Options may often include both actual and threatened danger. The clause varies according to individual contracts but invariably the master would not be required to put his ship or crew at risk. Options need to be exercised at key points of the voyage; these are: prior to loading, the continuation of loading when this has already commenced, prior to discharge and during discharge. The sort of options frequently found are those which allow the ship to load or discharge all or part of the cargo, as the case may be, at safe ports nominated by the charterer or, in the absence of timely instructions, at safe ports of the master's choosing.

Associated abbreviation:
addcomm address commission

Associated definitions:
rechartering sub-letting (*see* **sub-let clause** *above*)
assignment sub-letting (*see* **sub-let clause** *above*)

See also:
Strike clause
Sundry time charter-party clauses
Sundry voyage charter-party clauses

Sundry time charter-party clauses

Bunkers clause: Clause which specifies the amount of fuel and diesel required to be on board the vessel at the time of delivery and redelivery. It also sets out the price payable by the charterer to the owner for bunkers on board on delivery, and by the owner to the charterer for bunkers remaining on board on redelivery. These prices are subject to individual agreement and may be the current price at the place concerned or a price agreed between the parties to the contract. In some charter-parties, this clause includes the specification for the fuel and a requirement that any fuel supplied by the charterers is to conform to it.

Delivery clause and redelivery clause: These clauses may appear separately or together and vary in complexity according to the particular contract or charter-party form. The delivery clause may include the period of the charter, the place, time and hours of delivery and required notices to be given by the ship prior to arrival. The redelivery clause includes the place of redelivery and notices required to be given by the charterers to the owners.

Demise clause: A clause found in some time charters signifying that the existence of the charter does not denote that the charterer is considered to be the owner of the ship. A similar clause appears in some bills of lading stipulating that the contract of carriage is between the shipper or bill of lading holder and the shipowner. Bills of lading issued by charterers of a ship on behalf of the owner and master often contain this clause. It should be noted that this clause may be inconsistent with the laws of certain countries and may therefore be invalid in those countries. Also called the **identity of carrier clause**.

Drydocking clause: Clause which states whether the shipowner is entitled to put his ship into drydock during the period of the charter. If so, it may specify the notice which the owner is required to give the charterer and state which party pays for which of the associated costs. Generally, the ship will be off hire during the drydocking (*see* **Off hire clause** *below*).

Hire clause and **hire payment clause**: These two elements may be found separately or together. Hire is the money paid by the charterer to the shipowner for the hire of a ship taken on time charter (also the amount paid by the sub-charterer to the time charterer when the ship is sub-let). The hire clause specifies the rate of hire, that is, normally an amount per day or per 30 days or per dead-weight ton per month. The hire payment clause sets out the currency, timing and frequency of payment, all of which vary depending on the particular contract. As a rule, it is specified that the shipowner has the right to withdraw the ship from the service of the charterer if hire is not paid on time.

Off hire clause: Clause which sets out the circumstances in which hire money, payable by the charterer to the shipowner, may be temporarily suspended. These periods are known as **off hire periods**. The circumstances vary according to the individual contract but may include:

—inability on the part of the ship to comply with the charterer's instructions because of damage, defect or breakdown;
—arrest of the ship for reasons unconnected with the charterers;
—loss of time for which the ship is responsible;
—drydocking (this is often provided for in a separate clause).

Some charter-parties specify that the charterer has the option to add off hire periods to the period of the charter. This clause is also known as the **suspension of hire clause**.

Owners to provide clause and charterers to provide clause: These clauses, which normally appear separately, set out what the owners and charterers are required to provide and pay for. These requirements vary according to the particular contract and may include some or all of the following:

In the case of owners:

—provisions, wages and expenses of the master, officers and crew;
—insurance on the vessel;
—deck and engine room stores;
—winchmen, for example, one winchman per hatch.

In the case of charterers:

—fuel;
—taxes and dues arising from cargo carried;
—materials required for tank cleaning (cargo tanks);
—port charges;
—dock and harbour dues;
—loading, trimming and stowage costs, including dunnage;
—tugs.

Performance clause: Clause setting out the ship's fuel consumptions and speeds. These are guaranteed by the owner, and if not maintained give rise to a claim by the charterer for the cost of time lost or extra fuel consumed. There are normally exceptions or exclusions, for example, severe weather or an instruction by the charterer to reduce speed.

Supercargo clause: A supercargo is a person employed by a shipping company (which may include a shipowner or charterer) to supervise cargo handling operations. Some charter-parties contain a clause giving the charterers the right to put their supercargo on board, paying an agreed amount per day for meals and accommodation.

Associated abbreviation:
rob remaining on board

See also:
Sundry charter-party clauses (found in both voyage and time charters)
Sundry voyage charter-party clauses

Sundry voyage charter-party clauses

Agency clause: Clause which stipulates whether the owner or the charterer is entitled to appoint the ship's agent at the various ports.

Berth standard of average clause: Clause which sets out the contribution to be made by the charterer to any claim for loss and damage to cargo for which the shipowner is liable.

Cancelling clause or cancellation clause: Clause specifying the last date, known as the cancelling date, on which a ship must be available to the charterer at the agreed place. The ship must have arrived and notice of readiness tendered. The clause sets out the options and course of action if the ship arrives after the cancelling date or, in certain charter-parties, if the ship is merely expected by the owner to miss the cancelling date. These options vary but, typically, allow the charterer to cancel the contract or agree to a new cancelling date.

Excepted periods clause: Excepted periods are periods during which any time used to load or discharge does not count for the purpose of calculating demurrage or despatch other than by prior agreement. This clause sets out these periods, which vary from contract to contract but may include weekends, public holidays and certain periods of bad weather. This is also referred to as **suspension of laytime**.

Cesser clause: Clause which seeks to relieve the charterer of all responsibility under the contract once the cargo has been shipped. Often this clause incorporates a provision for the shipowner to have a lien on the cargo for freight, deadfreight and demurrage. In this case the clause is rightly termed a **lien and cesser clause**.

Sundry voyage charter-party clauses

Demurrage/despatch (dispatch) clause: Clause which specifies the rate of demurrage (and despatch, if applicable) payable in the event that the time allowed for loading or discharging, as the case may be, is exceeded.

Extra insurance clause: Clause which, typically, specifies that extra insurance on account of the vessel's age, class, flag or ownership to be for owners' account. Depending on the particular contract, a maximum amount may be agreed, or there may be a provision that, if no maximum is agreed, an amount be payable which is no greater than the lowest premium available in a particular insurance market, for example London.

Freight clause: Clause which stipulates when freight is due and when it is payable, and sets out the method of calculating it. These vary according to the particular contract.

Jettison clause: Clause in a bill of lading or charter-party setting out the circumstances under which a master is entitled to jettison goods from a ship.

Laytime clause: Clause which sets out the agreed rate of loading and discharging, or the number of days or hours allowed, or other agreed term, and details of excepted periods, such as week-ends, holidays and weather stoppages. In some charter-parties, loading, discharging and excepted periods are dealt with in separate clauses, particularly if the relevant terms and conditions are complex.

Negligence clause: Clause in a bill of lading or charter-party which seeks to relieve the shipowner or carrier of liability for losses caused by the negligence of his servants or agents.

Overtime clause: **Overtime** is any period outside normal working hours when work, if required, is available at an extra cost. Any of the parties may want to hasten the completion of loading or discharging for various reasons: cargo interests may want to avoid possible demurrage, the owner may have another cargo, provided his ship is ready in time. It is often agreed in charter-parties that the cost of overtime is payable by the party who orders it. Some contracts also contain a provision for apportionment of costs in instances of overtime being ordered by the port authorities or any Government agencies. In some contracts, the charterers are required to pay, in others the costs are apportioned on a 50/50 basis.

Owners' Responsibility Clause or **owners' responsibilities claus**e: Clause setting out the circumstances under which the owner of the ship is liable, or not liable, for loss or damage to the cargo. These circumstances vary according to the particular charter-party. In the case of the Gencon charter-party, the owners are only responsible in cases of "personal want of due diligence on the part of the Owners or their Manager to make the vessel in all respects seaworthy and to secure that she is properly manned, equipped and supplied, or by the personal act or default of the Owners or their Manager".

p&i bunker deviation: Clause giving the shipowner the right to proceed to any port, whether on the contracted route or not, for the purpose of taking on fuel.

278

Also called the **p&i bunkering clause**, **p&i bunker clause** or simply **bunkering clause**.

Seaworthy trim clause: A clause which requires the charterers to leave the vessel in seaworthy trim to the master's satisfaction between berths and ports, when loading or discharging. This situation arises when loading a cargo or part cargo, and when discharging a part cargo. To comply with the requirement, charterers must load or discharge, as the case may be, in such a way that, on completion of the particular operation, they leave the trim, that is, the relationship of the draughts forward and aft, in accordance with the master's requirements for putting to sea.

Shifting: Clause which sets out the implications to laytime and the apportionment of costs when a vessel is required to shift berths, normally by the charterer, shipper or receiver, when loading or discharging. In some contracts, the costs are borne by owners, in others, by charterers; generally, any time used counts as laytime. Since they are similar activities, shifting and warping (see below) are sometimes contained in the same clause.

Stevedore damage clause: Clause, varying from one contract to the next, which generally seeks to indemnify the shipowner against any damage done to the ship by the stevedores, since these are normally appointed by the charterers. There may be a provision for the owner to try and settle any claims directly with the stevedores.

Warping: Shifting a ship by means of her mooring ropes which may be a requirement of cargo interests to facilitate loading or discharging. Some charterparties contain a provision which sets out the implications to laytime and the apportionment of costs for this. In some contracts, the costs are borne by owners, in others, by charterers; generally, any time used counts as laytime. Since they are similar activities, warping and shifting (*see above*) are sometimes contained in the same clause.

Winch clause: Clause in a charter-party which makes provision for the use of the ship's winches by the charterer. The clause often includes a stipulation as to the number of winchmen to be made available by the shipowner and the responsibility for payment of shore winches, if these are used.

Associated abbreviations:
cl. clause
o/t overtime
p&i protection and indemnity (club)

See also:
Cancellation of a charter
Sundry time charter-party clauses
Sundry charter-party clauses (found in both voyage and time charters)

Surveys

Many surveys are carried out at different intervals for different purposes. The greatest number are surveys of ships done by classification society surveyors, mostly in order to maintain class (*see* **Classification societies**). Some are done by independent surveyors in connection with the charter of the ship or the condition or quantity of the cargo.

A **classification survey** is any survey carried out by a surveyor of a classification society which is done to ensure that the ship meets the minimum standards for continued trading set by the society. This could be a special survey, an annual surveyor an occasional survey.

A **special survey** is a stringent survey of a ship's hull and machinery carried out every five years for the purpose of maintaining class (*see* **Classification societies**). This survey may, at the request of the shipowner, be carried out on a continuous basis, when it is termed a **continuous survey** on a distributed basis (**distributed survey**). When the shipowner opts for a distributed survey, a planned programme is agreed.

In addition to the special survey, ships are required to undergo an **annual survey** in drydock to ascertain the condition of the hull and machinery. **Intermediate surveys** are also carried out depending on the ship's age and type. Different surveys are also carried out at different periods depending on the type of ship. These include a **bottom survey**, **propeller shaft survey** and **boiler survey**. **Occasional surveys** are carried out, for example, after repairs have been carried out or when ships are laid up.

A **statutory survey** is any survey required by a Government—it is not a classification survey but may be carried out by a classification society surveyor when authorised by the Government concerned.

Cargo surveys may be done in order to establish the quantity or condition of a cargo. This may be done, for example, before the cargo is loaded onto a ship or after discharge. Such a survey may be routinely carried out for a number of reasons, such as the establishing of the amount of freight payable, or the extent of a claim for shortage or damage against a carrier or terminal. When carried out before loading, such a survey is often termed a **pre-shipment survey**; when after discharge, it is called an **outturn survey**. When carried out by a single surveyor on behalf of two parties, such a survey is said to be a **joint survey**.

A **draught survey** is a survey undertaken at the port of discharge to determine the quantity of cargo on board a ship. The survey is in two parts: before and after discharge. Prior to discharge, the surveyor ascertains the draughts forward and aft and, taking into consideration the density of the water in which the ship is lying and any hogging or sagging, calculates the ship's displacement tonnage. He then sounds the ship's tanks to determine the quantity of fuel, fresh water and ballast on board. After discharge he repeats the procedure and arrives at a new displacement tonnage. After making allowances for any fuel and fresh water used or taken on board during discharge as well as any ballast pumped aboard, he calculates the quantity of cargo. This is sometimes used as the basis on which payment is made for bulk cargoes.

In the case of time chartered ships, two surveys are carried out, one at the beginning of the period of the charter, one at the end. An **on hire survey**, or **on hire condition survey**, is carried out at the time the ship is delivered by the shipowner to the time charterer. This is done in order to determine the condition of the ship at that time and this may be subsequently compared with her condition at the end of the charter, when an **off hire survey**, or **off hire condition survey**, is performed. In each case, the quantity of bunkers is ascertained for comparison with the amounts agreed in the charter-party. By agreement, the ship is inspected by one surveyor only or one surveyor for each of the two parties. Which party pays for the surveys and whether the time taken counts for the purpose of calculating hire money are matters agreed in the charter-party.

See also:
Classification societies

Tally (to)

Said of general cargo, to record the number of pieces at the time they are loaded into, or discharged from, a ship. This task may be performed by **tally clerks** working for the shipowner, the shipper or receiver, or the stevedore. The entries are made on **tally sheets** or in **tally books** and serve to verify the quantity of cargo loaded and discharged. A **tally** is therefore the physical count of pieces of cargo loaded into, or discharged from, a ship. The tally consists of the number of pieces together with their description and their **marks and numbers**, alternatively known as **shipping marks**. These are markings distinctively displayed on goods being shipped, or on their packaging, for ease of identification. They include the port or place of destination and a package number, if there is more than one.

Disputes can arise between the shipper and the ship as to the number of pieces or packages tallied on board. It is not normal for these pieces to be off-loaded for the purpose of tallying them again. It may also be impractical, especially when dealing with a large number of pieces, to count them again once they have been stowed in the ship, partly because they may not all be within view and partly because to count them again would cause the ship to be delayed. In such cases, the master will require a notation on the bill of lading which varies according to whether the tally reveals a larger or smaller number than that declared by the shipper. When larger by, say, four pieces, the notation will read **4 more in dispute, if on board to be delivered**. If smaller by four pieces, it will read **4 less in dispute, if on board to be delivered**.

On discharge from the ship, the stevedoring company issues an **outturn report**, a written statement in which the condition of the cargo discharged from the ship is noted along with any discrepancies in the quantity compared with the ship's manifest. This is also referred to an **over, short and damage report**. **To outturn**, said of cargo, is to be discharged from a ship. This term is normally qualified by the condition or quantity of the cargo, that is, whether it is damaged or whether the quantity is greater or less than the quantity on the ship's manifest. For example, a particular cargo **outturned 5 pieces short**. The **outturn weight** is the weight of a cargo ascertained when it is discharged from a ship. Freight on bulk cargoes is sometimes payable on the basis of this weight.

Discrepancies on discharge between the manifest and the outturn report may result in too much cargo or too little. Too much cargo discharged is known as an **overage, excess landing, overlanded cargo** or **overlanding**; missing cargo is termed a **shortage, shortlanded cargo** or a **shortlanding**.

Overlanded cargo may be further defined as cargo which has been discharged at a port for which it was not intended according to the ship's manifest. The ship's agent, on behalf of the shipowner or carrier, tries, by means of the shipping marks on the cargo and by contacting the ship's agents at the other discharge ports on the ship's itinerary, to identify the correct destination. In many instances, cargo which cannot be identified and disposed of within a certain period of time may be auctioned by the port authority.

In the case of shortlanded cargo, the ship's agent at the intended discharge sends a **cargo tracer**, by telex, fax or letter, to the agents at the other discharge ports on the ship's itinerary to determine whether this cargo was landed at one of these ports in error. If it has been discharged at a later port on the ship's itinerary, it is said to have been **overcarried**. In the event that it proves not to have been loaded in the first place, there is said to be a **non-shipment**. If all that is known is that it failed to reach its destination, there is said to be a **non-delivery**. Cargo delivered by the carrier to the wrong consignee is termed **misdelivered**.

Associated abbreviation:
os&d (report) over, short and damage report

Associated terms:
overcarriage
misdelivery

Tankers

A tanker is a ship designed for the carriage of liquid in bulk, her cargo space consisting of several, or indeed many, tanks. Tankers carry a wide variety of products, including crude oil, refined products, liquid gas and wine. Size and capacity range from the ultra large crude carrier of over half a million tonnes deadweight to the small coastal tanker. Tankers load their cargo by gravity from the shore or by shore pumps, and discharge using their own pumps.

A variety of different types of tanker has evolved. A number are mentioned here.

Acid tanker: ship with tanks made out of stainless steel or with a coating made of one of a variety of linings to prevent the acid cargo from penetrating the hull.

A number of safety features are required: ventilation must be such that the crew are not affected by gases which may build up; there will also be emergency equipment to deal with breathing or contact injuries.

Ammonia tanker or **ammonia carrier**: fully refrigerated tanker designed to carry ammonia in liquid form by means of refrigeration. The ammonia is carried in tanks which are kept separate from the ship's hull by an insulating barrier so as to help maintain the low temperature. Very often, ammonia tankers are also used to transport **propane**, a cargo which has similar requirements.

Asphalt tanker: ship used exclusively or predominantly to carry asphalt, a waste product of the oil refining industry. Basically a tanker, this ship has heating coils, since asphalt is viscous and solidifies unless it is kept at the correct heat.

Bitumen carrier: bitumen solidifies at normal temperatures and so must be kept hot when being loaded and discharged as well as during the voyage. This is achieved by means of heating coils in the tanks, with the temperature being regularly monitored. The ship has two longitudinal bulkheads dividing the ship lengthwise into three. Because of the temperature requirements, the cargo is carried in the centre tanks only.

Butane carrier: butane is carried in tanks within holds; it remains in liquid form by means of pressure and refrigeration. Such ships are also suitable for the carriage of propane.

Chemical tanker: tanker designed to carry liquid chemicals, such as acids, in bulk. Because of the necessity to ensure quality control for many chemicals, tanks in a chemical tanker are often coated or constructed of stainless steel. Depending on the type of cargo expected to be carried, these ships may be equipped with heating coils.

Edible oil carrier: type of tanker used to carry different types of oil destined for human consumption. Because many of these oils solidify when cool, heating coils are required in the cargo tanks to maintain the correct temperature. High standards of cleanliness must be achieved, including the cleaning of the pumps used for discharging.

lng carrier: ship designed to carry liquid natural gas (methane). The gas is held in a liquid state by pressure and refrigeration. The cargo-carrying capability consists of special tanks whose upper sections often protrude above deck height in domed or cylindrical form. Also known as a methane carrier.

lpg carrier: ship designed to carry liquid petroleum gas, such as butane or propane. These are carried in special tanks under pressure and at very low temperatures. The tanks are often rectangular in section and may be flanked by wing or hopper tanks used to carry water ballast.

lpg/ammonia carrier: dual-purpose tanker which is fully refrigerated and designed to carry ammonia in liquid form or lpg. Cargo is carried in refrigerated tanks which are kept separate from the ship's hull by an insulating barrier so as to help maintain the low temperature.

Parcel tanker: type of chemical tanker capable of carrying a number and variety of bulk liquids at the same time. This involves having a large number of segregated cargo tanks, often coated or constructed of stainless steel to ensure that the quality of the cargo is maintained, as well as a complex system of pipes to avoid contamination. The types of cargoes likely to be carried include coconut oil and palm oil, inorganic acids and cooled semi-gases.

Phosphoric acid carrier: tanker designed to carry phosphoric acid, a substance used for fertilisers. The cargo tanks are required to be of a high grade stainless steel which has resistance to pitting. The heating coils needed for this cargo need to be corrosion-resistant. There is a need to keep this cargo circulating as a sediment is otherwise created.

Product carrier or **products carrier**: tanker designed to carry a variety of liquid products varying from crude oil to clean and dirty petroleum products, acids, other chemicals and even molasses. The tanks are coated, this being a requirement of some of the products carried and the ship may have equipment designed for the loading and unloading of cargoes with a high viscosity.

Sulphuric acid carrier: because of the highly corrosive nature of this product, the cargo tanks are lined with one of a variety of linings or coatings. Heating coils are necessary to maintain the correct temperature. Sulphuric acid gives off noxious gases which have to be vented away.

ulcc: giant tanker of no official size but variously described as being one between 350,000 tonnes and 550,000 tonnes deadweight.

vlcc: large tanker of no official size but variously described as one between 100,000 tonnes and 350,000 tonnes deadweight.

Associated abbreviations:
lng liquid natural gas or liquefied natural gas
lpg liquid petroleum gas or liquefied petroleum gas
ulcc ultra large crude carrier
vlcc very large crude carrier

Associated definitions:
clean (petroleum) products or **white products** refined products such as aviation spirit, motor spirit and kerosene.
dirty (petroleum) products or **black products** crude oils, such as heavy fuel oils.

See also:
Ship types

Tides

Chart Datum is the datum of the chart below which the depths are charted. It is also the same plane as the tidal datum, so that the tidal height when added to the charted depth gives the true depth of water. By international agreement, Chart Datum is defined as a level so low that the tide will not frequently fall below it. In the United Kingdom, this level is normally approximately the level of lowest astronomical tide (*see below*).

HAT (**highest astronomical tide**) and **LAT** (**lowest astronomical tide**): the highest and lowest levels respectively which can be predicted to occur under average meteorological conditions and under any combination of astronomical conditions; these levels will not be reached every year. HAT and LAT are not the extreme levels which can be reached, as storm surges may cause considerably higher and lower levels to occur.

Tidal range is the depth of water between low water and the next or previous high water.

A **spring tide** is a tide whose range between high and low water is at its highest. Spring tides occur shortly after new and full moon.

MHWS (**mean high water springs**) and **MLWS** (**mean low water springs**): the height of mean high water springs is the average, throughout a year when the average maximum declination of the moon is 23 ½ degrees, of the heights of two successive high waters during those periods of 24 hours (approximately once a fortnight) when the range of the tide is greatest. The height of mean low water springs is the average height obtained by the two successive low waters during the same periods.

A **neap tide** is a tide whose range between high and low water is at its lowest. Neap tides occur shortly after first and third quarter. A ship which is unable to leave a port or place because of a neap tide is said to be **neaped**.

MHWN (**mean high water neaps**) and **MLWN** (**mean low water neaps**): the height of mean high water neaps is the average, throughout a year as defined for MHWS and MLWS above, of the heights of two successive high waters during those periods (approximately once a fortnight) when the range of the tide is least. The height of mean low water neaps is the average height obtained from the two successive low waters during the same periods.

The values of MHWS, MHWN, MLWN and MLWS vary from year to year in a cycle of approximately 18.6 years. In general the levels are computed from at least a year's predictions and are adjusted for the long period variations to give values which are average over the whole cycle. The values of lowest astronomical tide (LAT) and highest astronomical tide (HAT) are determined by inspection over a span of years.

MSL (**mean sea level**). Mean sea level is the average level of the sea surface over a long period, preferably 18.6 years, or the average level which would exist in the absence of tides. **MTL** (**mean tide level**) can be calculated by meaning the heights of MHWS, MHWN, MLWN and MLWS.

Tides

Slack water is still or almost still water which occurs when the tide is neither coming in nor going out.

Associated abbreviations:
HAT highest astronomical tide
LAT lowest astronomical tide
MHWN mean high water neaps
MHWS mean high water springs
MLWN mean low water neaps
MLWS mean low water springs
MSL mean sea level
MTL mean tide level

Associated definition:
draught widely used to denote depth of water

Time charter

The hiring of a ship by a charterer from a shipowner for a period of time. This type of arrangement is favoured by cargo interests who wish to control all the commercial aspects necessary to move cargo by sea.

Under this type of contract, the shipowner places his ship, with crew and equipment, at the disposal of the charterer, for which the charterer pays hire money. Subject to any restrictions in the contract, the charterer decides the type and quantity of cargo to be carried and the ports of loading and discharging. He is responsible for supplying the ship with bunkers and for the payment of cargo handling operations, port charges, pilotage, towage and ship's agency. The technical operation and navigation of the ship remain the responsibility of the shipowner. A ship hired in this way is said to be **on time charter**. The person or company who hires a ship in this way is the **time charterer**.

Occasionally, a charterer may take a ship on time charter for a single voyage only. Such an arrangement is known as a **trip charter**. This is as distinct from the more normal **period charter**, that is, a charter for a period of time which could be anything from a few months to a few years.

At the beginning of the period of the charter, the ship is delivered, that is, it is placed by the shipowner at the disposal of the charterer. This is done at the time and place agreed in the charter-party. The place of delivery is often a location, such as a pilot station, where it is relatively easy to verify the time of arrival and hence the time when the charter commences. Normally, an **on hire survey**, or **on hire condition survey**, is carried out as soon as practicable in order to determine the condition of the ship and the quantity of bunkers on board at the time of delivery. Once delivered, the ship is said to be **on hire**.

One of the first duties of the charterer is to instruct the master and the agents at the intended ports of call regarding the intended voyages, cargoes, bunkering schedule and on hire/off hire surveys.

During the period of the charter, the charterer pays the shipowner **hire money**, normally referred to simply as hire. This is normally expressed as an amount per day, or per deadweight tonne per month. It is paid at regular agreed intervals such as monthly or semi-monthly, normally in advance. It is important for hire to be paid on time since otherwise the shipowner has the right to **withdraw the ship from the service of the charterer**.

If during the charter the ship or an important piece of equipment breaks down, the ship is taken **off hire** by the charterer. Hire money is temporarily suspended until the breakdown is repaired. In practice, hire money may continue to be paid by the charterer, and refunded after the ship comes back on hire, together with a refund covering the amount of bunkers consumed during this period. The document detailing the off hire period is called the **off hire statement**.

At the end of the charter, the charterer **redelivers**, or hands back, the ship to the shipowner. This is done at an agreed port, often simultaneously with completion of discharge of the last cargo, or at a place or area such as within a range of ports. An **off hire survey**, or **off hire condition survey**, is carried out in order to determine the condition of the ship and the amount of bunkers remaining on board.

The contract for time charters is contained in a **time charter-party**, otherwise simply termed the **time charter**. There are a number of standard forms, such as those published by BIMCO. *See* **BIMCO time charter-parties** *for the NYPE 93 charter-party which is reproduced on pp. 32–46.*

Important elements in a time charter are:

—period of the charter;
—cargo exclusions;
—trading limits;
—hire rate and frequency of payment.

Alternative spelling:
off-hire

Associated abbreviations:
dly delivery
redly redelivery
t/c time charter

Associated definition:
to off hire to take (a ship) off hire

Associated terms:
delivery (of a ship)
redelivery (of a ship)
to time charter

Time charter

See also:
BIMCO (Baltic and International Maritime Council)
Sundry charter-party clauses (found in both voyage and time charters)
Sundry time charter-party clauses

United Nations Conference on Trade and Development (UNCTAD)

Established in 1964 and based in Geneva, Switzerland, the United Nations Conference on Trade and Development has been the focal point within the United Nations for the integrated treatment of trade and development and related issues in the areas of investment, finance, technology, enterprise development and sustainable development.

UNCTAD promotes the development-friendly integration of developing countries into the world economy. UNCTAD has progressively evolved into an authoritative knowledge-based institution whose work aims to help shape current policy debates and thinking on development, with a particular focus on ensuring that domestic policies and international action are mutually supportive in bringing about sustainable development.

The organization works to fulfill this mandate by carrying out three key functions:

- it functions as a forum for intergovernmental deliberations, supported by discussions with experts and exchanges of experience, aimed at consensus building;
- it undertakes research, policy analysis and data collection for the debates of government representatives and experts;
- it provides technical assistance tailored to the specific requirements of developing countries, with special attention to the needs of the least developed countries and of economies in transition. When appropriate, UNCTAD co-operates with other organizations and donor countries in the delivery of technical assistance.

In performing its functions, the secretariat works together with member Governments and interacts with organizations of the United Nations system and regional commissions, as well as with governmental institutions, non-governmental organizations, the private sector, including trade and industry associations, research institutes and universities worldwide.

In the 1960s and 1970s, UNCTAD gained authoritative standing:

- as an intergovernmental forum for North-South dialogue and negotiations on issues of interest to developing countries, including debates on the "New International Economic Order".
- for its analytical research and policy advice on development issues.

United Nations Conference on Trade and Development (UNCTAD)

UNCTAD is responsible for a number of conventions relating to maritime transport. In all cases, these will apply where contracting states, i.e. states who have signed up to these conventions, are involved, for example where a voyage involves a call at a port in a contracting state. Contracting states normally pass their own law or statute which often is some years after the date of the convention.

Convention on a Code of Conduct for Liner Conferences concluded at Geneva on 6 April 1974

This convention recognised the need for a universally acceptable code of conduct for liner conferences, taking into account the special needs and problems of the developing countries with respect to the activities of liner conferences serving their foreign trade.

The following were the fundamental objectives and basic principles of the Code:

(a) the objective to facilitate the orderly expansion of world sea-borne trade;
(b) the objective to stimulate the development of regular and efficient liner services adequate to the requirements of the trade concerned;
(c) the objective to ensure a balance of interests between suppliers and users of liner shipping services;
(d) the principle that conference practices should not involve any discrimination against the shipowners, shippers or the foreign trade of any country;
(e) the principle that conferences hold meaningful consultations with shippers' organizations, shippers' representatives and shippers on matters of common interest, with, upon request, the participation of appropriate authorities;
(f) the principle that conferences should make available to interested parties pertinent information about their activities which are relevant to those parties and should publish meaningful information on their activities.

The Code provides for sharing the cargoes of a conference between the national shipping lines of the countries involved and third party shipping lines. It provides for each of the national lines having an equal share, and for third party shipping lines to take a "significant part", such as 20%. This has given rise to the name 40:40:20 for this aspect of the Code.

The Code also deals with, and describes in detail the rules governing, loyalty arrangements between conferences and shippers. It covers consultation arrangements with shippers' organisations and shippers themselves in respect of rates, surcharges and service. It calls for a minimum of 150 days' notice of a general rate increase, and notice according to regional practice for currency surcharges.

United Nations Convention on the Carriage of Goods by Sea, 1978 concluded at Hamburg on 31 March 1978

Known widely as the Hamburg Rules, these are rules governing the rights and responsibilities of carrier and cargo interests which may be incorporated into a contract for the carriage of goods by sea either by agreement of the parties or statutorily.

United Nations Conference on Trade and Development (UNCTAD)

The provisions of this Convention are applicable to all contracts of carriage by sea between two different States, if:

(a) the port of loading as provided for in the contract of carriage by sea is located in a Contracting State, or

(b) the port of discharge as provided for in the contract of carriage by sea is located in a Contracting State, or

(c) one of the optional ports of discharge provided for in the contract of carriage by sea is the actual port of discharge and such port is located in a Contracting State, or

(d) the bill of lading or other document evidencing the contract of carriage by sea is issued in a Contracting State, or

(e) the bill of lading or other document evidencing the contract of carriage by sea provides that the provisions of this Convention or the legislation of any State giving effect to them are to govern the contract.

United Nations Convention on International Multimodal Transport concluded at Geneva on 24 May 1980

This convention recognised the following basic principles:

(a) that a fair balance of interests between developed and developing countries should be established and an equitable distribution of activities between these groups of countries should be attained in international multimodal transport;

(b) that consultation should take place on terms and conditions of service, both before and after the introduction of any new technology in the multimodal transport of goods, between the multimodal transport operator, shippers, shippers' organizations and appropriate national authorities;

(c) the freedom for shippers to choose between multimodal and segmented transport services;

(d) that the liability of the multimodal transport operator under this Convention should be based on the principle of presumed fault or neglect.

The convention concerns itself with the issuance of a multimodal bill of lading, the nature and contents of the bill of lading including provisions whether it is negotiable of non-negotiable, the liability of the multimodal transport operator including limitation of liability, liability of the consignor and procedures for claims.

United Nations Convention on Conditions for Registration of Ships concluded at Geneva on 7 February 1986

The general provisions of this convention are:

1. Every State, whether coastal or land-locked, has the right to sail ships flying its flag on the high seas.

2. Ships have the nationality of the State whose flag they are entitled to fly.

3. Ships shall sail under the flag of one State only.
4. No ships shall be entered in the registers of ships of two or more States at a time, subject to the provisions of paragraphs 4 and 5 of article 11 and to article 12.
5. A ship may not change its flag during a voyage or while in a port of call, save in the case of a real transfer of ownership or change of registry.

The Convention has provisions for the identification, ownership and manning of ships, and the role of flag states in respect of the management of shipowning companies and ships.

UNCTAD Minimum Standards for Shipping Agents

The Minimum Standards for Shipping Agents were prepared by the UNCTAD secretariat in close consultation with the organizations involved in shipping agency matters, in response to a request from the UNCTAD Ad hoc Intergovernmental Group to consider means of combating all aspects of maritime fraud, including piracy. The Committee on Shipping at its thirteenth session in March 1988, having endorsed these Minimum Standards, recommended their use as appropriate. They are non-mandatory in nature and are to serve as guidelines for national authorities and professional associations in establishing their own standards.

The objectives of these Minimum Standards are: (a) to uphold a high standard of business ethics and professional conduct among shipping agents; (b) to promote a high level of professional education and experience, essential to provide efficient services; (c) to encourage operation of financially sound and stable shipping agents; (d) to contribute to combating maritime fraud by ensuring improved services by better qualified shipping agents; (e) to provide guidelines for national authorities/professional associations in establishing and maintaining a sound shipping agency system.

Review of Maritime Transport

The UNCTAD secretariat also publishes the Review of Maritime Transport, an annual publication which provides comprehensive and up-to-date statistics and information on maritime and ancillary services. The Review focuses on developments concerning maritime activities in developing countries as compared with other groups of countries.

Associated abbreviations:
mto multimodal transport operator
UNCTAD United Nations Conference on Trade and Development

See also:
Liner and conference tariffs
Liner shipping—how it is structured

Vehicle carriers

There are a variety of ship types designed to carry cars, trucks, trailers and buses, as well as railway wagons. They are grouped here under the generic title "vehicle carriers" although this term is normally used to define a particular type of ship (*see* **car carrier** *below*).

Car carrier or **pure car carrier**: ship designed to carry unaccompanied new vehicles such as cars, trucks, trailers and buses. Replacing the bulk carriers which were originally used to carry cars on the outward leg and bulk cargoes on the return leg, the vehicle carrier has roll-on/roll-off type ramps which give access to a number of decks, typically 12 or 13. Hoistable decks allow height adjustment, enabling taller vehicles to be accommodated. Some car carriers have the flexibility to carry other vehicles such as trucks, trailers and buses, and these are sometimes referred to as **vehicle carriers** or **pure car and truck carriers**.

Car ferry: ship used frequently on short sea routes to carry passengers and very often cars as well. Cars are driven on and off ramps onto one or more car decks where they are parked for the duration of the crossing. Shore operations often involve the use of a linkspan or bridge which links the ship and shore at whatever angle is necessary at the particular berth. Ferries operating on routes other than very short ones may have cabins and other passenger facilities.

Ro-ro ship: ship whose cargo is driven or towed on and off by means of ramps. Typical cargoes are vehicles of different types, which are driven on and off the ship, and machinery which is loaded onto a special flat, such as a Mafi flat, and towed into position in the ship by a terminal tractor.

Train ferry: ship designed to carry rail wagons (railcars). These may be cargo wagons or passenger cars. The wagons are shunted onto train decks which have tracks laid on them. There are various configurations possible which determine the number of tracks. Pure train ferries carry only rail traffic while **vehicle/train ferries**, alternatively known as **train/vehicle ferries**, carry road vehicles as well. As an example, a vehicle/train ferry might have a railway track in the middle of the deck with two lines of road vehicles, one on either side.

Associated abbreviations:
ro-ro roll-on/roll-off
pcc pure car carrier
pctc pure car and truck carrier

See also:
Ship types

Voyage charter

Contract of carriage in which the charterer pays for the use of a ship's cargo space for one, or sometimes more than one, voyage. This is as distinct from a time charter which is the hiring of a ship for a period of time.

Under a voyage charter, freight is generally paid per unit of cargo, such as a tonne, based on an agreed (minimum) quantity, or as a lump sum irrespective of the quantity loaded. Different elements are involved in loading a cargo, making it safe and discharging it depending on the particular commodity (for example, lashing, securing and dunnaging, or trimming); what these are and who pays are the subject of agreement between the parties (*see also* **Freight**). In cases where the charterer has regular shipments from and/or to the same port, perhaps even owning terminal facilities, it is usual for him to control and pay for cargo handling.

In all cases, the shipowner pays all the operating costs of the ship.

The terms and conditions of the contract are set down in a document known as a **voyage charter-party** (charter-party is often referred to simply as a charter, hence **voyage charter** may refer to the document in which the contract is contained as well as the type of contract); there are many forms of voyage charter-party, most of which have been formulated to meet the needs of different commodities and different trades. Probably the best known is the Gencon, an all-purpose charter published by BIMCO and this is reproduced on pp. 294–296.

A ship chartered in this way is said to be **on voyage charter**.

Important elements of a voyage charter are:

—the freight;
—the laytime, that is, the time allowed by the shipowner to the charterer in which to load and/or discharge the cargo;
—the ship's carrying capacities, often expressed as a weight and as volumes (grain and bale capacities);
—the loading and discharging ports;
—the cancelling date, that is, the last date by which the ship must be made available to the charterer.

Normally, the charter-party will also contain provisions for delays, such as might be caused by strikes, war or ice.

Voyage charters are normally negotiated by shipbrokers on behalf of shipowners and cargo interests.

Associated abbreviation:
v/c voyage charter

Associated definitions:
To voyage charter Said of a charterer, to take a ship on voyage charter. Said of a shipowner, to charter his ship out on a voyage charter basis

Voyage charter

1. Shipbroker	
	2. Place and date
3. Owners/Place of business (Cl. 1)	4. Charterers/Place of business (Cl. 1)
5. Vessel's name (Cl. 1)	6. GT/NT (Cl. 1)
7. DWT all told on summer load line in metric tons (abt.) (Cl. 1)	8. Present position (Cl. 1)
9. Expected ready to load (abt.) (Cl. 1)	
10. Loading port or place (Cl. 1)	11. Discharging port or place (Cl. 1)

12. Cargo (also state quantity and margin in Owners' option, if agreed; if full and complete cargo not agreed state "part cargo" (Cl. 1)

13. Freight rate (also state whether freight prepaid or payable on delivery) (Cl. 4)	14. Freight payment (state currency and method of payment; also beneficiary and bank account) (Cl. 4)
15. State if vessel's cargo handling gear shall not be used (Cl. 5)	16. Laytime (if separate laytime for load. and disch. is agreed, fill in a) and b). If total laytime for load. and disch., fill in c) only) (Cl. 6)
17. Shippers/Place of business (Cl. 6)	(a) Laytime for loading
18. Agents (loading) (Cl. 6)	(b) Laytime for discharging
19. Agents (discharging) (Cl. 6)	(c) Total laytime for loading and discharging
20. Demurrage rate and manner payable (loading and discharging) (Cl. 7)	21. Cancelling date (Cl. 9)
	22. General Average to be adjusted at (Cl. 12)
23. Freight Tax (state if for the Owners' account (Cl .13 (c))	24. Brokerage commission and to whom payable (Cl. 15)
25. Law and Arbitration (state 19 (a), 19 (b) or 19 (c) of Cl. 19; if 19 (c) agreed also state Place of Arbitration) (if not filled in 19 (a) shall apply) (Cl. 19)	
(a) State maximum amount for small claims/shortened arbitration (Cl. 19)	26. Additional clauses covering special provisions, if agreed

It is mutually agreed that this Contract shall be performed subject to the conditions contained in this Charter Party which shall include Part I as well as Part II. In the event of a conflict of conditions, the provisions of Part I shall prevail over those of Part II to the extent of such conflict.

Signature (Owners)	Signature (Charterers)

Voyage charter-party (Gencon)

Voyage charter

PART II
"Gencon" Charter (As Revised 1922, 1976 and 1994)

1. It is agreed between the party mentioned in Box 3 as the Owners of the Vessel named in Box 5, of the GT/NT indicated in Box 6 and carrying about the number of metric tons of deadweight capacity all told on summer loadline stated in Box 7, now in position as stated in Box 8 and expected ready to load under this Charter Party about the date indicated in Box 9, and the party mentioned as the Charterers in Box 4 that:
The said Vessel shall, as soon as her prior commitments have been completed, proceed to the loading port(s) or place(s) stated in Box 10 or so near thereto as she may safely get and lie always afloat, and there load a full and complete cargo (if shipment of deck cargo agreed same to be at the Charterers' risk and responsibility) as stated in Box 12, which the Charterers bind themselves to ship, and being so loaded the Vessel shall proceed to the discharging port(s) or place(s) stated in Box 11 as ordered on signing Bills of Lading, or so near thereto as she may safely get and lie always afloat, and there deliver the cargo.

2. Owners' Responsibility Clause
The Owners are to be responsible for loss of or damage to the goods or for delay in delivery of the goods only in case the loss, damage or delay has been caused by personal want of due diligence on the part of the Owners or their Manager to make the Vessel in all respects seaworthy and to secure that she is properly manned, equipped and supplied, or by the personal act or default of the Owners or their Manager.
And the Owners are not responsible for loss, damage or delay arising from any other cause whatsoever, even from the neglect or default of the Master or crew or some other person employed by the Owners on board or ashore for whose acts they would, but for this Clause, be responsible, or from unseaworthiness of the Vessel on loading or commencement of the voyage or at any time whatsoever.

3. Deviation Clause
The Vessel has liberty to call at any port or ports in any order, for any purpose, to sail without pilots, to tow and/or assist Vessels in all situations, and also to deviate for the purpose of saving life and/or property.

4. Payment of Freight
(a) The freight at the rate stated in Box 13 shall be paid in cash calculated on the intaken quantity of cargo.
(b) *Prepaid.* If according to Box 13 freight is to be paid on shipment, it shall be deemed earned and non-returnable, Vessel and/or cargo lost or not lost.
Neither the Owners nor their agents shall be required to sign or endorse bills of lading showing freight prepaid unless the freight due to the Owners has actually been paid.
(c) *On delivery.* If according to Box 13 freight, or part thereof, is payable at destination it shall not be deemed earned until the cargo is thus delivered.
Notwithstanding the provisions under (a), if freight or part thereof is payable on delivery of the cargo the Charterers shall have the option of paying the freight on account of delivered weight/quantity provided such option is declared before breaking bulk and the weight/quantity can be ascertained by official weighing machine, joint draft survey or tally.
Cash for Vessel's ordinary disbursements at the port of loading to be advanced by the Charterers, if required, at highest current rate of exchange, subject to two (2) per cent to cover insurance and other expenses.

5. Loading/Discharging
(a) *Costs/Risks*
The cargo shall be brought into the holds, loaded, stowed and/or trimmed, tallied, lashed and/or secured and taken from the holds and discharged by the Charterers, free of any risk, liability and expense whatsoever to the Owners. The Charterers shall provide and lay all dunnage material as required for the proper stowage and protection of the cargo on board, the Owners allowing the use of all dunnage available on board. The Charterers shall be responsible for and pay the cost of removing their dunnage after discharge of the cargo under this Charter Party and time to count until dunnage has been removed.
(b) *Cargo Handling Gear*
Unless the Vessel is gearless or unless it has been agreed between the parties that the Vessel's gear shall not be used and stated as such in Box 15, the Owners shall throughout the duration of loading/discharging give free use of the Vessel's cargo handling gear and of sufficient motive power to operate all such cargo handling gear. All such equipment to be in good working order. Unless caused by negligence of the stevedores, time lost by breakdown of the Vessel's cargo handling gear or motive power – pro rata the total number of cranes/winches required at that time for the loading/discharging of cargo under this Charter Party – shall not count as laytime or time on demurrage.
On request the Owners shall provide free of charge cranemen/winchmen from the crew to operate the Vessel's cargo handling gear, unless local regulations prohibit this, in which latter event shore labourers shall be for the account of the Charterers. Cranemen/winchmen shall be under the Charterers' risk and responsibility and as stevedores to be deemed as their servants but shall always work under the supervision of the Master.
(c) *Stevedore Damage*
The Charterers shall be responsible for damage (beyond ordinary wear and tear) to any part of the Vessel caused by Stevedores. Such damage shall be notified as soon as reasonably possible by the Master to the Charterers or their agents and to their Stevedores, failing which the Charterers shall not be held responsible. The Master shall endeavour to obtain the Stevedores' written acknowledgement of liability.
The Charterers are obliged to repair any stevedore damage prior to completion of the voyage, but must repair stevedore damage affecting the Vessel's seaworthiness or class before the Vessel sails from the port where such damage was caused or found. All additional expenses incurred shall be for the account of the Charterers and any time lost shall be for the account of and shall be paid to the Owners by the Charterers at the demurrage rate.

6. Laytime
* (a) Separate laytime for loading and discharging
The cargo shall be loaded within the number of running days/hours as indicated in Box 16, weather permitting, Sundays and holidays excepted, unless used, in which event time used shall count.
The cargo shall be discharged within the number of running days/hours as indicated in Box 16, weather permitting, Sundays and holidays excepted, unless used, in which event time used shall count.
* (b) Total laytime for loading and discharging
The cargo shall be loaded and discharged within the number of total running days/hours as indicated in Box 16, weather permitting, Sundays and holidays excepted, unless used, in which event time used shall count.
(c) *Commencement of laytime (loading and discharging)*
Laytime for loading and discharging shall commence at 13.00 hours, if notice of readiness is given up to and including 12.00 hours, and at 06.00 hours next working day if notice given during office hours after 12.00 hours. Notice of

readiness at loading port to be given to the Shippers named in Box 17 or if not named, to the Charterers or their agents named in Box 18. Notice of readiness at the discharging port to be given to the Receivers or, if not known, to the Charterers or their agents named in Box 19.
If the loading/discharging berth is not available on the Vessel's arrival at or off the port of loading/discharging, the Vessel shall be entitled to give notice of readiness within ordinary office hours on arrival there, whether in free pratique or not, whether customs cleared or not. Laytime or time on demurrage shall then count as if she were in berth and in all respects ready for loading/ discharging provided that the Master warrants that she is in fact ready in all respects. Time used in moving from the place of waiting to the loading/ discharging berth shall not count as laytime.
If, after inspection, the Vessel is found not to be ready in all respects to load/ discharge time lost after the discovery thereof until the Vessel is again ready to load/discharge shall not count as laytime.
Time used before commencement of laytime shall count.
* Indicate alternative (a) or (b) as agreed, in Box 16.

7. Demurrage
Demurrage at the loading and discharging port is payable by the Charterers at the rate stated in Box 20 in the manner stated in Box 20 per day or pro rata for any part of a day. Demurrage shall fall due day by day and shall be payable upon receipt of the Owners' invoice.
In the event the demurrage is not paid in accordance with the above, the Owners shall give the Charterers 96 running hours written notice to rectify the failure. If the demurrage is not paid at the expiration of this time limit and if the vessel is in or at the loading port, the Owners are entitled at any time to terminate the Charter Party and claim damages for any losses caused thereby.

8. Lien Clause
The Owners shall have a lien on the cargo and on all sub-freights payable in respect of the cargo, for freight, deadfreight, demurrage, claims for damages and for all other amounts due under this Charter Party including costs of recovering same.

9. Cancelling Clause
(a) Should the Vessel not be ready to load (whether in berth or not) on the cancelling date indicated in Box 21, the Charterers shall have the option of cancelling this Charter Party.
(b) Should the Owners anticipate that, despite the exercise of due diligence, the Vessel will not be ready to load by the cancelling date, they shall notify the Charterers thereof without delay stating the expected date of the Vessel's readiness to load and asking whether the Charterers will exercise their option of cancelling the Charter Party, or agree to a new cancelling date.
Such option must be declared by the Charterers within 48 running hours after the receipt of the Owners' notice. If the Charterers do not exercise their option of cancelling, then this Charter Party shall be deemed to be amended such that the seventh day after the new readiness date stated in the Owners' notification to the Charterers shall be the new cancelling date.
The provisions of sub-clause (b) of this Clause shall operate only once, and in case of the Vessel's further delay, the Charterers shall have the option of cancelling the Charter Party as per sub-clause (a) of this Clause.

10. Bills of Lading
Bills of Lading shall be presented and signed by the Master as per the "Congenbill" Bill of Lading form, Edition 1994, without prejudice to this Charter Party, or by the Owners' agents provided written authority has been given by the Owners to the agents, a copy of which is to be furnished to the Charterers. The Charterers shall indemnify the Owners against all consequences or liabilities that may arise from the signing of bills of lading as presented to the extent that the terms or contents of such bills of lading impose or result in the imposition of more onerous liabilities upon the Owners than those assumed by the Owners under this Charter Party.

11. Both-to-Blame Collision Clause
If the Vessel comes into collision with another vessel as a result of the negligence of the other vessel and any act, neglect or default of the Master, Mariner, Pilot or the servants of the Owners in the navigation or in the management of the Vessel, the owners of the cargo carried hereunder will indemnify the Owners against all loss or liability to the other or non-carrying vessel or her owners in so far as such loss or liability represents loss of, or damage to, or any claim whatsoever of the owners of said cargo, paid or payable by the other or non-carrying vessel or her owners to the owners of said cargo and set-off, recouped or recovered by the other or non-carrying vessel or her owners as part of their claim against the carrying Vessel or the Owners. The foregoing provisions shall also apply where the owners, operators or those in charge of any vessel or vessels or objects other than, or in addition to, the colliding vessels or objects are at fault in respect of a collision or contact.

12. General Average and New Jason Clause
General Average shall be adjusted in London unless otherwise agreed in Box 22 according to York-Antwerp Rules 1994 and any subsequent modification thereof. Proprietors of cargo to pay the cargo's share in the general expenses even if same have been necessitated through neglect or default of the Owners' servants (see Clause 2).
If General Average is to be adjusted in accordance with the law and practice of the United States of America, the following Clause shall apply: "In the event of accident, danger, damage or disaster before or after the commencement of the voyage, resulting from any cause whatsoever, whether due to negligence or not, for which, or for the consequence of which, the Owners are not responsible, by statute, contract or otherwise, the cargo shippers, consignees or the owners of the cargo shall contribute with the Owners in General Average to the payment of any sacrifices, losses or expenses of a General Average nature that may be made or incurred and shall pay salvage and special charges incurred in respect of the cargo. If a salving vessel is owned or operated by the Owners, salvage shall be paid for as fully as if the said salving vessel or vessels belonged to strangers. Such deposit as the Owners, or their agents, may deem sufficient to cover the estimated contribution of the goods and any salvage and special charges thereon shall, if required, be made by the cargo, shippers, consignees or owners of the goods to the Owners before delivery.".

13. Taxes and Dues Clause
(a) *On Vessel* -The Owners shall pay all dues, charges and taxes customarily levied on the Vessel, howsoever the amount thereof may be assessed.
(b) *On cargo* -The Charterers shall pay all dues, charges, duties and taxes customarily levied on the cargo, howsoever the amount thereof may be assessed.
(c) *On freight* -Unless otherwise agreed in Box 23, taxes levied on the freight shall be for the Charterers' account.

Voyage charter-party (Gencon)

295

Voyage charter

PART II
"Gencon" Charter (As Revised 1922, 1976 and 1994)

14. Agency 207
In every case the Owners shall appoint their own Agent both at the port of 208
loading and the port of discharge. 209

15. Brokerage 210
A brokerage commission at the rate stated in Box 24 on the freight, dead-freight 211
and demurrage earned is due to the party mentioned in Box 24. 212
In case of non-execution 1/3 of the brokerage on the estimated amount of 213
freight to be paid by the party responsible for such non-execution to the 214
Brokers as indemnity for the latter's expenses and work. In case of more 215
voyages the amount of indemnity to be agreed. 216

16. General Strike Clause 217
(a) If there is a strike or lock-out affecting or preventing the actual loading of the 218
cargo, or any part of it, when the Vessel is ready to proceed from her last port or 219
at any time during the voyage to the port or ports of loading or after her arrival 220
there, the Master or the Owners may ask the Charterers to declare, that they 221
agree to reckon the laydays as if there were no strike or lock-out. Unless the 222
Charterers have given such declaration in writing (by telegram, if necessary) 223
within 24 hours, the Owners shall have the option of cancelling this Charter 224
Party. If part cargo has already been loaded, the Owners must proceed with 225
same, (freight payable on loaded quantity only) having liberty to complete with 226
other cargo on the way for their own account. 227
(b) If there is a strike or lock-out affecting or preventing the actual discharging 228
of the cargo on or after the Vessel's arrival at or off port of discharge and same 229
has not been settled within 48 hours, the Charterers shall have the option of 230
keeping the Vessel waiting until such strike or lock-out is at an end against 231
paying half demurrage after expiration of the time provided for discharging 232
until the strike or lock-out terminates and thereafter full demurrage shall be 233
payable until the completion of discharging, or of ordering the Vessel to a safe 234
port where she can safely discharge without risk of being detained by strike or 235
lock-out. Such orders to be given within 48 hours after the Master or the 236
Owners have given notice to the Charterers of the strike or lock-out affecting 237
the discharge. On delivery of the cargo at such port, all conditions of this 238
Charter Party and of the Bill of Lading shall apply and the Vessel shall receive 239
the same freight as if she had discharged at the original port of destination, 240
except that if the distance to the substituted port exceeds 100 nautical miles, 241
the freight on the cargo delivered at the substituted port to be increased in 242
proportion. 243
(c) Except for the obligations described above, neither the Charterers nor the 244
Owners shall be responsible for the consequences of any strikes or lock-outs 245
preventing or affecting the actual loading or discharging of the cargo. 246

17. War Risks ("Voywar 1993") 247
(1) For the purpose of this Clause, the words: 248
(a) The "Owners" shall include the shipowners, bareboat charterers, 249
disponent owners, managers or other operators who are charged with the 250
management of the Vessel, and the Master; and 251
(b) "War Risks" shall include any war (whether actual or threatened), act of 252
war, civil war, hostilities, revolution, rebellion, civil commotion, warlike 253
operations, the laying of mines (whether actual or reported), acts of piracy, 254
acts of terrorists, acts of hostility or malicious damage, blockades 255
(whether imposed against all Vessels or imposed selectively against 256
Vessels of certain flags or ownership, or against certain cargoes or crews 257
or otherwise howsoever), by any person, body, terrorist or political group, 258
or the Government of any state whatsoever, which, in the reasonable 259
judgement of the Master and/or the Owners, may be dangerous or are 260
likely to be or to become dangerous to the Vessel, her cargo, crew or other 261
persons on board the Vessel. 262
(2) If at any time before the Vessel commences loading, it appears that, in the 263
reasonable judgement of the Master and/or the Owners, performance of 264
the Contract of Carriage, or any part of it, may expose, or is likely to expose, 265
the Vessel, her cargo, crew or other persons on board the Vessel to War 266
Risks, the Owners may give notice to the Charterers cancelling this 267
Contract of Carriage, or may refuse to perform such part of it as may 268
expose, or may be likely to expose, the Vessel, her cargo, crew or other 269
persons on board the Vessel to War Risks; provided always that if this 270
Contract of Carriage provides that loading or discharging is to take place 271
within a range of ports, and at the port or ports nominated by the Charterers 272
the Vessel, her cargo, crew, or other persons onboard the Vessel may be 273
exposed, or may be likely to be exposed, to War Risks, the Owners shall 274
first require the Charterers to nominate any other safe port which lies 275
within the range for loading or discharging, and may only cancel this 276
Contract of Carriage if the Charterers shall not have nominated such safe 277
port or ports within 48 hours of receipt of notice of such requirement. 278
(3) The Owners shall not be required to continue to load cargo for any voyage, 279
or to sign Bills of Lading for any port or place, or to proceed or continue on 280
any voyage, or on any part thereof, or to proceed through any canal or 281
waterway, or to proceed to or remain at any port or place whatsoever, 282
where it appears, either after the loading of the cargo commences, or at any 283
stage of the voyage thereafter before the discharge of the cargo is 284
completed, that, in the reasonable judgement of the Master and/or the 285
Owners, the Vessel, her cargo (or any part thereof), crew or other persons 286
on board the Vessel (or any one or more of them) may be, or are likely to be, 287
exposed to War Risks. If it should so appear, the Owners may by notice 288
request the Charterers to nominate a safe port for the discharge of the 289
cargo or any part thereof, and if within 48 hours of the receipt of such 290
notice, the Charterers shall not have nominated such a port, the Owners 291
may discharge the cargo at any safe port of their choice (including the port 292
of loading) in complete fulfilment of the Contract of Carriage. The Owners 293
shall be entitled to recover from the Charterers the extra expenses of such 294
discharge and, if the discharge takes place at any port other than the 295
loading port, to receive the full freight as though the cargo had been 296
carried to the discharging port and if the extra distance exceeds 100 miles, 297
to additional freight which shall be the same percentage of the freight 298
contracted for as the percentage which the extra distance represents to 299
the distance of the normal and customary route, the Owners having a lien 300
on the cargo for such expenses and freight. 301
(4) If at any stage of the voyage after the loading of the cargo commences, it 302
appears that, in the reasonable judgement of the Master and/or the 303
Owners, the Vessel, her cargo, crew or other persons on board the Vessel 304
may be, or are likely to be, exposed to War Risks on any part of the route 305
(including any canal or waterway) which is normally and customarily used 306
in a voyage of the nature contracted for, and there is another longer route 307
to the discharging port, the Owners shall give notice to the Charterers that 308
this route will be taken. In this event the Owners shall be entitled, if the total 309
extra distance exceeds 100 miles, to additional freight which shall be the 310
same percentage of the freight contracted for as the percentage which the 311
extra distance represents to the distance of the normal and customary 312
route. 313

(5) The Vessel shall have liberty:- 314
(a) to comply with all orders, directions, recommendations or advice as to 315
departure, arrival, routes, sailing in convoy, ports of call, stoppages, 316
destinations, discharge of cargo, delivery or in any way whatsoever which 317
are given by the Government of the Nation under whose flag the Vessel 318
sails, or other Government to whose laws the Owners are subject, or any 319
other Government which so requires, or any body or group acting with the 320
power to compel compliance with their orders or directions; 321
(b) to comply with the orders, directions or recommendations of any war 322
risks underwriters who have the authority to give the same under the terms 323
of the war risks insurance; 324
(c) to comply with the terms of any resolution of the Security Council of the 325
United Nations, any directives of the European Community, the effective 326
orders of any other Supranational body which has the right to issue and 327
give the same, and with national laws aimed at enforcing the same to which 328
the Owners are subject, and to obey the orders and directions of those who 329
are charged with their enforcement; 330
(d) to discharge at any other port any cargo or part thereof which may 331
render the Vessel liable to confiscation as a contraband carrier; 332
(e) to call at any other port to change the crew or any part thereof or other 333
persons on board the Vessel when there is reason to believe that they may 334
be subject to internment, imprisonment or other sanctions; 335
(f) where cargo has not been loaded or has been discharged by the 336
Owners under any provisions of this Clause, to load other cargo for the 337
Owners' own benefit and carry it to any other port or ports whatsoever, 338
whether backwards or forwards or in a contrary direction to the ordinary or 339
customary route. 340
(6) If in compliance with any of the provisions of sub-clauses (2) to (5) of this 341
Clause anything is done or not done, such shall not be deemed to be a 342
deviation, but shall be considered as due fulfilment of the Contract of 343
Carriage. 344

18. General Ice Clause 345
Port of loading 346
(a) In the event of the loading port being inaccessible by reason of ice when the 347
Vessel is ready to proceed from her last port or at any time during the voyage or 348
on the Vessel's arrival or in case frost sets in after the Vessel's arrival, the 349
Master for fear of being frozen in is at liberty to leave without cargo, and this 350
Charter Party shall be null and void. 351
(b) If during loading the Master, for fear of the Vessel being frozen in, deems it 352
advisable to leave, he has liberty to do so with what cargo he has on board and 353
to proceed to any other port or ports with option of completing cargo for the 354
Owners' benefit for any port or ports including port of discharge. Any part 355
cargo thus loaded under this Charter Party to be forwarded to destination at the 356
Vessel's expense but against payment of freight, provided that no extra 357
expenses be thereby caused to the Charterers, freight being paid on quantity 358
delivered (in proportion if lumpsum), all other conditions as per this Charter 359
Party. 360
(c) In case of more than one loading port, and if one or more of the ports are 361
closed by ice, the Master or the Owners to be at liberty either to load the part 362
cargo at the open port and fill up elsewhere for their own account as under 363
section (b) or to declare the Charter Party null and void unless the Charterers 364
agree to load full cargo at the open port. 365
Port of discharge 366
(a) Should ice prevent the Vessel from reaching port of discharge the 367
Charterers shall have the option of keeping the Vessel waiting until the re- 368
opening of navigation and paying demurrage or of ordering the Vessel to a safe 369
and immediately accessible port where she can safely discharge without risk of 370
detention by ice. Such orders to be given within 48 hours after the Master or the 371
Owners have given notice to the Charterers of the impossibility of reaching port 372
of destination. 373
(b) If during discharging the Master for fear of the Vessel being frozen in deems 374
it advisable to leave, he has liberty to do so with what cargo he has on board and 375
to proceed to the nearest accessible port where she can safely discharge. 376
(c) On delivery of the cargo at such port, all conditions of the Bill of Lading shall 377
apply and the Vessel shall receive the same freight as if she had discharged at 378
the original port of destination, except that if the distance of the substituted port 379
exceeds 100 nautical miles, the freight on the cargo delivered at the substituted 380
port to be increased in proportion. 381

19. Law and Arbitration 382
* (a) This Charter Party shall be governed by and construed in accordance with 383
English law and any dispute arising out of this Charter Party shall be referred to 384
arbitration in London in accordance with the Arbitration Acts 1950 and 1979 or 385
any statutory modification or re-enactment thereof for the time being in force. 386
Unless the parties agree upon a sole arbitrator, the reference shall be 387
appointed by each party and the arbitrators so appointed shall appoint a third 388
arbitrator, the decision of the three-man tribunal thus constituted or any two of 389
them, shall be final. On the receipt by one party of the nomination in writing of 390
the other party's arbitrator, that party shall appoint their arbitrator within 391
fourteen days, failing which the decision of the single arbitrator appointed shall 392
be final. 393
For disputes where the total amount claimed by either party does not exceed 394
the amount stated in Box 25** the arbitration shall be conducted in accordance 395
with the Small Claims Procedure of the London Maritime Arbitrators 396
Association. 397
* (b) This Charter Party shall be governed by and construed in accordance with 398
Title 9 of the United States Code and the Maritime Law of the United States and 399
should any dispute arise out of this Charter Party, the matter in dispute shall be 400
referred to three persons at New York, one to be appointed by each of the 401
parties hereto, and the third by the two so chosen; their decision or that of any 402
two of them shall be final, and for purpose of enforcing any award, this 403
agreement may be made a rule of the Court. The proceedings shall be 404
conducted in accordance with the rules of the Society of Maritime Arbitrators, 405
Inc.. 406
For disputes where the total amount claimed by either party does not exceed 407
the amount stated in Box 25** the arbitration shall be conducted in accordance 408
with the Shortened Arbitration Procedure of the Society of Maritime Arbitrators, 409
Inc.. 410
* (c) Any dispute arising out of this Charter Party shall be referred to arbitration at 411
the place indicated in Box 25, subject to the procedures applicable there. The 412
laws of the place indicated in Box 25 shall govern this Charter Party. 413
(d) If Box 25 in Part I is not filled in, sub-clause (a) of this Clause shall apply. 414
* (a), (b) and (c) are alternatives; indicate alternative agreed in Box 25. 415
** Where no figure is supplied in Box 25 in Part I, this provision only shall be void but 416
the other provisions of this Clause shall have full force and remain in effect. 417

Voyage charter-party (Gencon)

296

Associated term:
Voyage charterer

See also:
BIMCO (Baltic and International Maritime Council)
BIMCO voyage charter-parties
Baltic Exchange
Laytime—calculation
Laytime—commencement
Time charter
Voyage charter—ship's position

Voyage charter—ship's position

When advertising a ship, the shipowner or his broker may describe her as being **open** on or about a certain date, that is, the date when she becomes free to take on new employment. She may be **spot**, available almost immediately, or even **spot prompt**, immediately. She may be fixed to perform an **interim voyage**, undertaken between the time when she is to perform the voyage for which she is being advertised and the time she actually performs it. Alternatively, she may **ballast** directly to the loading port, that is, proceed there without a cargo.

During the negotiating stage, the shipowner may have more than one ship **coming free** (becoming available) and may not know which one will perform the voyage. He may therefore offer a named ship or (**similar**) **substitute**, or a **vessel TBN** (**to be nominated**) or a **vessel TBA** (**to be advised**), or simply a **TBN** or a **TBA**. He will be required to **nominate**, or designate, the exact ship by a certain time before commencement of the charter.

The date when the vessel is expected at a port or place, for example the load port or the discharge port, is the **ETA** (**estimated time of arrival**). She may **come forward**, have an estimated date of arrival which is earlier than previously given, or **go back** (alternatively **drop back**) with an estimated date later than previously given. The charter-party may stipulate that several ETAs be given at agreed intervals prior to the ship's arrival at the load and discharge ports; these are normally given by the ship's master to the port agent and relayed to the charterer.

The **cancelling date** is the last date by which a ship must be available to the charterer at the agreed place at the commencement of the contract. If the ship is not available by that date, the charterer may have the option to cancel the charter, depending on the exact agreement.

In the case of a voyage charter, both the shipowner and the charterer will want to be informed of the vessel's progress while in port and will be notified by the agent, probably on a daily basis: a vessel's **ETR** (**estimated time of readiness**) is given in order to indicate when she is expected to be ready to take on cargo;

when she is actually ready, she is said to be **load ready**. Her **ETC, estimated time of completion** of loading (or discharging), **ETD, estimated time of departure** and **ETS, estimated time of sailing,** are given as indications at various times. Another way of expressing an indication of expectations for a ship is refer to her **prospects**. This could apply, for example, when indicating, or asking about, her arrival time or date of berthing, or date of completion of loading or discharging.

A ship's **itinerary** is a list of all the ports which the ship calls at on a particular voyage to load and discharge cargo; this list often includes her ETAs and ETSs. When incorporated into a set of instructions to the master of a ship for his next voyage, the itinerary may include ports where it is intended to take on bunkers. The **rotation** is the sequence in which the ship calls at these ports and, if in **geographical rotation**, the ship calls at each of the ports in turn utilising the most direct route.

Associated abbreviations:
eta estimated time of arrival
etc estimated time of completion
etd estimated time of departure
etr estimated time of readiness
ets estimated time of sailing
sim. sub. similar substitute
sub. substitute
tba to be advised
tbn to be nominated

Associated definitions:
nomination designation of a specific ship for a particular voyage by the shipowner
EDA estimated date of arrival. Strictly, this is more appropriate than ETA, especially when the date referred to is a long way off. However, it is less commonly used. The same applies to **EDS**, estimated date of sailing

Associated terms:
substitution
to substitute

See also:
Arrived ship
Time charter

Voyage estimate

Calculation of the profitability of a prospective voyage of a ship using estimated figures. In the case of a tramp shipowner, the estimate is used to compare two or more voyages in order to determine which is the most profitable. Similarly, a time charterer would compare two or more ships so as to charter the one which is least costly overall. The content of an estimate varies according to the type and terms of the charter and whether the calculation is being made by a shipowner or charterer. For an owner, the principal costs are the running cost of the ship (or hire money for a time charterer), bunker costs, port charges and canal dues together with ship's agency fees and any cargo handling costs; the revenue is the daily hire, in the case of a time charter, or the freight, less any commission in the case of a voyage charter.

Below is an example of a voyage estimate as suggested by the Baltic Exchange in the Baltic Code. It is based on "free in and out" (FIO) terms and full laytime and can be used for both dry cargo and tanker business.

Vessel .... Load port(s) ....

Discharge port(s) ....

Distance .... Vessel's speed/consumption ....

Expected bunker price ....

Fuel oil .... Diesel oil ....

Days at sea .... days in port ....

Total voyage time ....

Income Freight .... tonnes at ....

Less Commission .... %

Costs Loading port(s) costs ....

Bunkering port(s) costs ....

Discharge port(s) costs ....

Fuel oil .... days x .... tonnes x ...... $ per tonne

Diesel oil .... days x .... tonnes x ...... $ per tonne

Canal costs ....

Taxes/dues ....

Other costs ....

Gross voyage costs ....

Net voyage income ....

(freight less costs)

Voyage income .... in .... days = ... per day

Vessel's daily running cost ....

Profit or Loss per day (income less costs) ....

Voyage estimate

Associated definition:

voyage account Statement of the costs and revenue of a voyage of a ship made after the voyage is completed when the income and all actual costs are known

War risk surcharge

Insurance underwriters face wide ranging risks and these become greater as ships become more sophisticated and more expensive to build and repair. When shipping becomes at risk because of a war, underwriters announce that a specific area has become a war zone and shipowners entering this zone are liable to pay an extra insurance premium. Liner operators faced with this extra cost, and it can be a sizeable amount, will generally seek to receiver the extra cost from shippers by introducing a temporary surcharge called a **war risk surcharge**. This is applied to the freight and can be expressed as a percentage or as an amount per container. The calculation which shipping lines have to perform under these circumstances is to estimate the revenue which they will earn and divide the additional premium into it in order to determine the level of the surcharge. When underwriters announce that an area is no longer officially a war zone, shipping lines will withdraw the surcharge.

See also:
Liner surcharges

Waybill

Document, issued by a shipping line or shipowner to a shipper or charterer, which serves as a receipt for the goods and evidence of the contract of carriage. In these respects it resembles a bill of lading but, unlike a bill of lading, it is not a document of title; it bears the name of the consignee who has only to identify himself in order to take delivery of the cargo. Because it is not negotiable, the waybill is not acceptable to the banks as collateral security. The purpose of the waybill is to avoid delays to ships and cargoes which occur when bills of lading are late in arriving at the port of discharge or place of delivery. This document is also referred to as an **ocean waybill** or **sea waybill** and, when issued under a liner contract, a **liner waybill**.

Different waybills are available for different types of contract. In particular, the Baltic and International Maritime Council (BIMCO) publishes a variety of forms:

—The Blank Back Form of Non-negotiable Liner Waybill which, as its name suggests, has no conditions printed on its reverse but states on the front that it is subject to the carrier's standard terms and conditions. This enables it to be used by different shipping lines each having its own terms.

—Non-negotiable General Sea Waybill, codenamed **Genwaybill**, is issued pursuant to a voyage charter-party; the name, place and date of issue of the charter-party are specified on the face of the waybill.

—Non-negotiable Tanker Waybill, codenamed **Tankwaybill 81**, issued pursuant to a tanker charter-party, the details of which are specified on the face.

—Non-negotiable Chemical Tank Waybill, codenamed **Chemtankwaybill 85**, issued pursuant to a chemical tanker charter-party, the details of which are specified on the face.

—Non-negotiable Gas Tank Waybill for Use in the LPG Trade, codenamed **Gastankwaybill**, issued pursuant to an LPG (liquid or liquefied petroleum gas) charter-party, the details of which are specified on the face.

—Non-negotiable Liner Waybill, codenamed **Worldfoodwaybill**, issued in respect of liner contracts concluded with the UN/FAO World Food Pro-gramme in Rome.

—Combined Transport Sea Waybill, codenamed **Combiconwaybill**, issued in respect of a combined transport contract.

—Multimodal Transport Waybill, codenamed **Multiwaybill 95**, issued in respect of a multimodal transport contract.

See also:
Combined transport
Combined transport bill of lading
Multimodal transport bill of lading

Weather routing

Service offered by a Government department or private company whereby a shipowner or ship operator is provided with a route for his ship, devised by means of up-to-date weather predictions, which avoids severe weather con-ditions such as storms, fog and ice. This route is not necessarily the most direct but is expected to take less time since it avoids conditions which would require a reduction in speed. Additionally, the risks of heavy weather and, in extreme conditions, of injury to the crew, are reduced. A fee is charged for this service. Weather routing is also known as **ship routing**.

WNI Oceanroutes is a private company offering weather routing services. They describe the benefits as follows:

—Reduce fuel costs.
—Maintain schedule integrity.
—Lower insurance claims.
—Reduce asset damage.
—Improve intermodal connections.
—Improve crew safety.

Weather routing

Their information is derived from a complete range of environmental data, such as surface pressure charts, satellite data, winds and waves, sea conditions, ice and sea temperatures. They also factor in the nature of the cargo and the condition of vessels, like type, age, speed, draft, trim, deck load, stability and sea-handling characteristics.

Following the voyage WNI Oceanroutes can also prepare a post-voyage Preliminary Performance Evaluation (PPE) to be used by the vessel operator and the master to review the voyage in the light of weather experienced, the route taken and the performance of the vessel on that route. The PPE provides important vessel management information about fuel consumption and speed performance.

WNI Oceanroutes further describe the benefits in terms of making cost-effective voyages, along with resolving any disputes related to the charter-party by means of the following:

—Enhance voyage profitability
—Improve vessel performance
—Safeguard your interests in disputes
—Reduce fuel consumption
—Assure greater schedule integrity
—Upgrade your ETA tracking capability

WNI Oceanroutes provides two-fold protection to chartered ship operators: (1) improving voyage performance and (2) providing conflict-resolution tools.

By providing actual and reliable data related to your voyage, WNI Oceanroutes information is particularly useful in substantiating speed and fuel consumption issues.

Speed and bunker analysis

If given details of the charter-party as it pertains to speed and fuel consumption, WNI Oceanroutes' Speed and Bunker Analyses (SBA) can be used to show the actual time lost and fuel over-consumed during the voyage.

Voyage reconstruction

Voyage reconstruction can be provided for those voyages where weather routing was not utilised. WNI Oceanroutes provide a complete Preliminary Performance Evaluation and Speed and Bunker Report to compare against the reported weather, consumption, performance of the vessel and route selected. WNI Oceanroutes maintains a comprehensive historical weather database to handle all your vessel performance and forensic needs.

Weather Routing Inc., a US weather routing company, also provides daily en route weather updates together with a weather synopsis (*see below*), detailed forecast and a review of the current route.

"REQUESTS FOR OUR SERVICES are normally made days to a week in advance. To provide individualized service, tailored to your vessel, we will need particulars about your vessel—her speed, range, stability, handling, maximum acceptable winds and seas, etc.

A message with this information might be as follows:

TO: CAPTAIN—ANY VESSEL

SYNOPSIS: LARGE W'RN ATLANTIC STORM CENTERED NEAR 35N61W AT 08–15Z IS MOVING NE'WARD AT APPROX 15KTS. SYSTEM WILL ACCELERATE SOME AS IT CONTINUES NE'WARD MOVEMENT THRU THE 09TH, THEN SLOWLY TURN ENE'WARD AND SLOWLY WEAKEN ON 10TH INTO THE 11TH. ASSOCIATED WEAKENING COLD FRONT EXTENDS SW'WARD FROM STORM CENTER TO JUST NORTHWEST OF PUERTO RICO, AND WILL MOVE E'WARD THRU THE 09TH, PASSING NORTH OF VIRGIN ISLANDS TONIGHT AND THE LEEWARDS EARLY 09TH. THERE WILL BE A TROUGH OF LOW PRESSURE COVERING AN AREA FROM THE BAHAMAS E'WARD TO THE CARIBBEAN ISLANDS NEXT 2DAYS—KEEPING THE W'LY WINDS ACROSS THE N'RN CARIBBEAN ISLANDS DURING THAT TIME.

FURTHER WEST, RIDGE OF HIGH PRESSURE COVERING MUCH OF E'RN U.S. AND EXTREME W'RN ATLANTIC WILL DRIFT E'WARD THRU THE 11TH. AS A RESULT, NE-E'LY TRADES WILL RETURN TO THE CARIBBEAN ISLANDS LATE 10TH, CONTINUING THRU THE 11TH.

FROM VIRGIN GORDA TO ST. BARTS: WINDS SW-SSW/VARY/S-SSE'LY 8–17KTS THRU TONIGHT, BECOMING SW-W'LY 10–19KTS ON 09TH AND W-WNW/VARY/NW'LY 11–20KTS NIGHT 09TH THRU AFTERNOON 10TH. WINDS THEN BCM NE-E 12–20KTS (OCNL 20–23KTS IN/ABEAM ANEGADA PASSAGE) NIGHT 10TH, INCREASE TO NE-E 14–23KTS (OCNL 23–28KTS IN/ABEAM ANEGADA PASSAGE) ON THE 11TH.

WIND DRIVEN SEAS 2–3FT THRU TONIGHT, 2–4FT ON 09TH THRU THE 10TH, AND 3–5FT (OCNL 6FT) ON THE 11TH. SWELLS BECOMING SW-W'LY 4–8FT THRU TONIGHT, THEN W-NW'LY AND BUILDING 7–10FT ON THE 09TH, AND NW'LY 8–12FT (BUT LONG IN PERIOD) LATER NIGHT 09TH THRU THE 10TH. SWELLS THEN BCM NE-E 4–8FT ON THE 11TH MIXED WITH OCNL LONG PERIOD W-NW'LY SWELLS 5–9FT EARLY IN THE MORNING, WHICH WILL EASE FURTHER AS THE MORNING WEARS ON.

GENERALLY PARTLY CLOUDY SKIES TODAY, WITH SCTD SHWRS DEVELOPING LATE THIS AFTERNOON, CONTINUING THRU TONIGHT, BECOMING CLEAR TO PARTLY CLOUDY WITH ISOLATED SHWRS 09TH THRU THE 11TH."

Weights and measures

The unit on which freight is calculated differs depending on the type of cargo and the type of contract. Many different units may be used of which the following are the most common:

—**tonne**, also referred as a **metric ton**: 1,000 kg
—**ton**, or **long ton**: 2,240 lb
—**net ton** or **short ton**: 2,000 lb
—**cubic metre**: metric unit of volume
—**cubic foot**: Imperial unit of volume
—**teu**: twenty-foot equivalent unit; unit of measurement equivalent to one 20-foot shipping container. Thus a 40-foot container is equal to two teu's.

Weights and measures

—**feu**: forty-foot equivalent unit
—**lane metres**: unit of distance along the car deck of a ro-ro ship
—**board foot** (lumber): distance along the length of lumber
—**lump sum**: one amount irrespective of the quantity

Freight may be calculated in a number of ways, depending on the individual contract. The principal distinction is between the weight of a cargo and its measurement. Generally, carriers aim to earn freight on whichever calculation (out of the weight or the cubic measurement) brings the greatest revenue. Thus very often freight is quoted on a **weight or measurement** basis, also called **weight or measure**. In this case, the rate of freight is multiplied by whichever is the greater, the number of cubic metres or the number of tonnes. This method of quoting freight applies particularly in cases where the ratio of a cargo's weight to its volume (its **stowage factor**) is not certain.

A cargo which measures less than one cubic metre to one tonne is known as a **weight rated cargo** or **weight cargo**. Freight is generally payable **per tonne weight** (often simply termed **per tonne**). Such freight is said to be payable **on the weight**.

Conversely, a cargo which measures more than one cubic metre to one tonne is said to be **measurement rated cargo** or **measurement cargo**. Freight is normally payable **per cubic metre** and the freight is said to be payable **on the measure** or **on the measurement**.

Depending on the contract, the calculation of the freight may be based on the **intaken weight,** that is, the total amount of cargo loaded on the vessel, or possibly on the **outturn weight**, the quantity discharged. There may be a difference between these two weights, particularly in the case of bulk cargoes, because of circumstances such as wind (especially with fine cargoes), when a quantity of cargo can literally be blown away during cargo handling; this is known as **windage**. An allowance mayor may not be made for the moisture content of a bulk cargo. If it is, the freight may be based on the **dry weight**; if not, it is based on the **wet weight**.

Tanker cargoes are often quoted by means of a scale called Worldscale. *See entry under* **Worldscale** *for an explanation.* Alternatively, cargoes may be quoted on a lump sum basis.

Associated abbreviations:
cbm cubic metre
feu forty foot equivalent unit
lm lane metre(s)
ls lump sum
lt long ton
mt metric ton
nt net ton or nett ton
teu twenty-foot equivalent unit
w/m weight or measure, weight or measurement

Worldscale

Introduction to Worldscale Freight Rate Schedules

The concept of freight rate schedules originated during the 1939–45 War.

Before the War, rates of freight for tanker voyage charters were expressed in dollars or shillings and pence per long ton (there were 20 shillings to a pound, 12 pence in a shilling) and this meant that when a charterer required wide loading or discharging options it was necessary to agree many rates of freight.

During the War, first the British Government and later the US Government requisitioned shipping and owners received compensation on the basis of a daily hire rate.

However, from time to time, the Government were able to make requisitioned tankers available on a voyage basis to the major oil companies for their private use particularly during the period from the end of hostilities until control of shipping was relinquished. On such occasions, the oil companies paid freight to the Government concerned and the rate of freight, which was dependent upon the voyage performed, was determined in accordance with a scale or schedule of rates laid down by that Government.

The rates were calculated so that, after allowing for port costs, bunker costs and canal expenses, the net daily revenue was the same for all voyages.

Here then was the genesis of the principle for tanker rate schedules, namely that owners should receive the same net daily revenue irrespective of the voyage performed.

The last schedule of tanker voyage rates to be issued by the British Ministry of Transport gave rates effective 1 January 1946 and this schedule became known simply as "MOT". Similarly, the last rates to be issued by the United States Maritime Commission, which took effect from 1 February 1946, became known as "USMC".

In fact, Government control of shipping continued until 1948 and by that time the tanker trade had come to recognise the advantages of freight rate schedules and therefore, in the free market, the system evolved of negotiating in terms of MOT or USMC plus or minus a percentage as dictated by the demand/supply position in the market.

Between 1952 and 1962 a number of different schedules were issued as a service to the tanker trade by non-governmental bodies: Scales Nos 1, 2 and 3 and then Intascale in London, ATRS in New York.

Then in 1969 there came the joint London/New York production issued to replace both Intascale and ATRS called the "Worldwide Tanker Nominal Freight Scale", more usually known under its code name "Worldscale".

The full name is mentioned because it provides the opportunity to stress the word "nominal" and to emphasise that it was only during the period of Government control that the schedule rates were intended to be used as actual rates. Subsequently, it has been the freely negotiated percentage adjustments to the scale rates that has determined the actual rate used for the payment of freight.

Worldscale

Incidentally, with the introduction of Worldscale, it became the custom to express market levels of freight in terms of a direct percentage of the scale rates instead of a plus or minus percentage. This method is known as "Points of Scale" and thus Worldscale 100 means 100 points or 100 per cent of the published rate or, in other words, the published rate itself, sometimes referred to as Worldscale flat, while Worldscale 250 means 250 points or 250 per cent of the published rate and Worldscale 30 means 30 points or 30 per cent of the published rate. Under the older method these would have been referred to as plus 250 per cent and minus 70 per cent respectively.

During its life span, from September 1969 until the end of 1988, Worldscale was regularly revised for changes in bunker prices and port costs but the fixed daily hire element of $1,800 remained constant.

Finally, to bring the story up to date, "New Worldscale" was introduced with effect from 1 January 1989. However, in deference to the custom that emerged in the trade, the epithet "new" was soon dropped and now it is generally under-stood that "Worldscale" refers to the new scale, while the previous scale is called "Old Worldscale".

Until the introduction of Old Worldscale, the various scales issued in London were all based on the old MOT rate of 32/6d (thirty-two shillings and six pence) for the voyages Curaçao to London. Indeed, the daily hire element of $1,800 used for Old Worldscale was indirectly related to that rate in so far as this, at the rate of exchange of £1/$2.40 (as applied in 1969), was close to the sterling hire rate for its immediate predecessor Intascale.

It was only when a replacement for the old Worldscale was being considered that a systematic attempt was made to establish, by a series of lengthy exercises, the size of standard vessel and the relevant daily hire element that would provide the best practicable basis for a scale. It was concluded, from the results of these exercises, that a standard vessel with a carrying capacity of 75,000 tonnes and a daily hire element of $12,000 was likely to provide such a basis for a scale to be used during the 1990s.

Both "Worldscales" are the joint endeavour of two non-profit making organisations known as Worldscale Association (London) Limited and Worldscale Association (NYC) Inc standing of course for New York City. Each company is under the control of a management committee, the members of which are senior brokers from leading tanker broking firms in London and New York respectively.

Worldscale is available on a subscription basis and the annual fee entitles the subscriber not only to the Schedule itself but also to notices of all amendments and the right to request rates for any voyage not shown in the Schedule.

Worldscale and New Worldscale compared

	WORLDSCALE (1988)	NEW WORLDSCALE (1/1/89)
STANDARD VESSEL		
Total capacity	19,500 long tons	75,000 tonnes
Average service speed	14.0 knots	14.5 knots
Bunker consumption at sea	28 tons/day	55 tonnes/day
Purposes other than steaming	–	100 tonnes/voyage
In port	5 tons/day	5 tonnes/port
Grade of fuel oil	180 cst	380 cst
Port time	72 hours laytime plus 12 hours/port	72 hours lay time plus 12 hours/port
FIXED HIRE	$1,800/day	$ 12,000/day
VARIABLE COSTS		
(a) Bunker prices	Historical 6 month market average of prices up to 30 September and 31 March for the January and July revisions.	Worldwide average price for 380 cst during the month of September prior to the effective date ($74.50/tonne for 1989).
data source	Platts and others	Cockett Marine Oil
(b) Port costs	Port charges known to the Association at the end of March and September, the rate of exchange for local currency to US$ normally being the average over the same 6 months as used for bunker prices.	Based on information available up to end September, rate of exchange for local currency to US$ being the average applicable during September.
CANAL TRANSITS	30 hours for each transit of Panama or Suez Canal.	24 hours for each transit of Panama Canal, 30 hours for each transit of Suez canal.
RATES	US$/long ton	US$/tonne of 1,000 kg.
REVISIONS		
Frequency	Six monthly	Annual

Worldscale

	WORLDSCALE (1988)	NEW WORLDSCALE (1/1/89)
REVISIONS-cont.		
Effective date	1 January & 1 July	1 January
Interim revisions	As judged necessary	As judged necessary

Required freight levels for vessel size 280,000 tonnes dwt.

Below is a table of required freight levels (in points of New Worldscale) to attain a given daily hire under the New Worldscale for a variety of typical voyages from Ras Tanura in the Arabian Gulf. These freight levels are calculated using typical values of operational parameters (e.g. speed, consumption etc.) for this vessel size.

LOADING RAS TANURA

DISCHARGING	DAILY HIRE (US$)		
	6,000	12,000	18,000
ROTTERDAM (VIA CAPE)	34.5	45.25	55.75
ROTTERDAM (VIA SUEZ BALLAST)	34.25	43.0	51.5
LOOP TERMINAL (VIA CAPE)	30.5	41.75	53.0
YOKOHAMA	34.0	44.5	55.0
SINGAPORE	31.5	42.5	53.25
AIN SUKHNA	32.75	43.75	55.0

Associated abbreviations:
cst Centistokes
dwt deadweight

Index

Term	See under
24-Hour Advance Cargo Manifest Rule	Security
about	Chartering—offer and counter-offer
accept except	Chartering—offer and counter-offer
accomplish a bill of lading (to)	Bill of lading
accomplished	Bill of lading, Bill of lading as document of title
acid tanker	Tankers
ad valorem freight	Container freight, Conventional freight and the export contract
addendum to the charter	Charter-party
additional	Breakbulk liner ancillary charges
additional charge	Breakbulk liner ancillary charges
additional freight	Breakbulk liner ancillary charges, Penalties
address commission	Sundry charter-party clauses (found in both voyage and time charters)
address commission clause	Sundry charter-party clauses (found in both voyage and time charters)
ADR/AID classification	Dangerous goods
advance call	Protection and Indemnity Club (P&I club)
agency agreement	British International Freight Association (BIFA), Forwarding agent
agency clause	Sundry voyage charter-party clauses
agency fee	Ship's agent
agent	Ship's agent
air draught	Draught, Ship's dimensions and capacities
all in rate	Container freight, Conventional freight and the export contract
all purposes	Laytime—calculation
all time saved	Laytime—calculation
alliance	Liner shipping—how it is structured
alumina carrier	Bulk carriers
American Bureau of Shipping	Classification societies
ammonia carrier	Tankers
ammonia tanker	Tankers
Amwelsh 93	BIMCO voyage charter-parties
annual survey	Surveys
arbitration clause	Sundry charter-party clauses (found in both voyage and time charters)
arbitrator	Shipping
area differential	liner surcharges
arrival pilot station any time day or night Sundays and holidays included	Delivery and redelivery (time charter)
arrived ship	Arrived ship
as agent only	Bill of lading, Charter-party, Ship's agent
asphalt tanker	Tankers
assignment	Sundry charter-party clauses (found in both voyage and time charters)
Austwheat	BIMCO voyage charter-parties

Index

Term	See under
Austwheat Bill	BIMCO voyage charter-parties
autonomous port	Port types
average (laytime) (to)	Laytime—calculation
Average Freight Rate Assessment	London Tanker Brokers' Panel
averaged	Laytime—calculation
back to back conditions	Sub-charter
backfreight	Penalties
bale	Ship's dimensions and capacities
bale capacity	Ship's dimensions and capacities
ballast	Ballast
ballast (to)	Voyage charter—ship's position
ballast bonus	Ballast
ballast leg	Ballast
ballasting	Ballast
Baltic and International Maritime Council	BIMCO (Baltic and International Maritime Council)
Baltic Code	Shipbroker
Baltic Dry Index	Baltic Exchange indices
Baltic Exchange	Baltic Exchange
Baltic Exchange Capesize Index	Baltic Exchange indices
Baltic Exchange Clean Tanker Index	Baltic Exchange indices
Baltic Exchange Dirty Tanker Index	Baltic Exchange indices
Baltic Exchange Handymax Index	Baltic Exchange indices
Baltic Exchange LPG Index	Baltic Exchange indices
Baltic Exchange Panama Index	Baltic Exchange indices
Baltic Exchange Sale and Purchase Assessments	Baltic Exchange indices
Baltic Exchange Supramax Index	Baltic Exchange indices
Baltic Handy Index	Baltic Exchange indices
Baltime 1939	BIMCO time charter-parties
banana carrier	Dry cargo ships
bank	Shipping
bar draught	Draught
bareboat charter	Bareboat charter, Chartering
bareboat charter registry	Bareboat charter
bareboat charter (to)	Bareboat charter
bareboat charterer	Bareboat charter
bareboat charter-party	Bareboat charter, Chartering
Barecon 2001	Bareboat charter
barge	Shipping
barge-carrying ship	Dry cargo ships
Bargehire 94	Bareboat charter
basket of currencies	Currency adjustment factor
beam	Ship's dimensions and capacities
bearer	Bill of lading as document of title
berth	Berth
berth a ship (to)	Berth
berth charter-party	Berth
berth standard of average clause	Sundry voyage charter-party clauses
BIFA	British International Freight Association (BIFA)
bill	Bill of lading, Bill of lading as document of title, Bill of lading as evidence of contract of carriage, Bill of lading as receipt

Index

Index

Term	See under
coasting broker	Shipbroker
collier	Bulk carrier
Combiconbill	Combined transport, Combined transport bill of lading
Combiconwaybill	Combined transport, Combined transport bill of lading, Waybill
combined transport	Combined transport, Combined transport bill of lading
combined transport bill of lading	Bill of lading, Bill of lading as evidence of contract of carriage, Combined transport, Combined transport bill of lading
combined transport document	Bill of lading, Bill of lading as evidence of contract of carriage, Combined transport, Combined transport bill of lading
combined transport operator	Carrier
combined transport sea waybill	Combined transport, Combined transport bill of lading
come forward (to)	liner ship positions, Voyage charter—ship's position
come free (to)	Chartering—offer and counter-offer, Voyage charter—ship's position
commencement of laytime	Laytime—commencement
commercial operation	Ship operating costs
commodity rate	Container freight rates
common berth	Berth
common carrier	Carrier
common short form bill of lading	Bill of lading, Bill of lading as evidence of contract of carriage, Shipping documents
common user berth	Berth
company security officer	Security
competitive broker	Shipbroker
compression damage	Stowage
conference	Liner shipping—how it is regulated, Liner shipping—how it is structured
conference tariff	liner and conference tariffs
Congenbill	BIMCO voyage charter-parties
congested	Congestion
congestion	Congestion
congestion surcharge	Congestion, Liner shipping—trades
Conlinebill	Bill of lading
Conlinebooking	Bookings
con-ro ship	Multipurpose ships
consign (to)	Consignment
consignee	Consignment, Shipping
consignment	Consignment
consignment note	Consignment
consignor	Consignment, Shipping
consolidation	British International Freight Association (BIFA), Container freight, Forwarding agent
consolidator	Forwarding agent
consortium	Liner shipping—how it is regulated, Liner shipping—how it is structured
container	Containers and associated ancillary charges
container freight	Container freight
container freight station	Container freight
Container Security Initiative	Security
container/barge carrier	Multipurpose ships
container/bulk carrier	Multipurpose ships
container/pallet carrier	Multipurpose ships
Container/vehicle packaging certificate and declaration	Dangerous goods
containerised cargo	Cargo types

Index

Index

Term	See under
Federation of National Associations of Shipbrokers and Agents	Institute of Chartered Shipbrokers (ICS)
feeder	Liner shipping—trades
feeder additional	Breakbulk liner ancillary charges, Liner shipping—trades
feeder port	Liner shipping—trades, Port types
feeder ship (feeder vessel)	Breakbulk liner ancillary charges, Liner shipping—trades, Port types
Ferticon	BIMCO voyage charter-parties
Fertisov	BIMCO voyage charter-parties
Fertisovbill	BIMCO voyage charter-parties
Fertivoy 88	BIMCO voyage charter-parties
FIATA Bill of Lading	Shipping documents
FIATA Forwarder's Certificate Receipt (FCR)	Shipping documents
FIATA Multimodal Transport Bill of Lading (FBL)	Multimodal transport bill of lading
FIATA SDT (Shipper's Declaration for the Transport of Dangerous Goods)	Dangerous goods
FIATA Warehouse Receipt	FIATA Warehouse Receipt (FIATA FWR)
firm offer	Chartering—offer and counter-offer
first class ship	Classification societies
fix a ship (to)	Chartering—offer and counter-offer, Post fixture work
fixed on subjects	Chartering—offer and counter-offer
fixed rate call	Protection and Indemnity Club (P&I club)
fixed rate premium	Protection and Indemnity Club (P&I club)
fixture	Chartering—offer and counter-offer
flag	Flag
flag discrimination	Flag
flag of convenience	Flag
flag of necessity	Flag
flag out (to)	Flag
flag waiver	Flag
flashpoint	Dangerous goods
flat	Containers and associated ancillary charges
flatrack	Containers and associated ancillary charges
float-in float-out	Dry cargo ships
fob	Conventional freight and the export contract
fob charges	Cargo handling charges, Breakbulk liner ancillary charges, Conventional freight and the export contract
fob's	Breakbulk liner ancillary charges
FONASBA General Agency Agreement	BIMCO sundry documents
FONASBA International Broker's Commission Contract	BIMCO sundry documents
FONASBA Standard Liner Agency Agreement	BIMCO sundry documents
forests products carrier	Bulk carriers
forty foot equivalent unit	Weights and measures
forty footer	Containers and associated ancillary charges
forwarder	Forwarding agent
Forwarder's Certificate of Receipt	Forwarder's Certificate of Receipt (FIATA FCR)
Forwarder's Certificate of Transport	Forwarder's Certificate of Transport (FIATA FCT)
forwarding agent	Forwarding agent, Shipping

Index

Term	See under
Gastime	BIMCO time charter-parties
Gasvoy 2005	BIMCO voyage charter-parties
geared ship	Ship types
gearless ship	Ship types
Gencon	BIMCO voyage charter-parties, Both to blame collision clause, Voyage charter
general average clause	Bill of lading-common clauses
general cargo	Cargo types
general cargo ship	Ship types
general declaration	Convention on Facilitation of International Maritime Traffic
general ice clause	Ice clause
general purpose container	Containers and associated ancillary charges
general rate increase	Liner and conference tariffs
Gencon	Both to blame collision clause
general ice clause	Ice clause
generals	Cargo types
Genwaybill	Waybill
geographical rotation	Voyage charter—ship's position
Germanischer Lloyd (Germany)	Classification societies
go back (to)	Liner ship positions, Voyage charter—ship's position
governing law clause	Sundry charter-party clauses (found in both voyage and time charters)
grain	Ship's dimensions and capacities
grain capacity	Ship's dimensions and capacities
Grainvoy	BIMCO voyage charter-parties
Grainvoybill	BIMCO voyage charter-parties
grid haulage rate	Inland haulage
gross register tonnage	Ship's dimensions and capacities
gross registered tonnage	Ship's dimensions and capacities
gross terms	Charter freight terms
gross tonnage	Ship's dimensions and capacities
groupage	Container freight, Forwarding agent
groupage bill of lading	Bill of lading, Bill of lading as evidence of contract of carriage, Forwarding agent
groupage operator	Forwarding agent
half height container	Containers and associated ancillary charges
half-height	Containers and associated ancillary charges
Hamburg Rules	United Nations Conference on Trade and Development (UNCTAD)
handover charge	Container freight, Inland haulage
handymax	Bulk carriers
handy-sized bulk carrier	Bulk carriers
harbour master	International Harbour Masters' Association (IHMA)
hazardous cargo additional	Dangerous goods
hazardous cargo surcharge	Dangerous goods
head charter	Sub-charter
head charterer	Carrier, sub-charter
head charter-party	Sub-charter
heavy lift additional	Cargo handling charges, Breakbulk liner ancillary charges
heavy lift cargo additional	Breakbulk liner ancillary charges
heavy lift extra	Cargo handling charges
heavy lift ship	Dry cargo ships
heavy lift surcharge	Cargo handling charges, Breakbulk liner ancillary charges
heavy weight additional	Breakbulk liner ancillary charges
Heavyconreceipt	Charter-party bills of lading, waybills and cargo receipts
Hellenic Register of Shipping (Greece)	Classification societies
high cube reefer	Containers and associated ancillary charges

Index

Index

Index

Term	See under
non vessel owning carrier	Carrier, Shipping
non vessel owning common carrier	Carrier, Shipping
non-conference line	Liner and conference tariffs, Liner shipping—how it is structured
non-delivery	Tally
non-negotiable bill of lading	Bill of lading as document of title
non-negotiable sea waybill	Shipping documents
non-reversible	Laytime—calculation
non-shipment	Tally
Norgrain 89	BIMCO voyage charter-parties
not otherwise enumerated	Liner and conference tariffs
not otherwise specified	Liner and conference tariffs
note protest (to)	Bunkers
notice of readiness	Arrived ship
notice of re-delivery	Delivery and redelivery (time charter)
notice to the trade	Congestion, liner surcharges
Nubaltwood	BIMCO voyage charter-parties
Nubaltwoodbill	BIMCO voyage charter-parties
Nuvoy-84	BIMCO voyage charter-parties
Nuvoybill-84	BIMCO voyage charter-parties
NYPE 93	BIMCO time charter-parties
occasional survey	Surveys
ocean waybill	Waybill
off hire	Charter documentation, Time charter
off hire (condition) survey	Delivery and re-delivery (time charter), Lloyd's agents, Post fixture work, Surveys, Time charter
off hire (to)	Time charter
off hire clause	Sundry time charter-party clauses
off hire periods	Sundry time charter-party clauses
off hire statement	Charter documentation, Time charter
offer	Chartering—offer and counter-offer
offer firm (to)	Chartering—offer and counter-offer
off-hire	Charter documentation, Time charter
oil/bulk/ore carrier	Multipurpose ships
on bareboat charter	Bareboat charter
on demurrage	Penalties
on hire	Charter documentation, Time charter
on hire survey	Charter documentation, Delivery and redelivery (time charter), Post fixture work, Surveys, Time charter
on hire (condition) survey	Charter documentation, Post fixture work, Surveys, Time charter
on the berth	Berth
on the measure	Weights and measures
on the measurement	Weights and measures
on the weight	Weights and measures
on time charter	Time charter
on voyage charter	Voyage charter
on-carriage	Combined transport
on-carrier	Carrier, Combined transport
on-carry (to)	Carrier, Combined transport
once on demurrage, always on demurrage	Demurrage
one safe berth	Berth
open	Voyage charter—ship's position
open conference	Liner shipping—how it is structured
open hatch bulk carrier	Bulk carriers
open rate	Liner and conference tariffs

326

Index

Index

Term	See under
round the world service	Liner shipping—trades
Royal Institution of Naval Architects	Royal Institution of Naval Architects (RINA)
running day	Laytime—calculation
Ruswood	BIMCO voyage charter-parties
Ruswoodbill	BIMCO voyage charter-parties
safe berth	Berth
Safety Management Certificate	Ship's documents, International Safety Management (ISM) Code
safety management system	The International Safety Management (ISM) Code
Safety Radio-telegraphy Certificate	Ship's documents
said to contain	Bill of lading as receipt
sailing card	Liner ship positions
sailing schedule	Liner ship positions
sale and purchase	Sale and purchase (s&p)
sale and purchase broker	Ship broker
Saleform 93	Sale and purchase
Salescrap 87	Sale and purchase
sand carrier	Dry cargo ships
sand dredger	Dry cargo ships
Scancon	BIMCO voyage charter-parties
Scanconbill	BIMCO voyage charter-parties
scope of the voyage	Bill of lading—common clauses
sea water	Draught
sea waybill	Waybill
seasonal tropical zone	Freeboard and load lines
seasonal winter zone	Freeboard and load lines
seaworthy trim clause	Sundry voyage charter-party clauses
secretariat	Liner and conference tariffs, Liner shipping—how it is structured
security	Security
self-sustaining containership	Ship types
self-trimmer	Bulk carriers
self-trimming ship	Bulk carriers
self-unloader	Bulk carriers
SEP Programme	Security
separations	Stowage
service agreement	Liner contracts
service contract	Liner contracts
sheep carrier	Dry cargo ships
shifting	Sundry voyage charter-party clauses
ship agent	BIMCO (Baltic and International Maritime Council), Ship's agent
ship broker	Shipbroker, Institute of Chartered Shipbrokers (ICS)
ship broking	Shipbroker
ship management	InterManager—International Ship Managers' Association (ISMA), ISMA Code
ship operating costs	Ship operating costs
ship routing	Weather routing
ship security officer	Security
ship security plan	Security
ship supplier	International Ship Suppliers' Association
shipbroker	BIMCO (Baltic and International Maritime Council), Shipbroker, Shipping
shipbroking	Institute of Chartered Shipbrokers (ICS), Shipbroker
shipmanager	Chamber of Shipping, InterManager—International Ship Managers' Association (ISMA)

Index

Term	See under
Standard Barge Bareboat Charter Party	BIMCO sundry documents
Standard Contract for the Sale of Vessels for Demolition	BIMCO sundry documents
Standard Crew Management Agreement	BIMCO sundry documents
Standard Disbursements Account	BIMCO sundry documents
Standard Marine Fuels Purchasing Contract	BIMCO sundry documents
Standard Ship Management Agreement	BIMCO sundry documents
Standard Shipping Note	Shipping documents, Standard Shipping Note (SSN)
Standard Slot Charter Charter Party	BIMCO sundry documents
Standard Statement of Facts (Long Form)	BIMCO sundry documents
Standard Statement of Facts (Oil and Chemical Tank Vessels) (Long Form)	BIMCO sundry documents
Standard Statement of Facts (Oil and Chemical Tank Vessels) (Short Form)	BIMCO sundry documents
Standard Statement of Facts (Short Form)	BIMCO sundry documents
Standard Time Sheet (Long Form)	BIMCO sundry documents
Standard Time Sheet (Short Form)	BIMCO sundry documents
Standard Transportation Contract for Heavy and Voluminous Cargoes	BIMCO sundry documents
Standard Volume Contract for Contracts of Affreightment	BIMCO sundry documents
statement of facts	Charter documentation, Laytime—calculation, Post fixture work
statutory survey	Surveys
steamship line	Shipping
stem a berth (to)	Berth
stevedore damage clause	Sundry voyage charter-party clauses
stevedoring charges	Ship operating costs
storage charges	Penalties
stow deadweight (to)	Conventional freight and the export contract
stowage	Stowage
stowage factor	Conventional freight and the export contract, Ship's dimensions and capacities, Weights and Measures
stowage plan	Stowage
strategic alliance	Liner shipping—how it is structured
strike clause	Strike clause
strike-bound	Strike clause
strip (to)	Container freight, Containers and associated ancillary charges
stuff (to)	Container freight, Containers and associated ancillary charges
sub-charter	Chartering, Sub-charter
sub-charter (to)	Chartering, Sub-charter
sub-charterer	Chartering, Sub-charter
sub-freight	Chartering, Sub-charter
sub-hire	Chartering

Index

Term	See under
tropical fresh water timber freeboard	Freeboard and load lines
tropical fresh water timber load line	Freeboard and load lines
tropical load line	Freeboard and load lines
tropical timber freeboard	Freeboard and load lines
tropical timber load line	Freeboard and load lines
tropical zone	Freeboard and load lines
trucking company	Shipping
tug/supply ship	Dry cargo ships
tween decker	Ship types
twenty foot equivalent unit	Ship's dimensions and capacities, Weights and measures
twenty footer	Containers and associated ancillary charges
ulcc	London Tanker Brokers' Panel, Tankers
unclean (bill of lading)	Bill of lading as receipt
uncon	Containers and associated ancillary charges
uncontainerable	Cargo types, Containers and associated ancillary charges
uncontainerisable	Cargo types
UNCTAD	Liner shipping—how it is regulated, United Nations Conference on Trade and Development (UNCTAD)
UNCTAD Liner Code	Liner shipping—how it is regulated
United Nations Conference on Trade and Development	Liner shipping—how it is regulated, United Nations Conference on Trade and Development (UNCTAD)
unenumerated	Liner and conference tariffs
unit loads	Cargo types
unitisation	Cargo types
unitised	Cargo types
universal bulk carrier	Bulk carriers
unless used	Laytime—calculation
vehicle carrier	Dry cargo ships, Vehicle carriers
vehicle/train ferry	Vehicle carriers
vessel TBA (to be advised)	Liner ship positions
vessel TBN (to be nominated)	Liner ship positions
vessel to be advised	Chartering—offer and counter-offer, Voyage charter—ship's position
vessel to be nominated	Chartering—offer and counter-offer, Voyage charter—ship's position
vlcc	London Tanker Brokers' Panel, Tankers
Volcoa	Contract of affreightment
volume-realted discount	Liner contracts
vouchers	Charter documentation
voyage account	voyage estimate
voyage charter	Chartering, Voyage charter
voyage charter (to)	Voyage charter
voyage charterer	Voyage charter
voyage charter-party	Chartering, Charter-party, Voyage charter
Voyage Charterparty Laytime Interpretation Rules 1993 (VOYLAY RULES)	BIMCO sundry documents
voyage estimate	Voyage estimate
voyage number	liner ship positions
wagon demurrage	Penalties
war clause	Sundry charter-party clauses (found in both voyage and time charters)
war risk surcharge	Liner surcharges, war risk surcharge

Index

Term	See under
war, strikes, ice clause	Bill of lading—common clauses
warehouse to warehouse	British International Freight Association (BIFA)
warehousekeeper	Shipping
warping	Sundry voyage charter-party clauses
water density	Draught
waybill	Bill of lading, Charter-party bills of lading, waybills and cargo receipts, Waybill
weather permitting	Laytime—calculation
weather routing	Weather routing
weather working day	Laytime—calculation
weight cargo	Weights and measures
weight or measure	Conventional freight and the export contract, Weights and measures
weight or measurement	Conventional freight and the export contract, Weights and measures
weight rated cargo	Weights and measures
weight ton	Conventional freight and the export contract
wet cargoes	Cargo types, Conventional freight and the export contract
wet weight	Weights and measures
wheeled cargo	Cargo types
when where ready on completion of discharge	Delivery and redelivery (time charter)
whether in berth or not	Arrived ship, Laytime—commencement
whether in free pratique or not	Arrived ship, Laytime—commencement
whether in port or not	Arrived ship, Laytime—commencement
white products	Tankers
wide laycan	Chartering—offer and counter-offer
winch clause	Sundry voyage charter-party clauses
windage	Weights and measures
winter draught	Draught
winter freeboard	Freeboard and load lines
winter load line	Freeboard and load lines
winter marks	Freeboard and load lines
winter North Atlantic freeboard	Freeboard and load lines
winter North Atlantic load line	Freeboard and load lines
winter North Atlantic timber freeboard	Freeboard and load lines
winter North Atlantic timber load line	Freeboard and load lines
winter timber freeboard	Freeboard and load lines
winter timber load line	Freeboard and load lines
winter zone	Freeboard and load lines
withdraw the class (to)	Classification societies
withdraw the ship from the service of the charterer (to)	Time charter
withdrawal of class	Classification societies
without guarantee	Chartering—offer and counter-offer
woodchip carrier	Bulk carriers
woodpulp carrier	Bulk carriers
workable hatches per day	Laytime—calculation
working day	Laytime—calculation
working day of 24 consecutive hours	Laytime—calculation
working day of 24 hours	Laytime-calculation
working hatch	Laytime-calculation
working time saved	Laytime-calculation
World Customs Organisation	Security
Worldfood	BIMCO voyage charter-parties

336

Term	See under
Worldfoodreceipt	BIMCO voyage charter-parties, Charter-party bills of lading, waybills and cargo receipts
Worldfoodwaybill	Waybill
Worldscale	Worldscale
zone haulage rate	Inland haulage